THE TRUTH OF
POETRY

THE TRUTH OF POETRY

POETRY

Tensions in Modern Poetry
from Baudelaire to the 1960s

MICHAEL HAMBURGER

METHUEN
London and New York

First published in 1969 by Weidenfeld & Nicolson

Reissued 1982 by Carcanet New Press Ltd
208-212 Corn Exchange Buildings, Manchester M4 3BQ

First published as a University Paperback in 1982 by
Methuen & Co. Ltd
11 New Fetter Lane, London EC4P 4EE

Published in the USA by
Methuen & Co.
in association with Methuen, Inc.
733 Third Avenue, New York, NY 10017

© 1969 and 1982 Michael Hamburger

Printed in Great Britain by J. W. Arrowsmith Ltd, Bristol

British Library Cataloguing in Publication Data
Hamburger, Michael
    The truth of poetry.
    1. Poetry—19th century—History and criticism
    2. Poetry—20th century—History and criticism
    I. Title
    809.1'034   PN1261
    ISBN 0-416-34240-X (University paperback 781)

Library of Congress Cataloging in Publication Data
Hamburger, Michael.
    The truth of poetry
    (University paperbacks)
    Reprint. Originally published: London:
Weidenfeld & Nicolson, 1969. With new postscript.
    Includes bibliographical references and index.
    1. Poetry, Modern—19th century—History and
criticism. 2. Poetry, Modern—20th century—
History and criticism. I. Title.
PN1261.H35   1982   809.1   82-6357
ISBN 0-416-34240-X (pbk.)   AACR2

CONTENTS

The author's thanks are due to the Bollingen Foundation of New York for a Fellowship awarded to him while this book was a project which might never have been carried out without their help.

PREFACE

WHAT makes 'modern poetry' modern? What makes it more difficult than any other poetry, if indeed it is more difficult than the poetry of Pindar, say, or Dante, or Shakespeare, or Donne, or Góngora, or Blake? Could it be that lyrical poetry after Baudelaire has tended to become different *in kind* from any that preceded it? And, if so, does this change mean that the poets in question were no longer trying to make the same *kinds* of statement as their predecessors?

These are some of the questions that worried me when I started preparing this book, well over ten years ago. What was clear to me even then was that an answer to them called for much more knowledge not of poetry, but of poets and poems, than I was ever likely to acquire. Despite all the distinct traditions and national peculiarities that have continued to affect the practice of poets, the 'modernity' of 'modern poetry' is an international phenomenon. I had read English, American, German, French and Italian poets in their own languages. I had not read the Spanish, Portuguese, Spanish-American, Portuguese-American, Russian, Polish, Yugoslav, Czechoslovakian, Hungarian, Greek, Dutch or Scandinavian poets – to mention only some of the nationalities that ought to have been included in a comprehensive study. Though I have tried hard to extend my reading to poets accessible to me only in or through translations, I found that more often than not such reading did not sink in. My book, in any case, was never intended to be a survey of all the major poets who have written 'modern' poems. Even within the languages that I know I have omitted poets who may be at least as good as those who are mentioned or dealt with at some length. At the same time I have tried to do justice to the diversity of poetry after Baudelaire. Instead of confining my enquiry to a single line of development defined in advance as 'modern,' I have concentrated on the tensions and conflicts apparent in the work – or behind the work – of every major poet of the period, beginning with the work of Baudelaire himself.

If too much emphasis falls on what poets have said about their poetry rather than on their poems themselves, the reason is that the more strictly critical procedure would have demanded minute analyses of hundreds of poems, many of them in foreign languages. Poems, not poetry or theories about poetry, were my starting-point; but very rigid limits had to be set to a book whose subject, in both time and space, is very nearly limitless. Whatever 'modern poetry' may be, its inception can easily be traced back beyond Baudelaire and beyond such poets as Edgar Allan Poe to whom Baudelaire and his successors have traced their literary ancestry. The antecedents had to be left out; but some awareness of them, I hope, will be implicit in my remarks on the poetry dealt with in this book, no less than an awareness of many poems and poets that could not be quoted or mentioned.

An international anthology like Hans Magnus Enzensberger's *museum der modernen poesie* (Frankfurt, 1960), with translations of all the texts, would help to make up for these necessary omissions, but no comparable anthology has yet been compiled for English-speaking readers. One extremely useful companion to my book is *The Poem Itself*, edited by Stanley Burnshaw and published in 1960 by Holt, Rinehart and Winston, New York. This volume contains analyses of poems by French, German, Spanish, Portuguese and Italian poets, as well as the texts and literal English renderings. Another is the anthology *Modern European Poetry*, edited by Willis Barnstone and others, published by Bantam Books, New York, in 1966. Many other anthologies and critical studies, such as those by C. M. Bowra, could be listed here; but the nature of my study prohibited much reference to secondary material. Even the sketchiest of bibliographies, too, would have overburdened a study that ranges as widely and freely as this one.

Lastly, I should like to emphasize again that this book is not a history of modern poetry, but an attempt to understand its nature, assumptions and functions. This accounts for many obvious and not so obvious omissions. Others arose from a reluctance to repeat what I have written elsewhere or what critical opinion generally has already established. Since the present decade is touched upon, a history would have degenerated into a survey. My only hope was to stick to what I felt to be the crucial issues.

M.H.
London, 1968

1

PUERILE UTOPIA AND BRUTAL MIRAGE

1   IN 1951 Professor Henri Peyre undertook a brief survey of what he regarded as the more outstanding contributions to the study of Baudelaire. Even at that time, before the centenary of the publication of *Les Fleurs du mal* in 1957 and the centenary of Baudelaire's death in 1967, Professor Peyre felt called upon to deal with some 350 books and articles. The importance of Baudelaire, then, can be taken for granted here, both as the father of modern poetry – 'le premier voyant, roi des poètes, un vrai Dieu'[1]* to cite Rimbaud's deification – and as the prototype of the modern poet whose vision is at once sharpened and limited by a high degree of critical self-awareness. 'With Baudelaire,' Paul Valéry wrote, 'French poetry has at last transcended national frontiers. It has found readers everywhere; it has established itself as the very poetry of modern times.'[2]

Baudelaire was also the author of the last book of poems to become an international best-seller.[3] That this success was posthumous is as relevant to the history of literature as to Baudelaire's life, its extreme wretchedness and its peculiar heroism. A childless man with little interest in the future, Baudelaire derived no comfort from the anticipation of his post-dated success. To write for those unborn was like writing for the dead. Baudelaire's heroism, which at one time he connected with his cult of the dandy – 'the man who never comes out of himself' – was one of deliberate self-containment. With complete

*'The first of seers, king of poets, a true God.'

sincerity, Baudelaire could say that he 'would be content to write only for the dead'.[4]

The vast body of critical and biographical literature about Baudelaire points to another development that is very much part of the situation of poets later than he; I mean the disproportion between the demand for poetry itself and the demand for literature about poetry. Very few, if any, serious poets since Baudelaire have been able to make a living out of their work; but thousands of people, including poets themselves, have made a living by writing or talking about poetry. This anomaly – paralleled in many ways, as it is, by economic developments conducive to a proliferation of middle-men in all trades and industries – has not only produced conscious or unconscious reactions apparent in the political commitments of several outstanding modern poets, but has also affected the very substance of their work. Ezra Pound's economic theories, and long passages of his *Cantos*, are one obvious instance; Bertolt Brecht's Communism, and his attempts to produce a functional poetry for the man in the street, are another. In this regard, too, Baudelaire was the prototype; not least because he wavered between the aristocratic and the revolutionary positions, sure only about his bitter rejection of the bourgeois and capitalist order that had no place for him. More than any other poet of his time Baudelaire was aware of living in a civilization in which commodities had taken over from things, prices from values; and whenever later poets have turned their attention to economics their thinking has tended to revolve around a theory of values. This is as true of Pound as of Brecht, of T.S.Eliot as of William Carlos Williams.

Even Baudelaire's dilemma has been examined and probed from almost every possible angle – aesthetic, social, psychological, existential, political and theological. Of all the contradictory judgements of his work – beginning with Victor Hugo's attribution to Baudelaire of his own creed of 'Art for the sake of progress,' Sainte-Beuve's advice to him to 'cultivate his angel' and to 'let himself go,' Barbey d'Aurevilly's description of Baudelaire as 'un de ces matérialistes raffinés et ambitieux' incapable of envisaging any kind of perfection other than a material one, followed by the inconsequential warning that 'after *Les Fleurs du mal* only two choices remain to the poet who made them bloom: either to blow out his brains or to become a Christian' – very few need to be considered here. Almost from the beginning Baudelaire was seen as progressive and re- actionary, original and banal, classical and modern, a Christian, a Satanist and a materialist, a consummate craftsman and a bad writer, a rigorous moralist and a man incapable of sincerity.[5] Most of the fundamental disagreements about Baudelaire's attitudes and intentions are due to his own self-contradictions; and he was conscious enough of these self-contradictions to make a general plea for 'a right in which everyone is interested – the right to contradict oneself.' The truth embodied in Baudelaire's work cannot be extracted from this or that con- fession, this or that apodictic line of verse, but only from the tensions to which his self-contradictions are the surest clue.

2   One reason why Baudelaire remains so fascinating a phenomenon, despite a great deal in his work that has lost its power to give us the 'frisson nouveau' experienced by Victor Hugo in reading *Les Fleurs du mal*, is that Baudelaire bequeathed not only his poetry, but also his dilemma, to generations of later poets and critics. Jean-Paul Sartre's 'existential psycho-analysis' of Baudelaire,[6] which uses what is known about this poet's life to demonstrate that 'men always have the kind of lives they deserve,' is one of several studies of Baudelaire that concentrate on his dilemma rather than on his work. In it Baudelaire's 'negative capability' assumes an exemplary significance, not least because Baudelaire's extreme self-awareness induced him to document his own failings and his own suspicion that he might be 'inferior to those whom he despised.' Baudelaire, in fact, came so close to Sartre's conviction that 'man is never any- thing but an imposture' that he did not mind leaving the kind of evidence that Sartre could bring against him. Baudelaire's existential dilemma was an acute one, and some of its implica- tions – such as his doubts as to his identity both as a man and as a poet – will be taken up in later chapters of this book. What concerns me at this point are Baudelaire's uncertainties about the function of poetry.

In studying any recent movement in European poetry, or the work of any individual poet later than Baudelaire who has made

3

some striking innovation, we are almost sure to be faced with problems which may not be intrinsic to the poetry itself, but which determine the nature of our approach to it and divide the judgements of its critics. The private reader can avoid them; the critic or teacher of modern literature cannot. These problems can be traced back considerably further still, but Baudelaire was the poet who lingered at the crossroads of modernity. His critical works show the same momentous hesitations as his poetry; momentous, because he knew the allurements of every direction which later poets were to take, not excluding headlong retreat; and so does the life of this Romantic-Classical-Symbolist poet, conservative pariah, dandy and spokesman of the underworld, solitary and 'man of crowds,' blasphemer and Christian apologist. Both his theory and his practice reveal a conflict between two radically different, if not incompatible, conceptions of the nature and functions of poetry. This conflict corresponds to a crisis which is not confined to literature or the arts; to a greater or lesser extent it has come to affect every activity that involves public or cultural values. Basically it may be the old question of ends and means; but at a time when few people agree as to what are the ultimate ends of human activity, every art, science and craft that was once considered a means tends to assume the character and importance of an ultimate end.

Baudelaire was one of the earlier exponents of the doctrine that the writing of poetry is an autonomous and autotelic activity. 'La poésie,' he wrote in 1859, 'ne peut pas, sous peine de mort ou de déchéance, s'assimiler à la science ou à la morale; elle n'a pas la Vérité pour objet, elle n'a qu'Elle-même.'[7]* It might be objected that this statement occurs in an essay on Gautier, the originator of the French school of 'art for art's sake,' and that Baudelaire was the kind of sympathetic and empathetic critic who tends to assume the point of view of his subject, especially where that subject is also a personal friend. But Baudelaire made similar claims in other essays. That on Barbier (1861), a Socialist poet whose artistically undistinguished verse had some influence on Baudelaire, precisely because of the truth

*'Death or deposition would be the penalty if poetry were to become assimilated to science or morality; the object of poetry is not Truth, the object of poetry is Poetry itself.'

which it conveys, contains the aphorism: 'La poésie se suffit à elle-même.'*

Baudelaire, however, was also an extreme opponent of the same view. 'Le temps n'est pas loin,' he had written in 1852, 'où l'on comprendra que toute littérature qui se refuse à marcher fraternellement entre la science et la philosophie est une littérature homicide et suicide.'† And again in the same year: 'La puérile utopie de l'école de l'art pour l'art, en excluant la morale, et souvent même la passion, était nécessairement stérile.'‡ Lastly, a passage that reads less like a critical judgement than like an intimate confession, akin to Baudelaire's remark that 'art is prostitution' and that 'all books are immoral':8 'Le goût immodéré de la forme pousse à des désordres monstrueux et inconnus. . . . La passion frénétique de l'art est un chancre qui dévore le reste; et comme l'absence nette du juste et du vrai dans l'art équivaut à l'absence d'art, l'homme entier s'évanouit; la spécialisation excessive d'une faculté aboutit au néant.'9§

A great number of other passages could be adduced from Baudelaire's writings for either side of the argument; to do full justice to Baudelaire, they would have to be related to his practice as a poet and to his development as a man. Nor would Baudelaire be the great poet and critic that he is if he had made no attempt to reconcile these conflicting views of poetry. In practice he did so by the allegorical use of urban imagery to act as a link between the actual and the timeless, the phenomenon and the Idea; by combining a new realism with his search for the archetypes.‖ How far he remained from a consistent symbolism, how deeply rooted in the rhetorical and didactic

---

*'Poetry is sufficient to itself.'

†'The time is not distant when it will be understood that all literature which refuses to march fraternally between science and philosophy is a homicidal and suicidal literature.'

‡'The puerile utopia of art for art's sake, by excluding morality and often even passion, was inevitably sterile.'

§'The immoderate love of form produces monstrous and unprecedented disorders . . . The frantic passion for art is a canker that devours all the rest; and since the complete absence of the right and the true in art amounts to a lack of art, the entire man perishes; the excessive specialization of any one faculty ends in complete annihilation.'

‖A good example is the 'gibet symbolique' of *Un Voyage à Cithère* which is also the actual gibbet seen by Gérard de Nerval on the (then British) island of Cerigo, as recorded in his *Voyage en Orient. Les Femmes du Caïre* (1882).

tradition of French verse, can only be exemplified here by a single poem of his maturity, *Causerie*. In consecutive lines of this sonnet he likens his heart to something which the beasts have eaten:

> Ne cherchez plus mon coeur; les bêtes l'ont mangé

and to a palace befouled by the mob:

> Mon coeur est un palais flétrie par la cohue.

The clash between these disparate analogies, which the remaining five lines of the sestet vainly try to resolve, is so disturbing just because Baudelaire was not a Symbolist, but an allegorical poet. If *Causerie* remains a successful poem it is because Baudelaire's allegories do their work even within the bounds of a single line; and they do so because of the compressed rhetoric he had learnt from the classical poets, both French and Latin.

On the level of theory, several attempts to reconcile the two views occur in his last essays. 'Le beau,' he wrote in 1863, 'est fait d'un élément éternel, invariable, dont la qualité est excessivement difficile à déterminer, et d'un élément relatif, circonstanciel, qui sera, si l'on veut, tour à tour ou tout ensemble, l'époque, la mode, la morale, la passion.'10* In the same year Baudelaire wrote his ill-fated letter to Swinburne to thank him for his laudatory article on *Les Fleurs du mal*; Baudelaire continues: 'Permettez-moi, cependant, de vous dire que vous avez poussé un peu loin ma défense. Je ne suis pas aussi moraliste que vous feignez obligeamment de le croire. Je crois simplement "comme vous sans doute" que tout poème, tout objet d'art bien fait suggère naturellement une morale. C'est l'affaire du lecteur. J'ai même une haine très décidée contre toute intention morale exclusive dans un poème.'11†

The morality of a poem, then, should be implicit, and there is a relation between this implicit morality and the artistic merit

---

*'Beauty consists of a timeless, invariable element, whose character is exceedingly difficult to define, and of a relative, circumstantial element which we can attribute to the period, the fashion, morality or passion, each in turn or all at once.'

†'Allow me, however, to tell you that you've gone a little too far in defending me. I am not so much of a moralist as you obligingly pretend to believe. I simply believe "like you no doubt" that every poem, every work of art that is well made naturally and necessarily suggests a certain morality. That's the reader's business. I even feel a decided loathing for any exclusively moral intention in a poem.'

of a poem. But Baudelaire does not claim, as later critics have claimed, that the reader has no business to enquire into these moral implications. And of course there is also the very different tone of a later letter, one of Baudelaire's last, in which he confessed that he put his whole heart, his most tender feelings, all his religion – in a disguised form – and all his hatred into that 'terrible book.'[12] It is also worth noting that, despite his partial allegiance to the 'art for art's sake' school, Baudelaire at no time found it necessary to evolve a kind of literary criticism that would concentrate on the aesthetic and stylistic aspects of a poem. His critical essays are brilliant examples of the synthetic, as distinct from the analytical, approach, and they are the work of a man concerned with the public function of the arts as much as with their inner laws. As a critic Baudelaire had more in common with Matthew Arnold than with his acknowledged master, Poe, or his acknowledged disciple, Mallarmé.

But it was Baudelaire the aesthete, the dandy and the Satanist who was acclaimed in the decades that followed his death. Admirers of Villiers de l'Isle-Adam could easily identify themselves with the perpetrator of squibs like this one: 'If a poet demanded of the State the right to keep a couple of bourgeois in his stable, people would be very much astonished; but if a bourgeois asked for some roast poet, people would think it quite natural.' This epigram had all the ingredients required by the *fin de siècle* aesthetes: the anti-humanism, the fine insolence, the tacit equation of the artist with the aristocrat. Even the moralists were taken in by Baudelaire's various masks. Henry James summed up one view of Baudelaire's poetry when he wrote: 'Our impatience is of the same order as that which we should feel if a poet, pretending to pluck the Flowers of Good, should come and present us, as specimens, a rhapsody on plumcake and eau de Cologne.'[13]

3   In 1866, shortly before Baudelaire's death, Mallarmé underwent the crisis known as 'les nuits de Tournon,' during which he lost his religious faith. The outcome of this crisis was his essay *Le Livre, instrument spirituel*, and the sudden discovery that 'everything, in the world, exists in order to culminate in a book.'[14] What Bauledaire had described as a 'puérile utopie' was established in all seriousness; and Baudelaire, together with Poe, was worshipped as its founder. One would be inclined to ascribe Mallarmé's statement to his youth or to the momentary thrill of having found a substitute for religious faith; but throughout his mature life he expounded an aesthetic doctrine which had its origin in this early crisis. As late as 1894, in his Oxford lecture *La Musique et les lettres*, he made this astonishing statement (though he himself described it as an exaggeration): 'Yes, indeed, Literature exists, and if you like, Literature alone exists, to the exclusion of everything else.' Though this new cult of literature and art derived from the poets, critics and metaphysicians of German Romanticism, in Mallarmé's case it was combined with Platonic or neo-Platonic influences. The same lecture makes this clear, or as clear as Mallarmé's truly jewelled, hard but many-faceted prose style can be said to make anything clear: 'At my risk aesthetically, I set down this conclusion ... that Music and Letters are the alternate face, here enlarged towards darkness, there sparkling, with certainty, of a phenomenon, the only one, I have called it the Idea.'[15] Art, according to Mallarmé, 'simplifies the world,' because by virtue of an inward state the artist reduces external phenomena to their single parent Idea.

What Schiller called the 'aesthetic education of man' most certainly derives from Plato; but it was also Plato who had his doubts as to the fitness of poets to conduct it. The very reason why literature now 'aspired towards the condition of music' was the uncomfortable awareness that the written word, after all, is a medium that resists the purification required of it. The significance of Mallarmé's 'simplification' was that the external world, which already to Delacroix and Baudelaire had been only a 'dictionary,' a 'store of images' or a 'forest of symbols' from which the artist selects his material, has now become no more than 'a brutal mirage.'[16] Whereas Baudelaire's allegories served to link the phenomenon to the Idea – or else served the purely artistic purpose of appealing to more than one sense at a time, by the use of synaesthesia – Mallarmé's withdrawal to a wholly subjective symbolism of the inward state severed all connection between the poet and that 'relative circumstantial' sphere in which extra-artistic values apply. In the most literal sense of the word, art had become a religion, with its own dogma, its artist-saints, and even its own asceticism, summed up by Villiers de l'Isle-Adam's *Axel* in the aphorism much admired by Mallarmé: 'Vivre? Les serviteurs feront cela pour nous!'* It is no wonder, then, that outside the field of aesthetics Mallarmé's thinking was indeed 'puerile' and inept. What could be more so than his prophecy, from the same lecture: 'If in the future, in France, there is a rebirth of religion, it will be the amplification into a thousand joys of the celestial instinct [instinct de ciel] in each man'? Baudelaire would have laughed at such a *niaiserie*.

Rimbaud's reaction was even more extreme. Although he criticized Baudelaire for 'living in too artistic a milieu' and for failing to invent new forms, he also deified the master in words already cited. Yet while Mallarmé withdrew into the sanctum of Art, Rimbaud prepared to take the next step, to re-create the world by the power of his imagination. Whereas Mallarmé merely disparaged 'le mirage brutal, la cité, ses gouvernements, le code,'† and could therefore devote himself to the refinement of his medium, Rimbaud was in active rebellion against society, morality and even God. It followed that art could be only a means to this end, a weapon of revolt; and when Rimbaud recognized his spiritual defeat in this greater struggle, the mere weapon became a worthless thing. On the rough draft of the work that recorded his struggle and defeat, *Une Saison en enfer*, he scribbled these words: 'Maintenant je puis dire que l'art est une sottise.'‡

Together with Lautréamont, whose *Chants de Maldoror* was almost contemporary with *Une Saison en enfer*, Rimbaud became the precursor of Surrealism and other experimental movements of this century. It is worth remembering, therefore, that Rimbaud and Lautréamont regarded their own experiments as failures; not on artistic grounds, but because the wheel had come full circle: as Baudelaire predicted, the hypertrophy of art must inevitably lead to its atrophy. Rimbaud's recantation took the form of silence; his rebellion had been too wholehearted and too extreme to permit such a conciliatory half-measure as Verlaine's *Sagesse*. Rimbaud's renunciation of literature was as complete as his former faith in the power of the written word –

*'As for living, our servants can do that for us.'
†'... that brutal mirage, the city, its governments, the law.'
‡'I can say now that art is an imbecility.'

9

but in the written word as a means of changing the world. As for Lautréamont, he recanted in his last work, *Poésies*; the creator of *Maldoror*, whose search for a kindred spirit had culminated in sexual intercourse with a shark, and who had exclaimed, 'moi seul, contre l'humanité!'* now advocated a return to the 'impersonal poetry' of the classical period and to moral. conformism. 'The aim of poetry,' he now wrote, 'should be practical truth.'17

The wheel had come full circle – by 1873! But the history of literature shows no reluctance to repeat itself; and no wonder, since it's made by individuals whose aspirations and follies are not determined by history alone, nor by those literary and philosophical 'trends' in which historians are forced to deal. The same wheel is turning still; rather more sluggishly, perhaps, but steadily all the same. Mallarmé's lecture of 1894 shows no awareness at all of the implications so clear to the historian's hindsight. Two years later Hofmannsthal wrote to Stefan George, Mallarmé's German disciple, asking him to receive an Austrian friend, Count Joseph Schönborn ('of the Bohemian branch of the house'), who was on a visit to Germany. George replied indignantly, 'You write a sentence, my dear friend: "he belongs to life, not to any of the arts" which I would almost regard as a blasphemy. If a man belongs to no art, has he the right to claim that he belongs to life at all? What? At the very most in semi-barbaric ages.'18

Later in his life it became evident enough to George that he was indeed living in a semi-barbaric age; and it may even have occurred to him that the gulf fixed by the arrogance of his letter was as acute a symptom as any of this barbarism. Hofmannsthal certainly knew it, and gave up lyrical poetry; and so did Yeats know it, for he included the aristocracy and the poor in his ideal order, as well as the artist (a rather more humane variant of Baudelaire's triad of 'respectable beings': 'The priest, the warrior and the poet. To know, to kill and to create'19).

It was inevitable that 'life' should counter-attack. Max Nordau's *Degeneration* appeared in 1893. Tolstoy's tract *What Is Art?* appeared in 1897 and 1898. Already in 1887 Tolstoy had written to Romain Rolland: 'Our whole trouble today is due to this: that the so-called civilized people, supported by the

*'I alone, against humanity!'

learned and the artists, are a privileged caste, like the priesthood; and this caste has the faults of every caste. It debases and dishonours the principle in whose name it was formed. What we call our learning and art is nothing but boundless humbug, a great superstition which usually takes us in as soon as we have emancipated ourselves from the superstitions of the Church.'[20] Tolstoy's attack on Shakespeare followed in 1903. No more recent pronouncement has improved on Tolstoy's description of Shakespeare as 'a fourth-rate artist' whose 'power of characterization was nil.' In *What Is Art?*, however, Tolstoy was mainly concerned with the modern aestheticism which he also castigated in *The Kreutzer Sonata*.

Tolstoy's literary judgements were so distorted by the inner crisis which he suffered at this time – a crisis of self-revulsion and self-reproach – and by his position in a society that had only lately ceased to be feudal, that they can be taken seriously only as a symptom of what was to come. The vitalism of Nietzsche was a much more shattering influence in the West. Though on the side of aestheticism, Nietzsche had undertaken the job of relating this doctrine to the philosophical situation in Europe; he showed that the religion of art was 'the last metaphysical activity within European nihilism.' He related it to his religion of the anti-Christ, his immoralism and his own version of Darwinism, 'the will to power.' Another little turn of the wheel, and barbarism revealed a new face. The Nietzschean revolution produced the strange phenomenon of the cultured man with a passionate hatred for culture, the artist ashamed of art. 'To read Rimbaud or the Seventh Canto of *Maldoror*,' André Gide confessed in his diaries, 'makes me ashamed of my works, and disgusted with everything that is a mere product of culture.'

How classical Baudelaire's attitude seems in view of this later *trahison des clercs*, the intellectual's abject desertion to the enemy's side! 'Tout ce qui est beau et noble,' Baudelaire believed, or at least asserted, 'est le résultat de la raison et du calcul.'[21]* True, the new vitalism was a development of aestheticism, with the stress not on beauty, but sensation; it was aestheticism released from its ethical, social and cultural inhibitions. Baudelaire, who had 'foresuffered all,' knew its temptations too; hence his warning against the excesses of art-worship,

*'Everything beautiful and noble is the result of reason and calculation.'

which would not only play into the hands of the barbarians, but turn artists themselves into the worst enemies of art.

4   This brief sketch has confined itself to the attitudes and statements of imaginative writers. To arrive anywhere near completeness – as far as anything so selective, drastic and spasmodic can arrive at completeness – it would have to trace the dilemma of literary criticism, whose history runs exactly parallel with the one I have attempted to outline. In its effort to keep pace with the imaginative writers, much of the most intelligent criticism of our time has become 'Criticism for Criticism's sake,' as D.J.Enright has called it. Although, as long ago as 1924, Edwin Muir wrote that 'all criticism is criticism for criticism's sake,'22 his observation does not contradict Enright's; for Muir continued: 'It is a moral habit carried over into art.' Instead of mediating between the work of art and a non-specialist public, it has become as specialized and as difficult as modern poetry is reputed to be; more difficult often, because poetry has its own way of communicating complex perceptions, and because the critics have added their own complexities to those of their texts. There are signs at present that the reaction to the New Criticism may grow as violent and as perverse as Tolstoy's protest against the debilitating effect of art. In fact Tolstoy's exasperation was mild compared to that of Professor Erich Heller's *The Disinherited Mind*, with its insistence that 'the poetry is the ideas, and the ideas are the poetry.' This was anti-aestheticism with a vengeance, in that it led the author to condemn Rilke's *Duino Elegies* because its ideas are wrong, and to conclude that Kafka 'had good reason to decree that his writings should be burnt.'

Erich Heller's pronouncements on the relationship between truth and poetry are a drastic formulation of opinions very widely held, but rarely expressed with anything like his eloquence, by persons whose quarrel with modern poetry is either that they do not 'understand' it or that they disagree with what they do understand. 'Without that all-pervasive sense of truth which bestows upon happier cultures their intuitive order of reality,' Heller wrote in *The Disinherited Mind*, poetry – in company with all the other arts – will be faced with ever increasing demands for ever increasing 'creativeness.' For the 'real order' has to be 'created' where there is no intuitive conviction that it exists. The story of the rise of the poet from the humble position of a teller of tales and a singer of songs to the heights of creation, from a lover of fancies to a slave of imagination, from the mouthpiece of divine wisdom to the begetter of new gods, is a story as glorious as it is agonizing. For with every new form in poetic creativity the world as it is, the world as created without the poet's inventions, becomes poorer; and every new impoverishment of the world is a new incentive to poetic creativeness. In the end the world as it is is nothing but a slum to the spirit, and an offence to the artist. Leaving its vapours behind in audacious flight, his genius settles in a world wholly created by the creator-poet: *Gesang ist Dasein.*[23]

Despite its wild generalizations – beginning with the evocation of those mythical 'happier cultures' in which poets 'tell tales' and 'sing songs' – this passage does say something apt about the developments culminating in Mallarmé's disparaging reference to the external world as a 'brutal mirage.' Yet it is difficult to understand how and why the modern poet's inventions come to impoverish the world. This presupposes readers of poems like Rilke's *Duino Elegies* whose response to the poetry is so pedantically literal and abjectly passive that they abandon the world they know in favour of the world 'created' for them by Rilke, bursting into song in order to 'be.' Yet even Rilke's most devoted admirers and disciples did no such thing. It is Heller's own literal approach to poetry that is at fault. He treats every work of literature, imaginative and historical alike, as though its primary function were to expound a body of beliefs and ideas:

To make poetry is to think. Of course, it is not *merely* thinking. But there is no such activity as 'merely thinking,' unless we confine the term to purely logical or mathematical operations. Language is not quite so stupid as some of our analytical philosophers seem to assume. It knows what it does when it allows us to say that we 'think of someone,' and when it calls actions deficient in kindness or imagination 'thoughtless.' 'Thinking' and 'thought' in these phrases are no mere manner of speaking. The words mean what they say: thought and thinking. And if we have it on authority still higher than Goethe's or Mr Eliot's that in the beginning was *logos*, the word, the thought, the meaning, we should think twice before we answer the question whether or not a poet thinks.[24]

Of course we should; but the real question for a reader of poetry is *how* a particular poet is thinking in a particular poem or part of a poem, and how this mode of thinking works in relation to the totality of what the poem enacts. In his eagerness not to compromise with the aesthetes Heller goes so far as to assert that

the reasons why one should, or should not, accept the beliefs inherent in Rilke's later poetry are not different in kind from the reasons why one should, or should not, accept the beliefs of Marxism, or of the Oxford Group, or of anthroposophy. To say, 'but he is merely a poet' (and not, I suppose, a sectarian hawker, an ideologist or a political propagandist) is to suggest that, by his profession, he is less capable of perceiving truth than others; to say, 'but his poetry is too beautiful to be true' is to insinuate that the closer the poetry is to truth, the less successful it will be as art, because all truth is necessarily ungainly.25

This argument is so preposterously oversimplified as to be meaningless. Even in this century there have been poets like Brecht who wanted their verse to be understood as Heller asks us to understand all poetry. Brecht, among other things, was a 'political propagandist'; but Brecht also knew that in being that he was reversing the main trend of poetry in his time, a trend of which he considered Rilke a representative. Heller's insistence that everywhere and at all times 'the poetry is the ideas, and the ideas are the poetry' slurs over the very distinctions which it is the main business of criticism to establish; and his constant appeals to moral, metaphysical and religious criteria which are never stated or defined greatly weaken his case against those modern poets, like Rilke, who glorified the poetic imagination. A numinous 'truth' or 'logos' is an ineffectual weapon in the hand of a critic who sets out to expose the pseudo-beliefs of poets, yet can also write: 'We have become so democratic in our belief of thought that we are convinced that Truth is determined by a plebiscite of facts.' Heller is fond of quoting Pascal's remark about 'the heart's reasons' of which reason is ignorant; but he forgets that to Pascal, a mathematician after all, it was 'la *dernière* démarche de la raison de connaître qu'il y a une infinité de choses qui la surpassent.'* Heller's impatience with the facts of literature – that is, with the specific poem or play from which he extracts a text for his sermon against modern

*'. . . the last resort of reason to realize that countless things are beyond it.'

literature as a whole – makes him a bad reader. As such, he can only confirm the prejudices of those who think that poetry is only a 'beautiful' way of saying things that can be said in prose. That function is not only obscurantist but utterly unhelpful, since it cuts the knot which literary criticism should endeavour to untie. It may be that the aesthetic order will never again be re-integrated with a larger one, as Kierkegaard set out to do in Baudelaire's lifetime. What is certain is that it can't be done by merely holding out Dante as a yardstick for all and sundry, and finding that Shakespeare and Goethe – not to mention Hölderlin and Rilke – were too modern to pass the test. Nor can it be done by merely returning to Matthew Arnold's position in 1863, before Art – at least in England – had proclaimed her independence from Life, and saying that 'poetry is simply the most beautiful, impressive and widely effective mode of saying things, and hence its importance.'[26] Arnold was a great critic because he tried to maintain a proper balance between the various functions of poetry, as T.S.Eliot, with very different premises and aims, did in his time; whereas most of the New Criticism has failed to grapple with the dilemma at all. Yet the dilemma was implicit in I.A.Richards' dictum that 'it is never what a poem *says* that matters, but what it is.' Erich Heller's literalism simply reverses the dictum; but the dictum itself implied that what a poem says is something different, and separable, from what it is; and that the discerning reader is the one most conscious of this difference. What criticism has failed to do is to account for this difference without losing sight of at least one of the various functions of literature, or giving it up as a bad job. The analytical method is incomplete if it doesn't end by reassembling the parts; and this final process is as liable as any other synthetic process to produce a new machine.

5   Both as a poet and as a critic, Baudelaire's practice was more classical than is generally granted. Because he was an allegorical poet, rather than a Symbolist, most of his poetry conforms to Samuel Johnson's classical prescription that 'the business of a poet is to examine, not the individual, but the species, to remark general properties and large appearances; he does not number the streaks of the tulip, or describe the different

shades in the verdure of the forest. He is to exhibit in his portraits
of nature such prominent and striking features, as recall the
original to every mind; and must neglect the minuter discriminations. . . .'27 Baudelaire's attitudes, on the other hand, were
bound to reflect his situation in his own age, and particularly
the isolation which, as Frank Kermode has emphasized in
Romantic Image, was the common predicament of the Romantics
and Symbolists. Baudelaire's self-contradictions, and his dilemma
itself, were due to the almost intolerable strain of being a
classical, or near-classical, artist in a modern society.

Baudelaire, therefore, fell into the confusion which is my
chief concern in this chapter: to attribute a social, ethical and
even religious significance to preoccupations that were in fact
aesthetic. The confusion is very common; few persons of
aesthetic sensibility are not sometimes guilty of it. What it
amounts to in this particular context is the failure to distinguish
between our response to what is ugly and our response to what
is evil. The confusion is made all the easier because the aesthetic
order touches on the moral in the sense of *mores* or *moeurs*; and
the words 'sordid' and 'squalid' seem to apply to both orders.
(W.H.Auden made the connection in his line, 'New styles of
architecture, a change of heart.') But Baudelaire chose exactly
the right word to characterize the utopia of 'art for art's sake':
'puerile,' because it is children who are least capable of making
the distinction, most apt to base ethical judgements on physical
appearances (though very young children are not put off by
physical ugliness).

This confusion has led to two other, related confusions. In
asserting their belief in 'art for art's sake' many writers have
failed to distinguish between their personal motive for writing
and the function of all literature. For a modern poet to say that
he writes for the poem's sake is neither strange nor shocking; it
is simply another way of saying that he is neither a knave nor a
fool. The error arises when the poet proceeds to identify his
motive with the nature or function of poetry itself, or when he
constructs a philosophy of life on the laws of his craft or on his
personal situation as a poet. It was the ideal of Gottfried Benn
to write 'the absolute poem, the poem without faith. The poem
without hope, the poem addressed to no one, the poem made of
words which you assemble in a fascinating way.'28 Absolute

poems are 'phenomena, historically ineffective, without practical consequences. That is their greatness.' But Gottfried Benn published his poems; and he didn't even disdain such aids to publication as the radio talk, the public lecture and the press interview. Mere publication would have sufficed to make his poems historically effective, and to give them practical consequences. To point out this inconsistency is not to convict Benn of hypocrisy; I do so to indicate that communication is a function intrinsic to poetry, even where the poet is aware of no wish to communicate anything in particular, where he writes for the dead or for no one. A poem can be a monologue; but it is a monologue spoken aloud.

The second error is to suppose that there must be a fixed ratio between the degree of autonomy attained by a work of literature, and its quality; that this ratio depends on the poet's belief; and that a poet who acknowledges no commitment to anything other than his art is therefore incapable of writing a bad poem, let alone a vulgar poem. Commitment, again, is not only a matter of conscious attitudes; merely to write is to commit oneself, and to reveal a commitment that cannot possibly be confined to the aesthetic order. Villiers de l'Isle-Adam, for instance, owes most of his reputation to his attitude; as a writer of fiction he was inferior to many of the popular novelists of his time. And as Baudelaire remarked, there is also the vulgarity that consists in insulting a crowd.

The poet as aesthete is the poet turned specialist, the poet who cannot see further than his specialization and turns it into a creed. In so far as he approved the 'art for art's sake' school, Baudelaire showed that he couldn't resist the general trend towards specialization. His solitude was against him. His cult of dandyism – as 'the last refulgence of heroism in decadent ages'[29] – was his desperate attempt to make sense of his solitude; it was one of a long succession of auxiliary religions to which artists have resorted merely to keep going at all. Yet it was Baudelaire the classicist who noted in his journal, under the heading of *Dandyisme*: 'Who is the superior man? He is not the specialist. He is the man of leisure and of general education. To be rich and love work.'[30] But Baudelaire for the greater part of his life was anything but rich, and he hated work. So he became the first to complain of the 'immense nausea of advertisements,' a

borderline nausea, half aesthetic, half moral, which he inter-
preted as disgust with the 'sordid' materialism of the age. At the
same time he knew that – except in its highest, Platonic reaches
– aestheticism is also materialism, and that it was his own
aestheticism that divided him from the crowd. 'As for me, who
sometimes find it in myself to assume the ludicrous role of
prophet, I know that I shall never find there the charity of a
physician. Lost in this vile world, buffeted by the crowd, I am
like a man tired out, who, looking back, into the deep chasm of
years, sees nothing but disillusionment and bitterness, and
looking forward, sees only a cataclysm that contains nothing
new, neither knowledge nor grief.'[31]

By the time he had wholly emerged from this vicious circle
and acquired the 'charity of a physician,' Baudelaire had almost
ceased to write; but there are more traces of that charity in his
earlier work than he allowed himself to admit. Baudelaire
feared nothing so much as that the spiritual passion which he
put into his poetry might be mistaken for the false spirituality of
the age; that is why he wrote that the one important thing was
'to be a great man and a saint *in one's own eyes*' (*pour soi-même*).

In judging Baudelaire's pronouncements on society, politics,
ethics and religion, it is essential to distinguish between two
kinds: those made by the specialist concerned only with his own
trade, a trade for whose products there was little demand at the
time, and those which have the special value of a vantage point
which he indicated in his journal: 'I have no convictions, as
people of my century understand the word, because I have no
ambition.' There is no point in trying to make sense of the
former kind – other than biographical and historical sense; to
do so is to be confronted with a Baudelaire who was a socialist,
a conservative and a fascist, a mystical pantheist and an ortho-
dox Catholic, a Satanist, a puritan and a pagan, etc., etc. It is
also essential to distinguish between what Baudelaire thought as
a man and what he thought as an artist. Thus Baudelaire wrote:
'Je ne crois pas qu'il soit scandalisant de considérer toute infraction à la morale, au beau moral, comme une espèce de faute
contre le rythme et la prosodie universels.'* This is an example

---

*'I do not think it is shocking to consider every infraction of morality, of the
morally beautiful, as a kind of offence against the universal rhythm and prosody.'
Théophile Gautier.

of the auxiliary religion; it is a statement designed to throw a very flimsy bridge across the gulf between the aesthetic and the ethical orders. The fact is that Baudelaire the man didn't believe in a 'universal rhythm and prosody' which would have co-ordinated the aesthetic and the ethical functions of poetry without any effort on the poet's part; but the artist would have liked to believe in it, and the pseudo-belief was useful to a poet.

There is no need to despair of modern poetry because it calls for distinctions of that kind, or to deny oneself the pleasure of reading it for fear of being corrupted by its 'wrong' ideas. It is up to the critic and the reader to recognize the auxiliary religions where they have become part of the poetry instead of merely helping to support the poet in a difficult job. I doubt that a reader who is not a poet (or indeed a reader who isn't Rilke) could live for long by the aesthetic religion implicit, and occasionally explicit, in Rilke's *Duino Elegies*; but that reader could still be the wiser for having entered into an experience that wouldn't otherwise have been his; and by entering into it, I mean wholeheartedly, without prejudgement. If the experience leaves a deposit of ideas, rather than sensations, these will have to be put in their place at a later stage. The discrimination demanded then is no different from that which life demands of us; the people and things we come up against aren't labeled 'good' or 'bad.' True and false ideas appeal to us in every news-paper, not to mention the advertisements that nauseated Baudelaire.

Yet the thing itself tells no lies; this is as true of the poem as an object well and honestly made (and A.E.Housman said that poetry is 'more physical than intellectual'[32]) as of purely physical products. In both cases we may have to dissociate it from the claims that have been attached to it, even from claims imprinted on the thing itself. If this growing need to discrimi-nate and to dissociate is bewildering, conducive to Tolstoy's exasperation with literature and to Baudelaire's disgust with life, or else to cynicism, indifference and deliberate philistinism, literature also provides a remedy; it has the power to make new associations between the things which, in life, tend more and more to 'fall apart.' The distinction of modern poetry is that it has concentrated on numbering 'the streaks of the tulip'; but again and again it has shown its power to universalize the particular, to give a new centre to experiences which by all the classical criteria should be peripheral, because they are the experiences of specialists. The modern poet may 'number the streaks of the tulip' and not only think, but hope, that he has left it at that; but, whether he likes it or not, he has said something new about flowers, and about men.

2

THE TRUTH OF POETRY

1   THAT poetry embodies or enacts truth of one kind or another has hardly ever been denied by poets themselves, even by poets who have gone further than Baudelaire in the search for a syntax liberated from prose usage, for an imagery not subservient to argument, or for a diction determined more by acoustic values than by semantic exigencies. It is an error to assert that poetry since Baudelaire's time has developed only in one of those directions. Different poets have explored different possibilities of development; and quite a number of considerable poets no less modern than those who would trace their descent from Mallarmé have taken none of those directions, but aspired to a bareness and directness of statement that far exceeds anything demanded by the strictest classical canons. To Dryden the words that make up a poem were 'the image and ornament' of the thought which it was the primary function of that poem to 'convey to our apprehension,'[1] though Dryden was writing about verse translation, and even his practice as a poet and translator of poetry does not always accord with so rigid a definition. The modern poets in question differ from Dryden in having no use for ornament, and no use for images or metaphors that are ornamental in the sense of merely adding grandeur or dignity to their thoughts. The important thing for the readers and critics of modern poems is not to expect too simple or constant an approach to the many kinds of truth which different kinds of poems are able to convey.

Reviewing Bonamy Dobrée's *The Broken Cistern* in 1954, Donald Davie quoted this well-known passage from A.E. Housman's 1933 lecture *The Name and Nature of Poetry*:[2]

> Poems very seldom consist of poetry and nothing else; and pleasure can be derived also from their other ingredients. I am convinced that most readers, when they think they are admiring poetry, are deceived by inability to analyse their sensations, and that they are really admiring, not the poetry of the passage before them, but something else in it, which they like better than poetry.

Davie went on to comment:

> I.A.Richards, in *Practical Criticism*, proved that this was so. Now Bonamy Dobrée argues that poetry nowadays has few readers of this sort; and this, too, though it cannot be proved, seems very likely. The surprising thing is that he thinks this is a pity. One would think that if the poet no longer has many readers of this sort he is well rid of them. But Professor Dobrée believes that poetry can be a civilizing influence even on people who read poems for something other than their poetry. This is, to say the least, highly questionable, for *Practical Criticism* seemed to prove also that if poetry was read in this wrong-headed way it was a debilitating influence, not civilizing at all.

It would be pleasant to be able to agree with Davie that 'poetry nowadays has few readers of this sort'; but quite a number of them are still to be met at public poetry readings, in university seminars and in other unlikely places. 'Poetry,' Housman said in the same lecture, 'is not the thing said, but a way of saying it. Can it then be isolated and studied by itself? For the combination of language with its intellectual content, its meaning, is a union as close as can well be imagined.' If critics as expert as Professor Dobrée insist on separating 'the thing said' from 'the way of saying it,' or insist that poetry, after all, is 'the thing said,' as Professor Heller has done, readers of that sort will most probably be met for a long time to come; and not only in those countries where any other sort of reader is considered ideologically suspect. Even after Symbolism, Imagism, Futurism, Expressionism, Surrealism, and the new Concrete poetry, not only critics and readers, but poets too, remain divided on those questions to which Baudelaire could not give an unequivocal answer; and the division, in many cases, remains an inner division, one of those quarrels with himself out of which a poet, as Yeats said, makes poetry.

Donald Davie himself once wrote an eloquent appeal for a kind of poetry that 'must reek of the human' and show no 'loss of faith in conceptual thought'; and, as he argued at the time, in *Articulate Energy*,[3] such a poetry would have to return to a syntax more logical than dynamic. Though his own position has probably changed since that time, his analysis of modern poetic syntax, and of the philosophical and psychological changes that led to its adoption, is still valid. Above all, he was right to stress the importance of poetic syntax:

It is from that point of view, in respect of syntax, that modern poetry, so diverse in all other ways, is seen as one. And we can define it thus: *What is common to all modern poetry is the assertion or the assumption (most often the latter) that syntax in poetry is wholly different from syntax as understood by logicians and grammarians.* When the poet retains syntactical forms acceptable to the grammarian, this is merely a convention which he chooses to observe. But never before the modern period has it been taken for granted that all poetic syntax is necessarily of this sort. This is, surely, the one symbolist innovation that is at the root of all the technical novelties that the symbolist poets introduced. Later poets could refuse to countenance all the other symbolist methods and still, by sharing, consciously or not, the symbolist attitude to syntax, they stand out as post-symbolist.

In the same study Donald Davie quoted a comparison by Paul Valéry between Mallarmé's poetic syntax – a syntax, incidentally, which Mallarmé also succeeded in carrying over into prose – and the 'attitudes of men who in algebra have examined the science of forms and the symbolical part of the art of mathematics. This type of attention makes the structure of expressions more felt and more interesting than their significance or value.' Davie's conclusion was that 'the syntax of Mallarmé appeals to nothing but itself, to nothing outside the world of the poem.'[4]

Yet Mallarmé has also been seen as the representative of a tradition as old as poetry itself. Elizabeth Sewell, from whose book *The Structure of Poetry* Davie quoted the remark by Valéry, has made just that connection in her later book, *The Orphic Voice*.[5] There she cites Mallarmé's own reference to the Orphic tradition: 'l'explication orphique de la terre, qui est le seul devoir du poète et le jeu littéraire par excellence';* and her book has the singular merit of relating the 'postlogic' of modern poetry – as exemplified in the syntactic developments analysed by Donald Davie – with developments in science and thought. She has no doubts at all about the capacity even of modern poetry to embody truth: 'Poetry puts language to full use as a means of thought, exploration and discovery, and we have so far just about made a beginning and no more on its potential usefulness.' The operative words are 'exploration' and 'discovery', since the crucial distinction between an expository syntax and the syntax of post-Symbolist poetry has to do with the later poets' readiness to explore truths rather than to assert them. Elizabeth Sewell shows that there is a precedent for the exploratory procedure not only in the poetry of all periods but also in philosophy and speculative science. Poetry, she suggests, has the same aim as religion, myth and science; and 'that is truth, taken in its most simple everyday sense.' This function of poetry has been summed up once and for all in the Preface to *Lyrical Ballads*: 'Poetry is the breath and finer spirit of all knowledge, carrying sensation into the midst of the objects of science itself.'

2   The poetry of Mallarmé and his successors carried sensation – image, music and gesture – into realms that were once considered accessible only to abstract thought and logical argument. Not many poets before them were as consistent or deliberate in working out a syntax close to 'the logic of consciousness itself,' as Susanne K. Langer has put it,[6] though Hölderlin's syntactical contractions, ellipses and suspensions are as daring as anything in Mallarmé; and Hölderlin, too, quite consciously worked for a poetry as 'alive' as possible, in which the very processes of thinking and feeling and imagining are enacted.

Nevertheless, the quarrel is not over. What Susanne Langer calls the 'artistic interest' of poetry continues to clash with what she calls the 'propositional' – sometimes, indeed, within the work of a single poet or even within the structure of a single poem. One may accept the view of an aesthetician like Susanne

*'. . . that Orphic interpretation of the earth, which is the poet's one task and the supreme literary game.'

Langer that all art is 'abstract' – in a special sense which she defines[7]* – and symbolic; that 'the relation of poetry to the world of facts is the same as that of painting to the world of objects; actual events, if they enter its orbit at all, are motifs of poetry, as actual objects are motifs of painting. Poetry, like all art, is abstract and meaningful.' Yet at the same time one may find oneself responding primitively to the 'propositional interest' of a line like Mallarmé's

> La chair est triste, hélas! et j'ai lu tous les livres

or Yeats's

> Man has created death

though both are excellent examples of pseudo-factual assertions whose meaningfulness is not detachable from their contexts. In the early, still somewhat Baudelairean poem by Mallarmé (*Brise marine*), as in the Yeats poem, the single line, because it is a syntactical unit, still makes a kind of appeal more characteristic of classical verse than of Mallarmé's later, more subtly organized poetry, in which every image and cadence is intricately related to every other, and even punctuation is discarded. Another way of putting it is that the Romantic convention of confessional poetry still dominates Mallarmé's early poems, as it did the poems of Baudelaire, to a degree that invites a 'propositional interest' rather than an artistic one. The proposition in Mallarmé's poem *L'Azur*, that 'Heaven is dead' ('Le ciel est mort'), can hardly fail to arouse a response akin to our response to Nietzsche's claim, made in prose, that 'God is dead.' Mallarmé's proposition does not fill a whole line; but the apostrophizing of 'matter' in the same line – 'Vers toi, j'accours! donne, ô matière . . .' – makes a link so important in the history both of thought and of art, so essential also to an understanding of Mallarmé's development as an artist, that it is difficult to resist an interpretation that would leave the context out of

---

*'Artistic abstraction, being incidental to a symbolical process that aims at the expression and knowledge of something quite concrete – the facts of human feeling, which are just as concrete as physical occurrences – does not furnish elements of genuine abstract thought. The abstractive processes in art would probably always remain unconscious if we did not know from discursive logic what abstraction is. . . . For science moves from general denotation to precise abstraction; art, from precise abstraction to vital connotation, without the aid of generality.'

account. It was the realization that poets do not need to provide that kind of evidence – in this case, a variation of Nietzsche's discovery that the death of God makes 'art the last metaphysical activity within European nihilism,' with the corollary that this modern art may have to be ultimately materialistic, however spiritual and quasi-religious the impulses behind it – which led Mallarmé and his successors to evolve a poetry no longer conducive to the literal interpretation of isolated lines or parts of lines.

This realization does not necessarily imply a 'loss of nerve' on the part of modern poets, as Donald Davie suggested in *Articulate Energy*, or an impoverishment of poetry, as Bonamy Dobrée regretted in *The Broken Cistern*. The ontological or psychological truths conveyed in statements like 'Man has created death' and 'Le ciel est mort' have not been taken out of poetry, even where poets have come to resist the temptation to formulate them directly. Poets still think, as well as feel and imagine; but the thinking and the feeling and the imagining have tended more and more to be rendered as the indivisible process which, intrinsically, they have always been. 'Imagination,' said the French poet Saint-Pol Roux, in 1923, 'is a reaping before the sowing. Reason is imagination that has gone stale.'[8]*

What is hardly questionable is that the understanding of poems as poems has been hindered by nothing so much as by the direct assertions that could be detached from them – that is, by those passages in them that seem most immediately understandable. Some assertions of that order, like this notorious one glossed by W.H.Auden, have seemed to cry out to be detached because they are so quotable:

If asked who said Beauty is Truth, Truth Beauty! a great many readers would answer 'Keats.' But Keats said nothing of the sort. It is what he said the Grecian Urn said, his description and criticism of a certain kind of work of art, the kind from which the evils and problems of this life, the 'heart high sorrowful and cloyed,' are deliberately excluded. The Urn, for example, depicts, among other beautiful sights, the citadel of a hill town; it does not depict warfare, the evil which makes the citadel necessary.

Art arises out of our desire for both beauty and truth and our knowledge that they are not identical.[9]

*'L'Imagination, c'est la moisson d'avant les semailles. La raison, c'est de l'imagination qui a de la bouteille.'

Critics more inclined to Platonism or to Elizabeth Sewell's Orphic tradition would probably disagree with Auden's interpretation; and that precisely is the trouble with general assertions of that order. Auden is certainly right to point to the strictly poetic function of those words within that particular poem. But when he goes on to state that poets write out of the knowledge that beauty and truth are not identical, he is telling us something about poets like Auden, and not necessarily about poets like Keats, whose assertion or proposition remains controversial, a debating point for critics and aestheticians; and that, at best, is an incidental function of poetry.

3 W.H.Auden himself received only incidental mention in Hugo Friedrich's widely read study of the development of modern poetry, *Die Struktur der modernen Lyrik*;[10] and once again we are reminded that there is no such thing as a single modern movement in poetry, wholly international, and progressing in a straight line from Baudelaire to the middle of this century (the period covered by Hugo Friedrich's book). Friedrich does tend to concentrate on a single line of development – that towards 'pure,' 'absolute' or hermetic poetry – and his academic specialization is in the Romance languages, in which that line of development has been much stronger than in the Anglo-Saxon, Slavic or Scandinavian language areas. In English poetry especially, every step forward in the direction of pure or hermetic verse has been followed by at least two paces backwards, or by what used to be called a period of 'consolidation.' The history of Imagism – the most promising of the Anglo-Saxon varieties of modernism – is a case in point. Yet Baudelaire, as I have tried to show, was a moralist as well as an aesthete; and it is the moral concerns of the non-hermeticists that have brought them back again and again to modes of poetic utterance that diverge from the line of development traced by Hugo Friedrich. Characteristically, the mere passing reference to Auden is matched by a similar one to Bertolt Brecht, a poet not affected by Friedrich's linguistic specialization. If Baudelaire is to be taken as a starting point – and Friedrich does begin with Baudelaire – the dilemma inherent in modern poetry has to be taken into account. Baudelaire, after all, was one of the first poets to grapple with some of the realities of the modern megalo-politan scene; and the English-language poets from T.S.Eliot to Auden, from William Carlos Williams to Philip Larkin and Charles Tomlinson, have excelled at kinds of poetry that respond much more faithfully than Baudelaire's to specific localities and ways of life. The assimilation of experienced and observed realities into poetry, that is, into the diction, imagery and rhythmic structure of verse, is a process seemingly at odds with the trend towards abstraction, as understood by Susanne Langer, or towards the essential autonomy of art. Yet wherever major poetry has been written in the past century, or in any other, the two opposing impulses have met, imagination (or 'inwardness') has fused in some new way with outer experience.

Hugo Friedrich puts all the stress on what he calls the 'destruction of reality' in modern poetry, beginning with Baudelaire and his 'depersonalization of poetry, at least in as much as the lyrical word no longer proceeds from the unity of poetry with the empirical self.'[11] Yet he grants that this unity was characteristic only of the confessional poetry of the Romantic period, so that Baudelaire's 'depersonalization' can be seen as a return to classical premises. (That was how Eliot's advocacy of impersonality in literature linked up both with his modernism and with his preference for classicism.) With Rimbaud the thrust of imagination does assume a vehemence that warrants Friedrich's notion of a 'destruction of reality' by certain modern poets. He is also right to remark on the 'empty transcendentalism' of much modern poetry, citing Rimbaud's recourse to 'angels without God and without a message.' (A whole genealogy of such angels could be traced from Rimbaud to Stefan George, Rilke, Wallace Stevens and Rafael Alberti, and Friedrich does make the connection between Alberti's angels and those of Rimbaud.) In Rimbaud, too, Friedrich finds evidence of 'a process of dehumanization' characteristic of the development of modern poetry – but again, one must object, only of that line of development which Friedrich chooses to pursue. He quotes this line from Mallarmé's *Hérodiade*:

Du reste, je ne veux rien d'humain

and claims that 'it could serve as a motto for Mallarmé's entire work.'[12] But this is a poem in dialogue form, and it is Herodias who speaks, in a work by a poet who had severed 'the unity of poetry with the empirical self' much more thoroughly than Baudelaire. Friedrich himself quotes Mallarmé's famous remark to Degas that 'poems are made not of ideas but of words.' True, Friedrich also quotes this personal confession by Mallarmé in a letter to Cazalis of 1866: 'After I had found nothingness I found beauty'; and there is no denying that a profound nihilism underlies the extreme aestheticism of the late nineteenth and early twentieth centuries.

It is the one-sidedness of Friedrich's view of what constitutes modern poetry that allows him to make generalizations like the following: 'To call a thing by name means to spoil three quarters of one's pleasure in a poem ... this applies to Mallarmé, as to almost all the lyrical poetry after him'; or: 'The modern poem avoids acknowledging the objective existence of the objective world (including the inner one) by descriptive or narrative elements.' Yet elsewhere he admits that 'there is also a poetry crowded with things,' though 'this abundance of things is subject to a new way of seeing and combining, to new stylistic devices; it is material for the lyrical subject's power to arrange it as he pleases';[13] and he speaks of Francis Ponge as a writer of 'a poetry that has no other content than things. . . .' 'The subjects of his free verse poems are called bread, door, shell, pebble, candle, cigarettes. They are captured so factually that one critic (Sartre) has spoken of a "lyrical phenomenology." The ego that captures them is fictitious, a mere carrier of language. This language, however, is anything but realistic. It does not so much deform things as make them so inert, or impart so strange a vitality to things inert by nature, that a spooky unreality is created. But man is excluded.'

I have already suggested that man can never be excluded from poetry written by human beings, however impersonal or abstract; and of Francis Ponge's poems in particular one could equally well say that they render not things, but a way of looking at things and experiencing things. Ponge, it is true, has expressed severe misgivings about the anthropocentric view of a universe that has become 'nothing more than man's field of action, a stage on which to exercise his power'; but this, too, is a view of man. Elsewhere, in his book *Liasse* (1948), Ponge has written: 'People say that art exists for its own sake. This means nothing to me. Everything in art exists for men.' As for his approach to things – an attempt to put men back into the natural universe, and relate them to its phenomena – he has commented: 'My method most certainly is not one of contemplation in the strict sense of the word, but rather of one so active that the naming follows immediately; it is an operation with pen in hand, so that I see closer analogies in alchemy . . . and quite generally in action, too (including political action), than in some sort of ecstasy that originates only in the individual and rather makes me laugh.'

As Werner Vortriede has shown,[14] Symbolist practice rests on the assumption of a magical correspondence between the inner and outer worlds, an assumption which he traces back to Novalis and other theorists of German Romanticism. 'Psychologically speaking,' he remarks, Mallarmé's use of symbols and Symbolist practice generally is a 'secularized mysticism'; psychologically speaking, because the Symbolists were perpetually producing analogies of the poetic process itself. Yet at least in his earlier years, Mallarmé still spoke of 'understanding' poems, saying that our pleasure in a poem consists in our *gradual* understanding. The reader, therefore, is invited to participate in a process of exploration. Francis Ponge's reference to alchemy brings us up once more against the peculiar interchangeability of subject and object in so much modern poetry. Rilke's so-called 'thing poetry' in his *Neue Gedichte* is another striking instance. This has usually been seen as a highly subjective poet's attempt to emulate the practice of painters and sculptors in their concern with the visual and tactile qualities of the physical world. Rilke's *Der Panther*, one seeming triumph of poetic objectivity in that collection, is as much a poem about the poetic process as a poem about a panther: the caged animal's gaze, which encounters only images unrelated to the panther's true nature, images that enter the panther's eyes but 'cease to be' when they reach his heart, like the bars of the first stanzas, with no 'world' behind them – all these are analogies of the poet's alienated 'inwardness.' But that, too, is 'psychologically speaking,' and there is no need for us to enquire into the psychological machinery. What makes the poem successful is that the poet *has* found a correspondence that works – Eliot's 'objective correlative' – and rendered it in such a way as not to distract us with allusions to his state of mind. Baudelaire's poem *L'Albatros*, psychologically speaking, is a similar poem, but Baudelaire still felt obliged to explain and resolve his analogy between the animal and the poet 'whose giant's wings prevent him from walking,' much as Rilke's panther is a 'great will' paralysed by the lack of anything on which to exercise itself. Baudelaire's explanation turns his albatross into a metaphorical bird, less interesting in itself than Rilke's panther; and it allows the unsympathetic or literal-minded reader to object that poets, not being birds or angels, don't have wings, let alone giant's wings. The comparison detracts from both the bird and the poet, because even the most rigorously sustained simile always implies that the two things compared are not, in fact, identical. Whatever its psychological and philosophical premises, therefore, Mallarmé's recourse to freely floating, unanchored and unexplained images enriched the resources of poetry; artistically speaking – that is, in terms of effects rather than causes – it absolved later poets from the stale dichotomy of mind and things.

4   Language itself guarantees that no poetry will be totally 'dehumanized,' regardless of whether a poet attempts to project pure inwardness outwards – as Rilke often did – or to lose and find himself in animals, plants and inanimate things. The exact balance between the expression of feeling and penetration of the world outside may be a problem for poets when they are not writing poetry, as well as for those of their critics whose main interests are psychological and philosophical. If the poem succeeds, the problem is resolved in that poem: within its bounds a magical correspondence does indeed prevail. Something of this interchangeability seems to attach even to the latest experiments in a kind of poetry that neither expresses nor records anything at all, but makes words and their interrelationships its only material; significantly enough, this kind of poetry has been described both as 'abstract' and as 'Concrete' poetry.

William Carlos Williams is another poet whose work is crowded with people, places and things. As in Ponge's work, this involvement was an active one, based on the reciprocity of imagination and external reality. It is usual to label Williams with the prescription 'no ideas but in things,' a parenthesis that occurs in his poem *A Sort of Song*:[15]

> Let the snake wait under
> his weed
> and the writing
> be of words, slow and quick, sharp
> to strike, quiet to wait
> sleepless.
>
> – through metaphor to reconcile
> the people and the stones.
> Compose. (No ideas
> but in things) Invent!
> Saxifrage is my flower that splits
> the rocks.

To begin with, this is a dynamic poem of discovery; and the words in brackets are not a prescription, .but part of an experience – a part of the experience, incidentally, which could not be rendered in terms of the two 'images' or things dominant in the poem, the snake and the saxifrage. In later poems Williams evolved a meditative style that no more excludes direct statement of ideas than does that of Eliot's *Four Quartets*; and even here he has to resort to the language of ideas in order to convey his purpose – akin to Ponge's opposition to the anthropocentric exploitation of the universe – 'through metaphor to reconcile the people and the stones.' A later poem, *The Desert Music*, adds a reflection on the character of Williams's involvement with the outside world:

> to imitate, not to copy nature, not
> to copy nature
>
> NOT prostrate to copy nature
> but a dance . . . ![16]

The line that follows carries us right back into the physical world, so that once more the lines quoted lose their prescriptive character and become part of an experience that is also a discovery. In both cases it is impossible, and irrelevant, to say whether Williams has written a poem about the poetic process or about people and things.

Nor is there any real inconsistency between the procedure in the earlier poem, *A Sort of Song,* and Williams's words in another, later poem, *The Host* – words that have also been detached from their context and treated as a kind of manifesto:

> it is all
>   according to the imagination!
> Only the imagination
>   is real! They have imagined it
>   therefore it is so[17]

Here Williams is not even speaking primarily about poetry or art, but about religious belief – which to him, a non-believer, is imagination – and as always the general observation proceeds from his encounter with people, places and things, from a specific occasion which he does not so much narrate as dynamically re-enact in words that render both an inner and an outer experience.

Read out of context, 'Only the imagination is real' becomes a statement which one would be inclined to attribute not to Williams, but to his American contemporary who seems to represent the opposite pole of modern poetry, Wallace Stevens – a poet as self-contained as Williams was open to everything around him. Yet the diction and, above all, the syntax and metre of the immediate context – with that word 'they' which switches without transition from the general statement to the people of the poem, the 'tall negro evangelist,' the 'two Irish nuns' and the 'white-haired Anglican' – bring us back at once to Williams and the urgency of immediate experience. Philosophically, Williams and Stevens meet in that passage, as extremes are apt to meet in modern poetry, since the possibilities of poetic expression are always being pushed to the limits. When such a limit has been reached, a poet may swing back to the other side. Yet the principle of imagination was no less present in the words on either side of the parenthesis in *A Sort of Song,* the words 'compose' and 'invent.' If there is a seeming contradiction between 'no ideas but in things' and 'Only the imagination is real' it has to do with language itself.

One thing that Williams had in common with Wallace Stevens, as with Ezra Pound and T.S.Eliot and almost every significant poet of his time, was a constant concern with the possibilities and limits of language, including the contradiction inherent in it as the material of poetry. In his profound and perceptive essay *The Poet as Fool and Priest*[18] the late Sigurd Burckhardt showed why language itself forbids total abstraction in poetry or prose:

There can be no non-representational poetry; the very medium forbids. MacLeish's 'A poem should not mean but be' points to an important truth, but as it stands it is nonsense, because the medium of poetry is unlike any other. Words must mean; if they don't they are gibberish. The painter's tree is an image; but if the poet writes 'tree,' he does not create an image. He *uses* one; the poetic image is one only in a metaphorical sense. . . . Words already have what the artist first wants to give them – meaning – and fatally lack what he needs in order to shape them – body.

This fundamental, but easily overlooked, characteristic of language points to one of the limits that Williams came up against, as all the one-time Imagists did. Incidentally, it also disposes of Erich Heller's fears about the arrogance of those – like Mallarmé, Rilke or Stevens – who set themselves up as 'creator poets,' and it modifies all definitions of the functions of poetry which – like Susanne Langer's – are based on a consideration of all the arts. Burckhardt goes on to explain why poets – and not only modern poets – have often gone out of their way to make their language 'difficult' (just as other poets, or the same poets at other times, have cultivated a simplicity of diction equally far removed from the literary or non-literary styles of discourse prevalent in their time):

Ideally, the language of social intercourse should be as window-glass; we should not notice that it stands between us and the meaning 'behind' it. But when chemists recently developed a plastic coating which made the glass it was spread on fully invisible, the results were far from satisfactory: people bumped into the glass. If there were a language pure enough to transmit all human experience without distortion, there would be no need for poetry. But such a language not only does not, it cannot exist. Language can no more do justice to all human truth than law can to all human wishes. In its very nature as a social instrument it must be a convention, must arbitrarily order the chaos of experiences, allowing expression to some, denying it to others. It must provide common denominators, and so it necessarily falsifies, just as the law necessarily inflicts injustice. And these falsifications will be the more dangerous the more 'transparent' language seems to become, the more unquestionably it is accepted as an undistorting medium. It is not windowglass but rather a system of lenses which focus and refract the rays of an hypothetical unmediated vision. The first purpose of poetic language, and of metaphors in particular, is the very opposite of making language more transparent. Metaphors increase an awareness of the distortion of language by increasing the thickness and curvature of the lenses and so exaggerating the angles of refraction. They shake us loose from the comfortable conviction that a grave is a grave is a grave. They are semantic puns, just as puns are phonetic metaphors; though they leave words as sounds intact, they break their semantic identity.

Poetic language, then, resorts to what Brecht, in a very different connection, called 'alienation effects.' Metre and rhyme, Burckhardt shows, are such effects, until they become a 'binding convention of poetry' and lose their 'dissociative force.' Commenting on the song from *The Tempest*, 'Full fathom five . . .' he shows that in order to be rich the word in poetry 'must first become strange.' Dislocations of normal syntax, as in Mallarmé, are another device of that kind. 'A word that can function simultaneously as two or more different parts of speech, a phrase which can be parsed in two or more ways – to the despair of all grammar teachers – simply extends the pervasive incertitude of poetry from words to their connections into statements.'

Yet as soon as such things as rhyme, metre and inversion have become poetic conventions, poets may have to reverse the whole process in order to produce the necessary alienation. They may even try to do without metaphoric language of any kind, since non-poetic discourse, too, is full of metaphors. If poetic or discursive conventions tend towards formality and intricacy, they will explore the possibilities of simple colloquial language, as Blake and Wordsworth did in the eighteenth century, or as Williams did in ours.

In this context Burckhardt takes up William Empson's analysis of ambiguity and shifts 'the emphasis a little,' as he puts it – a modest understatement on his part:

He [Empson] made us aware that one word can – and in great poetry commonly does – have *many meanings*; I would rather insist on the converse, that many meanings have *one word*. For the poet, the ambiguous word is the crux of the problem of creating a medium for him to work in. If meanings are primary and words only their signs, then ambiguous words are false; each meaning should have its word, as each sound should have its letter. But if the reverse is true and words are primary – if, that is, they are the corporeal entities the poet requires – then ambiguity is something quite different: it is the fracturing of a pristine unity by the analytic conceptualizations of prose.

The distinction leads Burckhardt to his main contention that the nature of language itself forces poets into the dual roles of fool and priest, since 'the poet's purpose is to tell truths – truths which escape the confines of discursive speech. And to do so he is committed to the word, even the negative, as in some sense physically present. How, then, can he express negations?' Burckhardt finds the answer in Shakespeare's 116th sonnet, though the function of negatives and negation in more recent poetry is a special one that will concern me in another chapter. For the present, Burckhardt's conclusion that 'the poet must always be half fool, the corrupter of words,' is worth bearing in mind, just because it is his analysis of passages from Shakespeare that led to it. The contradictions inherent in language itself are not confined to poetry after Baudelaire, though modern poets have experienced them most acutely.

The poet would be much safer [Burckhardt writes] if he did not commit himself to the Word, but in ironic detachment exploited the infinite ambiguities of speech. Or he could retreat to the safety of a sacro-religious order, give up his claim to verbal priesthood and turn 'mouthpiece.' Both roads have been taken – but they lead to self-abnegation. . . . Where the philosopher seeks certitude in the sign – the 'p' of propositional calculus – and the mystic in the ineffable – the 'OM' of the Hindoos – the poet takes upon himself the paradox of the human word, which is both and neither and which he creatively transforms in his 'powerful rhyme.' This rhyme is his deed; it dissociates, dissolves the word into its components – mark and bark – but simultaneously fuses it into a new and now sacramental union.

5   The purpose of poets, then, is 'to tell truths,' but in ways necessarily complicated by the 'paradox of the human word.' From Baudelaire onwards (and long before Baudelaire) poets have grappled endlessly with that basic paradox; and

since the writing of poetry is a 'deed' – a process of exploration and discovery – the truths told are of a special kind. Certainly there have been times when, even in verse, the emphasis fell on the elegant and decorous exposition of truths that were already the common property of writer and reader; but those were periods of a cultural homogeneity – or of a cultural exclusiveness – unknown to any of the poets with whom I am concerned. 'One of the most difficult things in writing poetry,' Wallace Stevens remarked with a matter-of-fact dryness not really surprising in a poet active long after Mallarmé, 'is to know what one's subject is. Most people know what it is and do not write poetry, because they are so conscious of that one thing. One's subject is always poetry, or should be. But sometimes it becomes a little more definite and fluid, and the thing goes ahead rapidly.'[19] In other words, it is the poem that tells the poet what he thinks, not *vice versa*; and Stevens remarks on just that peculiarity of poets – an aspect of what Keats called their 'negative capability' – in a later letter:[20] 'Some people always know exactly what they think. I am afraid that I am not one of those people. The same thing keeps active in my mind and rarely becomes fixed. This is true about politics as about poetry.' Yet the thinking does crystallize – in poems; and Stevens could also write: 'It made me happy the other day to find that Carnap said flatly that poetry and philosophy are one. The philosophy of the sciences is not opposed to poetry any more than the philosophy of mathematics is opposed.'[21]

Mallarmé, Valéry, Stevens and Jorge Guillén are some of the poets who have tried to think in purely poetic terms, much as a mathematician thinks in purely mathematical terms – without direct reference, that is, to concerns that may well have been theirs when they were doing other things. As Mallarmé wrote in 1867, he created his work 'only by *elimination*.' This elimination, active also in the work of later poets, is certainly akin both to the abstractions of mathematics and to the trend towards abstract forms in the visual arts that began with the post-Impressionists; but since words have meanings independent of the special functions that poetry lends to them, such analogies should never be taken too literally. Even Stevens combined elements of verbal clowning with his philosophical seriousness, which was priestly in the precise sense that Burckhardt defined.

Stevens began with a belief in poetry for poetry's sake: 'What I am after in all this is poetry, and I don't think that I have ever written anything with any other objective than to write poetry.'[22] It was only when he tried to explain this belief to himself and to others that he came to relate it to preoccupations that were by no means purely aesthetic.

It is the paradox inherent in language itself that makes the theories and occasional pronouncements of poets more confusing, more obscure and often more self-contradictory than their practice. Pierre Reverdy, for instance, wrote in 1948 that 'the poet has no subject at all. . . . His work is valuable just because it adduces no reason for its discontinuity and its process of fusing with incompatible things.' In a radio discussion with Francis Ponge and Jean Cocteau the same poet said that 'form is only the visible part of content – the skin.' The two statements seem to contradict each other, though both make sense when applied to Reverdy's poetry, or to that of many other poets of his time. In the first instance Reverdy was thinking of a subject that could be paraphrased in prose, translated or abstracted from its medium into that of logical discourse. In the second instance he was thinking not of that kind of subject, but of the peculiarly poetic thinking and feeling and imagining that do indeed determine the form of a poem, especially where that form is 'organic' or 'free.' Both statements, therefore, say something about the indivisibility of form and content in poetry, and both imply a distinction between content and subject.

Genuine differences between poets do arise over the value that each attributes to the public functions and implications of poetry – functions and implications that are very far from having been eliminated once and for all by Mallarmé's dictum that 'poems are made not of ideas but of words,' or by MacLeish's 'a poem should not mean but be.' These, in any case, are half-truths, as Burckhardt argued, since words can never be totally severed from the connection with ideas and meaning. Nor does one need to be a Marxist to recognize that all poetry has political, social and moral implications, regardless of whether the intention behind it is didactic and 'activist' or not. Contrary to what Hugo Friedrich has asserted, a very good case could be made out for the special humanity of much modern poetry, a concern with humankind as a whole all the more intense for being 'depersonalized' as much Romantic poetry was not, because the more confessional of the Romantic poets were primarily interested in their own individuality and in those things that made them different from other people.

Quite apart from moral or political commitments as such – and I shall have more to say of these, as of the persistence of Romantic-Symbolist attitudes in poets otherwise modern – the mere practice of poetry as an art whose medium is language has social implications which have been given special prominence this century, as by the Austrian critic and aphorist Karl Kraus, all of whose copious writings on society and literature are based on the analysis of the many uses and abuses of language. If poets are writers whose use of language is necessarily critical, because whatever else a poem may be it cannot be a good poem unless every word in it has been weighed, they have an inescapable function that has been stressed even by a writer as much at odds with his own society and its values as Ezra Pound: 'Has literature a function in the state, in the aggregation of humans, in the republic . . .? It has. . . . It has to do with the clarity and vigour of "any and every" thought and opinion. . . . When this work goes rotten – by that I do not mean when they express indecorous thoughts – but when the very medium, the very essence of their work, the application of word to thing goes rotten, i.e. becomes slushy and inexact, or excessive or bloated, the whole machinery of social and individual thought and order goes to pot.'[23] That was also the view of Karl Kraus, who was far from sharing Ezra Pound's political enthusiasms at this time. These political enthusiasms have a great deal to do with the extent to which Pound remained rooted in the Romantic-Symbolist aesthetic; but, however limited his view of social realities, Pound was passionately concerned with them in a way that Mallarmé, for instance, was not: 'In proportion as his work is exact, i.e. true to human consciousness and to the nature of man, as it is exact in formulation of desire, so it is durable and so it is useful; I mean it maintains the precision, and clarity of thought not merely for the benefit of a few dilettantes and "lovers of literature," but maintains the health of thought outside literary circles and in non-literary existence, in general individual and communal life.'[24] Nor is there any confusion about ideas and words, the meaning and the being of poetry, in

Pound's definition of great literature, in the same work, as 'merely language charged with meaning to the utmost possible degree.'

'Human consciousness' and 'the nature of man' – these two concepts alone indicate why poetry can never exclude man, as long as it is written by human beings rather than machines (and even machines are designed and made by men). What poetry can exclude, especially where words are picked up at random, split up into their components or left to form visual or sonic patterns on the page, is individuality; but where those exercises are meaningful, they reveal something about language, and language brings us back to 'human consciousness' and 'the nature of man.'

Octavio Paz has explained why 'poetry is a food which the bourgeoisie – as a class – has proved incapable of digesting.'[25] Poetry, he argues, has tried in different ways to abolish 'the distance between the word and the thing,' and this distance is due to the self-consciousness of civilized men and their separation from nature. 'The word is not identical with the reality which it names because between men and things – and, on a deeper level, between men and their being – self-consciousness interposes.' Modern poetry, according to Paz, moves between two poles, which he calls the magical and the revolutionary. The magical consists in a desire to return to nature by dissolving the self-consciousness that separates us from it, 'to lose oneself for ever in animal innocence, or liberate oneself from history.' The revolutionary aspiration, on the other hand, demands a 'conquest of the historical world and of nature.' Both are ways of bridging the same gap and reconciling the 'alienated consciousness' to the world outside.

Yet both tendencies may be at work within the same poet, and even within the same poem, just as a poet may combine the function of priest and fool, hater and lover of words. Octavio Paz, too, has written: 'What characterizes a poem is its necessary dependence on words as much as its struggle to transcend them.'[26] The dependence has to do with the poet's involvement in history and society, the transcendence with the magical short cut back to nature and to the primitive unity of word and thing. Both correspond to general human concerns, though many people may be unaware of the tensions and complexities inherent in their relationship with words or with things. An extraordinary degree of alienation from language, even as a medium of simple communication, has become more and more widespread in 'advanced' societies, as one can see in television interviews with young people incapable of uttering a simple short sentence not helped out by 'sort of' and 'you know.' The causes of this non-articulation may well be closely connected with the 'word-scepticism' which underlies many of the practices of modern poets (and which Hofmannsthal attributed to a basic split between the conventions of language and the reality of particular things).[27] The truth of poetry, and of modern poetry especially, is to be found not only in its direct statements but in its peculiar difficulties, short cuts, silences, hiatuses and fusions.

3

LOST IDENTITIES

1   MALLARMÉ's experience of nothingness – 'le néant'
– was not without precedent in pre-Symbolist poetry. Leopardi
had known it, and Baudelaire had his 'abyss.' When, at the end
of the last poem in *Les Fleurs du mal*, Baudelaire addressed Death,
the 'old captain,' and went on:

> Nous voulons, tant ce feu nous brûle le cerveau,
> Plonger au fond du gouffre, Enfer ou Ciel, qu'importe?
> Au fond de l'Inconnu pour trouver du *nouveau!*

> (So fiercely our brains burn, we're driven to
> Plunge down into the chasm – Heaven or Hell, who cares? –
> Right down into the Unknown to find the *new*.)

he was also signposting the future development of Symbolist
poetry, Mallarmé's beauty that is found in the very abyss that
Baudelaire invoked. This plunging into the abyss, so as to find
something new, demanded the abandonment of that 'empirical
self' which was still very much in evidence in other poems of
Baudelaire. It was left to Mallarmé to remove all traces of it
from his later poetry, and to Rimbaud to record what happens
to the 'empirical self' when it is systematically destroyed so as
to make it a vehicle, 'a drunken vessel,' for poetry. 'On me
pense' ('I am being thought') Rimbaud announced to his friends
in 1871, and 'Je est un autre' ('I is another'). In the same letter
of May 1871, he declared: 'Le poète se fait *voyant* par un long,
immense et raisonné dérèglement de tous les sens.'1*

*The poet turns himself into a visionary by a long, drastic and deliberate
disordering of all his senses.'

42

It is only in his early, more argumentative than visionary poems that Rimbaud still felt it necessary to negate. So in *Ce qu'on dit au poète à propos de fleurs* :

> Mais, Cher, l'Art n'est plus, maintenant,
> – C'est la vérité – de permettre
> A l'Eucalyptus étonnant
> Des constrictors d'un hexamètre;[2]

> (But, friend, it's no longer Art –
> And this is the truth – to allow
> The astonishing Eucalyptus
> An hexameter's constrictors.)

or:

> Dis, non les pampas printaniers
> Noirs d'épouvantables révoltes,
> Mais les tabacs, les cotonniers!
> Dis les exotiques récoltes!

> (Speak of no pampas in the Spring
> Black with atrocious revolution,
> But tobacco, cotton plants!
> Speak of exotic crops brought in.)

The whole of this argument between Romantic and realistic attitudes, or between aestheticism and utilitarianism, is a variation on Heinrich Heine's prophecy in his *Confessions* of 1854 that poets of the future would have to contend with a 'democratic rage against love poetry. Why sing of roses, you aristocrat? Sing of the democratic potato, which keeps the people alive.' Rimbaud's poem includes a near-paraphrase of that remark:

> Surtout, rime une version
> Sur le mal des pommes de terre!

> (Above all, rhyme a version
> All about potato blight.)

The new freedom of the imagination in Rimbaud's later work could dispense with arguments, though the great negation that preceded this freedom and made it possible is invoked very economically in *L'Eternité* :

> Là pas d'espérance,
> Nul orietur.[3]

43

> (There no hope remains,
> Nul orietur.)

By the time he wrote the free verse of *Mouvement* and the prose poetry of *Les Illuminations* and *Une Saison en enfer* Rimbaud was anticipating Surrealism, Dadaism and even the latest pop art, as in *Délires II*, with its dismissal of 'the celebrities of painting and of modern poetry' as ludicrous, and its list of substitutes, including 'erotic books with incorrect spelling' and 'popular colour prints.' Not only his own 'empirical self,' but human identity in general, had become so dubious as to be freely inter-changeable: 'To every being several *other* lives seemed to me due. This gentleman doesn't know what he's doing: he is an angel. This family is a brood of dogs. In front of several men I chatted aloud with a moment in one of their other lives – in that way I've loved a pig.'

It is the work of two other French poets of the period, Corbière and Laforgue, that took up the argument in Rimbaud's early poem between Romantic-Symbolist aestheticism and a bitter awareness of unromantic realities – a polarity that corresponds to Baudelaire's *spleen* and *idéal*, and one that he could compress into lines like

Eldorado banal de tous les vieux garçons[4]

(Trite Eldorado of every old bachelor's dreams)

his description of Cythera, Aphrodite's isle. Corbière, like Baudelaire, never succeeded in totally dissolving his 'empirical self.' He remained a confessional poet, though an anti-Romantic one, a confessional poet with a vengeance. Most of his work is a self-exposure of self-centred Romantic attitudes; and negation is one mode of its pervasive irony.

2   'Je rime, donc je vis,' Tristan Corbière wrote in *Le Poète contumace*; but this existential affirmation of art for art's sake – if not life for art's sake – has to be read in its context, the half-lyrical, half-dramatic exposition of a poet's existence, as experienced by him and as seen by others, in its social setting. Here, as elsewhere, Corbière's irony creates a multiple self-

portrait which, according to the angle of vision, presents caricatures and even a blank:

> C'est bien moi, je suis là – mais comme une rature.

> (Yes, it's me all right – I'm there – but like an erasure.)

Positives and negatives are so well balanced as to cancel each other out:

> Dans mes dégoûts surtout, j'ai des goûts élégants;
> Tu sais: j'avais lâché la vie avec des gants. . . .

> (In my distastes above all I have elegant tastes;
> You know, with gloves on I let go of life. . . .)

Baudelaire, too, had cultivated that disgust and that desperate elegance, accusing himself in the prose poem *A une heure du matin* of having 'distributed handshakes . . . without having taken the precaution of buying gloves.' But Baudelaire's prose poem is a justification of the poet as pariah and aristocrat in a bourgeois world. Corbière's poem, among other things, is a demolition of that last refuge, since one of his perspectives is that of the poor Breton community to which he belonged and did not belong. Corbière's gloves serve not to protect his poetic integrity and superiority as a poet, but to 'let go of life' in style and make the most, poetically, of his self-destruction.

Corbière was obsessed by negations and doubts as to his own reality. In a different spirit from Rimbaud – without Rimbaud's plunge into frenzied imagination – he played with the *disjecti membra* of the empirical self in *Bonsoir*:

> Ses chants? . . . C'était d'un autre; il ne les a pas lus.

> (His songs? . . . Those were by someone else. He never read them.)

In *Déclin* and *Pauvre garçon*, there is the juggling with 'nothing' – a simple 'Rien' not dignified with the metaphysical overtones of Mallarmé's 'le néant.'

> Oh! comme il était Rien! . . .

> (Oh, how he was Nothing! . . .)

> Serait-il mort de chic, de boire ou de phtisie?
> Ou peut-être, après tout, de rien . . .
> > > > ou bien de moi,

> (Could he have died of *chic*, of drink or of consumption?
> Or maybe, after all, of nothing . . . or of me?)

the 'me' being the Muse – as Destroyer, akin to Baudelaire's Beauty in the duel with whom 'the artist cries out in terror before being vanquished.'[5]

Although, in his *Epitaphe*, Corbière presented himself as a *poseur*, he refused to escape from multiple, fluid identity, as many Symbolist poets did, into a succession of *personae* or to a simple, consistent poetic mask. Corbière's self-portraits are the most truthful rendering in poetry of what Keats had said in prose about the 'chameleon' character of the poet, who is 'the most unpoetical of anything in existence, because he has no Identity – he is continually in for and filling some other body.'[6] Corbière's limitation was that he was intent on exposing that lack of identity – too truthful, perhaps, or too literal or too preoccupied with his own wretchedness to project himself into persons or things and 'fill some other body.' Corbière carried out one half of Keats's prescription for 'strengthening one's intellect' – to 'make up one's mind about nothing'; but he failed in the other half – 'to let the mind be a thoroughfare for all thoughts, not a select party.'[7] His poetry always returns to the self that was not a self but a 'mélange adultère de tout.'

In that same poem, *Epitaphe*, he wrote of his poses that were not poses, because he was too conscious of posing:

> Ne fut *quelqu'un*, ni quelque chose.
> Son naturel était la *pose*.
> Pas poseur, posant pour *l'unique*;
> Trop naïf, étant trop cynique;
> Ne croyant à rien, croyant tout.
> – Son goût était dans le dégoût.
>
> (Was neither *anyone* nor anything.
> Was most himself when posturing.
> Not a *poseur*, posed for the *One*, not all;
> Too naïve, being too cynical;
> Believing in nothing, too credulous:
> Put all his gusto into feeling disgust.)

Even when Corbière writes about a toad, he does not identify himself with the toad but compares himself to it; and I have already suggested why poetic comparisons are odious. In the same way his sonnet to his dog Sir Bob becomes a poem about himself, a comparison to the literal dog's advantage – the dog is purebred and English, unlike his master – but detrimental to all but the autobiographical interest of the poem.

Corbière was truly modern, nonetheless, not only because of the dilemma that was his constant theme, but in the tone and diction of his verse. His colloquialism, for one thing, was an effective break with poetic conventions that retained a strong hold on Baudelaire; and the potentialities of his colloquial diction were to be appreciated outside France, even if later French poets, on the whole, preferred the example of Rimbaud's 'alchemy of the word' or of Mallarmé's hermetical symbolism. Something of Corbière's tone, with its understatements, its diffidence, and its self-mockery, intermingled with the tone of Laforgue in T.S. Eliot's early poems, and Ezra Pound acknowledged a similar debt to Corbière's 'hard-bit lines,' calling him 'perhaps the most poignant poet since Villon, in very much Villon's manner.'[8] The hardness and roughness that Pound admired in Corbière is mainly a quality of his diction. Despite Eliot's greater debt to Laforgue, it was Eliot who came closer than Pound to the tone of such lines as these from Corbière's *Rapsodie du sourd*:

> Vous ne me direz mot : je ne répondrai rien . . .
> Et lors rien ne pourra dédorer l'entretien.

> (You will not breathe a word : nothing I shall reply
> And nothing then will spoil our colloquy.)

The literal appeal of Corbière's work is inseparable from his limitations. His poems are exercises in truthfulness, a truthfulness seemingly confined to the self-confessions of a man whose recurrent complaint is that he has no self, of a lover who has no beloved :

> Et ma moitié : c'est une femme . . .
> Une femme que je n'ai pas.[9]

That is Corbière's theme. But there is another truth of poetry which has to do not with its theme, not with what it says, but with what it does. The very thoroughness and daring of Corbière's self-exposures releases an energy whose vibrations are positive, though his theme is not. The very elusiveness of his empirical self leads him to an inevitable confrontation with a void that was not his alone, though existential thinkers had not yet vulgarized its universality. In the same poem, *Paria*, that confrontation is at least implied:

> Je ne connais pas mon semblable;
> Moi, je suis ce que je me fais.
>
> (I've yet to meet the man who's like me;
> Like me? I'm what I make myself.)

Those lines are followed by a quotation from Pascal, who well in advance of the existentialists confronted the void and realized that we do in fact make ourselves what we are by a choice. Technically, Corbière's poetry rarely goes beyond the confrontation; but his diction and tone are stripped of those rhetorical and grandiloquent trappings which belong not only to literary conventions but also to the beliefs and attitudes and opinions behind them – the beliefs and attitudes and opinions that treat human identity as something given, not made. Because Baudelaire did not dispense with a certain traditional vocabulary, as Corbière did, his work has invited all sorts of theological interpretations that may well be largely irrelevant to it. In that respect, too, Corbière – who died in 1875, only eight years later than Baudelaire – was a considerable innovator.

His use of the vernacular and direct statement places him in a line of development other than that of Symbolism; but again it must be stressed that modernity should not be looked for only in poets who aspired to the autonomy of the image and to a diction as remote as possible from common usage. Pound and Eliot were not alone in taking up the innovations of Corbière. German translations[10] appeared just when the twentieth-century modernist movement was gathering impetus, and at least two of the early Expressionist poets, Hoddis and Lichtenstein, combined Corbière's irony with a grotesque or deliberately trivial imagery not unlike his own. Apart from related tendencies in some of the work of Verlaine and all of that of Laforgue – Corbière's near-contemporaries – French modernism, too, has not been exclusively hermetic. Apollinaire, Blaise Cendrars, Max Jacob, Paul Eluard and Pierre Reverdy are a few of the twentieth-century French poets who did not scorn the vernacular and found the naïve tone conducive to subtle effects.

Corbière's own development was towards subtlety and delicacy, *Les Amours jaunes* was to be followed by *Mirlitons*, and the
few short poems in this series which he lived to complete have a
lightness of texture, a tenderness and playfulness more reminiscent of Ronsard than of Villon. Here Corbière's essential ironies
are taken for granted, and the poet is rid of the compulsion to
define his own identity by negatives and paradoxes, as he did
succinctly in the shorter of his two poems called *Epitaphe*. This
posthumous poem is like a final summing-up of Corbière's
'negative capability' in the form of a laconic inventory:

> Mélange adultère de tout:
> De la fortune et pas le sou,
> De l'énergie et pas de force,
> La Liberté, mais une entorse.
> Du coeur, du coeur! de l'âme, non –
> Des amis, pas un compagnon,
> De l'idée et pas une idée,
> De l'amour et pas une aimée

> (Adulterate mixture of everything;
> Without a bean, rich as a king,
> Full of energy and yet effete,
> Free to go anywhere, with twisted feet.
> No heart? Yes, plenty, but no soul,
> With friends enough, yet not one pal,
> Crammed with ideas, but none to guide him,
> Loving, with never a girl beside him),

ending with the unresolved paradox:

> Il mourut en s'attendant vivre
> Et vécut s'attendant mourir.

> (Waiting for life to start he died
> And lived awaiting death.)

Baudelaire also spent his life 'waiting to live'; but there was a
great deal more literary posing in Baudelaire's poetry than in
these stark lines. When Corbière wrote that 'his nature was to
pose' he must have meant something other than insincerity. His
posing has to do with the very dilemma which he recorded, not
with the manner in which he recorded it. Where the 'empirical
self' has become as dubious as it was to Corbière, self-confession,
however truthful, cannot escape from the unreality that is its

49

subject matter. The 'self' written about becomes no more than a multiplicity of alternatives, possibilities and potentialities. Like Keats, Baudelaire, too, was well aware of this, and his prose poem *Les Foules* (Crowds) suggests the way out taken by himself at times, by later poets consistently:

Multitude, solitude: terms that, to the active and fruitful poet, are synonymous and interchangeable. A man who cannot people his solitude is no less incapable of being alone in a busy crowd.
The poet enjoys the incomparable privilege that he can, at will, be either himself or another.[11]

In the same prose poem he writes of the man who 'can gorge himself with vitality at the expense of the human race' because he has 'a love of disguise and of the mask.'

All that is repetitive and limited in Corbière's work comes of his failure to pose in this sense. Yet for the same reason he tells us more than any other poet of his time about what it was that made the need for masks so acute and imperative at the end of the Romantic period. From now on a poet's self was what he chose to make it, his identity to be found only in the bodies that he chose to fill.

3   Although his life was even shorter than Corbière's, Jules Laforgue was not only the more sophisticated ironist, but a poet who transcended many of the limitations of the confessional mode. Like Corbière and Mallarmé, and Baudelaire before them, Laforgue began with a late phase of the 'malheur d'être poète,' that 'Weltschmerz' which, increasingly, had consisted in having no world worth grieving over – and as an inevitable consequence very little self to do the grieving. After his early collection *Le Sanglot de la terre*, with its Baudelairean parodies of Christian devotion, Laforgue continued where Corbière left off in the *Mirlitons* poems. To self-mockery and colloquialism he added a delight in verbal clowning, as in the dedication of his next collection to Paul Bourget and its pun on 'pour cent' (per cent) and 'pur sang' (pure blood):

> En deuil d'un Moi-le-Magnifique
> Lançant de front les cent pur-sangs
> De ses vingt ans tout hennissants ...

From this time onwards, until his death some five years later in 1887, Laforgue's formal experiments gave his work an increasing range, especially as regards rhythm and an *enjambement* that served to counteract the tendency of French verse to be sententious and aphoristic. The example of Corbière is suggested not only by Laforgue's use of such words as *chic*,* one of Corbière's favourite words, but by an obsession with negatives and non-identity:

> Je vivotais, altéré de *Nihil* de toutes
> Les citernes de mon Amour? ...
>
> Oh! qu'il n'y ait personne et que Tout continue!
> Alors géhenne à fous, sans raison, sans issue!
>
> . . . .
> Et que Jamais soit Tout bien intrinsèquement.
>
> (I sort of lived, sustained by the Nihil of all
> The cisterns of my Love? ...
>
> Oh, how there's nobody and how All goes on!
> Gehenna for madmen, then, without reason or consequence!
>
> . . . .
> And Never, quite intrinsically, is All.)

In *Complainte de cette bonne lune*, the poem from which T.S. Eliot adapted his line 'la lune ne garde aucune rancune' in *Rhapsody on a Windy Night* and the 'prickly pear' passage in *The Hollow Men*, Laforgue coins the portmanteau word '[la céleste] Eternullité,' an invention as typical of his verbal ingenuity as of his capacity to make the endemic nihilism amusing – in poems aptly called 'Complaints.' Laforgue's melancholy was as genuine as Corbière's; and, like both Corbière and Rimbaud, he experienced a self-alienation which the ironic reference to 'Moi-le-Magnifique' helps us to understand. That 'I-the-Magnificent' is the 'egotistical sublime' of Romantic poetry, most magnificently and magniloquently present in the poetry of Victor Hugo, who survived Corbière and was still vociferously alive when Laforgue, like Verlaine, resolved to 'wring the neck of rhetoric.'† This was in 1882. In a letter of that year Laforgue wrote about his first collection: 'I'm disgusted with it: at that time I wanted to be

---

*E.g. 'en ce Paris, jardin/ Obtus et chic.' *Préludes autobiographiques.*

†Laforgue quoted Verlaine's 'l'éloquence, tords-lui son cou' in his letter to Charles Henry of July 1884.

eloquent, and that gets on my nerves these days. To indulge in eloquence seems to me to be in such bad taste, so simple-minded.'[12] Writing to his sister two years later, about his more sophisticated later poems, Laforgue returned to this matter: 'I find it stupid to mouth big words and play at eloquence. Now that I'm more sceptical and don't take off so easily and, at the same time, master my language in a more minute, more clown-like way, I write little poems of fancy, with only one end in view: to produce something original at any price.' In the same letter he admits that 'life is gross – true enough – but, by God, when it comes to poetry, let's be as exquisite as carnations.'

Just as Corbière could only identify himself with the fishermen of Brittany to the extent of seeing himself as they saw him – exacerbating his self-consciousness and his sense of being different by that partial identification – so Laforgue could find no substitute for the 'Moi-le-Magnifique' that had become absurd and vulgar. The Romantic-Symbolist aesthetic told him that 'poetry should not be an exact description (like a page of a novel) but be bathed in dream.' His irony could serve to mediate between 'gross' realities and delicate fantasies; but that same irony attested that the observer and the dreamer must remain as irreconcilable as the empirical and the poetical selves. Not surprisingly, therefore, Laforgue's poems render a self-estrangement as extreme as that of Rimbaud and Corbière:

> – Voyons, qu'est ce que je veux ?
> Rien. Je suis-t-il malhûreux !

That grammatical dislocation in *Autre complainte de l'orgue de Barbarie* corresponds exactly to Rimbaud's 'Je est un autre,' with the important difference that Laforgue avoids confessional sententiousness by slipping into buffoonery and mocking both the alienation and the unhappiness that have become poetic commonplaces. At the same time, there is a shift of emphasis from the alienated sensibility to the world around it, for the reader is free to attribute that refrain not to the poet's voice, but to the barrel-organ of the title. Laforgue's subtlety has hit on the 'objective correlative,' one of whose modes is the *persona*.

Elsewhere (*Complainte du sage de Paris*) Laforgue plays intricate variations on the 'loss of identity' theme, with a resourcefulness and inventiveness much greater than Corbière's:

... Sans songer : suis-je moi ? Tout est si compliqué !
Où serais-je à présent, pour tel coche manqué ?

(Without reflecting: Am I myself? It's all so complicated!
Where should I be at present, for what missed coach?)

The 'missed coach' of those lines links the 'loss of identity' theme
– the 'heart,' in the same poem, that 'rhymes with nothing' and
therefore questions its own authenticity – with Laforgue's awareness of the many possibilities open to a self that has become fluid
or volatile. Baudelaire had already made the connection between
'the love of disguise and of masks' and a 'passion for voyaging.'
Laforgue's voyages and travels, like Baudelaire's, are valuable
only as possibilities :

Oh ! qu'ils sont pittoresques, les trains manqués ...

(How picturesque they are, the trains we've missed ...)

or the boats, in the same posthumous poem, 'seen from the
jetty's edge.' The 'missed trains' are also an instance of
Laforgue's increasing ability to draw his images from the
workaday world, much as he extends his identity theme from
self-confession to general reflections like this, in *Nobles et
touchantes divagations sous la lune* :

Pas un Moi qui n'écume aux barreaux de sa cage
Et n'épluche ses jours en filaments d'ennui

(No self that does not foam against its bars
And pluck its days out into threads of boredom).

In that caged 'I' the panther of Rilke's poem is implicit as
well as Gottfried Benn's 'Gitter-Ich,' a concept which, in Benn's
work, implies a total separation of the empirical and the poetical
selves, and a total withdrawal of the latter from society. Yet
Laforgue's poem is an admirable example of his ability to
liberate the poetical self from its cage. The theme of his poem
is constriction and frustration; but its images draw so freely on
the trivia of modern urban life, as well as on nature, that the
pervasive melancholy becomes an attribute not of the poet, but
of the world around him. Laforgue's truly metaphysical wit
breaks the bars of his cage, as when he invites the Infinite to
show its credentials :

Infini, montre un peu tes papiers !

Though in another poem[13] Laforgue lamented that his 'great metaphysical distresses had been reduced to little domestic worries,' that was his strength as a poet, since the metaphysical concerns were not lost, but merged in an imagery that related them to the everyday experience of others. T.S. Eliot's appropriation of whole lines and passages from Laforgue, not to mention his more general indebtedness to the diction and mood of Laforgue's poetry, shows how completely Laforgue succeeded in being original – even thirty and forty years after his death. For *La Figlia che piange* alone Eliot took over the lines 'Penche, penche ta chère tête, va/Regarde les grappes des/Premiers lilas' from *Dimanches* and 'l'amour s'échange/Simple et sans foi comme un bonjour' from *Pétition* or the earlier *La Vie qu'elles me font mener*, as well as the last stanza of the posthumous poem beginning 'Oh! qu'une d'Elle-même....' Even the self-alienation and the nihilism that Laforgue shared with other poets of the age were not only redeemed by his inventiveness and wit, but turned to positive advantage by the extraordinary mobility of his poems, their rhapsodic structure that was to be adapted both for *The Waste Land* and for Pound's *Cantos*. Without deliberately writing whole poems in persons other than his own, Laforgue availed himself of the multiple selves at his disposal, freely switching from one to another; this enabled him to create one of the prototypes of the modern poem, especially the modern longer poem. Being the 'Lord Chancellor of Analysis,' as he called himself in *Dimanches*, he was well aware of these multiple selves:

> ... et ce sieur que j'intitule
> Moi, n'est, dit-on, qu'un polypier fatal!
> . . . .
> Quand j'organise une descente en Moi,
> J'en conviens, je trouve là, attablée,
> Une société un peu mêlée[14]

> (... and that gentleman whom I call
> Me, is no more, they say, than a fatal octopus!
> . . . .
> When I organize a descent into myself
> There, I confess, round the table I find
> A company somewhat mixed).

More than any other poet of his time Laforgue knew how to make use of the 'company somewhat mixed' that he found inside himself, letting each member of it speak in turn within the same poem. His use of the word 'organize' in this context is another instance of his readiness to include even the jargon of modern bureaucracy and commercialism – ironically and playfully, of course, but all the more effectively for that. Like Rilke and Eliot after him, Laforgue found modern tourism a particularly rich source for images of depersonalization. Corbière, like Baudelaire, had contrasted the sight visited with the sight imagined in poems like *Vésuves et Cie,* but it was Laforgue who wrote of 'this Grand Hotel of the anonymous,' in the context of a poem about a broken-off love affair, *Arabesques de malheur.* In Rilke's poem *Wendung* (Turning-Point), written some thirty years later, a hotel room becomes the very paradigm of modern loneliness, anonymity and fortuitousness – a connection already made in Laforgue's line, in the same poem, 'Ma Destinée est demimorte! . . . ,' and the context, too, is the failure to love. This failure, in both cases, has to do with the loss of a fixed personal identity, as Laforgue – almost unironic and quite unambiguous for once – shows in *Dimanches* ('Bref, j'allais me donner'):

> Bref, j'allais me donner d'un 'Je vous aime'
> Quand je m'avisais non sans peine
> Que d'abord je ne me possédais pas bien moi-même.
>
> (Mon Moi, c'est Galathée aveuglant Pygmalion!
> Impossible de modifier cette situation.)
>
> Ainsi donc, pauvre, pâle et piètre individu
> Qui ne croit à son Moi qu'à ses moments perdus,
> Je vis s'effacer ma fiancée
> Emportée par le cours des choses . . .
>
> (In short, I was about to give myself away
> With an 'I love you' when not without distress
> I realized that I didn't quite
> Possess myself in the first place.
>
> My Self, that's Galatea blinding
> Pygmalion! No way out of that.

> Poor pale and paltry individual, then,
> Who doesn't believe in his Self except
> At his lost moments,
> I saw my fiancée
> Fade out, carried away by the course of things . . .)

Laforgue's acute awareness that the age is one of 'no absolutes; but compromises;/ All is no more, all is allowed' (*Pétition*) has its exact parallel in the formal evolution of his poetry. To the rhapsodic structure the later poems add half-rhymes (as in *Air de biniou*: 'phrases'/ 'choses,' 'jalouse'/ 'prise'), more and more metrical and rhythmic irregularity, more and more enjambement, culminating in the free, partly unrhymed, verse of posthumous poems like *Dimanches* and *Pétition*. The effect of all these innovations is to render the casualness and permissiveness that are Laforgue's theme, summed up in the line 'Oh! que tout m'est accidentel!'15*

In the last, valedictory, poems – the *Derniers vers* – tenderness and compassion have largely replaced Laforgue's preoccupation, inherited from his predecessors, with his own alienation, isolation and unhappiness. Like T.S.Eliot's early poems – whose formal and thematic links with Laforgue are so close as to give one second thoughts about the twentieth-century 'revolution' in poetry – Laforgue's last poems subordinate self-confession and even self-expression to a critique of modern life, or perhaps life at any time:

> Nous ne serons jamais plus cruels que la vie
> Qui fait qu'il est des animaux injustement rossés
> Et des femmes à jamais laides . . .
>
> (We shall never be more cruel than life
> Which authorizes the existence of animals unjustly thrashed
> And of women for ever ugly . . .)

The refrain of that poem, *Simple agonie*, is a counsel of despair – 'break up everything.' Stylistically, there is a significant trend towards the 'simplicity' of the title, a trend not confined to this one poem. Paradox and irony are no longer the clowning of a divided self; they have become part of a vision of human existence as a whole, and all references to the poet's personal

*'Oh, how to me all is fortuitous!'

predicament illustrative of a wider concern with the cruelty and fortuitousness of life.

Yet that distinction, in modern poetry at least, is an artificial one. Baudelaire, Rimbaud, Corbière and Laforgue had all experienced a point where individual identity breaks down, becoming a non-self or a vehicle for other persons or things. It matters little whether, in the poem *Moeurs*, Laforgue reflects as a moralist on love-making in general, describing it as 'virtuosities for two and yet so lonely,' and asking 'Can you be the key to oblivion's harbours?'; or whether, in *Sur une défunte* and the last of the *Derniers vers*, he resorts to the first person singular to render the same anguish of fortuitousness, recapitulating love under the shadow of death:

> Et je ne serais qu'un pis-aller
> Comme l'est mon jour dans le Temps,
> Comme l'est ma place dans l'Espace . . .

> (And I shall be no more than a last resource
> As is my day in Time,
> As in my place in Space . . .)

The internal jingle on 'place' and 'espace' – though a truly functional rhyme in this context, since the place fits into space, and a more than aural relation is established – recalls Laforgue's metaphysical clowning. In a poem from the same sequence, *Le Mystère des trois cors*, Laforgue had even experimented with a kind of pure poetry different from Mallarmé's, a nonsense poetry akin to that of Edward Lear, T.S.Eliot's and Edith Sitwell's light verse and the Dadaist verse of Kurt Schwitters and Jean Arp. The last made a principle of semantic fortuitousness; and there are passages in earlier poems by Laforgue that place him in the company of Rimbaud and Mallarmé as an initiator of the many kinds of free association practised by twentieth-century poets. Though, like Corbière, Laforgue was apt to repeat himself – and to be aware of repeating himself (me répéter, oh! mal de tête . . .)[16] – these repetitions have to do with his sensitive response to everyday experiences, to experiences that repeat themselves. Both in theme and in style Laforgue's range was remarkably wide. His use of half-rhymes, some thirty years before Wilfred Owen's in English, and his gradual approximation to free verse in the late poems are two of the more obvious instances of his technical inventiveness. His diction struck a rare balance between the colloquial and the ingeniously or wittily allusive; and this balance corresponds to one between expressiveness and receptiveness in his imagery.

Laforgue is usually included among the Symbolist poets, but this is misleading if one thinks of Symbolism not just as the new poetry written after Baudelaire and the Parnassians, but as a particular kind of poetry tending towards hermeticism and aspiring 'to the condition of music.' Many of Laforgue's innovations brought poetry closer not to music, but to speech; not to the exclusive aestheticism of Mallarmé or Villiers de l'Isle-Adam, but to an existential and moral involvement in the cruelties of life. It is to the empirical self that Laforgue referred in the lines about his 'day in Time,' his 'place in Space.' His poetical self – with its masks of buffoon and ironist, romantic dreamer and desperate metaphysician – had no need to fear that it would vanish without trace in 'celestial Eternullity,' one of many passing guests in 'the Grand Hotel of the anonymous.'

4 The Symbolists proper had no place for the empirical self in poetry. However 'subjective' their work, the one thing that must not appear in it was the everyday person, the citizen and employee, the family man or *poète maudit* who might well have no servant to do his living for him. The Romantic poets' alienation from society, and from their social selves, was far from having been overcome, but it was to be taken for granted, not confessed, mused upon or lamented in poetry – except under the cover of a mask that served to make it impersonal. This, again, does not mean that doubts about personal identity were resolved. Paul Valéry, the most consistent practician and theorist of pure poetry after Mallarmé, was as worried by the question of personal identity as Baudelaire, Rimbaud, Corbière and Laforgue before him; but it is his prose that tells us so explicitly: 'Our I, is it perhaps isolated from its environment, preserved from being *Everything*, or from being *Anything whatever*, rather as the movement of my watch is in my waistcoat pocket? ... It is no use appealing to our memory; it gives us much more evidence of our variation than of our consistency. ... In our desires, our regrets, our researches, in our emotions and passions, and even in the efforts that we make to know ourselves, we are the toys of absent things – which don't even need to exist in order to act upon us.'[17]

Clearly, it was not the poets alone who grappled incessantly with this question of discontinuous identity. Valéry's remarks on it occur in his most substantial essay on society and politics. Nietzsche, after Schopenhauer, had thought in a radical way about 'the principle of individuation,' and Bergson had related consciousness to time. The new depth psychology asked the same questions and suggested answers quite as destructive of conventional views. Alienation of a different kind was a key concept in Marxian sociology. The novelists, too, explored streams of consciousness and disrupted traditional narrative structures based on the old unities of character, action and time. Yet there was a special reason why lyrical poets should return again and again to these matters. Lyrical poetry, by its very nature, has always been less concerned with continuous, historical or epical time, with *chronos*, than with *kairos* and what Joyce called epiphanies, moments in which experience or vision is concentrated and crystallized. Lyrical poetry, therefore, was more dependent on the unity of inner experience – that is, of the experiencing consciousness – than on that sequence of outer events which provided a framework for verse or prose narrative. Although this unity was not necessarily one of what Hugo Friedrich calls the empirical self – he seems to assume that the confessional 'I' of Romantic poetry was always identical with the poet's 'empirical self,' and that this identity is a norm from which later poets deviated, whereas it has always been the exception – doubts about the consistency of the self were bound to add to the lyrical poet's awareness of his peculiar freedom to escape from it altogether and 'fill some other body.'

The poets from Valéry to Pound and Pessoa made ample and various use of that freedom. The truth of poetry became inseparable from what Oscar Wilde called 'the truth of masks.' Hugo von Hofmannsthal's obsession with the fortuitousness and discontinuity of the empirical self caused him to abandon lyrical poetry, turning from the dramatic monologue or *persona* to 'lyrical drama' – a kind of short verse play in which the characters scarcely interact – and, by gradual progression, to the

drama proper.* To the endemic doubts about personal identity
Hofmannsthal added a profound scepticism about language and
the power of words to render what only gesture or dance can
convey – the self stripped of all its empirical accidents. Valéry,
Yeats, Eliot and Lorca are a few of the poets who shared those
preoccupations, though each found his own way out of the same
maze of complexities; and each, at least momentarily, was
brought up against the inescapable realities of the empirical
self – inescapable even for one of the actors celebrated in poems
by Hofmannsthal:

> Doch wenn das Spiel verlosch und sich der Vorhang
> Lautlos wie ein geschminktes Augenlid
> Vor die erstorbne Zauberhöhle legte
> Und er hinaustrat, da war eine Bühne
> So vor ihm aufgetan wie ein auf ewig
> Schlafloses aufgerissnes Aug, daran
> Kein Vorhang je mitleidig niedersinkt:
> Die fürchterliche Bühne Wirklichkeit.
> Da fielen der Verwandlung Künste alle
> Von ihm, und seine arme Seele ging
> Ganz hüllenlos und sah aus Kindesaugen.[18]

> (Yet when the play was fading, and the curtain
> Came down in silence like a painted eyelid
> Over the magical cavern emptied now of life,
> And he stepped out, a stage appeared before him
> Like a wide, sleepless eye for ever open
> On which no curtain mercifully falls:
> The terrifying stage, reality.
> Then all the arts of transformation dropped
> From him, and his poor soul walked quite unclothed
> And gazed from a child's eyes.)

*This development is traced in my Introduction to Hugo von Hofmannsthal: *Poems and Verse Plays*, and *Selected Plays and Libretti* (New York and London, 1961, 1963), German version: *Hugo von Hofmannsthal: Zwei Studien* (Göttingen, 1964). Though very relevant to my present theme, it cannot be recapitulated here without undue simplification or repetitiveness.

4

MASKS

1   HOFMANNSTHAL, who studied the new psychology
in a critical phase of his life, believed that the age of individualism had ended. Extreme doubts, like his or Valéry's, about the
consistency and limits of the self led not only to an acute
scepticism but to a new mysticism which Valéry called 'mysticism without God' and Hofmannsthal spoke of in his Chandos
Letter as 'the situation of a mystic without a mystique.'[1]
Hofmannsthal also spoke of his 'word-scepticism' and of his
'word-mysticism'; and in Valéry's writings we find the same
analytical intellectualism always on the brink of the irrational.
The thinking of both writers was intricate to the point of self-
contradiction. Doubts as to what constituted the self did not
absolve them from those quarrels with themselves which,
according to Yeats, generate poetry. 'The I, perhaps, is no
more than a conventional notion,' Valéry wrote, 'as empty as
the verb to be.'[2] Paradoxically, this dubious 'I' was in the
greatest danger of falling into solipsism – a danger closely bound
up with the aesthetic of pure autotelic art from the beginning,
but increasingly apparent to poets, like Valéry and Gottfried
Benn, who drew on philosophy and the sciences for support of
their artistic practice. Valéry's poem *Fragments du Narcisse* and
his *Cantate du Narcisse* are only the most blatant instances of his
preoccupation with solipsism. Nearly all his dramatic works,
including the late unfinished *Faust* plays, revolve around this
theme; and always the autonomy not only of art, but of the

mind, is confronted with temptation in the shape of love or death or a combination of the two.* His Narcissus says to the Nymph:

> Je suis seul. Je suis moi. Je suis vrai . . . Je vous hais.

> (I'm alone. I am I. I am real . . . I hate you.)

And the nymph's reply, later in the cantata, includes the reproach:

> Ton crime est d'ignorer tous les coeurs alentour.

> (Your crime is to be unaware of all the hearts around you.)

Valéry's Faust is similarly tempted by his secretary, Luste. This makes him just human enough to be scorned by a figure still more solipsistic, the 'Solitary' or 'The Only One' of the second *Faust* fragment. These dramatic works are cited here because they exemplify the paradox: Valéry's plays not only revolve around the theme of solipsism, but show his incapacity to 'create' or enter into characters different from himself. His impersonal lyrical poetry avails itself of the freedom to 'fill some other body.' Yet his first *Faust* play contains passages as unmistakably autobiographical or even confessional as this one:

To tell the truth, my friend, I neither love nor hate the past, nor my books which are the fragments or the fruits of it. They are no longer me. I can't find myself in the past. . . . Does an EGO have a past? The word *past* has no meaning for it. I lived . . . and then I . . . more than lived! How can I put it? My fate has been so absolutely unique, I can only express it by a metaphor. . . . I suppose that living is a kind of movement, starting from the place and date of birth and ending at the place and date of death. The sum of a lifetime rises at one point of the horizon, emerges from the mists and the tender shades of childhood. The high noon of feelings and desires, of knowledge, thought, and affection begins its reign. . . . The light grows precise and hard. The star of strength and certitude reaches its meridian, sinks, and vanishes. . . . Man is a sort of Mayfly who never relives that single day, which is his whole life. The sun of his being never shines twice, and whatever it shines on is always without precedent

---

*As in *Sémiramis* (1934): 'I have given to each thing its pasture. My night to flesh, my flesh to Love; Love to Death.'

for him, from the novelty of his birth to the novelty of his death. . . .
Whereas I, my friend, with the help of mysterious powers, saw my
day of life continue on under the fatal horizon. The other side of
nature, the antipodes of creation, were revealed to me. I made the
real voyage round the real world. . . . The boldest, the most unprecedented idea that occurs to me cannot ever seem new to me. . . .[3]

The uniqueness of Valéry's Faust is less convincing than his
solipsism, if only because the language here, even in the
original, lacks the distinction of Valéry's poems. But *Mon Faust*
is a kind of morality play; and the moral is that Faust's first and
last words are 'No.' This is pointed out to him by the Fairies
who are close relatives of the Nymph in the *Narcissus Cantata*.
The moral is also pointed out by 'Le Solitaire,' who negates
himself by remarking: 'As soon as there is only myself there is
nobody.' Valéry's extreme scepticism negated itself. The autonomous mind despised its own ideas, taking refuge in form –
because 'the shaped work,' as Hofmannsthal said, 'disposes of
the problem.' Valéry's Faust put it differently: 'Ideas cost
nothing. Form is what matters.'[4]

Outside his poetry Valéry, like Hofmannsthal, was a 'word-
sceptic'; and the 'word-scepticism' arose from the same awareness of the uniqueness of that which art seeks to express, and the
inescapable commonness of words. 'If words could express it,'
'Le Solitaire' says about his own icy habitat, 'it wouldn't be
much. Everything that can be said is nothing. You know what
humans do with what can be expressed. All too well. They turn
it into a base currency, an instrument of imprecision, a lure, a
trap for mastery and exploitation. Reality is absolutely incom-
municable. It resembles nothing, signifies nothing; nothing can
represent or explain it; it has neither duration nor place in any
conceivable order or universe. . . .'[5] Like Hofmannsthal and
other post-Symbolists, Valéry turned to mixed media – the
fusion of words with music, décor, gesture and dance in
Amphion and *Sémiramis*, of words with music only in the *Narcissus
Cantata* – out of an aversion to the 'base currency' of words.
These media did not describe or relate; they enacted: and
Valéry's aversion extended to the epic and descriptive modes:
'What can be recounted cannot count for much!'[6]

'The principal personages of a poem,' on the other hand, 'are
always the sweetness and vigour of the verse.'[7] Form could

dispose of every kind of problem – including the problematical or solipsistic personage of the writer – because, as Hofmannsthal put it, 'form is mask, but without form neither giving nor taking from soul to soul.'[8] Valéry's too rigid distinction between purposive or 'instrumental' prose, which he compared to walking or running, and a poetry that is like dancing, having 'no other end but itself' (*Eupalinos*), points to a dichotomy in his own nature. Valéry admitted as much when, in the Preface to *Monsieur Teste*, he wrote of being afflicted with the 'mal aigu de la précision.' The precision and lucidity of Valéry's thinking became an affliction because of the 'positive electron' in him that repeated monotonously: 'There is only I. There is only I. There is only I, I, I. . . .'[9] Poetry also released him from a kind of thinking that examines its own processes and frequently ends by biting its own tail; and, once again, it made no difference that Valéry wanted his poetry to communicate nothing, to have no other end but itself. Valéry's insistence on conscious and deliberate composition, rather than 'inspiration,' is as paradoxical as the rest of his thinking. 'Skilled verse,' he wrote in *Au Sujet d'Adonis*, 'is the art of a profound sceptic. It presupposes an extraordinary freedom with respect to the whole of our ideas and sensations. The gods in their graciousness give us an occasional first line *for nothing*; but it is for us to fashion the second, which must chime with the first and not be unworthy of its supernatural elder. All the resources of experience and of the mind are not too much to render it comparable to the line which was a gift.'[10]

The scepticism of which Valéry writes there is a freedom, not a compulsion, to argue and rationalize. It is the freedom that Keats described so well – the freedom to 'make up one's mind about nothing, to let the mind be a thoroughfare for all thought, not a select party.' This freedom and openness, combined with the utmost concentration on the poem's peculiar demands, is nothing other than 'inspiration.' Valéry recognizes this when he states that 'all the resources of experience and of the mind' are needed to match the given line with the made lines – a disguised tribute to the unconscious factors in the act of writing. Because, as a critic and thinker, Valéry was afraid of these factors, his pronouncements on poetry are far from revealing a method or even a consistent view of the art. At one moment he asks for '*As much consciousness as possible*';[11] at another he writes: 'I can be interested only in things I cannot invent'[12] – and his definition of a poem is 'a kind of machine for producing the poetic state of mind by means of words.'[13] Machines are invented and deliberately constructed; yet Valéry was interested in poems. He cited his own *La Jeune parque* as an example of those of his poems which 'had as a starting-point merely one of these impulses of the "formative" sensibility which are anterior to any "subject" or to any finite, expressible idea.' 'Another poem began merely with the hint of a rhythm, *which gradually acquired a meaning.*'[14] When Valéry declared that he liked 'those lovers of poetry who venerate the goddess with too much lucidity to dedicate to her the slackness of their thought and the relaxation of their reason'[15] he can only have meant that the quality of a poet's thought and reason are evident in 'exercises' – like *La Jeune parque* – as far removed as possible from those matters to which thought and reason are usually applied; and that is beyond dispute. Keats, too, said that 'to make up one's mind about nothing' – that is, to suspend deliberate and purposive thought – is a means of 'strengthening one's intellect.'

Valéry was like Mallarmé, his master, in using reason to defeat reason. The aim of the poetry he admired was '*enchantement*,' as he said, and a 'feeling of generalized rapture' which he placed 'at the opposite pole from everything intended and performed by prose. ... It was the remoteness from man which ravished me.'[16] His Semiramis is 'unthinkable and therefore divine'; and all the craft and intelligence that he applied to his lyrical poems served to make them 'remote from man.' Yet Valéry's scepticism – that of a twentieth-century thinker familiar with the scientific and political trends of the age – made him aware of the limits of the 'pure' or 'absolute' poetry in which he excelled: 'Pure poetry is in fact a fiction deduced from observation,' he wrote in 1928;[17] and in 1920 he explained why it could not be more than a fiction:

Nothing so pure can coexist with the circumstances of life. We only traverse the idea of perfection as a hand passes with impunity through a flame; but the flame is uninhabitable, and dwelling places on the serene heights are necessarily deserted. I mean that our leaning toward the extreme rigours of art – toward the logical result of premises suggested to us by earlier successes – toward a beauty ever more conscious of its origins, ever more independent of all *subjects*, and of the vulgar attractions of sentiment as well as the blatant effects of eloquence – all this overenlightened zeal resulted perhaps in an almost inhuman state. That is a general truth: metaphysics, ethics, and even the sciences have experienced it. Absolute poetry can only proceed by way of exceptional marvels; works composed entirely of it constitute the rarest and most improbable portion of the imponderable treasures of a literature.[18]

Valéry's mythical solipsist, 'Le Solitaire' of his *Faust*, also has his being on those 'necessarily deserted' heights; and his state is more than 'almost' inhuman.

Apart from the 'sweetness and vigour' of his verse, the personages or masks of Valéry's pure poems are mythical or archetypal, and rarely human. Since he wrote in traditional verse forms and by no means avoided either the 'attractions of sentiment,' whether vulgar or not, or the 'blatant effects of eloquence' – invocations, apostrophes, epithets more emotive or decorative than functional – his most celebrated poems now read like nineteenth-century works. His modernity is more apparent in his prose writings than in his poetry, for the very reason that his prose writings demand to be judged by what they say, rather than by what they are and do. If consciousness of the age is to be looked for in a poet's images, above all, and in gestures that involve rhythm, cadence, syntax and diction, Laforgue was a more modern poet than Valéry, though Laforgue's work ended before Valéry's began. Valéry's choice of the word 'sweetness' (*douceur*) is significant in this connection: even Baudelaire recognized the peculiarly modern potentialities of harshness and dissonance. The epithets 'vulgar' and 'blatant' are other key words pointing back to the fastidious aestheticism of the *fin de siècle*.

Yet the root of Valéry's lack of modernity as a poet was his solipsism – a solipsism modern enough in itself, since it was nourished by the scientific and philosophical preoccupations of his time. When Valéry dropped the mask of form as in the late prose and free verse poems which he called *poésie brute* – crude or raw poetry – his empirical self enacted no terrible vengeance, comparable to that in Yeats's *The Circus Animals' Desertion*. The mystical and mythical sun-worship of the canonical poems is presented empirically in terms of direct personal experience in the poem *Au Soleil*, and for once Valéry exchanges the 'pure self'* of his earlier poetry for one that is conditioned and domestically informal:

Au Soleil

Au soleil sur mon lit après l'eau
Au soleil et au reflet énorme du soleil sur la mer,
Sous ma fenêtre
Et aux reflets et aux reflets des reflets
Du soleil et des soleils sur la mer
Dans les glaces,
Après le bain, le café, les idées
Nu au soleil sur mon lit tout illuminé
    Nu, seul, fou
    Moi![19]

(In the Sun

In the sun on my bed after water
In the sun and in the vast reflection of the sun on the sea,
Beneath my window
And in the reflections and in the reflections of the reflections
Of the sun and of the suns on the sea
In the mirrors,
After bathing, coffee, ideas
Nude in the sun on my bed drenched in light
    Nude, alone, mad
    Myself!)

Because that poem contains no active verb, its syntactical movement culminates in the final exclamation, 'Moi!' – after convolutions that render the intricacies of Valéry's mode of perception in images of multiple reflection. *Au Soleil* is an authentic self-portrait, and an authentic twentieth-century poem in its resort to an organic structure that sacrifices 'sweetness' to rightness. It is not a great or even outstanding poem because it lacks tension; and it lacks tension because there is something relaxed and complacent about this nudity, so different from the nakedness of the heart implied, but not enacted, by the word 'fou.' The circus animals have deserted, but coffee and ideas

*'Le moi pur,' which in *La Politique de l'esprit* (*Variété* III) Valéry described as being 'created' by men, as time is created by the human mind. English version by Denise Folliot and Jackson Mathews in *Valéry: History and Politics*, New York and London, 1962.

seem to be an adequate substitute. In *Psaume devant la bête* Valéry recapitulates both the solipsism •and the dichotomy between mind on the one hand and love and death on the other that pervades his whole work:

> Amour ni mort ne sont point pour l'esprit:
> Manger l'étonne et dormir lui font honte.

> (Not love nor death is palpable to the mind:
> Eating astounds it, of sleeping it is ashamed.)

And he tries in vain to relate himself to the 'dying animal' by divining the number of its limbs and the shape of its body:

> Mais c'est par quoi je puis concevoir d'autres choses
> Que moi-même...

> (But that is how I can conceive of things other
> Than myself...)

Yet again 'myself' is the last word; and the *persona* who speaks in the concluding poem of this sequence is the *Idée-maîtresse*, not a woman or even archetype of woman, but an idea abstracted from the self. 'You are my Madman-because-of-me: YOUR IDEA,' she says to the poet who has been 'fused' with her in love.

Speaking of the logician and the poet in his Oxford lecture *Poésie et pensée abstraite*,[20] in which he argued that abstract thought and poetry are not incompatible, Valéry expressed his 'sincere belief' that 'if each man were not able to live a number of other lives besides his own, he would not be able to live his own life.' The masks of Valéry's formal poems enabled him to live lives other than his own in his imagination, and his prose works do indeed go a long way towards reconciling the logician with the poet, always granted that 'there is no theory that is not a fragment, carefully prepared, of some autobiography,' as Valéry remarked in the same lecture. If the logician in him, the abstract thinker, contradicted himself at times, that, too, can be understood biographically; the self-contradictions occur at those points where the abstract thinker and the poet were not at one. Valéry's limitation was that his work shows so little awareness of lives other than those of the artist and the abstract thinker, that he had such difficulty in getting himself to believe and feel that anyone but these existed. Though Valéry has a place in the

Orphic tradition of poetry, Elizabeth Sewell, its interpreter and historian as well as an authority on Valéry, says of it that 'it lies with life and words, not with pure forms; misunderstanding this, Mallarmé and Valéry lead into an impasse into which a great deal of contemporary poetry has followed them.'[21] And again, in connection with Wordsworth's poem *On the Power of Sound*: 'Wordsworth speaks up for harmony, language and mankind, and this is extremely important in view of what was to happen later with the Orphic line in Mallarmé and Valéry. Each of them would have preferred, absolutely, either music or silence above the "impurity" of human language. It is most interesting to see Wordsworth in this poem rule that out long beforehand as reaction and *impietas*, poetically, humanly and theologically.'

2　　'Pure' or 'absolute' poetry did not end with Valéry, but it was never to be quite so pure or absolute again, even in the case of poets who professed an aesthetic similar to Valéry's, as Gottfried Benn continued to do in the second half of this century. Even so pure and often abstract a poet as Jorge Guillén, who learnt much from Valéry, has this to say about him:

Poésie pure, then, 'pure poetry'? This platonic idea could never take form in a concrete body. None among us* dreamed of such absolute purity, none desired it, not even the author of *Cántico*,[22] a book which can be defined negatively as the antithesis of Valéry's *Charmes*. . . . In the tradition of Edgar Allan Poe, Valéry believed scarcely or not at all in inspiration – on which these Spanish poets were always dependent: *Muse* to some, *ángel* to others, *duende* (a familiar demon) to Lorca. . . . A power alien to reason and will, providing those deep, unforeseen elements that constitute the *gracia* of the poem. . . . Valéry took a rather perverse pleasure in discoursing on the 'manufacture of poetry.' 'To create,' a proud term, 'to compose,' a sober professional term, do not imply manufacture. Valéry was above all an inspired poet. . . . Empty or near-empty formalism is a monster invented by incompetent readers, or is to be applied only to incompetent writers. If there is to be poetry, it will have to be human. How could it be otherwise? Inhuman or super-human poetry has perhaps existed. But a 'dehumanized' poem is a physical and metaphysical imposssi-

*The Spanish poets of the generation that included Lorca, Alberti, Guillén, Salinas, Cernuda, Aleixandre and Alonso.

bility, and the phrase 'dehumanization of art,' coined by our great philosopher Ortega y Gasset, rang false from the very beginning.[23]

Valéry was one of those poets – so shocking to Erich Heller – who claimed that poetic 'creation' or *poesis* is godlike,[24] though with ironic reservations that diminish the arrogance of his claim. Jorge Guillén explicitly dissociates himself from that theological analogy: 'The poet feels that word "poetry" in its full etymological meaning. (But this "creation" will always be secondary to that of the first Creator, of the book of Genesis. All poets are in this sense *poètes du dimanche*, of the Sunday following the Saturday on which Jehovah rested.)' Of other poets younger than Valéry, Rilke and Wallace Stevens evolved theories in which *poesis* or 'making' assumed a more than aesthetic and technical significance; and Gottfried Benn based all his thinking on the Nietzschean acceptance of both nihilism and total aestheticism as necessary consequences of the discovery that 'God is dead.' Benn's essential solipsism was another link with Valéry, though his vehement and unironic assertions presupposed a severance of the poet from the logician that made much of his critical prose as ecstatic and syntactically unconventional as his verse. Yet the opposite is true of some of Benn's last poems, which seem to abjure magic as thoroughly as the poems of so many poets everywhere writing after the Second World War. Benn's practice in those poems belies the theory of 'absolute poetry' which he never substantially modified in his prose writings of those years.

Valéry's German contemporary, Stefan George, also began as a disciple of Mallarmé, whom he visited in Paris; but from the beginning, George took over little more than the outward stance and gesture of pure Symbolism – the exclusiveness and disdain of 'vulgar' literature, the cult of masks not only as form and style but as a disguise, rather than an extension, of the empirical self often indistinguishable from mere pose and masquerade, and a preference for the artificial to the natural. Had George written in French, he would have been regarded as a *Parnassien* rather than as a Symbolist, though his choice of *personae* like Heliogabalus links him with the international *décadence* of the 1890s. For all its fastidiousness and calculated euphony, George's earlier poetry does not attain the freedom of Symbolist poetry, by which I mean the freedom of a poem to establish its own relations and references, a sign language not to be deciphered in terms other than its own. Many of George's most memorable lyrical poems are in fact confessional poems in an older mode, though their surface is hard and chiselled, less Romantic than classicizing. In his later poetry George broke the Symbolist prohibition against didacticism, as re-formulated in his own pronouncement: 'In poetry – as in all artistic activities – anyone still possessed with the craving to "say" something, to have some kind of "effect" or "influence," is not even worthy of entering the precincts of Art.'25 One has only to compare the style of that pronouncement with Mallarmé's prose style in essays and lectures to understand why George's practice was bound to break his own rule: the gesture of that aphorism contradicts what the words say. The pronouncement was aimed at others, as George's later poetry was aimed at others – with a gesture of scornful superiority that asserts and imposes itself, rather than trying to explore a truth much more complex than its expression here. As for the 'effect' and 'influence' of George's writings, it is enough in this context to mention that they were considerable and controversial.

It was George's cult of masks, above all, that gave his work the range expected of a major poet. In theme and form his poems ranged from classical and Biblical antiquity to mediaeval and modern Europe, from oriental exercises reminiscent of those by the early nineteenth-century poets Platen and Rückert, to blank verse, rhymed songs as metrically varied as those of Verlaine, and unrhymed lyrics no less various in rhythm. The word 'exercise' is apt in this context not only because Valéry used it to describe *La Jeune parque*, but because George's masks were chosen and donned with a degree of deliberation that seems to bear out Valéry's theory, derived from Poe, that poems can be assembled or manufactured like machines. Yet despite George's historical and formal range, both Hofmannsthal and Rilke excelled him in the use of *personae*, because both had a gift of empathy that enabled them to 'fill some other body' and make it speak with a voice not muffled by the mask. With rare exceptions – and these are usually confessions in which George's own voice penetrates the mask – the consistently stiff and opaque surface texture of George's poems reminds us that metal and cardboard are not skin. Because George's empirical self was rarely enlarged and enriched by an imaginative identification with what it was not, but only made use of masks as disguises, his work as a whole has become more like a museum or waxwork cabinet than like an assembly of living voices.

3   W.B. Yeats is not included in Hans Magnus Enzensberger's 'museum of modern poetry'; and if Mallarmé's practice defines the nature of Symbolism, Yeats was no more a Symbolist poet than George was. Nor was he a 'modernist' poet in the sense given to that word by Laura Riding and Robert Graves in *A Survey of Modernist Poetry*;[26] but, at least after *The Green Helmet* (1910), Yeats was a modern poet in diction and imagery. Laura Riding and Robert Graves seem to exclude Yeats from serious consideration as a modernist by the simple reference to him as 'Mr Yeats, who, observing that his old poetical robes have worn rather shabby, acquires a new outfit'; but, almost more than any other British poet of the time, Yeats accorded with their own definition of what modernist poetry ought to be: a poetry that 'would derive its excellence neither from its reacting against civilization by satiric or actual primitivism, nor from its proved ability to keep up with or keep ahead of civilization. It would not, however, ignore its contemporaneous universe, for the reason that it would not be stupid. . . .'

Yeats's early poetry did ignore 'its contemporaneous universe'; but so did Valéry's and Stefan George's and most of the best poetry written in the late 1880s and 90s – poetry based on the assumption that the 'contemporaneous universe' was a 'brutal mirage.' So in Yeats's *The Song of the Happy Shepherd* (from *Crossways*, 1889):

> New dreams, new dreams; there is no truth
> Saving in thine own heart. . . .
> Dream, dream, for this is also sooth.

Archaisms like 'thine' and 'sooth' were to be thoroughly expunged from Yeats's vocabulary and the 'contemporaneous universe' admitted into both his diction and his imagery; but something of that Romantic-Symbolist distrust of the 'real' and 'objective' world was carried over into Yeats's maturity, into the long quarrel between his empirical self and his 'anti-self,' between the circumstantial and the archetypal. Out of that quarrel he did indeed make magnificent poetry – not as modern, perhaps, as the poetry of those who had come to terms from the start with their 'contemporaneous universe,' but far more likely than theirs to survive its occasions and phenomena. Yeats's two selves debate in *Ego Dominus Tuus*, the dialogue poem that introduces his prose book *Per Amica Silentia Lunae* (1918).

And I would find myself and not an image

the one voice says and the other comments:

> That is our modern hope and by its light
> We have lit upon the gentle, sensitive mind
> And lost the old nonchalance of the hand;
> Whether we have chosen chisel, pen or brush
> We are but critics, or but half create. . . .

The first voice, *Hic*, represents the rational, liberal, sceptical and individualistic culture of the period. Stefan George utterly condemned it, though he was its product. Yeats, as a poet, was quite as reluctant to be 'timid, entangled, empty and abashed'; but where other poets resorted to irony in their dealings with the empirical self, or banished it entirely in favour of a mask, Yeats allowed the self and the anti-self, the circumstance and the image, to engage in perpetual combat: the 'tragic war' of that poem. Like Nietzsche, whom he read in 1902 and 1903, Yeats had a horror of psychological dishonesty – the kind of dishonesty or self-delusion that would have allowed him to suppress his motives for constructing a second, heroic and poetical self.

> The rhetorician would deceive his neighbours,
> The sentimenta'ist himself; while art
> Is but a vision of reality.
> What portion in the world can the artist have
> Who has awakened from the common dream
> But dissipation and despair?

The 'double' or 'anti-self' to whom *Ille* looks for an alternative to 'dissipation and despair' seems to predominate in Yeats's later poetry, but never to the total exclusion of his opposite. Just as in this poem the traditional blank verse frequently yields to non-iambic conversational rhythm, and formal imagery to realistic metaphors like 'The struggle of the fly in marmalade,' Yeats always preserved something of the 'gentle, sensitive mind' that responds to the unheroic, unplatonic realities of life. The 'cold eye' that his anti-self urged him to cast 'on life, on death' could also blink, observe, laugh and weep. If we did not know that, if the poetry did not tell us so, the injunction would leave us as cold as that stoical eye.

Yeats's 'anti-self' or 'antithetical self,' like Nietzsche's 'super-man,' 'comes but to those who are no longer deceived, whose passion is reality.'[27] This 'reality,' of course, is a timeless, absolute one, and the search for it the desperate resort of those 'who have awakened from the common dream' – Mallarmé's 'brutal mirage' – and can draw no sustenance from the pursuits and values of the majority. Yeats does not conceal the despera-tion and extremity that were his starting-point. 'But the passions, when we know that they cannot find fulfilment, become vision.' As the psychologists know, they can also become something very different; but vision is what they did become in Yeats's case.

The longer he lived, the more justice Yeats did to those passions which *can* find fulfilment; and this again has to do with his own personal development. 'I have grown happier with every year of life as though gradually conquering something in myself, for certainly my miseries were not made by others but were a part of my own mind.'[28] Yet Yeats could no more be satisfied with the expression of personal happiness than with the expres-sion of personal miseries: 'If I wrote of personal love or sorrow in free verse, or in any rhythm that left it unchanged, amid all its accidence, I would be full of self-contempt because of my egotism and indiscretion, and foresee the boredom of my reader. I must choose a traditional stanza, even what I alter must seem traditional. I commit my emotion to shepherds, herdsmen, camel-drivers, learned men, Milton or Shelley's Platonist, that tower Palmer drew. Talk to me of originality and I will turn on you with rage. I am a crowd, I am a lonely man, I am nothing. Ancient salt is best packing.'[29]

Those words were written towards the end of Yeats's life. They sum up not only Yeats's practice as a poet but the situation of all those poets after Baudelaire – as well as Whitman and Browning, older contemporaries of Baudelaire – who resorted to masks in order to turn the lonely man into a crowd, negative identity into positive multiplicity or universality of being. As

Yeats implies, and Hofmannsthal made explicit, poetic form itself can act as a mask. When the empirical self came back into poetry – not because poets took it more seriously than before, but because they were no longer interested in their own loneliness and uniqueness, and therefore had no further use for discretion – forms tended to be free and relaxed. Yeats wanted tension and intensity above all; and to achieve them he had to practise what he called 'active virtue,' something that went against the grain of his empirical self. 'Active virtue,' he wrote in *Per Amica Silentia Lunae*, 'as distinguished from the passive acceptance of a code, is therefore theatrical, consciously dramatic, the wearing of a mask.' The high degree of consciousness in all this saved Yeats from being taken in by his masks, or from substituting them for his own face. The same consciousness made him more modern and more original than he wanted to be. No 'traditional stanza' chosen by Yeats in his maturity could ever be mistaken for another poet's work. Tradition, in fact, was Yeats's alibi, as novelty has been the alibi of poets strenuously modernist; and much of that tradition was no less a creation of Yeats's imagination and will as his 'anti-self.' His modern relativistic premise is very evident in this passage, from the same work: 'Some years ago I began to believe that our culture, with its doctrine of sincerity and self-realization, made us gentle and passive, and that the Middle Ages and Renaissance were right to found theirs upon the imitation of Christ or some classic hero.' The mere lumping together here of the Middle Ages and the Renaissance, of Christ and some classical hero, gives Yeats's modernity away.

That modernity was Nietzschean – at once sceptical and irrational, psychologically probing and ecstatic. 'People much occupied with morality always lose heroic ecstasy,'[30] Yeats wrote to Dorothy Wellesley; and 'Bitter and gay, that is the heroic mood.' Yeats's tragic gaiety, his exaltation in strength, were Nietzschean; and so was his admission in another of these letters: 'When I am ill I am a Christian and this is abominable.' Yet in the same letter Yeats censures 'a type of man for whom I have no respect. Such men have no moral sense.' He calls himself 'anarchic as a sparrow,' and means the Nietzschean immoralism that wanted ecstasy at any cost. Yet he also exclaimed: 'O, my dear, I have no solution, none' – because the heroic ecstasy and the immoralism belonged to his anti-self, and this anti-self was a poetic mask truly valid only in Yeats's poetry and not in those spheres, like politics and social life and even literary criticism, to which Yeats vainly tried to apply its 'philosophy.' Yeats suggested as much in his little poem *Politics*, a rejoinder to Thomas Mann's statement that 'in our time the destiny of man presents its meaning in political terms':

> How can I, that girl standing there,
> My attention fix
> On Roman or on Russian
> Or on Spanish politics?

One ironic aspect of that poem is that Thomas Mann shared Yeats's dilemma and Yeats's doubts, exemplified for him in Chekhov's 'Am I not fooling the reader, since I cannot answer the most important questions?' – words with which Mann identified himself in his essay on Chekhov. Thomas Mann, too, had been profoundly and permanently shaken by Nietzsche's nihilistic aestheticism, though he tried hard in his later years not to drop the mask of the conscientious humanist and moralist to whom Yeats's lines are addressed. In *Politics*, therefore, Yeats's anti-self is quarrelling not only with his own empirical self, but with Mann's anti-self: a mask is arguing with a mask.

The Circus Animals' Desertion recapitulates the whole quarrel between Yeats's empirical and poetical selves, allowing psychological honesty to have the last word. The circus animals of the poem – 'Lion and woman and the Lord knows what' – all the emblems and archetypes gathered by Yeats from folklore, history, literature, religion and theosophy, are dismissed very much as Shakespeare's Prospero dismisses Ariel and Caliban, abjuring his 'rough magic.'

> Heart-mysteries there, and yet when all is said
> It was the dream itself enchanted me:
> Character isolated by a deed
> To engross the present and dominate memory.
> Players and painted stage took all my love,
> And not those things that they were emblems of.

We are brought back to what Yeats had written about half a century earlier:

> there is no truth
> Saving in thine own heart. . . .
> Dream, dream, for this is also sooth.

But since Yeats had not given up his quarrel with himself, even the despair of this ending had to be heroic and theatrical. Half-rhymes and syncopated rhythms still mark the limit of his informality; and not only is the mask of form upheld, but even his specimens of squalid reality are packed so tight in their 'ancient salt' as to recall the 'heroic ecstasy' that is their opposite:

> Those masterful images because complete
> Grew pure in mind, but out of what began?
> A mound of refuse or the sweepings of a street,
> Old kettles, old bottles, and a broken can,
> Old iron, old bones, old rags, that raving slut
> Who keeps the till. Now that my ladder's gone,
> I must lie down where all the ladders start,
> In the foul rag-and-bone shop of the heart.

It was left to other poets – some of whom Yeats half accepted, half rejected with an ambivalence rooted in his quarrel with himself – to liberate those specimens of squalid reality from their packing, to make both themselves and their poetry thoroughly at home 'in the foul rag-and-bone shop of the heart.' Measured against Mallarmé, Yeats was not a thorough-going Symbolist, because tradition kept him from discarding the syntax of discourse and argument. Where his poems are hermetic it is because of their occult and esoteric allusions, not because of their syntactic structure. Nor did Yeats observe the following prescription of Mallarmé: 'The work of art in its complete purity implies the disappearance of the poet's oratorical presence. The poet leaves the initiative to the words, to the clash of their activated differences. The words ignite through reciprocal reflection, like a flash of fire over jewels. Such reflections replace that afflatus apparent in the old lyrical aspiration or the enthusiastic impetus of the sentence.'[31] Yeats's 'oratorical presence' is very much in evidence throughout his work, though much of the oratory stems from his masks or his anti-self. Even Yeats's empirical self makes its presence felt, in colloquial diction, in speech rhythms and in the constant tension between 'heroic ecstasy' and bitter experience. Yet *The Circus Animals' Desertion* is only one of several impassioned valedictions, in which the Romantic-Symbolist assumptions[32] are confronted with that which was to supersede them, with

> the sort now growing up
> All out of shape from toe to top ...

Yeats's resort to an anti-self and a great variety of masks was a desperate one because in his heart he knew that, although great poetry could still be made out of his defiance of what 'the age demanded,' he was widening the gap between empirical and imaginative experience, whereas those whom he despised for

> Their unremembering hearts and heads,
> Base-born products of base beds –

were doing their best to close it. His letters, essays and auto- biographies are full of partial recognition of what it was that prevented him from being wholly modern. Writing of the political poets of the thirties, their 'cult of sincerity, that refusal to multiply personality which is characteristic of our time,' he commented: 'I can seldom find more than half a dozen lyrics that I like, yet in this moment of sympathy I prefer them to Eliot, to myself – I too have tried to be modern.'[33] Of the same poets he says: 'They have pulled off the mask, the manner writers hitherto assumed. . . .' The comment is perceptive and truthful, especially in the reference to a 'moment of sympathy' – for it was his Nietzschean anti-self's conviction that pity and compassion are symptoms of weakness, of Christan 'slave morality,' which divided Yeats from those poets, and from much more than those poets. The hesitation and uncertainty are equally evident in his remarks on Wilfred Owen, whom he excluded from the anthology, giving these reasons to Dorothy Wellesley: 'He is all blood, dirt and sucked sugar stick (look at the selection in Faber's Anthology – he calls poets "bards," a girl "a maid" and talks about Titanic wars).'[34] Yeats's own anthology is full of verse with the very defects and archaisms for which he censures Owen. In his verse testament, *Under Ben Bulben*, Yeats, or Yeats's anti-self, wrote:

> You that Mitchel's prayer have heard,
> 'Send war in our time, O Lord!'
> Know that when all words are said

> And a man is fighting mad,
> Something drops from eyes long blind,
> He completes his partial mind. . . .

The section on war poetry in Yeats's Oxford Introduction says[35] much the same thing, but Yeats's uncertainty and scruples are revealed in the qualifying phrase '*If war is necessary, or necessary in our time and place*, it is best to forget its suffering as we do the discomfort of fever . . .' and the repetition of 'if war is necessary' after the far more tentative comment, 'That too may be a right way of seeing war. . . .' Yeats knew perfectly well that the First World War, at least after its initial phase, was not waged by men who were 'fighting mad,' but men who were half crazed with the 'passive suffering' from which he flinched, because it was incompatible with 'heroic ecstasy.' Yeats's multiple personality included the perceptive and unheroic moralist who wrote of our time:

> The best lack all conviction, while the worst
> Are full of passionate intensity.

Yeats was also right in pointing out that lyrical poets before Baudelaire and the Symbolists had worn masks, even if they were only the masks of style, form and decorum – not the *personae* that abound in Symbolist and post-Symbolist verse. We may quarrel with some of Yeats's masks, and voice our objections to the dramatic postures of his anti-self; but it would be absurdly literal to condemn his poetry for not embodying the whole of the truth which he knew all the time. 'Elaborate modern psychology sounds egotistical,' Yeats thought, 'when it speaks in the first person, but not those simple emotions which resemble the more, the more powerful they are, everybody's emotion, and I was soon to write many poems where an always personal emotion was woven into a jewelled pattern of myth and symbol.' Those 'simple emotions' included atavistic and coarse ones; but we know better than ever that 'everybody's emotion' is atavistic or coarse at times. Almost more than any other poet's of his period, Yeats's lyrical verse demands to be read with the kind of adjustments that we make for dramatic poetry; and the first person in a lyrical poem should never be identified, in any case, with the poet's empirical self. Whether primarily confessional or primarily dramatic, the first person in lyrical poetry serves to convey a gesture, not to document identity or establish biographical facts. Only where poets forget this does the first person become 'egotistical,' and usually boring as well. Yeats's multiple selves are never boring; and they convey a great many different gestures, of a great many different orders. Those lines about war from *Under Ben Bulben*, for instance, say something true and psychologically valid about the fighting instinct, for all their irrelevance to modern war and their dubious political implications. As with all but nakedly didactic verse, it is up to the reader to respond to the dramatic gesture without jumping on to the stage. There is scarcely a modern poet worth reading who does not call on his reader to understand and allow for 'the truth of masks.'

5

ABSOLUTE POETRY
AND
ABSOLUTE POLITICS

1   As LONG as Romantic-Symbolist attitudes prevailed
in poetry – and they have attracted poets right up to our time,
even though the practice of these poets may have had little to
do with Symbolism – there has been a tendency towards
extreme political views, more often conservative or reactionary
than progressive. The reasons for this are so complex that it is
best not to attempt a general explanation here, but to examine
a few outstanding cases. Yet the following general observations
must be made.

Romantic-Symbolist attitudes presuppose a high degree of
isolation or alienation from society. Ever since Baudelaire poets
have felt themselves to be pariahs or aristocrats – if not both at
once – in societies dominated by bourgeois values and institutions. Baudelaire's gibes at 'democratization' and 'syphiliza-
tion' are typical reactions of an aristocrat-pariah who is
excluded from the benefits of capitalist industry as much as
from solidarity with the working classes. That, of course, is a
simplification, since it implies that Baudelaire's attitudes were
determined by his economic and social status, whereas a moral
and aesthetic revulsion from modern commercialism may well
have been a more powerful motive. Yeats, who could identify
himself with the Protestant Anglo-Irish gentry and with the
Catholic peasantry, but not with the urban middle and working
classes, defined the gentleman as 'a man whose principal ideas
are not connected with his personal needs and his personal

success.'[1] We may assume that Baudelaire was a gentleman in
that sense, though the case of Yeats himself shows that conscious
attitudes are one thing, the subconscious pressure of 'personal
needs' and personal ambition another.

What Laura Riding and Robert Graves wrote about the
generation of early twentieth-century modernists applies to their
Romantic-Symbolist predecessors also:

> As a generation writing in the limelight of modernism it has an
> over-developed historical sense and professional self-consciousness. It
> is mentally uncomfortable – shrewd, nervous, suspicious of itself. It
> rejects philosophy and religion in the old drivelling romantic sense,
> but would make an intellectual system – a permanently accessible
> mental cock-tail – that would be a stiff, sane, steadying combination
> of both. It cares so much that in all matters where the plain reader is
> accustomed to meet with earnest conviction of one kind or another
> in the poet, it is hysterically, gruesomely 'I-don't-care-ish.' It is like
> a person between life and death: everything that would ordinarily
> seem serious to him now seems a tragic joke. This nervousness, this
> superior sort of stage-fright, is aggravated by the fact that in the new
> synthesis of values – even in the system that he is attempting to
> realize for himself – the historically-minded modernist poet is
> uncertain whether there is any excuse for the existence of poets at
> all. He finds himself in a defensive position; and in sympathy with
> his position; but also with the system that has put him in this
> position.[2]

The same writers also point out:

> Genuine professional modernism inclines rather toward the two
> extremes of radicalism and conservatism, or aristocraticness and
> rough-neckedness; not so much out of militant opposition to
> bourgeois liberalism as out of peripatetic avoidance of a crowded
> thoroughfare – bourgeois liberalism, being a position of compromise
> between all extremes, is the breeding place of settled, personally
> secure convictions.

The two extremes may assert a simultaneous pull on the same
poet. Baudelaire succumbed to revolutionary frenzy at the time
of the 1848 barricades. Yeats was the spokesman both for
'aristocraticness' and for 'rough-neckedness.' Nor was it Irish
nationalism alone that Yeats celebrated in the uprising of 1916,
writing: 'A terrible beauty is born.' Violent upheaval itself has
fascinated and excited the imagination of Romantic-Symbolist

poets almost regardless of their political sympathies. Alexander Blok was one of many such poets who became victims of the revolutions which they glorified.

The one thing constant in the attitude of Romantic-Symbolist poets is the rejection of the very fabric of modern civilization; and even Robert Graves, a poet whose formative years were spent in the trenches, has been unable to reconcile his poetic creed with the utilitarianism dominant in every advanced country, whether capitalist, Socialist or Communist. Whatever Graves's political views – and they are known to be moderate and liberal – the creed professed in his Foreword to *The White Goddess* could not be more profoundly romantic, and therefore reactionary:

> The function of poetry is religious invocation of the Muse; its use is the experience of musical exaltation and horror that her presence excites. But 'nowadays'? Function and use remain the same; only the application has changed. This was once a warning to man that he must keep in harmony with the family of living creatures among which he was born, by obedience to the wishes of the lady of the house; it is now a reminder that he has disregarded the warning, turned the house upside down by capricious experiments in philosophy, science and industry, and brought ruin on himself and his family. 'Nowadays' is a civilization in which the prime emblems of poetry are dishonoured. In which serpent, lion and eagle belong to the circus-tent; ox, salmon and boar to the cannery; race-horse and greyhound to the betting-ring; and the sacred grove to the saw-mill. In which the Moon is despised as a burnt-out satellite of the Earth and woman reckoned as 'auxiliary state personnel.' In which money will buy almost anything but the truth, and almost anyone but the truth possessed poet.[3]

Robert Graves is mundane and scrupulous enough to be aware that a creed so deeply incompatible with the aims and pursuits of the majority cannot be related to political realities at all. He has been a non-political poet ever since he arrived at that poetic creed; and he has been fortunate enough not to be forced into the position of having to commit himself politically. In a sense all the poets with Romantic-Symbolist attitudes have been non-political, in as much as their values have sprung from the imagination, and the imagination is too radical and utopian to adjust to political issues proper. Yet ever since Thomas

Mann's *Reflections of a Non-Political Man* (1917), and his later reversal of its anti-democratic argument, it has been clear that to be non-political or anti-political at a time when 'the destiny of a man presents its meaning in political terms' is almost inevitably to be conservative or reactionary – at least under régimes that perpetuate an established structure of power and privilege. The imagination, in our time, has also tended to be primitivist, out of a reaction against the complexities and pluralism of a culture which it cannot assimilate. Yeats's 'ceremony of innocence,' which is 'drowned' in our time, is one instance of the many lost Edens invoked or created by the poetic imagination; Robert Graves's matriarchal order is another. The temptation for poets, therefore – a temptation which Graves resisted, but Yeats did not – has been to succumb to political movements that spring from a related primitivism, a related reaction against cultural pluralism. Italian and Spanish Fascism, German National Socialism, the Action Française, are a few right-wing movements of that kind; but so is Anarcho-Syndicalism, a left-wing movement that appealed not only to Spanish intellectuals but to English poets such as Herbert Read. If that left-wing movement has declined, it is because its primitivism – that is, its opposition to modern industrialism and urbanization – was so radical and consistent as to make it incapable of using the existing machinery of power, as right-wing primitivism did with a ruthlessness and duplicity that need no exemplification here.

The politics of poets would be of limited interest if their temptations were utterly different from those of other people; but a revolt of the imagination or of the instincts against an ever more intricately organized civilization is general enough. A sociologist, Professor Michael Polanyi, has written about 'the tension between a positivist scepticism and a modern moral perfectionism in our time' which 'has erupted with vast consequences.'[4]

It has erupted in two directions, towards art and philosophy and towards politics. The first was a move towards extreme individualism, the second, on the contrary, towards modern totalitarianism. These two movements may appear diametrically opposed, yet they are but alternative solutions of the equation which required *the joint satisfaction of a belief in moral perfection with a complete denial of moral motives*.

A man looking at the world with complete scepticism can see no grounds for moral authority or transcendent moral obligations; there may seem to be no scope then for his moral perfectionism. Yet he can satisfy it by turning his scepticism against existing society, denouncing its morality as shoddy, artificial, hypocritical, and a mere mask for lust and exploitation. Though such combination of his moral scepticism with his moral indignation is inconsistent, the two are in fact fused together by the joint attack on the same target. The result is a moral hatred of existing society and the alienation of the modern intellectual. The effect on his inner life goes deep. His scepticism-cum-perfectionism scorns any expression of his own traditional morality. . . . Divided against himself, he seeks an identity safe against self-doubt. Having condemned the distinction between good and evil as dishonest, he can still take pride in the honesty of such con-demnation. Since ordinary decent behaviour can never be safe against the suspicion of sheer conformity or downright hypocrisy, only an absolutely a-moral meaningless act can assure man of his complete authenticity. All the moral fervour which scientific scepti-cism has released from religious control and then rendered homeless by discrediting its ideals, returns then to imbue an a-moral authen-ticity with intense moral approval. . . . This theme has prevailed in Continental thought since a century ago Dostoevsky first described murder as an experiment in moral scepticism and, soon after, Nietzsche repudiated all traditional conceptions of good and evil as hypocritical. . . . These are some individualistic solutions of the conflict between scepticism and perfectionism. They unite the two opposites in a moral nihilism charged with moral fury. This paradoxical combination is new in history and deserves a new name; I have called it *moral inversion*. In public life moral inversion leads to totalitarianism.

The work of W.B.Yeats abounds in instances of a 'moral nihilism charged with moral fury'; and his sympathy with right-wing totalitarian movements was shared by poets as various as Rainer Maria Rilke, Wallace Stevens, Ezra Pound, Gottfried Benn and the Futurist F.T.Marinetti. The conservatism of Hugo von Hofmannsthal and T.S.Eliot was less nihilistically based, less 'charged with moral fury'; but Hofmannsthal took up the dangerous slogan 'conservative revolution' – a concept also dear to the various nationalist factions that prepared the way for Nazism in Germany and Austria – and Eliot's 'idea of a Christian society' was so absolute and utopian as to be irreconcilable with liberal democracy. Stefan George's cult of 'Caesarism' had obvious affinities with the Caesarist antics of Mussolini, though George did not succumb to the advances of the National Socialist leaders, whose plebeian 'rough-neckedness' was uncongenial to his fastidious 'aristocraticness.'* (Hofmannsthal found George's 'aristocraticness' altogether 'too bourgeois'; and it is true that the whole trend towards sectarian cultural élites was a bourgeois phenomenon. Yet it was an aristocratic disciple of Stefan George, Count Stauffenberg, who tried to assassinate Hitler.) In every case these sympathies were qualified by important reservations. In most cases they were of short duration, contradicted by other statements or decisions, or positively withdrawn if and when knowledge of political realities came to outweigh the attraction of political gestures. Yet there is no getting away from the fact that the 'moral perfectionism' of all these poets could not come to terms with 'bourgeois liberalism,' that their imagination rejected its assumptions and institutions even where their reason acknowledged that it gave them what they needed most, the freedom to dissent, assert their own values and despise 'the common dream.'

2   Yeats's attitude to Irish and European Fascism has been examined by Conor Cruise O'Brien,[5] who not only documented it in detail but related it to Yeats's poetry.

This attitude was complicated both by Yeats's ambiguous position as a Protestant in the Irish nationalist movement – politically anti-British, but with strong linguistic, cultural and social ties to England – and by vacillations due to periodical retreats into non-political privacy. 'And always,' O'Brien comments, 'in the long phases of withdrawal, he tended to write of all politics with a kind of contempt, a plague-on-both-your-houses air. (Contempt for politics is of course a characteristic Conservative stance.)' As O'Brien points out, 'the two main currents in Yeats's active politics' were 'his Anglophobe Irish nationalism and his authoritarianism.' Yet, with very few exceptions, even Yeats's directly political poems render much more than those currents. At times his apocalyptic imagination could transform a political occasion into a universal

---

*See the chapter, *Stefan George: Perilous Prophet*, in Peter Viereck: *Dream and Responsibility*, Washington, D.C., 1953, pp. 25–35.

myth, as in the case of *Leda and the Swan*, cited by O'Brien. Only Yeats's own note on the poem recalls the circumstances of its inception, the invitation by the editor of a political review to contribute a poem: '. . . Then I thought "Nothing is now possible but some movement from above preceded by some violent annunciation." My fancy began to play with Leda and the Swan for metaphor, and I began this poem: but as I wrote, bird and lady took such possession of the scene that all politics went out of it, and my friend tells me that his "conservative readers would misunderstand the poem." '

O'Brien shows how the forces in Yeats 'that responded to the hatred, cruelty and violence welling up in Europe' produced prophetic poems like *The Second Coming* and the last part of *Nineteen Hundred and Nineteen*. Yeats's opinions and sympathies, like his 'active politics,' have become irrelevant to those poems. What matters is their powerful evocation of forces which few of his contemporaries recognized (though Hofmannsthal, who died in 1929, ten years before Yeats, did recognize them in his late play *Der Turm*: Hofmannsthal noted that the 'imagination is conservative,' but his own imagination could be as prophetic and apocalyptic as Yeats's). O'Brien's comments on *Leda and the Swan* say all that needs to be said about the way in which the poems profited by Yeats's 'fanatic heart,' by the capacity for hatred that makes Yeats's politics unacceptable to O'Brien and the majority of Yeats's readers.

In the poetry, however, the raw intimations of what is impending – the telepathetic waves of violence and fear – make themselves known, not in the form of calculated practical deductions, but in the attempt to reveal, through metaphoric insight, what is actually happening and even, in a broad sense, what is about to happen. The poet, like the lady, is

> so caught up,
> So mastered by the brute blood of the air

that he does indeed take on the knowledge of what is happening with the power to make it known. The political man had his cautious understanding with fascism, the diplomatic relation to a great force; the poet conveyed the nature of the force, the dimension of the tragedy. The impurities of his long and extraordinary life went into his devious and sometimes sinister political theories and activities.

87

The purity and integrity – including the truth about politics as Yeats apprehended it – are in the poetry concentrated in metaphors of such power that they thrust aside all calculated intent: the bird and lady take possession of the scene.

Yeats is one of the writers whom Frank Kermode has called 'the new apocalyptics.'[6] Kermode, too, is worried by the discrepancy between Yeats's moral relativism and the beliefs, or half-beliefs, of which he made use for his poetry. 'At bottom,' Kermode writes, 'he was sceptical about the nonsense with which he satisfied what we can call his lust for commitment. Now and again he believed some of it, but in so far as his true commitment was to poetry he recognized his fictions as heuristic and dispensable, "consciously false." "They give me metaphors for poetry," he noted.' Yet the discrepancy remains; and we shall see how later poets came to distrust metaphor itself, because it lends itself to a kind of double-dealing, unacknowledged shifts and transferences from one order of reality to another. Kermode writes of Yeats's 'retreat to myth and to the rituals of the occult; on the one side were the shopkeeping logicians, on the other the seductive and various forms of unreason.' O'Brien has shown how that very retreat to myth could thwart the poet's original intentions, and redeem the poem from its occasion. Elsewhere, as Kermode observed, the very reverse occurred: pragmatic reality asserted itself in Yeats's diction, deflating his fury and replacing apocalypse with experience: 'What saved him in the end was a confidence basic to the entire Euopean tradition, a confidence in the common language, the vernacular by means of which from day to day we deal with reality as against justice. Everything depends upon a power

> To compound the imagination's Latin with
> The lingua franca et jocundissima.

In the same way, Yeats, though he entertained the fictions of apocalypse, renovation, transition, saw the need to compound them with the *lingua franca* of reality.'

This, however, applies only to the poetry, as Kermode goes on to say. 'The dreams of apocalypse, if they usurp waking thought, may be the worst dreams,' he writes, and quotes Dewey's remark that 'even aesthetic systems may breed a disposition towards the world and take overt effect.' In Yeats Kermode sees one instance of 'totalitarian theories of form matched or reflected by totalitarian politics'; and 'the only reason why this is unimportant is that he had no influence upon those who might have put his beliefs to an operational test.'

From whatever angle we look at it, Yeats's case is paradoxical, not least because he made his poetry out of a quarrel with himself, rather than resolutions of that quarrel – though the resolutions, too, matter, since they account for Yeats's extraordinary progression from melancholy romantic reverie to prophetic or starkly realistic encounters with 'the Savage God,' so that in his old age he could write lines as new, intense, yet seemingly effortless as

> A barnacle goose
> Far up in the stretches of night; night splits and the dawn breaks
> loose;
> I, through the terrible novelty of light, stalk on, stalk on;
> Those great sea-horses bare their teeth and laugh at the dawn.[7]

Yeats's capacity to change, to learn even from younger men like Ezra Pound, also makes it likely that he would have revised his political sympathies had he lived long enough to experience the cataclysms which he invoked. Despite his use of masks, Yeats did not allow an aesthetic system or any other to insulate him against shocks and disturbances and breakdown. 'To speak of one's emotions without fear or moral ambition, to come out from under the shadow of other men's minds, to forget their needs, to be utterly oneself, that is all the Muses care for.'[8] Beneath all Yeats's masks we sense the need to be 'utterly oneself,' though it was only the masks that enabled him to render the multiplicity of that self without loss of intensity and concentration, or the universality which he owed to tradition and found in the great lyric and tragic poets before him: 'That shaping joy has kept the sorrow pure, as it had kept it were the emotion love or hate, for the nobleness of the arts is in the mingling of contraries, the extremity of sorrow, the extremity of joy, perfection of personality, the perfection of its surrender, overflowing turbulent energy, and marvellous stillness. . . .' Since 'we believe only in the thoughts which have been conceived not in the brain but the whole body,' at least as far as poetry is concerned, Yeats's opinions obtrude far less than do those of other poets more consistently modern than he, such as Ezra Pound. Yeats himself wrote in his late *General Introduction for My Work*, 'I hated and still hate with an ever growing hatred the literature of the point of view.' Apart from a few conspicuous lapses, Yeats's poetry conveys to us not only the moral fury but the tragic insight of the poet who wrote before the Second World War:

> Civilization is hooped together, brought
> Under a rule, under the semblance of peace
> By manifold illusion; but man's life is thought,
> And he, despite his terror, cannot cease
> Ravening through century after century,
> Ravening, raging, and uprooting that he may come
> Into the desolation of reality. . . .⁹

Whatever our point of view, and whatever Yeats's when he wrote those lines, even so general and undramatized a statement must convince us, not only because the modulation and control of the blank verse are masterly, but because the statement is true; and events which Yeats did not live to experience have made its truth not less but more apparent.

If we do consult Yeats's opinions, we find that all of them have a corrective or complement in his own writings. His pro-Fascist leanings, for instance, are modified by the admission, 'I am no nationalist, except in Ireland for passing reasons,' and those 'passing reasons' must not be left out of account; also by his psychological observation: 'All empty souls tend to extreme opinion. It is only in those who have built up a rich world of memories and habits of thought that extreme opinions affront the sense of probability. Propositions, for instance, which set all the truth upon one side can only enter sick minds to dislocate and strain, if they enter at all, and sooner or later the mind expels them by instinct.'¹⁰ Most of the extreme opinions and attitudes in Yeats's work are those of his anti-self. The Yeats who confessed, 'I have no solution, none,' was the reasonable man who despaired of 'perfection of the life,' knowing that the kind of perfection that he wanted for his work could not be obtained without the help of his 'circus animals,' of that mask of style which even the prose writer could rarely bring himself to discard.

3   Yeats's participation both in the Irish literary revival and in the political developments that were so closely linked with it exacerbated his moral and artistic dilemmas. Yet the choice between 'perfection of the life' and 'perfection of the work' was familiar to poets who had less opportunity than Yeats to let the apocalyptic imagination encroach on active politics. Paul Valéry, too, remarked: 'Whoever says Work says Sacrifice. The crucial question is to decide what one is going to sacrifice: one needs to know *who, who is going to be devoured*.'[11] As a French intellectual, however, Valéry was saved from apocalyptic proclivities by the tradition of sceptical, analytical and psychologically probing intelligence – a tradition going back to the French moralists of the seventeenth century and beyond them, to Montaigne – which his prose works continued, despite his 'exercises' in absolute poetry. Yeats could never have written: 'A political or artistic opinion should be something so vague that under the same semblance the same individual can always accommodate it to his moods and his interests; justify his action; explain his vote.'[12] Yeats's definition of the gentleman – one instance of his indebtedness to English culture and morality – forbade so deliberate a relativism.

In the same way, Valéry's very French reluctance to make a fool of himself prevented him from indulging in prophecy when, in writings like *La Politique de l'esprit* or *Regards sur le monde actuel*, he dealt with public and general issues, the 'crisis' in European civilization of which his poetry has so little to say, as compared with Yeats's apocalyptic awareness that 'things fall apart, the centre cannot hold.' Pronouncements of the same order by Hugo von Hofmannsthal, but especially his lecture *Das Schrifttum als geistiger Raum der Nation* (1927), show how prudent it was of Valéry to exercise this kind of restraint. Hofmannsthal's theme has a great deal in common with Valéry's. As social critics and cultural politicians both men were profoundly disturbed by the changes not only in the institutions but in the mentality of Europe between the two wars. Indeed, Valéry's analysis, in *La Politique de l'esprit*, of what technology and conformism were doing to that mentality is more devastating than Hofmannsthal's fears, in his lecture, about the centrifugal *hubris* of his contemporaries. Yet Valéry's 'horror of prophecies' prompted him to conclude his analysis with an admission that he had 'no solution, none,' did not know what would become of the human species, and could only advise his audience to be prepared for anything, 'or almost anything.' Hofmannsthal attempted a synthesis; and in doing so he used the words 'conservative revolution,' crossing the dangerous borderline between cultural analysis and active politics, between diagnosis and prescription. Hofmannsthal was not a Fascist or sympathizer with Fascism, and the National Socialists were to ban his works because of one Jewish, or 'non-Aryan,' grand-parent; but 'conservative revolution' became the slogan of a number of extreme nationalist and near-Fascist groups in Austria and Germany. Hofmannsthal's exasperated conserva-tism, quite different in spirit and intent from the programme of any political faction of that or a later period, was modified by irony, self-criticism and liberalism in his imaginative works. In the public address, his poetic imagination proposed a solution more rhetorical and more drastic, because the poetic imagination tends towards utopia, apocalypse and prophecy when it is not engaged with the kind of realities that engaged Hofmannsthal as a story-teller and dramatist.

Valéry knew his limitations. He knew that literary men are well qualified to offer social and cultural criticism, but tend to have 'no solution, none,' when it comes to the choice of evils inseparable from practical politics. Besides, Valéry's pervasive scepticism and his individualism always on the verge of solipsism made it difficult for him to take politics seriously. 'All politics,' he wrote,. 'are founded on the indifference of the majority of those involved; otherwise, no politics would be possible.'[13] At best he could be a cynical observer of events to which he attached less importance than to changes in the intellectual habits and processes of his contemporaries: 'Great events, perhaps, are only such for little minds. To more attentive minds it is the imperceptible and continuous events that count.' Valéry, therefore, has next to nothing to say about the political movements and conflicts that were sweeping away his own individualist and bourgeois culture, though he excelled at the analysis of 'more attentive minds.' For all their political indis-cretions, both Yeats and Hofmannsthal were on more intimate terms with the *Zeitgeist*, more responsive to the tremors and rumblings of a violent age. One reason is that both men were less inclined to solipsism than Valéry, more involved in the human condition generally, and more concerned with particular societies, their own.

4   The German critic and philosopher Walter Benjamin, who became a Marxist in his later years, once remarked that Fascism 'aestheticizes politics,' whereas Communism 'politicizes art.'[14] He cites the Italian Futurist Marinetti as an instance of the Fascist apocalyptic who finds his satisfaction in war, proclaiming *'fiat ars – pereat mundus'*; and he comments: 'That, clearly, is the consummation of l'art pour l'art.'

There is enough truth in that generalization to make one wonder whether there is any middle way between the 'aestheticization' of politics and the 'politicization' of art. In the period that extends from the initiation of the 'art for art's sake' principle to the 1920s – and *l'art pour l'art* was proclaimed as early as the 1830s by Théophile Gautier – that middle way was often found in practice, though rarely in theory. From the start there was a tendency for poets to confuse the autonomy of art with the autonomy of the artist, a confusion that came easily to an age in which the artist was worshipped as a hero and 'representative man.' Paradoxically, that 'representative man' insisted on his uniqueness, indeed, on all that separated and isolated him from humanity as a whole. Hence the pervasive uneasiness of poets about their 'empirical selves' and the cult of masks or of impersonality which turned their uneasiness into a new imaginative and moral freedom. Without this freedom, used in a great variety of ways by a great variety of poets throughout Europe and America, there would have been no modern poetry of the kind that flourished internationally in the first half of the twentieth century. All the best poems of C. P. Cavafy, for instance, are historical *persona* poems that owe their subtlety and vividness to that freedom – so much so that Cavafy's empirical self is present only in its disguises, fulfilled itself only in its transformations. To a lesser degree this applies to most of the outstanding modern Greek poets, with their special ability to merge a modern sensibility in the figures and landscapes of history or myth. In the work of George Seferis personal experience – including political experience, doubts and fears about the state of his country, exile, loss, deprivation and recovery – is transformed with such delicacy into the figures and images that are its 'objective correlative' that only irrelevant biographical information could prompt one to separate his empirical from his poetic self. So seemingly effortless and complete a transposition demands something other than a readiness to put on masks; in the case of Seferis the rival claims of aesthetics and experience have been truly reconciled, by an impersonality that is not an artistic device, but a conviction that the whole is greater than the part, the individual consciousness less important than what it contains. A similar conviction informs the work of T.S.Eliot, but the traditions to which he looked for sustenance of his impersonality were less easy to take for granted, less close at hand, more diversified, and more problematical. Eliot's early preoccupation with the work of Laforgue and Corbière, the self-questioners *par excellence*, indicates some of his difficulties.

Paul Valéry said that 'tradition and progress are two great enemies of the human race'[15] – an example of his ingenious and mischievous humour – but went on to investigate the ambivalent, if not positively hostile, attitudes of nineteenth-century poets to progress in the sciences and technology. Edgar Allan Poe is cited as a writer of the Romantic period who opposed such progress, but made use of new discoveries in his works. In Poe's succession, Villiers de l'Isle-Adam, that out-and-out aesthete, was also one of the fathers of modern science fiction, in his novel *L'Eve future*. Romantic-Symbolist poetry, on the other hand, could not make even such ambiguous use of the sciences, because its specialization was an aesthetic one which inevitably conflicted with the increasing specialization of scientific enquiry and with a technology felt to be as materialistic as it was ruthlessly antagonistic to 'the ceremony of innocence.' Valéry's own work shows the extent of the rift between intellectual curiosity in prose and mythopoeic atavism in verse.

That rift could be satisfactorily closed or mended by those poets who worked in the more technically backward areas of Europe and America, or could draw without too much strain on memories of such a background. The Spanish poet Juan Ramón Jiménez, for instance, was still able to believe that 'any one who progresses in one discipline (poetry, for example, religion, art or science, etc.) will inevitably progress in all others even though he may not consider them individually to be his.'[16] The same poet attempted to reconcile the anti-progressive bias of Romantic-Symbolist poets with a humanist affirmation of liberal democracy; and so did his contemporary Antonio Machado and most of the next generation of Spanish poets, the generation of Lorca, Alberti, Aleixandre, Alonso, Guillén and Cernuda. In 1941, Jiménez redefined the terms 'democracy' and 'aristocracy' in such a way as to minimize their social and political incompatibilities. Yet the poetic imagination is revealed in his identification of 'aristocracy' with the peasantry, because 'there is no more exquisite form of aristocracy than living out of doors.'[17] It is difficult to imagine any poet with a metropolitan background making that pronouncement in 1941 without hearing the mocking cackle of the sociologists at his back. Even Yeats's preference for the peasantry is regarded as a reactionary gesture – and Yeats was an Irishman. Jiménez, true, made it clear that his aristocracy was not the aristocracy of birth, which Yeats also glorified; but like Yeats he believed that 'always and in everything one must end with poetry, which is the unequalled expression of aristocracy.'

These are the words of a poet who proved his preference for liberal democracy by leaving his country after the Civil War. That political and moral choice is one thing, the premises of Romantic-Symbolist poetry are another. As a poet, Jiménez could not conceive of a civilization without roots in nature and tradition. In another essay of that period he specifically distinguished poetry from literature. 'The literary man scarcely ever makes a mistake,' he noted; 'he nearly always catches the plates he has tossed into the air, and if one falls it falls on somebody else's head. The poet customarily loses some plates, but they do not fall on any head, they are lost in the infinite because he is a good friend of space.' The literary man, in other words, knows what he is doing and what he wants to do; but 'poetry is never realized by everyone, it always escapes and the true poet, who is usually an honourable person because he has the habit of living with truth, knows how to let it escape. . . .' Jiménez concludes that 'literature is a state of culture, poetry a state of grace, before and after culture.'

Jiménez was perfectly right in implying that the primacy of the imagination in poetry forbids the total integration and assimilation of poetic values into any social or cultural order that exists in the modern world; and he was equally right to keep his political and moral choices separate from his knowledge that this is so. 'The imagination is autonomous,' he wrote, 'and I am an imaginative autonomist.'[18] Unlike so many of his fellow poets, however, he recognized the bounds of the autonomous imagination and refrained from aggressive sallies beyond its bounds. That was the purpose of his distinction between poetry and literature, the art exercised for its own sake, instinctively, and the craft 'obsessed by the external world which it has to incorporate.' Because poetry is 'a state of grace' – 'the poet, when mute or when writing, is an abstract dancer, and if he writes, it is out of an everyday weakness, for to be truly consistent he ought not to write. He who ought to write is the literary man.'[19]

Yeats, Valéry and Hofmannsthal were a few of the many poets in the Romantic-Symbolist tradition who were fascinated by the mute arts, aspiring not so much to 'the condition of music' as to the condition of silence; and 'dance,' as Frank Kermode has written, 'is the most primitive, non-discursive art, offering a pre-scientific image of life, an intuitive truth. Thus it is the emblem of the Romantic image. Dance belongs to a period before the self and the world were divided, and so achieves naturally that "original unity" which modern poetry can reproduce only by a great and exhausting effort.'[20] Jiménez suggests that it is literature, not poetry, which ought to make that 'great and exhausting effort.' As a Spaniard it was easier for him than for most of the poets with whom Frank Kermode dealt in *Romantic Image* to preserve 'the ceremony of innocence,' and attain the simplicity and nakedness celebrated and enacted in his poem from *Eternidades* (1918) about poetry that begins

> Vino, primero, pura
> vestido de inocencia
>
> (Pure at first, she came,
> Clothed in innocence),

traces an intermediary stage of sophistication and adornment, but ends in praise of a poetry that has learnt to undress again, wholly this time, a 'naked poetry.' In a poem from the same collection Jiménez asks for that 'intelligence' which provides 'the exact names of things,' and asks that his word may be 'the thing itself,' so that through him those who have no knowledge of things may reach them. As Rilke, Williams and Ponge did in very different ways, Jiménez puts himself at the disposal of things, losing himself in order to find himself. This transposition, too, required a 'great and exhausting effort' on the part of poets confronted with things that were artifacts of the new technology. Jiménez had the advantage of not being provoked to pseudo-political gestures by the things that confronted him, since they were part of nature or of a way of life still largely pre-industrial. He could leave it to 'literature' to accept or reject those other things, products of the machine age.

5   At the heart of every Romantic-Symbolist poet's aesthetic, then, there is a private religion, a *religio poetae* irreconcilable with the exigencies of the public world. In the case of Jiménez, his image of the 'abstract dancer' betrays it. Essentially and inescapably, the abstract dance is non-political, solitary and anachronistic; but since it cannot be mute, because the poet's medium is words, the abstract dancer interrupts his dance to engage in 'literature,' if only by explaining himself to himself and looking for the link, never doubted though invisible, between his solitary performance and the needs of humanity as a whole.

At that point he must be prepared to 'go out of himself,' to meet others half-way and understand that in the social and political spheres imaginative values are not, and cannot be, absolute without a clash of autonomous imaginations. If he fails to make that adjustment he will align himself with absolute political creeds, mistaking their monomania for a dedication akin to his own, and seduced by promises of order.

Again and again readers of modern poetry are dismayed by revelations, often posthumous, that their favourite poets, 'gentle' and retiring and 'sensitive' persons, admired the most violent and ruthless politicians of their time. Yeats, at least, did not pretend to be gentle, and neither did D.H.Lawrence or Gottfried Benn. The strangest case of all is that of Rainer Maria Rilke, because Rilke's extreme eclecticism, apparent in the many successive phases of his work, as in the multiplicity of his masks and *personae*, did rest on an explicit profession of gentleness, sensitiveness and compassion. Unlike his slightly older contemporary Stefan George, Rilke began not with a rigid aesthetic canon and a stance of rigorous exclusiveness, but a readiness to respond to almost any experience and avail himself of almost any literary model that came his way. After the Romantic practice of much of his early verse he followed the Naturalists – George's chief aversion – in a poetry of pity that drew on the megalopolitan scene of his time, mainly by a self-identification with its outcasts, the poor, the sick and the oppressed. Then came the pseudo-Christian and pseudo-mystical lyricism of the *Stundenbuch*, anticipated, it's true, by a good many of the more personal poems in *Das Buch der Bilder* – and the reaction against its subjectivity in the 'thing poems' of *Neue Gedichte*, written under the influence of Rodin and Cézanne as a deliberate attempt to apply the disciplines of the visual arts to poetry. In the critical years between 1908 and the completion of the *Duineser Elegien* and *Sonette an Orpheus* in 1922, Rilke proved receptive to many new trends in poetry, in the other arts and in society, a seemingly cosmopolitan mind at home in the palaces and slums of Europe, in touch with aristocrats and working men, open to the 'pure' poetry of Valéry as to the less 'pure' poetry of Supervielle and to the decidedly committed poetry of the politically revolutionary German Expressionists. It is in the poems written, but not collected, in this period that Rilke's diverse experiments made him a decidedly modernist poet, far in advance of his near-coevals, George and Hofmannsthal. (Hofmannsthal, in any case, had turned to drama and various forms of imaginative or expository prose in his desperate endeavours to bridge the gap between Romantic-Symbolist art and society.)

It was not till 1956, thirty years after Rilke's death, that his *Lettres milanaises, 1921–1926*,[21] written in French to the Italian Duchess Aurelia Gallarati-Scotti, showed him to have been as ambiguous about the new nationalism in Europe as he had been about the First World War. His notorious rootlessness did not prevent him from telling the Duchess that 'internationalism' and 'humanism' are no more than abstract ideas – and this in the context of defence of Mussolini's Fascism. To the same correspondent he wrote:

It would have been difficult for me to be a soldier anywhere else, but I could have been one with conviction and enthusiasm in one of those countries, if I had been born there: an Italian soldier, a French soldier, yes, I could have been one, confraternally, to the point of the supreme sacrifice: to such an extent does nationality in those two countries seem to us bound up with gesture, with action, with the visible example. Amongst you, even more than in France, blood truly is *one* and, at some moments, the idea, borne along by this blood, can also be *one*.[22]

In his admiration for Mussolini Rilke was in good company, including Yeats, Wallace Stevens, Ezra Pound and D.H. Lawrence; but these writers had not flirted with Romain Rolland's pan-European pacifist movement, as Rilke had, or made semi-autobiographical fiction out of the sufferings of a sensitive pupil in a military academy, as Rilke had done in his story *Die Turnstunde*, as well as glorifying military honour and self-sacrifice in his most popular prose work, *Die Weise von Liebe und Tod des Cornets Christoph Rilke* (1899). That same early work had announced the theme of a mystique of blood and race which Rilke expounds in the letter with a vicarious and devious patriotism which may well have made the Duchess smile, if she did not share the high religious seriousness characteristic of most of Rilke's female correspondents.

There is a recurrent vacillation in all Rilke's work between the *personae* of aristocrat and pariah, a vacillation especially apparent in the Parisian episodes of *Die Aufzeichungen des Malte Laurids Brigge*, as in the section headed *Bibliothèque Nationale*. The vacillation goes back to Baudelaire, whose presence is so conspicuous in those episodes. In *Malte Laurids Brigge*, too, Rilke writes of the need for masks: 'I had never seen masks before, but I realized at once that there must be masks,'[23] and the mask that Brigge puts on takes possession of him, driving out his familiar self, though the identity and character of the mask are dubious and undefined. Rilke's extraordinary richness as a lyrical poet is inseparable from a 'negative capability,' a gift of empathy, which, outside his poems, led him into almost every conceivable absurdity. No other poet of his time had so fluid a personality, so wide a range of masks and styles; but also of sympathies and attitudes which exclude and contradict one another as soon as we look at them·from a pragmatic or logical point of view. That is why inestimable harm has been done to Rilke's work by the posthumous publication of his letters and private documents.

6. Early in 1927, not many months after Rilke's death, his daughter wrote to Hugo von Hofmannsthal to tell him of plans for the posthumous publication of work by Rilke and ask Hofmannsthal's advice and cooperation. Hofmannsthal, who believed that the era of bourgeois individualism was over, and who had evolved a doctrine of impersonality not unlike that of T.S.Eliot, replied:

> ... If I felt my death drawing very close, I should leave instructions in a sense almost diametrically opposed. I should do all I could – in so far as anything can be done in this disconnected world of ours – to suppress all those tiresome and often indiscreet statements about a productive individual and his works, all that diluting chatter, or at least to deprive it of nourishment as far as possible by the removal of private letters and notes, by putting difficulties in the way of that inane biography-mania and all indecencies of that kind. My idea would be to really entrust the hardly explicable phenomenon that once existed here, R.M.R. or H.H., to death, even to oblivion if need be (except in the hearts of a few loyal men and women), and leave the works to engage unaided in their hard secret struggle with the next hostile decades....[24]

It may look as though Rilke's reputation had not only withstood these hostile decades, but reversed the usual process by turning hostility into unstinted homage. Editions of his poems, prose works and letters, translations into countless languages, biographies, memoirs, critical studies and academic theses have jostled one another at a rate that must be almost unique in modern literature. To many of his readers Rilke was not a poet, but *the* poet, the reincarnation in his time of the archetypal Orpheus whose myth he revived and celebrated in the *Sonnets*. Yet his work appealed to many different kinds of readers and satisfied many different needs. It was as exquisitely musical and pictorial as the poetry of the French Symbolists and their German successor, Stefan George, yet without being deliberately recondite and exclusive; and though firmly based on an aesthetic akin to theirs, it was open to that order of reality which had been the province of the opposing school, the Naturalists. It ranged from the intense self-communion of the *Stundenbuch* to the seemingly social preoccupations of the *Buch der Bilder* and the seeming absorption in things of the *Neue Gedichte*. During the critical years that followed, Rilke came to terms with the new styles and energies that might so easily have left him stranded. Like Yeats, and unlike Valéry, George or Hofmannsthal, he entered yet another new phase as a distinctly 'modern' – post-1914 – poet. Most important of all, as far as his reputation is concerned, he annexed so much 'life' to a basically autonomous art, so much of the language of religious mystical communion to a basically individualistic outlook, that like no other poet of his time he seemed to offer a new existential philosophy and a new morality. This philosophic and didactic function can be discounted as one of those misunderstandings on which, as he said, the fame of artists rests; but it has become as difficult to separate from Rilke's fame as our knowledge of his person from his poetry.

Hofmannsthal knew that his own choice entailed other diffi-culties and dangers, and foresaw the eclipse which his own work was to suffer during those hostile decades; but, now that Rilke's struggle has begun in earnest, it will soon be all too clear that Hofmannsthal's warning was apt and right. Four decades after Rilke's death the spate of publications continues as though nothing had happened; but more and more readers of poetry turn from Rilke's poetry with a feeling little short of disgust. The myth so beautifully sustained in his later poetry has been blasted by a barrage of biographical 'indecencies'; the philosophy well and truly debunked by critical examinations.

If poetry, as well as poets, were subject to the moral criteria which one applies to the actions and decisions of public figures, it would be reasonable to blame Rilke for some of the posthumous indignities which his work has suffered. It was he who wrote those copious letters with an unmistakable squint at posterity. It was he who sowed the seeds of the philosophical and theologi-cal criticism that has discredited his most ambitious work, in confessions and manifestos like his *Letters to a Young Poet, Letter from a Young Artisan* and his letters to his Polish translator about the *Duino Elegies*. Almost from the start Rilke claimed an absolute authority. His early autobiographical story *Ewald Tragy* contains this casual remark: 'I am my own legislator and King;

there is no one above me, not even God.' Yet as far as his poetry is concerned this question of responsibility is simply irrelevant. The truth of poetry is of a different order. If we cannot dissociate the poetry from the pretensions and vanities – let alone the harmless foibles – of the man, it is we who are the losers; and only a small part of Rilke's poetry calls for a 'suspension of disbelief.' The part in question – mainly sections of the *Duino Elegies* and *Sonnets to Orpheus* – is that in which Rilke made the mistake of formulating his private *religio poetae*, instead of using it to write poetry. That private religion was an auxiliary religion with little relevance or validity outside and beyond Rilke's poetry. The angels of the *Duino Elegies*, for instance, are not to be confused with the angels of theology, since they were secular angels, the functionaries not of faith but of imagination. Like the angel of Wallace Stevens, they were 'necessary angels of the earth' within an imaginative system, but nowhere else; and indeed there is an extraordinary accordance between the private religions of Rilke and Wallace Stevens, both of whom were theologians of the poetic imagination, hierophants of the earthly, but especially of things and places. 'Life is an affair of people and places,' Stevens wrote. 'But for me life is an affair of places and that is the trouble.'[25]

That was Rilke's trouble, too, though he could never have said so as bluntly and straightforwardly. Rilke's crisis poems of the years 1912 to 1914, particularly the poems *Wendung*, *Klage*, *Narziss* and *Waldteich*, render his awareness of what he had lost by being unable to relate himself to people – people as independent agents, not as *personae* to be filled with his own 'inwardness' – as completely as he had related himself to landscapes, plants, animals and artifacts. In other words, Rilke knew that his relation to people had been no different from his relation to those things which do not and cannot answer back. His Narcissus poem contains the line

Er liebte, was ihm ausging, wieder ein

(Back into himself he loved that which went out of him)

an admirably precise description of the whole process by which Rilke assimilated the world to his imagination without ever giving any part of himself away in a more than imaginative involvement. The woodland pond of *Waldteich* is an image of the same seeming reciprocity of world and mind, a reciprocity threatened or broken by the awareness that there are storms and oceans beyond the woodland pond's stillness, 'turned in upon itself.' In a poem of the same period, *To Hölderlin*,[26] Rilke adds this comment to his Narcissus, pond and mirror images:

> Seen
> Sind erst im Ewigen. Hier ist Fallen
> das Tüchtigste.

> (Lakes
> don't exist till eternity. Here
> falling's the best we can do.)

And the poem *Wendung* (Turning-Point)[27] hinges on the distinction between the active contemplation by which things or places can be assimilated and transformed, and human relations that demand a measure of self-sacrifice, a love that gives as well as takes:

> Werk des Gesichts ist getan,
> tue nun Herz-Werk
> an den Bildern in dir, jenen gefangenen; denn du
> überwältigtest sie: aber nun kennst du sie nicht.

> (Work of seeing is done,
> now practise heart-work
> upon those images captive within you, for you
> overpowered them only; but now do not know them.)

7   Rilke's political inconsistencies and absurdities may seem to have nothing to do with that personal crisis, a crisis that was never resolved in his life, as distinct from his work. Yet the failure to love others instead of projecting himself into them, 'overpowering' them and exploiting them imaginatively, is not really distinct from Rilke's failure to see the political world as anything other than a screen on which to project his private feelings and attitudes. Both failures were those of an 'imaginative autonomist,' a maker of 'supreme fictions' who could not get himself to believe in those realities which defy the creative imagination.

The term 'supreme fictions' is another borrowing from

Wallace Stevens, whose *religio poetae* was almost identical with Rilke's. 'What makes the poet the potent figure that he is, or was, or ought to be,' Stevens wrote, 'is that he creates the world to which we turn incessantly and without knowing it, and that he gives to life the supreme fictions without which we are unable to conceive of it.'[28] The poet 'has had immensely to do with giving life whatever savour it possesses. He has had to do with whatever the imagination and the senses have made of the world.' 'The world about us would be desolate except for the world within us.' 'Besides, unreal things have a reality of their own, in poetry as elsewhere.' Poetry 'is an interdependence of the imagination and reality as equals.' 'It comes to this, that poetry is a part of the structure of reality.' All these statements from Wallace Stevens's *The Necessary Angel* are part of what he called 'poetry's mystical theology,' the formulation of which in Rilke's *Duino Elegies* has given so much offence to his Christian and humanist critics alike. 'The major poetic idea in the world is and always has been the idea of God,' Wallace Stevens also wrote;[29] and : 'After one has abandoned a belief in God, poetry is the essence which takes its place as life's redemption.' The poet becomes 'the priest of the invisible,' words that recall Rilke's to his Polish translator about the 'bees of the invisible.' In both cases the imagination has taken the place of that transcendent order on whose existence outside the imagination most of the great religions insist.

This 'mystical theology,' then, is at once materialistic – since its starting point is empirical – and irrational, if not antirational. For all his emphasis on thinking in poetry – an emphasis just as marked in Rilke – Stevens said that 'rational beings are canaille,'[30] and: 'The poem reveals itself only to the ignorant man,' because 'poetry must resist the intelligence almost successfully.' Above all, the 'real' must not be confused with the rational or even with the realistic mode in the arts. Reality has to be transformed by the imagination before it is truly perceived. That is what Stevens meant in saying that 'in the long run, the truth does not matter.' This truth is a fixed truth, the truth held on to once and for all either by reason or by faith. Poetry, on the other hand, is a perpetual two-way traffic between experience and imagination. Poets like himself, Stevens said repeatedly, are 'thinkers without final thoughts,'

In an always incipient cosmos,
The way, when we climb a mountain,
Vermont throws itself together.[31]

There are also poets with final thoughts, of course, and Stevens distinguished between 'adherents of the imagination' and 'adherents of the central,' whose ambition is 'to press away from mysticism toward that ultimate good sense which we term civilization.'[32] T.S.Eliot and Hofmannsthal were 'adherents of the central,' Rilke and Stevens, on the other hand, cannot be tied down by a philosophically anchored criticism. Every over-all interpretation of Rilke's or Stevens's thought – rather than of their thinking – must treat it as though it were definitive, as though their discoveries were codifications, their flashes of recognition (within a particular context) the articles of a creed. The result is like using a lasso to catch a humming-bird.

'Poetry is a satisfying of the desire for resemblance,'[33] Stevens wrote. The satisfying of this desire is rarely contained within the bounds of a poet's beliefs, even if he is a poet who holds beliefs. The imagination picks up its resemblances wherever it can find them. If it needs angels it will take them from a religion which the poet cannot accept, or actively opposes, as Rilke opposed Christianity. Unscrupulous as such habits may seem, not only Christian mystics but sober apologists and preachers are equally apt to borrow metaphors and analogies from worldly pursuits which they have no intention of glorifying. The medium of language is to blame.

Granted that Stevens's and Rilke's thinking scarcely 'works' outside the sphere in which poetic processes, or their analogues, apply, we are forced every day of our lives to allow for specializations of this order. Railway tickets can't be cashed at the bank, though they represent money. To write great poetry is quite enough for one man to achieve in 'this disconnected world of ours.' That the truths of some poetry are partial and provisional truths does not make them less valuable. It is up to the reader of poetry not to approach it with expectations and demands which it cannot, by its nature, fulfil.

8   In taking issue with the 'politicization of art,' in the form of what he took to be a Marxist rejoinder to his poem *The*

Idea of Order at Key West, Stevens remarked parenthetically: '(I am pro-Mussolini personally).'[34] This casual admission is almost irrelevant to Stevens's poetry, not excluding the poem *Mr Burnshaw and the Statue*[35] that was his answer to political criticism. In that poem Stevens sees Communism as directed towards an unreal and unrealizable future, as a utopian religion that denies the thing in favour of the idea. Stevens's mysticism, like Rilke's, begins with the visible world:

> the apple in the orchard, round
> And red, will not be redder, rounder then
> Than now ...

Fascist ideology does not enter into the poem. Yet a predilection for the past is as much a premise of Stevens's poetry as it is of Yeats's, Rilke's, Eliot's and Ezra Pound's; and one could well argue that all these poets' treatment of the past is no less utopian than the Marxist ideology which Stevens opposed in the poem. This, again, has to do with the poetic imagination, which is 'conservative,' as Hofmannsthal said, because the past is less abstract than the future. However elusive as a whole, the past is a repository of fragments that are palpable to the imagination and can therefore be 'shored against one's ruins.'

Rilke's opposition to the machine, which 'threatens all we have acquired as long as it does not obey but lays claim on the mind,'[36] belongs to the same Romantic-Symbolist complex; and so does the anti-capitalism of a sonnet in the same sequence, No. XIX of Part II of the *Sonnets to Orpheus,* in which Rilke shows his ability, also apparent in passages of the *Duino Elegies,* to incorporate the idioms and phenomena of contemporary civilization into a kind of poetry that is radically antagonistic to them. The money that 'lives somewhere in the pampering bank, acting familiar with thousands,' is contrasted with the figure of the blind beggar, a figure that recalls Rilke's early *Buch der Bilder*:

> In den Geschäften entlang ist das Geld wie zuhause
> und verkleidet sich scheinbar in Seide, Nelken und Pelz.
> Er, der Schweigende, steht in der Atempause
> alles des wach oder schlafend atmenden Gelds.

> (In the length of those shops money's as though in its place,
> at home, and seems to dress up in silk, carnations and furs.

He, the silent, stands in the breathing-space
of all that money which breathes as it sleeps or stirs.)

Here we come up against the dilemma of all the many poets
who thought if only briefly that Fascism offered an alternative
to the primacy of economics in both capitalism and Marxism,
a primacy obscured in Fascist ideology by emotionally primitivist gestures. Rilke did not live to see how far Fascism would go
in its mechanization of the mind. Wallace Stevens did; and in
a later letter [37] he wrote: 'For a long time, I have thought of
adding other sections to the *Notes* [*toward a Supreme Fiction*] and
one in particular: *It Must Be Human.*'

> The heaven of Europe is empty, like a Schloss
> Abandoned because of taxes . . .

Stevens had written in *The Greenest Continent* (1945), and in the
tenth of Rilke's *Duino Elegies* there are related images of
desolation characterizing modern Europe, like the 'market of
consolations,' bounded by the church 'bought ready made,'

> reinlich und zu und enttäuscht wie ein Postamt am Sonntag

(clean, disappointed and shut like the post office on a Sunday).

This is the negative use of modernity also to be found in T.S.
Eliot and Ezra Pound's *Mauberley* sequence, as in much modern
poetry, other than that by Communists and Futurists, written up
to the Second World War. There is no complete agreement as to
what the imaginations of the different poets of this period
wanted to conserve; but all looked to the past, all were preoccupied with tradition as something alive and precious, more
alive and more precious than the paraphernalia of contemporary
civilization. In a late poem, *Recitation after Dinner*,[38] Stevens
found this metaphor for tradition (which means 'carrying over,'
an active sense that is often forgotten by those who use words
less attentively and scrupulously than the poets) :

> It has a clear, a single, a solid form,
> That of the son who bears upon his back
> The father that he loves, and bears him from
> The ruins of the past, out of nothing left,
> Made noble by the honour he receives,
> As if in a golden cloud. The son restores
> The father. He hides his ancient blue beneath

> His own bright red. But he bears him out of love,
> His life made double by his father's life,
> Ascending the humane . . .

In their concern with things on the one hand, a supreme (and aesthetically satisfying) fiction on the other, these poets were inclined to forget Stevens's addendum, *It Must Be Human*, if that is taken to mean that every kind of human need, not only the aesthetic and imaginative, must be taken into account. Commenting on the work of St-John Perse, a poet who has continued to write imaginatively 'absolute' poetry even after the Second World War, Kathleen Raine has pointed to 'an element entirely absent from the writings of St-John Perse – the human as such. The poet stops short, in his account of man, precisely with what is (in terms of all the higher religions) precisely human in man, his individual being. The gods whom he invokes are old pantheistic gods. . . .'[39] I shall have more to say elsewhere of the longing for primordially uncomplicated ways of life in certain poets who put up a desperate fight against complexities intractable to the imagination; but Stevens's words could also mean that the supreme fiction cannot be other than human, because the imagination is a human faculty, however little use it may have for human manifestations like those listed in E.E. Cummings's love-hate poem about humanity:

> humanity i love you because you
> are perpetually putting the secret of
> life in your pants and forgetting
> it's there and sitting down
>
> on it
> and because you are
> forever making poems in the lap
> of death Humanity
>
> i hate you[40]

The same ambivalence pervades other poems by Cummings, like the one beginning

> pity this busy monster, manunkind,
> not[41]

or the one beginning 'what if a much of a which of a wind,' in which every sort of destruction – even of the universe – is cheerfully accepted because

the most who die, the more we live.[42]

These are playful poems, intended to disturb and make fun of the solemn humanitarian commonplaces. That, too, is one of the useful functions of poetry, though to the puritanical and literal-minded the playfulness of Cummings will seem as irresponsible as Rilke's and Stevens's delight in the rich resources of both formal and informal language, simply as the material for intricate inventions.

As even Yeats recognized, the 'politicization of art' in this century has placed too great a burden of responsibility on the poetic imagination. Rilke, that almost monomaniacally dedicated poet, at one time considered giving up poetry to become a country doctor. And Yeats wrote:

> I think it better that in times like these
> A poet's mouth be silent, for in truth
> We have no gift to set a statesman right.[43]

The more heavily their social conscience came to weigh on poets, the more difficult it became for them to produce a body of work as consistent in quality as that of Yeats, Rilke, Stevens or St-John Perse. Such major work required the kind of specialization to which many poets no longer feel they have a right, a specialization not only of craft but of vision; 'One of the essential conditions to the writing of poetry,' Stevens wrote in a letter,[44] 'is impetus. That is a reason for thinking that to be a poet at all one ought to be a poet constantly. It was a great loss to poetry when people began to think that the professional poet was an outlaw or an exile. Writing poetry is a conscious activity. While poems may very well occur, they had very much better be caused.' Only very few poets opposed to the Romantic-Symbolist aesthetic – usually on conscientious grounds – have found it possible to be poets constantly; many more have lost impetus not only because of economic or political pressures, but because of a deep distrust of the autonomous imagination and its atavistic affinities.

6

MULTIPLE
PERSONALITIES

1   WALLACE STEVENS made little use of *personae*.
Language itself served him as a mask: the mask of style. The
conflict between empirical and poetic identity was enacted by
his vocabulary and diction, extreme artifice and preciosity on
the one hand, the bare blunt vernacular on the other. This is
especially true of his early poems, such as *The Comedian as the
Letter C*, with its many erudite, archaic or exotic words whose
function is like that of a clown's costume and make-up:

> The responsive man,
> Planting his pristine cores in Florida,
> Should prick thereof, not on the psaltery,
> But on the banjo's categorical gut,
> Tuck, tuck, while the flamingoes flapped his bays.
> Sepulchral señors, bibbling pale mescal,
> Oblivious to the Aztec almanacs,
> Should make the intricate Sierra scan.[1]

Most of his earlier poems – like so many of Rilke's – are poems
about poetry, or about the poetic process, though they draw on
a wide range of sensuous experience. Many of them come close
to the kind of near-nonsense sound poems which Edith Sitwell
was writing in the same period, from her *Bucolic Comedies* to *Gold
Coast Customs*. Stevens's little poem *Life Is Motion* (from *Har-
monium*, 1923) is a good example:

> In Oklahoma,
> Bonnie and Josie,

> Dressed in calico,
> Danced around a stump.
> They cried,
> 'Ohoyaho,
> Ohoo' . . .
> Celebrating the marriage
> Of flesh and air.

Yet the last two lines bring us up against Stevens's constant preoccupation with the interaction and interplay of mind and world, that celebration of the earthly which was also Rilke's *religio poetae* and his justification for writing poems about the poetic process. In a few late poems like *Irrlichter* (1924) Rilke too could be a comedian of language; and mannerism was his temptation at all times, as it was the temptation of Stevens.

The great variety of *personae* which Rilke added to his verbal virtuosity cannot be traced or listed here. What needs to be said is that they do not maintain a more or less consistent mask, as do the *personae* of Stefan George or of W.B.Yeats's later poems, *personae* supported by the mask of a single style. This does not mean that Rilke is a lesser poet. It means that he was more susceptible to disturbances of the balance between his empirical and poetic selves. The uncertainty of his opinions and sympathies has to do with the same susceptibility. The need for masks is even more marked in the early work of Hugo von Hofmannsthal, which arose from a state of boundless empathy, of totally fluid identity, as ecstatic as it was hard to bear. His lyrical *personae* ranged from a ship's cook to the Emperor of China, from childhood to old age, from the mythical past to the contemporary world, with a magical mobility which he came to ascribe to a pseudo-mystical condition, a 'pre-existence' whose alternative was commitment to the social world. The transition can be traced in his 'lyrical dramas,' short verse plays whose characters do not interact, because all are lyrical *personae*, with no social current between them that would permit dialogue. Gradually the lyrical drama gives way to drama proper – at the cost of lyrical poetry. Stefan George, on the other hand, excluded dramatic interaction on principle. His dialogue poem *Der Mensch und der Drud* (The Man and the Faun), from the late collection *Das Neue Reich*, is a confrontation of two radically distinct *personae*, less capable of communicating than those in Hofmannsthal's early *Idylle*, a poem seemingly of the same kind.

2   If art is regarded as essentially symbolic, whether or not it employs a deliberate symbolism, difficulties about the empirical and poetic selves of lyrical poets come to seem a pseudo-problem. Susanne K. Langer, for instance, writes: 'Poetry does, indeed, *make life appear in certain ways*, but that is not commenting on it. Comment itself when used as a poetic element is not the poet's comment, but the imaginary speaker's who makes it in the poem. His name may be simply "I"; but that again is a part of poetic creation.'[2] Yet the poets will not oblige, and continue to worry about their literal or empirical selves.

If that were not so Juan Ramón Jiménez need not have written his poem *I Am not I* (*Eternidades*, 1916–17), one of many poems about the empirical self written by modern poets such as Dámaso Alonso, Pedro Salinas, Jorge Guillén, Vladimir Mayakovsky and Ezra Pound. That the 'I' of lyrical poetry is a creation or function of the poem has not seemed self-evident enough to those poets to deprive them of a recurrent theme:

> Yo no soy yo.
> Soy este
> que va a mi lado sin yo verlo;
> que, a veces, voy a ver,
> y que, a veces, olvido.
> El que calla, sereno, cuando hablo,
> el que perdona, dulce, cuando odio,
> el que pasea por donde no estoy,
> el que quedará en pié cuando yo muera.
>
> (I am not I.
> I am he
> who walks at my side without my seeing him;
> whom, at times, I go to see
> and whom, at times, I forget.
> He who, composed, is silent when I speak,
> he who, gentle, forgives when I hate,
> he who walks about where I am not,
> he who will stand up straight when I die.)

That the poetical self should be outside time and space is marvellous enough to warrant a poem so simple and so right; and there is another poem related to it in Jiménez's collection *Belleza* (1917–23), the poem *Cenit* (Zenith):

> Yo no seré yo, muerte,
> hasta que tú te unas con mi vida
> y me completes así todo;
> hasta que mi mitad de luz se cierre
> con mi mitad de sombra
> – y sea yo equilíbrio eterno
> en la mente del mundo:
> unas veces, mi medio yo, radiante;
> otras, mi otro medio yo, en olvido.
>
> Yo no seré yo, muerte,
> hasta que tú, en tu turno, vistas
> de huesos pálidos mi alma.
>
> (I shall not be I, death,
> until you are one with my life
> and so complete me;
> until my half of light is joined
> to my half of darkness
> – and I am balanced for ever
> in the mind of the world:
> now, this side of me, shining,
> now, that side, obscured.
>
> I shall not be I, death,
> until you, in your turn, dress
> my soul in pale bones.)

In both these poems the empirical, literal self has a real function, if only by contrast with the other self which the poem may indeed be said to create, much as death is shown to do in *Zenith* by completing the empirical self. Much of the moral and metaphysical basis of both poems is traditional; and indeed Jiménez was one of those poets – Yeats and Stevens were others – who succeeded in being modern without being modernistic. 'When modernism, imagism or surrealism for instance, produces a great poem,' Jiménez wrote, '(and it has produced, is producing and will continue to produce great poems), then it ceases to be called surrealism, imagism or modernism and once more is called poetry.'[3] The problem of multiple personality became most acute in those poets to whom tradition was not something given and self-evident – as to the majority of modern Spanish and Greek poets – but something to be selected from the *musée imaginaire* of literary history, to be renovated and restored. The naked diction of Jiménez was achieved when he had shed extraneous literary accretions. It issued from his empirical self as well as from his imaginative or imaginary self; and tradition saw to it that, however 'autonomous,' his imaginative and imaginary self would not be wholly isolated. The death to which Jiménez looked for completion is a republic.

3   Multiple personality was the dilemma of both Ezra Pound and T.S. Eliot, Americans at odds with the pluralism of their own national culture, renovators and restorers of selected exhibits in the *musée imaginaire*. Eliot's way was to make the selection as narrow and rigorous as possible, to confine and refine his empirical self – almost to the point of evanescence, in his later years, and at the expense of his poetic self. In quality and coherence, Eliot's poetry benefited by a discipline that was a true self-sacrifice; but as Yeats said, 'Too long a sacrifice can make a stone of the heart.' Eliot's work as a lyrical poet ended prematurely although, as his other works attest, he continued to develop. The rigour and coherence forbade a late lyrical phase that would surely have been as different from that of the *Four Quartets* as the last essays are from the earlier or the late plays from *Murder in the Cathedral* and *The Rock*. Both Pound and Eliot used *personae* with a freedom unprecedented either in the dramatic monologues of the late nineteenth century or in the twentieth-century adaptations of that mode, including those by Pound himself in his *Personae* proper. In these some kind of historical background and unity had to be maintained. In *The Waste Land* and the *Cantos*, on the other hand, Imagist technique – originally devised for the short poem only – was extended to the long poem. The *personae*, too, became multiple and fluid within a single poem, shifting and switching freely in time and space. Yet whereas Eliot's *Waste Land* had a centre outside the poet's self – a centre that may or may not be personified in the character of Tiresias – the centre of the *Cantos* remains a basically personal one, despite the even wider store of *personae*, historical instances and topographical fragments drawn upon.

To 'search for roots' is not only a biological absurdity but an admission that the seeker is rootless (or, since no man is truly rootless, that he is looking for roots of a kind more acceptable to him than those with which he is provided). From the first, Pound's 'search' for a tradition was bedevilled by the paradox that tradition can no more be searched for than roots, except in so far as that search means a growing awareness and recognition of what one's roots are. Politically, the paradox is exemplified in Pound's Fascism: like Rilke, another poet unsure of his national allegiances, Ezra Pound had to identify himself with the nationalism of a people to which he did not belong. Poetically, the paradox is exemplified in the extreme literariness of a writer who effectively revolted against the literary conventions obtaining when he began; or, to put it differently, in the extreme vacillation of Pound's poetic diction between what was native to his speech and what was taken over from books. Pound himself has referred to the 'Wardour Street' component in his early poems which in 1964 struck him as 'a collection of stale creampuffs.'[4] Pound's incomparable rhythmic innovations owed a great deal to his native vernacular, to the speech gestures – or 'sentence sounds,' as Robert Frost called them – which his archaic or bookish vocabulary so often neutralized. This had to do with the basic diffidence and uncertainty from which T.S. Eliot escaped into impersonality; a diffidence and uncertainty about American values, as opposed to those of European and Asiatic cultures, and about the poet's relationship to his readers.

In Pound's early poetry, up to and including his *Lustra* of 1916, there is an extraordinary preponderance of poems not about the poetic process – as in Stevens and Rilke – but about the poem's progress and reception in the world. The convention of the *envoi*, the poet's valediction to his poem, is modernized in a way that reveals not only Pound's preoccupation with the poet-critic-reader relationship but a self-consciousness scarcely precedented in poetry of any period. The effect is the opposite of that attained by writers of 'pure' or 'absolute' poetry. Although, like theirs, these poems move within their own confines, the repeated self-addresses deflect the reader's attention from the poem to its author. In *A Lume Spento* the very first poem, *Grace Before Song*, establishes this peculiar mode, though one may read it as a lyrical counterpart of the epic poet's traditional invocation of the Muse. Yet there is scarcely a poem in the collection that does not introduce the poet *qua* poet, questioning his function, antecedents and allegiances, either directly or by literary allusion and pastiche. These poems, of course, are juvenilia, and one must allow for the exclusively literary passions and enthusiasms characteristic of most young poets; but there is enough rhythmic variety and invention in *A Lume Spento* and *A Quinzaine for This Yule* to make them seem more than apprentice work. The poem *Histrion* is one of several that anticipate and elucidate Pound's later use of *personae*:

> No man hath dared to write this thing as yet,
> And yet I know, how that the souls of all men great
> At times pass through us.
> And we are melted into them, and are not
> Save reflexions of their souls.
> Thus am I Dante for a space and am
> One François Villon, ballad-lord and thief . . .
> 'Tis as in midmost us there glows a sphere
> Translucent, molten gold, that is the 'I'
> And into this some form projects itself.

By the time Pound published *Lustra* (in 1916, past the age of thirty) he had got rid of most, but by no means all, of the 'Wardour Street' impurities of his diction. Yet the self-exhortations and the pervasive self-consciousness about his status as a poet are as marked as in the earliest collections. Here are a few examples from *Lustra*:

> I beg you, my friendly critics,
> Do not set about to procure me an audience.
>
> I mate with my free kind upon the crags. . . .
> *Tenzone*

> O my fellow sufferers, songs of my youth,
> A lot of asses praise you because you are 'virile'. . . .
> *The Condolence*

I join these words for four people,
Some others may overhear them,
O world, I am sorry for you,
You do not know these four people.
                              Causa

You of the finer sense,
Broken against false knowledge,
You who can know at first hand,
Hated, shut in, mistrusted:

Take thought:
I have weathered the storm,
I have beaten out my exile.
                              The Rest

You are very idle, my songs.
I fear you will come to a bad end.
. . . .
But you, newest song of the lot,
You are not old enough to have done much mischief,
I will get you a green coat out of China
With dragons worked upon it,
I will get you the scarlet silk trousers
From the statue of the infant Christ in Santa Maria
    Novella,
Lest they say we are lacking in taste,
Or that there is no caste in this family.
                              Further Instructions

Come, my songs, let us speak of perfection –
We shall get ourselves rather disliked.
                              Salvationists

O chansons foregoing,
You were a seven days' wonder.
When you came out in the magazines
You created considerable stir in Chicago,
And now you are stale and worn out. . . .
                              Epilogue

Ezra Pound's empirical self – largely identical, as far as all
his poetry is concerned, with his literary role, rather than with
what one would usually call personal experience – is very far

from being absent here or anywhere else in his later work, despite the Imagism of certain well-known shorter poems. 'In the search for oneself,' Pound wrote at the same period,[5]

in the search for 'sincere self-expression,' one gropes, one finds some seeming verity. One says 'I am this, that, or the other,' and with the words scarcely uttered one ceases to be that thing.

I began this search for the real in a book called *Personae*, casting off, as it were, complete masks of the self in each poem. I continued in a long series of translations, which were but more elaborate masks.

Secondly, I made poems like 'The Return,' which is an objective reality and has a complicated sort of significance, like Mr Epstein's 'Sun and God' or Mr Brzeska's 'Boy with a Coney.' Thirdly, I have written 'Heather,' which represents a state of consciousness, or 'implies' or implicates it....

These two latter poems are impersonal.

As T.S. Eliot did also, Ezra Pound continued to grapple with multiple personality, the 'search for oneself' and different ways of reducing multiplicity to unity in a poem. Unlike Eliot, who adopted, or had himself adopted by, a single tradition that embraced religious, ethical and social values, Pound attempted to create his own system of values, his own canon of what should be known, admired and imitated. Eliot was able to attain a true impersonality, though one based less on imagination than on religious faith, an impersonality rendered in these lines from his last play:

> I've been freed from the self that pretends to be someone
> And in becoming no one, I begin to live.

The basis of Ezra Pound's system remained an aesthetic and imaginative one, though Donald Davie has explained why 'Pound's thoughts about style and styles of poetry cannot help but spill over into politics, ethics, economics.'[6] Pound's aesthetic specialization – admirable in itself, and as rich, as productive and seminal as a specialization can be – proved his undoing as soon as it was extended beyond the arts to society and economics. The reason is that Pound has never ceased to generalize from his own situation as a man dedicated to poetry – a situation necessarily anomalous in any modern society – and to build ideological structures on his grievances as a poet. These grievances were not selfish or petty. Bureaucracy and commercialism and usury are real evils, and Ezra Pound was right to oppose them; but the grounds of his opposition were always personal and emotional to a degree that forbade the subtle distinction which the realities of politics, ethics and economics demand. The 'history' in Pound's *Cantos* is another instance. It is a 'history' composed of fragments, and these fragments derive from personal predilections which, however wide and generous, are bound to be arbitrary or fortuitous because no one mind can encompass all the recorded facts of world history, let alone pronounce judgement on them, as Pound does explicitly or by the devices of quotation and juxtaposition of quotations. As Donald Davie writes, 'history, from now on, may be transcended in poetry, or it may be evaded there; but poetry is not the place where it may be understood.'[7]

Pound's dilemma has been the subject of so much discussion, controversy and explanation that it seems indecent to bring it up again. As Davie points out, Pound himself has shown a sporadic awareness of its cultural origins, as when he noted: 'Knowledge is NOT culture. The domain of culture begins when one has "forgotten-what-book" '; or when, in a musical context, he remarked on the differences 'between an art that has a culture behind it and an art,' like that of Pound's own *Cantos*, 'that is produced out of a solitary artist's struggle *against* the cultural condition he is born to.' The comparison between works by Boccherini and Bartók which occasioned the distinction (in Pound's *Guide to Kulchur*) does not warrant it, as it happens, and Pound's critical writings generally are no less eccentric, erratic and opinionated than the rest of his work. Pound's dilemma could be left alone if his own misgivings about his work were shared by those of his disciples who have praised him, and continue to praise him, for everything that is wrong with his poetry and the assumptions that underlie it. To put it briefly, Pound's totalitarian art – the 'new synthesis, the totalitarian,' called for in *Guide to Kulchur* – was a suppression of multiplicity, not an integration and ordering of it. Tradition cannot be created or imposed, any more than roots can be grafted on. Pound's own art, in the *Cantos*, remained essentially pluralistic and eclectic, just as his diction has remained impure, an amalgam of idioms drawn from the most heterogeneous conventions of speech and writing. If the *Cantos* have a unity, it is the unity of Pound's own memories and preoccupations. To demand that such a unity be accepted as a cultural synthesis is a totalitarian act.

Pound's critical writings are valid – and admirable – where he relies on his own experience as a poet and his own infectious enthusiasms for other people's poetry. His *ABC of Reading*[8] is a case in point. 'Ignorant men of genius,' Pound writes there, 'are constantly rediscovering "laws" of art which the academics had mislaid or hidden.' In so far as the *ABC of Reading* consists of such discoveries, rather than of general prescriptions, its aphoristic assertions are not only acceptable, but preferable to so-called scholarly arguments which only dress up prejudice and preference in a conventional pseudo-logic. As soon as Pound lays down the law – even in the important statement that 'poetry must be *as well written as prose*. Its language must be fine language, departing in no way from speech save by heightened intensity (i.e. simplicity). There must be no book words, no periphrase, no inversions' – one can object that a good many of Pound's own poems are full of 'book words,' and that some of them get away with it because their impetus and music are strong and new; that inversion can be a supremely poetic device, as in a grammatically daring line by Milton which Pound condemns;[9] and that periphrasis, too, has its strictly poetic uses.

As Pound himself says, 'One definition of beauty is aptness to purpose'; and there are as many kinds of poetic beauty as there are poetic purposes. It is characteristic of Pound's arbitrary assertiveness also to equate the German word 'dichten' (to make poetry) with 'condensare' (to condense). Etymologically 'dichten' is related not to 'dicht'(dense) but to 'dictare' (to reiterate) – a derivation completely at variance with Pound's Imagist aesthetic. In the same way, the 'exhibits' appended in Section Two of the book have a diversity at odds with the prescriptions in Section One – prescriptions to do with Pound's own advocacy of the kind of poetry that 'presents an intellectual and emotional complex in an instant of time,' the Imagist principle that governed the structure not only of his most successful short poems but of the *Cantos*. Too many of Pound's judgements on other poets make little sense except in relation to his own work; and though to some extent this is true of most poet-critics, and these have the inestimable advantage of knowing what they are talking about, criticism demands a measure of self-abnegation, a readiness to understand, if not to approve, the otherness of writers different from oneself. In his criticism as in his poetry and translations, Pound has no patience with anything that is not grist to his mill. The fact and circumstance that contradict him are ignored or distorted; the historical substrata of meaning violated, so as to yield him exemplars and exhibits.

All this has to be said again, and will have to be said again, as long as Pound's *Cantos* are compared to the epics of Dante and Milton, with such deductions as 'Pound's timeless frieze contains an enormously wider range of discriminations than Milton's arrangements of high-styled narrative and heavy conversations' (Hugh Kenner) or 'Landor complained that Dante left his characters in skeleton form, but Pound is able to clothe them with a phrase' (Henry Swabey).[10] There is no point in commenting on those judgements; their 'discriminations' are of the same order as Pound's when he writes not from experience or vision but partisanship. What must also be said is that Pound has acknowledged the one-sidedness of his thinking about culture and politics. 'My method of opposing tyranny,' he said in an interview with Donald Hall,[11] 'was wrong over a thirty-year period; it had nothing to do with the Second World War in particular. If the individual, or heretic, gets hold of some essential truth, or sees some error in the system being practised, he commits so many marginal errors himself that he is worn out before he can establish his point. . . . In writing so as to be understood, there is always the problem of rectification without giving up what is correct. There is the struggle not to sign on the dotted line for the opposition.' That sums up much of what is wrong with those passages of the *Cantos*, including *The Pisan Cantos*, that bear on the contemporary world, though their disjointed garrulousness is a poetic, as well as a moral, flaw. The widely praised 'What thou lovest well remains' passage of *Canto LXXXI* shows how both the stylistic and the thematic disjointedness can be mended as soon Pound permits himself a 'rectification' that proceeds from the same *metanoia*. It is no accident that the concluding lines of this passage, with its refrain of 'Pull down thy vanity,' are so close in cadence and tone to the later poetry of T.S.Eliot:

> Here error is all in the not done,
> all in the diffidence that faltered.

In *Canto CXVI*, too, a fragment of that section of the *Cantos* which was to correspond to Dante's *Paradiso*, Pound sets out

> To confess wrong without losing rightness

and does so with a directness and simplicity of diction too often sacrificed in the earlier *Cantos*:

> But the beauty is not the madness
> Tho' my errors and wrecks lie about me.
> (And I am not a demigod)

> The damn stuff will not cohere

> If love be not in the house there is nothing

> The voice of famine unheard.[12]

4   About Ezra Pound's range not of 'discriminations' but of curiosity, invention and adaptation there can be no question. His many styles and his many *personae* might easily be ascribed to several different poets if they had been published anonymously or under various pseudonyms, like the poems of Fernando Pessoa. For the same reason no other English-language poet of his time had so much to give to coevals or successors as diverse in practice and outlook as T.S.Eliot and Robert Duncan, Louis Zukofsky and Robert Creeley, Basil Bunting and Charles Olson, to mention only a few poets whose debt to Pound is not in doubt. T.S.Eliot's influence is far more elusive, though several generations of English poets, and a good many poets not English, felt it as strongly as others felt the influence of Pound. Ezra Pound's failure to 'make it cohere' may well have something to do with his heterogeneous following in a world increasingly heterogeneous. It is hardly possible to follow Eliot without following his particular choice, which was also a renunciation. Pound's multiplicity did not impair his energy: and one decidedly unifying factor in his work is his incomparable gift of *melopeia*, to use his own term, a musical mastery and rightness that has failed him only where the message

– in the form of ugly quotations from ugly sources – seemed more important to him than the medium.

T.S.Eliot's early *personae*, recognizably though not very closely related to the twentieth-century *personae* in Pound's *Hugh Selwyn Mauberley* and the *Moeurs Contemporaines* section of *Quia Pauper Amavi* (1919), receded or vanished in his later phase, especially in the *Four Quartets*. Many sections of the *Four Quartets* are in a voice which, although not to be identified with the poet's empirical self, is decidedly the poet's own voice, depersonalized not by masks but only by the reticence that was Eliot's at all times. Pound's extension of Imagist and *persona* technique to the longer poem, anticipated in his *Mauberley* sequence and in *Homage to Sextus Propertius* as in Eliot's *The Waste Land*, gave the *Cantos* a range and freedom denied to Eliot in his later phase. Yet it is a freedom that uses history and historical personages in a way that is wilful, sometimes irresponsible, and essentially egotistic, because we can rarely forget the manipulator of all those puppets, the ventriloquist behind all those masks. As a whole the *Cantos* stand or fall by their unifying purpose, and that unifying purpose cannot be looked for anywhere but in the author's mind, since his figures, scenes and dialogues have no other palpable unity. This is Pound's paradox and dilemma. The totalitarian synthesis, intended as an alternative to modern individualism and pluralism, brings us back more inescapably than most directly confessional poetry to the isolated individual who attempted it. Whereas a single *persona* permits an enlargement of both the poet's and the reader's experience, and the frankly confessional poem may permit an identification on the reader's part that bridges the gulf between individuals – as certain passages in the *Cantos* do, if detached from the whole – a large assembly of miscellaneous *personae* within a single poem has no such effect. *The Waste Land*, too, conveys a vision of life, indeed a judgement on life, more idiosyncratic and subjective than the direct expository statements in certain sections of the *Four Quartets*.

T.S.Eliot's problem, in fact, was not very different from Ezra Pound's, and some of his thinking on society and politics, though more cautiously formulated, was no less totalitarian in tendency. Both poets turned to Europe with an intense need nurtured by expectations more literary and romantic than realistic. Of the two, it was T.S.Eliot whose rejection of liberal, pluralistic and commercialized democracy was radical and total from the first. Ezra Pound could make his peace with Walt Whitman, as well as with Robert Browning, and his later quarrel with American bureaucracy and commercialism never prevented him from being deeply concerned with the history and institutions of his own country; but because they wanted Europe to be everything that America was not, neither Pound nor Eliot could accept those trends in contemporary Europe that were liberal, pluralistic and commercializing. Pound's disgust with England, when he left London in 1920, was at least as vehement as his earlier disgust with America. Those who died in the First World War died

> For an old bitch gone in the teeth,
> For a botched civilization ...
> . . . .
> For two gross of broken statues,
> For a few thousand battered books.[13]

Pound's antiquarian and literary view of Europe is apparent in those very lines. Most of the men who died in that war were not even aware of the 'broken statues' and 'battered books.' Whatever they thought they were dying for – and most of them, by the end of the war, knew that they were dying for nothing very much – it was not for the *musée imaginaire* that was Pound's and Eliot's refuge from the nastiness of modern civilization on both sides of the Atlantic.

One crucial difference between Pound's Hugh Selwyn Mauberley *persona* and Eliot's J. Alfred Prufrock is that Mauberley shares his creator's aesthetic preoccupations to such an extent that *Mauberley* cannot be regarded as representative of anything but those very specialized preoccupations:

> Turned from the 'eau-forte
> Par Jaquemart'
> To the strait head
> Of Messalina:
>
> 'His true Penelope
> Was Flaubert,'
> And his tool
> The engraver's.[14]

Of those lines one could say what Ezra Pound, not very aptly, said in 1917 about Laforgue, that 'he writes not the popular language of any country but an international tongue common to the excessively cultivated.'[15] George Orwell, it is true, declared that Eliot's early poems expressed 'the horror of an over-civilized intellectual confronted with the ugliness and spiritual emptiness of the machine age';[16] but one does not need to be 'excessively cultivated' or 'over-civilized' to understand and respond to *The Love Song of J. Alfred Prufrock*, because the experience rendered in it has a moral and social relevance far beyond Eliot's personal preoccupations as a poet and literary man. Orwell was wrong, I think, to argue that Eliot's early poems express 'a glowing despair,' the later 'a melancholy faith,' which 'turns its eyes to the past, accepts defeat, writes off earthly happiness as impossible, mumbles about repentance and prayer.' As I have tried to show elsewhere,[17] the *Four Quartets* hold out more hope of 'earthly happiness' than Eliot's early poems do; and even Eliot's early *personae* reveal his desire for an impersonality that is also a kind of universality, a transcendence of his own circumstances and specialized interests, an 'objective correlative' of subjective experience.

Yet this very craving for impersonality was so extreme and persistent as to imply an acute uneasiness about the empirical and social self. Hugh Kenner has called Eliot 'the invisible poet.' When, in *Lines for Cuscuscaraway and Mirza Murad Ali Beg*, Eliot sketched something like a self-portrait, the social mask is upheld by the third-person presentation, by an irony at his own expense quite different from the self-ironies of Corbière and Laforgue – which arose from the Baudelairean dualism of *spleen et idéal* – and by the conventions of nonsense verse. What those lines give away is no more than Eliot's awareness of the mask that served to keep others at a distance, the mask of the singularly evasive public man

> With his features of clerical cut,
> And his brow so grim
> And his mouth so prim
> And his conversation, so nicely
> Restricted to What Precisely
> And If and Perhaps and But –

a mask which he used in his critical writings also to disguise or palliate judgements quite as idiosyncratic as those of Ezra Pound.

Eliot's 'doctrine' of impersonality, as formulated in the essay *Tradition and the Individual Talent* of 1920, preceded his so-called 'conversion' to Christian orthodoxy and political conservatism. Like other 'doctrines' formulated in his critical writings, it was no more than an objective derivative of needs rooted in the peculiarities of his own nature and situation, those of a poet tormented beyond endurance by the fortuitousness and fragmentariness of modern civilization. 'The progress of an artist is a continual self-sacrifice, a continual extinction of personality,' Eliot wrote in the essay, telling us something important about himself, but not about the great majority of poets, whose personality was not so embarrassing to them as to need extinguishing. What was embarrassing to Eliot was that he had an individual personality susceptible to sufferings that were not shared by others, that were not even comprehensible to others, because they enjoyed and approved the things he abhorred. That had been the predicament of generations of poets before Eliot; but Eliot could not approve the predicament either, because it was the predicament of Romantic individualism, and Eliot wanted a classical coherence of the individual with society. A Christian society, therefore, had to be constituted in the teeth of centuries, in the teeth of the modern pluralism and liberalism that were penetrating even to the Christian churches and sects, not least to the Church of England; and the individual personality had to be extinguished, because it was tainted with heterodoxy and multiplicity. 'The more perfect the artist, the more completely separate in him will be the man who suffers and the mind which creates: the more perfectly will the mind digest and transmute the passions which are its material.' There is enough general truth in that statement – a truth about the poetic process – to divert one's attention from its assumption that the artist must be incompatible with the man. No such incompatibility is evident in the work of Villon, for instance, or in that of Racine, Milton, Dryden or Pope, to pick a few names from the pre-Romantic period. Similarly, the statement assumes that what distinguishes the man from the poet, the individual from the practitioner of an impersonal craft, is his sufferings. That, too, is a Romantic assumption, and one that tells us more about Eliot than his lines about the unpleasantness of meeting him.

Yet the primness and the grimness of his social mask had a good deal to do with the personal sufferings which Eliot succeeded in 'objectivizing' to a rare degree, in characters, situations, townscapes like those of the *Rhapsody on a Windy Night*, fragmentary visions and myths, fragmentary quotations and dialogues. For Eliot, if for no one else, impersonality worked; and it worked because it was not a literary or aesthetic doctrine, but a personal need. Renunciation and self-denial pervaded his work long before he found a religious justification for them. 'Poetry is not a turning loose of emotion, but an escape from emotion; it is not the expression of personality, but an escape from personality. But, of course, only those who have personality and emotions know what it means to want to escape from those things.' It is strange that Eliot should have allowed himself to repeat the word 'escape,' in this context, for it is that word which makes the 'impersonal' statement an intimate confession. To transmute personality and personal emotion, to merge them in their 'objective correlative,' is something different from wanting to escape from them. Eliot did want to escape from them, though the sufferings which he identified with them are much more poignantly present in his earlier work than in most directly confessional poetry. By the time that some of his emotions were emotions of joy or fulfilment, impersonality had become so inseparable from his poetic practice that he could rarely draw on them in poetry. One exception – touching rather than moving, because the mask of grimness and primness and impersonality has fallen, but the poetic power, too, has been lost – is the little poem, *A Dedication To My Wife*, that appeared with Eliot's last play, *The Elder Statesman*. Here, for the only and last time, Eliot's empirical and private self was allowed to make a public appearance; but the expression of 'the/Leaping delight/ That quickens my senses in our wakingtime/And the rhythm that governs the repose of our sleepingtime' is stated rather than enacted. The personal joy and fulfilment came too late for a more than theoretical revision of the whole notion of impersonality.

In very different ways, both Ezra Pound and T.S.Eliot tried to build bridges between the individualistic aestheticism inherited from the Romantic–Symbolist era and a more comprehensive art that would incorporate ethical, social and political values. Ezra Pound's vision has remained solitary, eclectic and essentially individualistic, despite his sincere and impassioned concern with history, Confucian ethics, monetary reform and many other matters not directly connected with the practice of poetry or of the other arts. T.S.Eliot's transcendence of both aestheticism and individualism brought him to the point where 'the poetry does not matter' (*East Coker*); but his 'continual self-sacrifice,' his 'continual extinction of personality,' was conducted with a rigour and austerity almost unprecedented in poetry. Eliot's vision, from the first, was ascetic, and the asceticism demanded a sacrifice not only of self-love, but of love and sympathy for all the grosser manifestations of humanity. For *Sweeney Agonistes*, his dramatic fragment of 1932, Eliot chose the epigraph from St John of the Cross: 'Hence the soul cannot be possessed of the divine union, until it has divested itself of the love of created beings.' This ascetic mysticism – more extreme in his early work than in that written after his reception into the Church of England – was as difficult to reconcile with an established religion as his political conservatism with the policies and principles (if any) of an established political party. Eliot's interest in a movement like the Action Française and his heresy-hunting in *After Strange Gods* (1934) and *The Idea of a Christian Society* (1939) show an anti-democratic, anti-pluralistic bias quite out of key with the mood of that British Conservative Union which Eliot, himself in a much more conciliatory mood, was to address in 1955.[18] As we can see in *Notes Towards the Definition of Culture* (1948), Eliot's thinking about society mellowed in his later years, no less than did his response to 'created beings' and his judgements on writers whose outlook or temperament he had once disliked; but the poetry for which he will be remembered, above all, makes no concession of that kind.

Unlike the religious creeds of almost all the major poets of his time, including Ezra Pound, Eliot's was not a *religio poetae*, based – however widely – on the requirements and processes of poetry. Both Rilke and Wallace Stevens could be described as agnostic or secular mystics, beginning with the love of 'created beings' or created things and ending with the transmutation of the created world into poetry, by a process that made them creators in their own right. Even Christian poets like Gerard Manley Hopkins have chosen to praise 'created beings' and created things, with that sensuousness which so austere a poet as Milton described as a distinguishing characteristic of poetry; and even Christian mystics like St John of the Cross found this sensuousness so indispensable to poetry that they borrowed the vocabulary and imagery of secular love in order to render a divestment 'of love of created beings.' T.S. Eliot's images of sensuous beauty, such as his recurrent garden and flower images, or 'the blown hair' and 'music of the flute' in *Ash Wednesday*, are greatly outweighed by images of sensuous disgust, by the ascetic mysticism that refuses to concede any beauty or meaning to sensuous experience or to 'created beings.' In the end the poetry did not matter and was either put away or hidden behind the small-talk demanded by an intrinsically trivial convention of social comedy, in Eliot's later plays.

Though Eliot's choice was to transplant rather than to uproot himself, becoming an English gentleman and pillar of the Church – not the American exile that Ezra Pound has never ceased to be – the tradition to which he dedicated himself is no longer familiar, or wholly comprehensible, to a good many younger poets and readers in England as well as in America. Eliot's bridge, too, was a precarious one. Though it served to carry him over from one environment to another, from one era to another, its structure was too delicate to permit much general traffic. Because of a social and cultural revolution with which he was out of sympathy, the public *persona* which he maintained with so much discretion, tact and fastidious care has less to say to his successors than the voice beneath it, a voice crying in the wilderness. Eliot renovated that wilderness, as Baudelaire and Laforgue did before him, with the paraphernalia of modern urban life, with street lamps, public houses and cheap hotels, though desert imagery is also pervasive in his work; but even Laforgue's mundane irony could not wholly cover the ascetic prophet's voice, older and more archetypal than the institutions to which Eliot gave his allegiance. This stern, harsh vision of the modern world, and indeed of secular life at any time – despite the romanticized evocations of past ages in *The Waste Land* and elsewhere – breaks through even in the later, more conciliatory

poems, as in the lines of *East Coker* that relegate 'the Almanach
de Gotha/And the Stock Exchange Gazette, the Directory of
Directors' to the same dark as 'Distinguished civil servants,
chairmen of many committees/Industrial lords and petty con-
tractors,' as well as 'eminent men of letters'; or in these lines
from *Burnt Norton*:

> ... the strained time-ridden faces
> Distracted from distraction by distraction
> Filled with fancies and empty of meaning
> Tumid apathy with no concentration
> Men and bits of paper, whirled by the cold wind
> That blows before and after time....

The mediating worldliness of the allusions to the *Almanach de
Gotha, Stock Exchange Gazette* and the rest may soon become an
anachronism to readers who have never heard of those publications, far less of all the literary and theological texts to which
Eliot alluded in his poems. This mediating worldliness was part
of Eliot's public *persona*, to which he sacrificed much of his
individuality. Yet the personality which Eliot chose to deper-
sonalize – to the extent of subordinating his poetic and
imaginative gifts to non-artistic ends – is present in everything
he wrote. We do not need to know anything about Eliot's
private life to have a stronger sense of the poet's presence than
in the work of less excellent poets who made free use of their
personal experience and their empirical selves. Eliot's 'escape
from personality' may have been justified in his case, because
ascetic mysticism has no use for 'the man who suffers' for private
and personal reasons; but since poetry itself, if it is good poetry,
strips its persons and characters of all that is merely accidental
and circumstantial, the principle of impersonality has no general
validity. To speculate what potentialities T.S.Eliot's sacrifice of
personality left unfulfilled in his poetry would be useless and
impertinent. What his work does tell us, and still conveys with
great power, is that he succeeded in reducing his multiple selves
to a unity and purity rare in modern poetry; and that, whatever
the emotion and the personality from which he wished to escape,
the man who suffered is as inescapable in his poetry as the mind
that shaped it.

5   In his lecture of 1953 on *The Three Voices of Poetry*[19] T.S.Eliot cites 'the German poet Gottfried Benn' and his 'very interesting lecture entitled *Probleme der Lyrik*' in connection with what Eliot called the first voice – 'the poet talking to himself – or to nobody.' Gottfried Benn differed from Eliot in acknowledging no other voice than the first. Though Benn wrote *persona* poems and even dramatic dialogues, he insisted that all good poetry is 'addressed to no one,' and specifically denied that poetry can have any public function. 'Works of art,' he wrote in 1930, 'are phenomena, historically ineffective, without practical consequences. That is their greatness.'[20]

Twenty-two years later, in the lecture *Probleme der Lyrik*, Benn disagreed with T.S.Eliot's very cautious suggestion that even in *poésie pure* the theme remains important in its own right. Benn's answer is that 'lyrical poetry has no other theme than the poet himself.'[21] It would seem, then, as though in 1952 and 1953 Gottfried Benn and T.S.Eliot were at variance over the same question that troubled Baudelaire a century before that time. Yet T.S.Eliot's polite references to Benn's views do not begin to convey the extent of their disagreement – that between a poet who had come to believe that 'the poetry does not matter' and a poet who believed that nothing but poetry matters. And there is a significant difference between Baudelaire's assertion that 'poetry has no other end than itself' and Benn's assertion that 'poetry has no other theme than the *poet* himself.'

Paul Valéry, whose concept of 'absolute poetry' Benn took over in his own critical and polemical writings, once described himself as 'insular,' meaning a peculiar self-containment which amounted to what I have called Valéry's tendency towards solipsism. As an instance of this peculiarity Valéry mentioned that he 'never felt the need to make others share his feelings on any subject.'[22] Gottfried Benn, some ten years later than Valéry's remark of 1937, declared: 'I am an isolationist. My name is Monroe.'[23] In Benn's case solipsism was far more than a tendency or a danger. It was the necessary premise of all his poetry and prose, as of his thinking about literature, society and the natural sciences. The very act of thinking, Benn repeatedly asserted, isolates the thinker from the rest of humanity. 'That which lives is something other than that which thinks,' he wrote in *Ausdruckswelt.*[24] Consciousness itself – largely identified with Schopenhauer's and Nietzsche's *principium individuationis* – becomes the cause of unbearable suffering, a kind of suffering which Nietzsche, in *The Birth of Tragedy*, had ascribed to 'the state of individuation' and condemned as 'intrinsically reprehensible.' Gottfried Benn, therefore, looked for a biological alternative to the consciousness that isolates and inflicts pain. Hence his cult of biological retrogression – the return to a primitive state in which consciousness is reduced or dissolved – and his advocacy of an art that is wholly expressive, to the point of severing traditional links between feeling and perception. 'There is no such thing as reality,' he declared; 'there is human consciousness which incessantly shapes, laboriously constructs, suffers and impresses its mental imprint on worlds out of its creative store.'[25]

Benn's glorification of primitive instincts has many analogies in the work of his contemporaries, but neither D.H.Lawrence nor the Futurists, Dadaists and Surrealists produced such a battery of intellectual arguments – derived from the sciences, from sociology and from aesthetics – in support of so frantic an anti-intellectualism. The characters and *personae* of Benn's early poems are presented negatively in so far as they are individuals. In the clinical poems of Benn's first collection, *Morgue* (1912), their individuality takes the form of sickness from which there is no release but in physical dissolution. So in *Mann und Frau gehen durch die Krebsbaracke* (Man and Woman Walk through the Cancer Ward):

> Hier schwillt der Acker schon um jedes Bett.
> Fleisch ebnet sich zu Land. Glut gibt sich fort.
> Saft schickt sich an zu rinnen. Erde ruft.

> (Around each bed already fields dilate.
> Flesh levels into land. Heat passes on.
> The sap prepares to flow away. Earth calls.)

Much the same is true of the characters in Benn's *Nachtcafé* (Night Café), whose individuality is reduced to such attributes as 'green teeth, pimples on his face,' 'conjunctivitis,' 'sycosis.' Sexual desire can create a kind of communication or community between human beings otherwise seen as so much diseased flesh. Like death, sexual desire dissolves such individuality as Benn grants his characters here, an individuality confined to externals, because there is no bridge from one person's inner life to another's. Where women are celebrated – as in *D-Zug* (Express Train) or *Untergrundbahn* (Underground Train) – it is for their capacity to release the male from his painful consciousness into what Benn once called 'bestial transcendence,'[26] a regression into instinct which he associated with the luxuriance of tropical vegetation:

> Durch all den Frühling kommt die fremde Frau.
> Der Strumpf am Spann ist da. Doch, wo er endet,
> ist weit von mir. Ich schluchze auf der Schwelle:
> laues Geblühe, fremde Feuchtigkeiten.
>
> Oh, wie ihr Mund die laue Luft verprasst!
> Du Rosenhirn, Meer-Blut, du Götter-Zwielicht,
> du Erdenbeet, wie strömen deine Hüften
> so kühl den Gang hervor, in dem du gehst!
>
> Dunkel: Nun lebt es unter ihren Kleidern:
> nur weisses Tier, gelöst und stummer Duft.
>
> Ein armer Hirnhund, schwer mit Gott behangen.
> Ich bin der Stirn so satt. Oh, ein Gerüste
> von Blütenkolben löste sanft sie ab
> und schwölle mit und schauerte und triefte . . .
>
> (Through all of Spring the alien woman walks.
> The stocking's foot is there. But where it ends
> is far from me. I sob upon the threshold:
> sultry luxuriance, alien moistures teeming.
>
> Oh, how her mouth squanders the sultry air!
> You brain of roses, sea-blood, goddess-twilight,
> you bed of earth, how coolly from your hips
> your stride flows out, the glide that is your walking.
>
> Dark: underneath her garments now it lives:
> white animal only, loosed, and silent scent.
>
> A wretched braindog, laden down with God.
> My forehead wearies me. Oh that a frame
> of clustered blooms would gently take its place,
> to swell in unison and stream and shudder . . .)

There is a surprising parallel between Benn's obsessions in this phase – which culminated in the ecstatic nihilism of such poems as *Palau*, written in the mid-twenties – and a passage in W.H.Auden's *Paid on Both Sides*:

> Could I have been some simpleton that lived
> Before disaster sent his runners here;
> Younger than worms, worms have too much to bear.
> Yes, mineral were best: could I but see
> These woods, these fields of green, this lively world
> Sterile as moon.[27]

Apart from the 'sterile' moon landscape of the closing lines this passage of Auden could be a paraphrase of the first of Gottfried Benn's *Gesänge* of 1913:

> O dass wir unsere Ururahnen wären.
> Ein Klümpchen Schleim in einem warmen Moor.
> Leben und Tod, Befruchten und Gebären
> glitte aus unseren stummen Säften vor.
>
> Ein Algenblatt oder ein Dünenhügel,
> vom Wind Geformtes und nach unten schwer.
> Schon ein Libellenkopf, ein Möwenflügel
> wäre zu weit und litte schon zu sehr.
>
> (Oh that we were our primal ancestors.
> A little lump of slime in tepid swamps.
> Our life and death, mating and giving birth
> a gliding forth out of our silent sap.
>
> An alga leaf or hillock on the dunes,
> shaped by the wind and weighted towards earth.
> A dragonfly's small head, a seagull's wing
> would be too far advanced in suffering.)

In Auden's 'charade' it is one character, John Nower, who touches briefly on this atavistic longing for mindlessness. The *personae* of Benn's early poems – his Icarus of 1915 and his Caryatid of 1916 are the outstanding instances – express no other craving than to 'bloom to death,' to be 'unbrained' or 'deforeheaded.' Because Benn attached no value to 'reality' in this early phase, his private and professional life (as a medical specialist) provided his poems with only negative images, symptoms of individuality to which he responded with disgust. His rejection of his empirical self was so drastic that he saw himself as leading two entirely distinct lives, the 'double life' of his autobiography. Far from wishing to link his empirical to his poetic self, he insisted on their complete separateness even when his poetic practice had come to contradict that insistence. By the time he published his autobiography, *Doppelleben* (1950), the *personae* and characters of his poems had become much more various and differentiated. The colloquial diction and relaxed rhythms in many of his later *persona* poems correspond to his readiness to admit the trivia of history and personal experience, if only as foils to the inward absolute; and his empirical self is very much in evidence in late poems like *Ideelles Weiterleben?* (Ideal Survival?):

> Bald
> ein abgesägter, überholter
> früh oder auch spät verstorbener Mann,
> von dem man spricht wie von einer Sängerin
> mit ausgesungenem Sopran
> oder vom kleinen Hölty mit seinen paar Versen –
> noch weniger: Durchschnitt,
> nie geflogen,
> keinen Borgward gefahren –
> Zehnpfennigstücke für die Tram,
> im Höchstfall Umsteiger. . . .
>
> (Soon
> a sawn-off, out-of-date
> man who died early or maybe late
> of whom one speaks as of a singer
> whose soprano is worn out
> or of poor little Todhunter and his handful of verses –
> even less: average,
> never flew in a plane,
> never drove a Borgward –
> pennies paid out on the tram,
> a return fare at the most. . . .)

The speaker of that poem is not Benn's 'lyrical I' of the earlier poems – the poetic self that uses 'reality' only as a fuel for a self-generated ecstasy, most intense when the outside world is utterly consumed and destroyed – but the social man and 'intellectual' who has distanced himself from the poet in order to appraise him from a worldly point of view. Though it remained difficult for Benn to identify himself with anyone but artists, his later *persona* poems, *Chopin* and *Gewisse Lebensabende* (The Evenings of Certain Lives), whose speakers are Rembrandt and Shakespeare, show a shift of emphasis to the empirical trivia and externals of human life. Benn's 'absolute poetry,' which he continued to advocate almost without modification to the end, is totally controverted both by the style and by the argument of these later poems. Shakespeare's reflections on his work in *Gewisse Lebensabende* – 'the Swan of Avon blows his nose' is an introduction that sets the tone – question his achievement quite as thoroughly as *Ideelles Weiterleben* questions Gottfried Benn's from a perspective outside the poet's isolated consciousness. The most extreme reversal of Benn's earlier tenets occurs in one of his last poems, *Menschen Getroffen* (People Meet), published shortly before his death in 1956. Though not a *persona* poem proper, *Menschen Getroffen* introduces characters whose distinction is that they are self-effacing, outwardly conventional and 'inwardly gentle and active as Nausicaa.' Benn, who had boasted of being a nihilist and amoralist in his poetry, though not in his life, concludes with three lines in which the poetry scarcely matters and the 'lyrical I' is as self-effacing as the characters to which the poem pays tribute:

> Ich habe mich oft gefragt und keine Antwort gefunden,
> woher das Sanfte und das Gute kommt,
> weiss es auch heute nicht und muss nun gehn.
>
> (Often I've asked myself, but found no answer,
> Where gentleness and goodness can possibly come from;
> Even today I can't tell, and it's time to be gone.)[28]

To grasp the full implication of that change of style – and far more than style – we have to compare later poems of this kind (and Benn continued to write poems in neo-Romantic or neo-classical modes) with his poems written in the 1920s, whose taut rhythm, regular rhymes and elliptic syntax sweep up the most diverse fragments of history, myth and conceptual thought into a flux wholly subjective and nihilistic, a primal flux that is the negation of every civilized order. So in the poem *Palau* (1925):

'Rot ist der Abend auf der Insel von Palau
und die Schatten sinken –'
singe, auch aus den Kelchen der Frau
lässt es sich trinken,
Totenvögel schrein
und die Totenuhren
pochen, bald wird es sein
Nacht und Lemuren.

Heisse Riffe. Aus Eukalypten geht
Tropik und Palmung,
was sich noch hält und steht
will auch Zermalmung
bis in das Gliederlos,
bis in die Leere
tief in den Schöpfungsschoss
dämmernder Meere.

('Evening is red on the island of Palau
and the shadows sink –'
sing, from woman's chalices too
it is good to drink,
deathly the little owls cry
and the death-watch ticks out,
very soon it will be
lemurs and night.

Hot these reefs. From eucalyptus there flows
a tropical palm concoction,
all that still holds and stays
also longs for destruction
down to the limbless stage,
down to the vacuum
back to the primal age
dark ocean's womb.)[29]

In Benn's poetry of that period there is no room for individual characters, though the poem *Die Dänin* (The Danish Woman) invokes an individual in the title only to reduce her to 'the Isolde of Nothingness' and celebrate her in terms of the flux that consumes all individuality. The poet's own voice, in the same poem, is as far removed as possible from the speaking voice of Gottfried Benn the man. Despite allusions to contemporary phenomena and concepts in *Die Dänin* – 'philosophia perennis' rhymes with 'tennis,' 'rewarding odds' with 'God's' – these poems are 'absolute' in their dissolution of the empirical self and its conditional, circumstantial consciousness.

6   Benn's early clinical poems suggest that his dual personality was assumed as a protection against multiple personality, against that identification with others, especially the sufferings of others, which both divides and enriches the self. As a doctor, Benn was remarkable for the very sympathy which all but his last poems not only suppress, but categorically negate on philosophical or pseudo-philosophical grounds reminiscent of Nietzsche's tirades against the Christian 'slave morality' or against Schopenhauer's principle of compassion; and Nietzsche was the fountainhead of all Benn's thinking and non-thinking, of his 'intellectualism' as of his irrationalism, of his aestheticism as of his professed nihilism. As a poet, Benn deliberately isolated and insulated his mind against other people, against social and historical realities that might have broken or withstood the flux of pure feeling, against anything adverse to the self-generated ecstasy which he called 'expression,' likening poetry to hallucinatory drugs. In this phase nothing but a total dualism between his empirical and poetic selves could make it possible for him to carry out both his functions: medical practice as a specialist in skin and venereal diseases was hardly conducive to ecstasy of any kind. Only a moral commitment, ruled out for Benn almost from the beginning by Nietzsche's 'transvaluation of all values,' might have linked his 'two lives.' That link was effected in some of his later poems, but in the teeth of all Benn's theories and attitudes.

The most extreme case of multiple personality and self-division in modern poetry is that of the Portuguese poet Fernando Pessoa (1888–1935). Like so many of his contemporaries – Pound and Eliot and Apollinaire are a few of them – Pessoa experienced a physical and cultural transplantation that may have something to do with his extraordinary development as a poet. (The term 'transplantés' was used by Rémy de Gourmont and distinguished by him from the term 'déracinés,' which had become a term of abuse in the mouths of early believers in the 'blood and soil mystique.')[30] As a child, Pessoa was taken to South Africa, spending his formative years in Durban and at an English-speaking public school. His early poems were written in English and collected in three volumes in 1922, after two earlier books of English poems published in 1918. Most of his mature work, written in Portuguese, was never published in his lifetime, though Pessoa returned to Portugal in 1905.

A posthumous sketch explains Pessoa's desperate resort to a division even of his poetic self into four distinct authors – Alvaro de Campos, Alberto Caeiro, Ricardo Reis and Fernando Pessoa – each of whom was allowed to write a kind of poetry which the other three did not and could not write.

The first stage of lyrical poetry is that in which the poet concentrates on his feelings and expresses them. If, however, he is a creature with mutable and multiple feelings, he will express a number of personalities, as it were, held together only by temperament and style. One further step, and we are confronted with a poet who is a creature with multiple and fictitious feelings, more imaginative than emotional, experiencing every state of mind more intellectually than emotionally. This poet will express himself in a variety of persons no longer unified by temperament and style, but by style alone; for temperament has been replaced by imagination, and emotion by intellect. One farther step on the way to depersonalization or, better, imagination, and we are confronted with a poet who becomes so much at home in each of his different states of mind that he gives up his personality completely, to the point where, by experiencing each state of mind analytically, he makes it yield the expression of a different personality; in that way even style becomes manifold. One last step, and we find the poet who is several different poets at once, a dramatic poet who writes lyrical poems. Each group of imperceptibly related states of mind thus becomes a personality with a style of its own and feelings that may differ from the poet's own typical emotional experiences, or may even be diametrically opposed to them. And in this way lyrical poetry draws close to dramatic poetry without assuming dramatic form.[31]

This was Pessoa's way of coping with the conflicts and tensions common to the poets of his time. Alvaro de Campos, for instance, is an out-and-out modernist, deriving from Whitman and from the Futurism of Marinetti, with preoccupations extraordinarily close to those of Hart Crane. Alvaro de Campos wrote odes in long rhapsodic, exclamatory, irregular lines, syntactically free and elliptic. Tradition, on the other hand, was maintained by the pagan and classical poet Ricardo Reis, who wrote meditative poems in regular stanzas, as terse and spare as the odes are effusive. Both these potentialities also characterize the work of Hart Crane, but the need to contain both within a single poet's work led Crane into modulations and inconsistencies of style which Pessoa was able to avoid. Alberto Caeiro, 'a bucolic poet of a complicated kind,' as Pessoa called him, wrote seemingly traditional reflections on the simple life which reveal a sophisticated and very modern revulsion from the awareness of multiplicity. Like Gottfried Benn, who claimed that the burdened consciousness of modern urban man amounted to a biological hypertrophy of the brain that would destroy the white races, Alberto Caeiro, a swain and shepherd familiar with Nietzsche, developed his 'metaphysic of not thinking':

> O que penso eu do mundo?
> Sei lá o que penso do mundo!
> Se eu adoecesse pensaria nisso.
>
> Que ideia tenho eu das coisas?
> Que opinião tenho sobre as causas e os efeitos?
> Que tenho eu meditado sobre Deus e a alma
> E sobre a criação do Mundo?
> Não sei. Para mim pensar nisso é fechar os olhos
> E não pensar . . .[32]

> (What do I think about the world?
> Do I know what I think about the world?
> If I were to fall sick I should think about it.
>
> What ideas do I have about things?
> What opinions about cause and effect?
> What conclusion have I reached about God and the soul
> And about the creation of the World?
> I don't know. For me, to think about that is to shut my eyes
> And not think . . .)

This is the modern poetic scepticism – an irrational scepticism – first recorded by Keats, the 'negative capability' so highly developed in Pessoa that he took the unprecedented step of inventing the authors of his poems, even writing prose dialogues in which one of them argues with another. In that poem by Caeiro another characteristically modern tendency emerges, the same tendency that prompted T. E. Hulme, Ezra Pound and others to evolve the theory of Imagism, out of a scepticism towards conceptual thought and a transference of faith to concrete visible phenomena. Caeiro's pantheism is one that can finally dispense with God, giving back God's attributes and glory to the visible world – much as Rilke did.

> Mas se Deus é as árvores e as flores
> E os montes e o luar e o sol,
> Para que lhe chamo eu Deus?
> Chamo-lhe flores e árvores e montes e sol e luar;
> Porque, se ele se fez, para eu o ver,
> Sol e luar e flores e árvores e montes,
> Se ele me aparece como sendo árvores e montes
> E luar e sol e flores,
> E que ele quer que eu o conheça
> Como árvores e montes e flores e luar e sol.

> (But if God is trees and flowers
> And mountains and moonlight and sun
> Why do I call him God?
> I call him flowers and trees and mountains and sun and
>   moonlight;
> For if, so that I can see him,
> He turns himself into sun and moonlight and flowers and
>   mountains and trees,
> If he appears to me as mountains and trees
> And moonlight and sun and flowers,
> It was his will that I should know him
> As trees and mountains and flowers and moonlight and sun.)

In Section VII of the same sequence Caeiro states that 'seeming is our only wealth,' a conclusion that follows from the anti-metaphysics of the passages quoted and these lines in Section V:

> O único sentido íntimo das coisas
> E elas não terem sentido íntimo nenhum.

> (The only meaning inherent in things
> Is that there is no meaning inherent in things.)

Ironically enough, even confessional poetry – poetry of the empirical self – has its place in the rich and multifarious opus of the four poets that were Fernando Pessoa (whose own name means 'person' – *persona* – mask!). Yet it was under his own name that Pessoa wrote his poem *Autopsicografia* (Autopsychography), concerned with the truth of masks, his true confession of the difficulty of telling the truth:

> O poeta é um fingidor.
> Finge tão completamente
> Que chega a fingir que é dor
> A dor que deveras sente.
>
> E os que lêem o que escreve,
> Na dor lida sentem bem,
> Não as duas que ele teve,
> Mas só a que eles não têm.
>
> E assim nas calhas de roda
> Gira, a entreter a tazão,
> Esse comboio de corda
> Que se chama o coração.
>
> (Poets feign and conceal,
> So completely feign and pretend
> That the pain which they really feel
> They'll feign for you in the end.
>
> And he who reads what they've done
> Never senses the twofold pain
> That's in them, only the one
> Which they never feel but feign.
>
> And so, to amuse our minds
> Round again to the start
> On its circular railway winds
> That toy train called the heart.)

Stylistically that poem is indeed by an author quite distinct from Pessoa's three other poetic media, though he had the advantage of drawing on the experiences of all four of them in presenting a paradox highly relevant to the self-concealment which, in so much modern poetry, is the prerequisite of self-expression. The sceptical intelligence at work in *Autopsicografia* is to be found in all Pessoa's work, even in the production of Alvaro de Campos, whose Nietzschean vitalism is as ambiguous as Nietzsche's own or as Gottfried Benn's, since both Nietzsche and Benn were 'intellectualists' in revolt against the intellect.

The *Ode marítima*, the most ambitious and most characteristic of the poems attributed to Alvaro de Campos, derives its power from an extreme tension between a sense of dynamic movement and an opposing sense of stasis – a tension also striking in the work of Gottfried Benn, who called one of his later collections *Statische Gedichte* (Static Poems), despite his cult of sheer energy. The *Ode marítima* vacillates between a vitalist, often brutalist, affirmation of the savagery not only of the sea itself, but of sailors, and a weary, gentle and tender return to an 'inner ocean' for ever at rest beneath the surface commotion. There is something morbidly masochistic about the intellectual's apostrophes to the sailors and his invocations of a 'horrible and satanic God, the God of a blood-pantheism.'

> Ah, torturai-me para me curardes!
> Minha carne – fazei dela o ar que os vossos cutelos atravessam
> Antes de caírem sobre as cabeças e os ombros!
> Minhas veias sejam os fatos que as facas trespassam!
> Minha imaginação o corpo das mulheres que violais!
> Minha inteligência o convés onde estais de pé matando!
> Minha vida toda, no seu conjunto nervoso, histérico, absurdo,
> O grande organismo de que cada acto de pirataria que se cometeu
> Fosse uma célula consciente – e todo eu turbilhonasse
> Como uma imensa podridão ondeando, e fosse aquilo tudo!

> (O, torture me in order to heal me!
> My flesh: make it the air that your knives slash
> Before they come down on heads and on shoulders!
> My veins the clothes pierced by your blades!
> My imagination the bodies of the women you violate!
> My intelligence the deck on which you murder!
> All my life – nervous, hysterical, absurd –
> The great organism in which each act of piracy when completed
> Becomes a conscious cell – and the whole of me seethes
> Like a vast billowing putrefaction, being all that you are!)

The 'I' of the poem, who glorifies savagery in these terms, is described as 'an engineer in Lisbon, – forced to be practical,

sensitive to everything./ Unlike you, tied down to this place,
even when I'm walking;/ Even when I'm acting, inert; even
when I have my way, feeble,/Static, broken, a cowardly defaulter
from your glory,/From your great strident energy, hot and
bloody!' The interpolation of 'Fifteen men on the Dead Man's
Chest/ Yo-ho-ho and a bottle of rum!' is drawn out into pure
brute noises: 'Eh-lahô-lahô-laHO-lahá-á-ááá-ààà. . . .' In the
spirit of the Futurists – rather than of Hart Crane, with his
historical and mythical preoccupations – machines and the
machine age are also celebrated in the *Ode marítima*, though
unlike Marinetti, Alvaro de Campos ascribed the cult of
machines to the waking and rational mind, not to daydream
fantasies of a 'blood pantheism,' so that a crucial distinction is
made between animal and mechanical energy. It is when the
engineer recovers from his frenzy that he turns to 'modern and
useful things,/ Freighters, steamers and passengers.' The bar-
barous fantasies – threaded with erotic, passively homosexual
overtones – are connected not with these modern phenomena
but with an obsolete schooner; and this schooner, in turn, is
associated with idyllic childhood reminiscences in stark contrast
with the same violent fantasies. In its drastic modulations,
therefore, the *Ode marítima* spans differences and distances as
great as those between the productions of the four poets whose
works were written by Fernando Pessoa; and the many potential
identities available to Pessoa are at least intimated within the
confines of this one poem. Yet the other poems of Alvaro de
Campos add to those potential identities. The ode *Grandes são
os desertos, e tudo é deserto* (Great Are the Deserts, and All Is
Desert) is not only related in theme and imagery to T.S.Eliot's
earlier poems, but as ironically understated as most of the *Ode
marítima* is hyperbolical.

> Acendo o cigarro para adiar a viagem,
> Para adiar todas as viagens,
> Para adiar o universo inteiro.
>
> Volta amanhã, realidade!
> Basta por hoje, gentes!
> Adia-te, presente absoluto!
> Mais vale não ser que ser assim.

(I light the cigarette to put off the journey,
To put off all journeys,
To put off the whole universe.

Come back tomorrow, reality!
Enough for today, gentlemen!
Take a break, absolute present!
Better not to be than to be like this.)

The whole poem is dominated by one question – to pack or not to pack the suitcase, to be or not to be; and its images, at once trivial and existential, give a new sardonic poignancy to a complex familiar since Baudelaire's and Laforgue's and Mallarmé's *poésie des départs*, a complex specifically recalled by the title of a related poem of Alvaro de Campos, *Là-bas, je ne sais où*:

Vida inútil, que era melhor deixar, que é uma cela?
Que importa? Todo o universo é uma cela, e o estar preso não
    tem que ver com o tamanho da cela.

(Useless life, better left behind, life is a cell?
What if it is? All the world is a cell, and to the imprisoned
    the cell's dimensions are not what matters.)

Fernando Pessoa's disguises were assumed out of the conviction that 'poetry is more true than the poet' – and it is not his practice alone that vindicates the conviction, though neither the practice nor the conviction could have occurred to poets immune to doubts about personal identity. With perfect sincerity Pessoa could write in a letter that 'Ricardo Reis writes better than I do, but with a purism that I consider excessive.' As in other poets before him, extreme doubts about personal identity turned into extreme doubts about reality itself. Again it is a poem by Alvaro de Campos, *The Tobacco Shop*, that combines the most minute concentration on an external reality, the tobacco shop itself, with a sense of dream-like unreality. Here Pessoa, or de Campos, anticipates not only existentialism but the *nouveau roman* and playwrights like Ionesco, by an identification of the poet with the tobacconist that effects a total break with Romantic-Symbolist conceptions of the poet: 'He will die and I shall die/ He will leave his sign and I, verses'; but, above all, by the deliberate accumulation of trivial or inconsequential details to produce an almost hypnotic effect. As in early poems by T.S.Eliot, irresolution and caprice yield new imaginative possibilities. The parenthesis '(If I married my washerwoman's daughter,/Perhaps I should be happy)' is one instance of Pessoa's encroachment here on the novelist's, as well as the dramatist's, preserves. As in the *nouveau roman*, seemingly fortuitious movements and actions are recorded as though for their own sake: 'The man has left the shop . . . the tobacconist has smiled.'

Pessoa's drastic resort to heteronyms gave him an extraordinary scope. Among other things, it enabled him to tell the whole truth about himself, about the multiple selves that elude biography. In his important letter of 19 January 1915 to Armando Cortes-Rodrigues he rightly insisted on the sincerity and truthfulness of his work. The poems of Caeiro-Reis-Campos, he writes, 'are a literature that I have created and lived, sincere because it is felt . . . felt in the other's person; written dramatically, but as sincere (in my grave sense of the word) as what King Lear says, though Lear is not Shakespeare, but one of his creations.'[33] Under his own name, Pessoa could write poems of many kinds, including the mystical *Initiation* that concludes: 'Neophyte, there is no death.' He needed Alvaro de Campos to render the modern experience of death-in-life ('I am nothing./I shall always be nothing'), just as he needed Ricardo Reis to produce pure poems, though in the same letter to Cortes-Rodrigues he wrote about 'the terrible importance of Life, that consciousness which makes it impossible for us to produce art only for art's sake, and the consciousness of having a duty towards ourselves and towards humanity.' Pessoa believed in 'the civilizing function of all works of art.' His sincerity, which required disguises and even at times 'the expression of a general truth through a personal lie,' is defined in the same letter by contrast with the insincerity of 'things written to shock . . . and those which do not contain a basic metaphysical idea, through which there passes no sense of the gravity and mystery of life.' He had no patience with the 'decoratively artistic,' with 'those who produce art for various inferior reasons, such as those who play, those who amuse themselves, those who decorate a drawing-room with good taste.' Yet his practice rests on the discovery that the greatest artist 'expresses with the greatest intensity, richness and complexity what in fact he does not feel at all.'

Even that is a simplification, corrected in Pessoa's poem *Autopsicografia.* It is the feelings of the empirical self which poetry enlarges, complements or even replaces with fictitious ones, but only because the empirical self is not the whole self, cramped as it is in its shell of convention, habit and circumstance.* Pessoa's disguises did not impair his truthfulness because he used them not to hoodwink others, but to explore reality and establish the full identity of his multiple, potential selves.

*Heteronymous poem sequences are included in two recent collections by British poets, Christopher Middleton's *torse* 3, London, 1962, and Geoffrey Hill's *King Log*, London, 1968. Although neither poet goes so far as to conceal his authorship of the poems in question, the function of Middleton's Herman Moon and Hill's Sebastian Arrurruz is not unlike that of Pessoa's fictitious poets. Both Middleton and Hill have resorted to invented authors for an extension of historical consciousness and stylistic range greater than the conventional *persona* poem, with its identifiable data, would easily permit. Both, even in their other work, are poets who differ from most of their contemporaries in having little use for their bare empirical selves or for the literalism that records immediate experience.

7

INTERNATIONALISM AND WAR

1   HISTORICALLY, the scope and variety of Pessoa's poems could be seen in relation to his need to create a modern Portuguese poetry – as he did, almost without competition or support from other poets. This need alone might have impelled him to become more than one poet. Something of Pessoa's variety is to be found in the work of Rilke, and in that of Ezra Pound, though neither went so far as to maintain four distinct and consistent *personae*; and neither was in a position quite as isolated as Pessoa's.

It goes without saying that Pessoa's innovations demanded an awareness of what was going on in other literatures. The great formative period of modernism – the years immediately before the First World War – was also the period when the arts, in Europe and the Americas, attained an extraordinary degree of internationalism, and this internationalism persisted even in the teeth of war, most remarkably in overtly neutralist and pacifist groups like the Dadaists. The patriotic war fever of individual poets made little difference; if they were modernists, as even Rilke was at heart, their art itself remained internationally based and orientated. Even when he wrote his *Fünf Gesänge* of 1914, poems celebrating war for war's sake on strictly individualist and emotional grounds, Rilke could not escape the cosmopolitanism which his very way of life re-affirmed after the end of the war. Rilke's brief war fever, in fact, had as little to do with patriotism as his flirtation with Fascism in later years; both were a residue of romantic and Nietzschean hero cults, very much as Yeats's attitudes were. With very few exceptions, the German and Austrian poets of the so-called Expressionist school – that is, the innovators and modernists younger than Rilke – were radically opposed to the war even if they served and died in it. Many of them were distinguished from their British and French counterparts by apocalyptic expectations which not only anticipated the outbreak of war but made them tend to see war as the inevitable prelude to a new era of brotherhood and world-wide social revolution. Something of this apocalyptic spirit informs Rilke's *Fünf Gesänge* too; and there was a time when Rilke was very much in sympathy with the political aspirations of those Expressionist revolutionaries who survived the war.

Enough has been written about 'war poetry' as such to make another examination of it superfluous. Nor as far as the modern period is concerned do I know of any one criterion by which a 'war poem' can be clearly distinguished from other kinds of poems, since peace has become a sequence of limited wars, either political or military, and even the distinction between soldiers' and civilians' verse, still applicable in the First World War, is of little more than technical relevance. The most memorable and characteristic poetry of the First World War was that produced by the impact of modern warfare on sensibilities essentially civilian. Modern war poetry, therefore, has become almost synonymous with anti-war poetry, from the work of Wilfred Owen, Siegfried Sassoon and Isaac Rosenberg, August Stramm, Georg Trakl and Giuseppe Ungaretti in the First World War to the less excellent work of combatants in the Second. By the end of 1915, when both Rupert Brooke and Julian Grenfell (a professional soldier) were dead, all but a few thick-skinned or obdurately romantic civilians were aware that the traditional affirmation of war in heroic or patriotic terms was no longer a decent subject for poetry.

This is not to say that patriotism had ceased to affect the attitudes of combatant poets, or that war no longer had its moments of glory and exhilaration. Charles Vildrac's *Relève*, for instance, rendered the joy of having 'come through' for the time being, a personal emotion as valid in the First World War as in any other. Guillaume Apollinaire continued to make verbal fireworks out of the lethal fireworks of the same war to the bitter end, not least in the ingenious analogies between love and war of his sequence *Ombre de mon amour*. In its detached and fair-minded way Edward Thomas's *This Is No Case of Petty Right or Wrong* . . . is a vindication of patriotism. Yeats's *An Irish Airman Foresees His Death*, on the other hand, is a vindication of heroism for its own sake, like Rilke's *Fünf Gesänge*. Though a poem connected with the war, one would hesitate to call it a war poem – not because Yeats, like Rilke, was a non-combatant, but because neither was responding to the realities of that particular war, as even non-combatant poets could and did. Stefan George's *Drei Gesänge*, published after the war, in 1921, is another instance of heroic attitudes upheld in spite of those realities.

Rilke could not possibly have foreseen the unprecedented wretchedness of the First World War when he wrote his poems, in August 1914; and the only reason why the *Fünf Gesänge* have shocked some of his readers is that they seem to contradict the internationalism of the modernist revolution in the arts, to which Rilke was incomparably closer than either Yeats or George. It is the work of combatant poets that shows most clearly and poignantly how that internationalism persisted, even on the battlefield and in the trenches. Jules Romains, whose Unanimist movement was closely associated with the pan-Europeanism of Romain Rolland, published his *Conjuration* in 1916:

> Europe! Je n'accepte pas
> Que tu meures dans ce délire.
> Europe, je cris que tu es
> Dans l'oreille de tes tueurs.
>
> (Europe! I will not accept
> Your death in this delirium.
> Europe, I'll shout that you are
> Into your murderers' ears.)

Even where internationalism was not a creed, it was part of the experience of the poets who were drawn into the war. Just as Charles Sorley had gone to Germany shortly before the war, to discover Hölderlin and Rilke and react with sceptical good humour to the institutions of the country, so the German poet

Ernst Stadler had become attached to England as a Rhodes scholar at Oxford. Both were killed in action before they had time to become war poets. Ernst Stadler was also one of four poets born in Alsace-Lorraine – René Schickele, Yvan Goll and Jean Arp were the others – to whom the compatibility of French and German culture was self-evident. Stadler translated French poetry, Goll and Arp were to write their poetry in both languages. The new philosophy of Bergson meant as much to T.E.Hulme in England as it did to Jules Romains in France; and Hulme, of course, was of seminal importance to Ezra Pound, Herbert Read, and the evolution of the entire Anglo-American Imagist movement.

Ezra Pound himself acknowledged his affinities with the Unanimist movement and the poetry of Jules Romains, Charles Vildrac, René Arcos and André Spire, saying that 'Spire and Arcos write "more or less as I do myself." '[1] In the same way Wyndham Lewis acknowledged the debt owed by his Vorticism and by all the modernist movements to Germany;[2] and Apollinaire, too, visited Germany and contributed to the Expressionist periodical *Der Sturm*. Apollinaire's French patriotism had special personal roots of which I shall have more to say; but in the poetry of René Arcos, too, the war is presented as an arbitrary and vicious interruption of European unity. So in *Les Morts*:

> Serrés les uns contre les autres
> Les morts sans haine et sans drapeau
> Cheveux plaqués de sang caillé
> Les morts sont tous d'un seul côté.

> (Pressed close against each other
> The dead without hatred or flag
> The hair stiff with congealed blood
> The dead are all on one side.)

Whether they began with preconceived pacifist ideals or were converted by the sheer brutality, boredom and waste of trench warfare; whether their protests were dignified and urbane or callow and hysterical as in much of later German Expressionist verse – the fact is that the poets were right about the war, the politicians and the press were wrong. Not only did Europe never recover materially from the war, but the terrible disparity between civilian and military experience created all sorts of rifts whose effects on life and literature can still be seen and felt even after a Second World War. The extreme political divisions after 1918 are only the most palpable of those rifts. It was the formative experience of war that caused Bertolt Brecht to break more completely than any other poet of his time with all the premises and practices of Romantic-Symbolist art, and it was in Germany, too, that the war between the generations became a commonplace in the inter-war period, as it did again after the Second World War. In Britain even such traditionalists of the old generation as Kipling, Chesterton, Newbolt and Alice Meynell did their best to mend the rift by expressing anger and guilt about the war, whereas young poets like Charles Sorley, for all his intelligence and his strictures on the 'sentimental attitude' of Rupert Brooke, remained trapped in conventions of diction and sentiment which his French and German contemporaries had discarded before the war. Yet the rift occurred in Great Britain also. In the immediate post-war poetry of Robert Graves and Edmund Blunden it became an inner one, a conflict between tendencies towards the pre-war nature idyll or faery romanticism and the new starkness. Such inner conflicts had to be fought out over a long period. Blunden's *Report on Experience*, his best-known poem about the disillusionment shared by so many survivors, appeared in his collection of 1929; Herbert Read's *The End of a War* as late as 1933, David Jones's *In Parenthesis* not until 1937.

In Germany, with no stable ruling class both able and willing to make the necessary adjustments and concessions, the war of the generations took such violent and irreconcilable forms that it seems to foreshadow all subsequent German history, including the present division of the country. At least four of the prominent younger poets became active revolutionaries, Werfel and Toller in the early inter-war period, Brecht and Becher up to the Second World War and beyond it. Already between the wars it became clear that the internationalism of 1912, the solidarity and unanimity of modernist writers everywhere, could not be restored. The very pacifism and fraternalism of the social revolutionaries hardened into an ideological commitment which raised barriers more impassable than national frontiers; and Fascist or nationalist ideologies claimed the allegiance of anti-

Communists. The effect of these ideological divisions on poetry can be traced in the development of German Expressionism in the twenties and thirties, in the English and American poetry that grew out of early Imagist practice – Ezra Pound's *Cantos* are the outstanding instance – as in the French poetry of Aragon, Eluard and other writers at one time associated with the Surrealist group. By the Second World War, several of the poets in question abandoned their modern, 'formalist' and individualistic practices in accordance with Communist or National Socialist collectivism. The later poetry of Johannes R. Becher, who became Minister of Culture in the German Democratic Republic, bears as little formal relation to his Expressionist work as *Le Crève-coeur* and *Les Yeux d'Elsa* do to Louis Aragon's poetry of the inter-war years.

The Second World War was the military continuation of the ideological conflicts that preceded it. As such, it was very much more predictable than the First World War, as far as intellectuals and artists were concerned. That is one reason why it produced far less poetry of outrage and pity comparable to the work of Wilfred Owen, Georg Trakl and Charles Vildrac, or the quiet eloquence of F. S. Flint's *Lament*:[3]

> The young men of the world
> Are condemned to death.
> They have been called up to die
> For the crime of their fathers.
>
> . . . .
> The young men of the world
> No longer possess the road:
> The road possesses them.
> They no longer inherit the earth:
> The earth inherits them.
> They are no longer the master of fire:
> Fire is their master;
> They serve him, he destroys them.
>
> . . . .
> The genius of the air
> Has contrived a new terror
> That rends them into pieces. . . .

In as much as it was an ideological war, the Second World War was fought too late; and much of its 'war poetry' was written before the outbreak of war by the politically engaged poets everywhere, just as much of the 'war poetry' of the First World War was written after 1918. What survived of the international humanism of 1912 was a lost cause before the Second World War began: Spain and Munich had marked its defeat. Herbert Read's *To a Conscript of 1940* can be read either as a 'war poem' of the Second World War or as a retrospective 'war poem' of the First; and, because censorship and repression had permitted no honest 'war poetry' to be published on the German side, the German poetry of the Second World War was written after 1945, and continues to be written, though it can no longer be clearly distinguished from an anti-war poetry directed against the threat of a Third World War.

The relevance of F. S. Flint's *Lament*, which concludes with the lines: 'Weep, weep, o women,/And old men, break your hearts' extends far beyond the events that occasioned it. After 1914 more and more poets ceased to 'possess the road,' if only because total war had ushered in the era of total politics. Whether poets wrote pure or impure poetry, in a new or in a conventional manner, ceased to be a question of personal choice or disposition in many parts of the world. Even where literature was not directed by government decrees, 'political consciousness' could act as an inward censor and director, forcing good poets to write bad poetry against the grain of sensibility and experience; or to exclude those layers of the personality that do not conform to the corporative image. Something of the excitement of 1912 persisted in certain groups; but after 1914 few poets were quite immune from new doubts about the validity of private aspirations of any kind, doubts that could turn into a bad conscience about being poets at all.

2   The most distinguished 'war poems' of the First World War combine formal innovation with a very personal response to the experience of war. This response could be unashamedly individualistic, as in Giuseppe Ungaretti's *Veglia* (Watch), written in 1915:

> Un'intera nottata
> buttato vicino
> a un compagno

massacrato
con la sua bocca
disgrignata
volta al plenilunio
con la congestione
delle sue mani
penetrata
nel mio silenzio
ho scritto
lettere piene d'amore

Non sono mai stato
tanto
attaccato alla vita[4]

(A whole night
thrust beside
a companion
massacred
his lips
in a snarl
turned to the full moon
his clogged hands
reaching out
into
my silence
I have written
letters full of love

Never with such a grip
have I
hung on to life)

In another poem written while on active service, *Pellegri-naggio* (Pilgrimage), Ungaretti speaks of the illusion needed to give him courage after hours of crawling about muddy trenches, an illusion which the fighting itself provides: 'A searchlight/over there/creates a sea/within the fog.' That sea image was to recur in Ungaretti's work up to his late poem *Finale*, and even the fog of the battlefield is recalled in the same late poem: 'A fumi tristi cedé il letto il mare,/Il mare' ('To sad vapours yielded her bed the sea/The sea') with a complete reversal of mood, since in *Finale* 'even the sea is dead.' Ungaretti's war poems could not have been written without his experience as a combatant; yet it is personal preoccupations, including his need to survive the war, that make them more than 'war poems.'

The same is true of the war poems of Georg Trakl, though it was an experience similar to that in Ungaretti's *Veglia* that drove Trakl to suicide in 1914, while he was serving on the Eastern front with the Austrian Army. His concern, too, was with the future, but not with his own. His *Lament*, like F.S.Flint's, has to do with the very quality of life and the 'image of man,' and the impact of specific war experiences does not make this poem different in any essential respect from his poems written before the war, with the same concerns and the same visionary concentration:

Klage

Schlaf und Tod, die düstern Adler
Umrauschen nachtlang dieses Haupt:
Des Menschen goldnes Bildnis
Verschlänge die eisige Woge
Der Ewigkeit. An schaurigen Riffen
Zerschellt der purpurne Leib.
Und es klagt die dunkle Stimme
Über dem Meer.
Schwester stürmischer Schwermut
Sieh, ein einsamer Kahn versinkt
Unter Sternen,
Dem schweigenden Antlitz der Nacht.[5]

(*Lament*

Sleep and death, the dark eagles
Around this head swoop all night long:
Eternity's icy wave
Would swallow the golden image
Of man; on horrible reefs
His purple body is shattered.
And the dark voice laments
Over the sea.
Sister of stormy sadness,
Look, a timorous boat goes down
Under stars,
The silent face of the night.)

As a literary figure Trakl was far from being either cosmopolitan or metropolitan. His contacts with other writers, even

those German Expressionists among whom historians of literature number him, were rare and marginal, though his early
reading of Rimbaud and other French poets affected his way of
writing. If Trakl's poetry became internationally accessible in
a way that the war poems proper of Wilfred Owen, Isaac
Rosenberg and Siegfried Sassoon did not, it was because Trakl's
imagery is archetypal rather than phenomenal, and because
his modernity has less to do with attitudes and experience than
with stylistic trends common to many different literatures and
literary movements. Trakl's last poem, *Grodek*, contains this line:

Und leise tönen im Rohr die dunklen Flöten des Herbstes.

(And softly the dark flutes of autumn sound in the reeds.)

With its 'Surrealist genitive' in a context otherwise traditionally elegiac that line could hardly be closer to these lines in
Lorca's *Romancero gitan* (1924–7):

Cantan las flautas de umbria
Y el liso gong de la nieve.

(The flutes of shadow sing
and the muted gong of the snow.)

Trakl was not a deliberately modernist or experimental poet,
like his older contemporary August Stramm (1864–1915),
whose Expressionism demanded nothing less than a new
vocabulary and a new grammar that reduced language to
essential kinetic gestures, by the total exclusion of impressionism
or description. Yet Stramm's war poems, with their onomato-
poeia and their neologisms, render more than a purely subjective
response to the experience of active service on the Russian front.
Frostfeuer (Frost Fire) renders one of the compensations of
extreme physical hardship:

Die Zehen sterben
Atem schmilzt zu Blei
In den Fingern sielen heisse Nadeln.
Der Rücken schneckt
Die Ohren summen Tee
Das Feuer
Klotzt
Und

Hoch vom Himmel
Schlürft
Dein kochig Herz
Verschrumplig
Knistrig
Wohlig
Sieden Schlaf.

(Our toes die
Breath melts to lead
In our fingers hot needles drain.
Our backs snail
Our ears hum tea
The fire
Logs
And
High from the sky
Your simmery heart
Shrinkily
Cracklingly
Snugly
Laps up
Seethy sleep.)

Stramm's poem *Schlachtfeld* (Battlefield), also written in 1915, succeeds in compressing the pity, horror and absurdity of the war into as few words as possible, though once more Stramm had to make up a high proportion of those words, or change the grammatical function of existing words, so as to charge them with the energy that he wanted:

Schollenmürbe schläfert ein das Eisen
Blute filzen Sickerflecke
Roste krumen
Fleische schleimen
Saugen brünstet um Zerfallen.
Mordesmorde
blinzen
Kinderblicke.

(Yielding clod lulls iron off to sleep
bloods clot the patches where they oozed
rusts crumble
fleshes slime
sucking lusts around decay.

Murder on murder
blinks
in childish eyes.)

The essential primitivism of Stramm's manner, akin to the simplication of planes and outlines practised by painters and sculptors of his time, does not prevent that poem from conveying a moral judgement of the war in which Stramm lost his life. 'To him,' Franz Marc wrote about Stramm, 'language was not a form or vessel in which thoughts are savoured, but a material from which he struck fire; or dead marble that he wanted to bring to life, like a true sculptor.' Soon after this tribute to Stramm, Franz Marc, too, was killed in the war; but it was not only the death of so many gifted men on both sides that impoverished poetry in the subsequent decades. Many of the survivors never recovered the zest or the conviction of the pre-war era, when revolution in the arts seemed capable of revolutionizing the very hearts and minds of a 'new humanity.' F.S.Flint was one of those survivors; and, like his *Lament*, Section IV of Ezra Pound's *E. P. Ode Pour L'Election de Son Sépulchre* commemorates the premature end of what should have been a new age:

> Died some, pro patria,
>   non 'dulce' non 'et decor' ...
> walked eye-deep in hell
> believing in old men's lies, then unbelieving
> came home, home to a lie,
> home to many deceits,
> home to old lies and new infamy;
> usury age-old and age-thick
> and liars in public places.

It is difficult to read those lines now without reflecting that their author was to lend his allegiance to a militant nationalism that differed from the old in being more shameless about its deceits and lies, total in its demands for obedience and conformity. That development, too, is of historical significance.

3   The various modern 'movements' of the immediate pre-1914 period and of the war years are also of interest to historians, but they are far less relevant to the work produced

159

at that time than the spirit of adventure and innovation that is common to them all. 'After Cubism and Unanimism,' Margaret Davies has recorded,[6] 'there had been Paroxysm, Futurism, Simultanism, Orphism, Dramatism, Beaudouin's "Synoptisme polyplan" (which tried to incorporate the technique of the cinema as well as musical construction), Dynamism, Modernism, and in England Vorticism and Imagism, in Russia Rayonnism.' Many more names could be added to the list, including Russian Futurism, German Expressionism and international Dadaism, followed by Surrealism, with its centre in Paris but affiliations throughout the world. If the very short poems of T.E.Hulme are taken to be prototypes of Imagist practice, the later development of the chief contributors to the Imagist anthologies is representative of the tendency of all such programmes to give way to individual needs. Apollinaire alone was associated with quite a number of the 'isms' listed by Margaret Davies. 'Expressionist,' on the other hand, is a label applied to such a range of works produced by German artists and writers in the course of several decades that it has come to serve as little more than a synonym for 'modernist.'[7]

Ernst Stadler, for instance, wrote poems as different from those of Georg Trakl as Trakl's are from those of Stramm or of Alfred Lichtenstein, another German poet killed in the war. All these poets are described as Expressionist, and all four were posthumously assembled in the anthology *Menschheitdämmerung* of 1920, which its editor called a 'symphony of recent poetry.'

What Stadler did share with other contributors to periodicals like *Die Aktion* and *Der Sturm* is an impatience with the old order both in society and in the arts, an impatience that generated images of doom and destruction – as in Georg Heym's poem *Der Krieg*, written some years before the outbreak of war, and in Stadler's own poem *Der Aufbruch* – but also of regeneration. The ironists Alfred Lichtenstein and Jakob van Hoddis trivialized their apocalypse, making it at once clownish, urbane and grotesque. Georg Trakl's apocalypse was rendered elegiacally, with a sustained gravity that recalls Hölderlin. Stadler was a realist and a vitalist. His poems on the East End of London – *Judenviertel in London* (Jewish Quarter in London) and *Kinder vor einem Londoner Armenspeisehaus* (Children at a London Soup Kitchen) – are striking examples of a manner not expressive or

Expressionist at all, because description is dominant in them and the squalor described does not assume the apocalyptic implications which Trakl could compress into a single image, in his poem *Das Herz* (The Heart):

> Am kahlen Tor am Schlachthaus stand
> Der armen Frauen Schar;
> In jeden Korb
> Fiel faules Fleisch und Eingeweid;
> Verfluchte Kost!

> (By the bare gate of the slaughterhouse there stood
> The crowd of poor women.
> Into every basket
> Rank flesh and entrails fell;
> Accursed fare!)

That image may derive from experience, like the 'stench of rotten meat and fish' that 'sticks to the walls' in Stadler's poem on the Jewish Quarter or the children 'filthy and in rags' queuing up for a free meal in his other London poem; but Stadler's much more elaborate descriptions in those poems fix the reader's attention on the scene itself, whereas Trakl's evoke a sense of evil and damnation that make the scene only incidental.

Another of Stadler's poems with an English setting, *Meer*, is as typical of his vitalism as the other two are of his realism; and one reason is that whereas the others are poems of compassion, *Meer* is a poem of self-expression. *Kinder vor einem Londoner Armenspeisehaus*, too, begins with the word 'I'; but after the introductory 'I saw,' the first person vanishes from the poem. In *Meer* the 'I' with which the poem begins is the true subject, in both senses of the word. From the very first line the sea becomes something inside the poet, as well as the water in which he bathes:

> In meinem Blute scholl
> Schon Meer. O schon den ganzen Tag. Und jetzt die Fahrt
>   im gelbumwitterten Vorfrühlingsabend. Rastlos schwoll
> Es auf und reckte sich in einer jähen frevelhaften Süsse,
>   wie im Spiel
> Sich Geigen nach den süssen Himmelswiesen recken.
>   Dunkel lag der Kai. Nachtwinde wehten. Regen fiel.

(Already in my blood
Sounded the sea. O that whole day it sounded. And now the journey
in early Spring, an evening fanned with yellow. Swell of the flood
Restlessly rising and reaching out in a sudden, arrogant sweetness,
           swell
Like that of violins reaching out for sweet empyrean meadows.
Dark lay the quay. Night breezes blew. Rain fell.)

That poem, too, contains a good deal of specific and localized imagery – Southampton Harbour, Dover and 'Shakespeare's Cliff,' the grating of broken shells in soft sand – but all these images are swept up in Stadler's long lines towards an elemental vision that is religious and erotic, as in Stadler's poem *On Crossing the Rhine Bridge at Cologne by Night*[8] or his celebrations of sexual love in *Leoncita*, *La Querida* and *Linda*. This cult of the 'dark gods' of the blood relates Stadler's work to that of Gottfried Benn and D.H.Lawrence, though Stadler's vitalism was palliated by his social concerns, his realism, and by a Christian mysticism that made him the German advocate and translator of Francis Jammes and Péguy. In his best poems the tension between these disparate affinities is sustained, despite a recurrent ambivalence and an occassional tendency to relapse into the vocabulary of the 1890s and of *art nouveau*. The ambivalence has to do with Stadler's celebration of an ecstasy that is always a dissolution of the self, as in his poem *Puppen* in which the prostitute's mouth is 'wie eine tolle Frucht die Lust und Untergang verheisst' ('like a mad fruit that promises pleasure and destruction'). Ecstasy and self-destruction are almost inseparably coupled in Stadler's poems, even where the context has no overtly erotic connotations.

As early as 1902, when Stadler was still working on the rather derivative verse collected in his first book, *Praeludien* (1904) – his second and last collection, *Der Aufbruch*, did not appear until 1913, not long before his death – he wrote in his essay *Neuland* that 'it is the future which all true art serves.' The title poem of Stadler's second collection renders his impatience for the future in military terms:

Aber eines Morgens
  rollte durch Nebelluft das Echo von Signalen,
Hart, scharf, wie Schwerthieb pfeifend. Es war
  wie wenn im Dunkel plötzlich Lichter aufstrahlen.

Es war wie wenn durch Biwakfrühe
 Trompetenstösse klirren,
Die Schlafenden aufspringen und die Zelte abschlagen
 und die Pferde schirren. . . .

(But one morning through hazy air the echo of signals rolled,
Hard, sharp, like a sword-blade swishing. It was as when
 sudden lights flare up in the dark.
It was as when bugle blasts blare through a bivouac dawn,
The sleepers leap up and break camp and harness the horses. . . .)

In this poem, too, Stadler's hedonism and the vitalism are
whetted by the possibility of sudden death. Much of the military
imagery is realistic enough, but the realism is true to modes of
warfare which the 1914–18 war made obsolete. Perhaps the
same applies to Stadler's vitalism, which is unlikely to have stood
up to the attrition of months in the trenches. Cruelly ironic
though it is that Stadler was killed by a British hand grenade
after writing his B. Litt. thesis on Shakespeare in English for
what he called 'dear old Oxford,' and killed in the very month
when he should have taken up his academic post in Toronto,
and killed in the very country, Belgium, where he had lived and
worked as a university lecturer, his early death in action accords
well with the pervasive ambivalence of his poetry. *Der Aufbruch*,
a pre-1914 poem, remained his only 'war poem'; and it is not a
poem about war, but about living keenly, dangerously and
unreservedly, in a way as different as possible from that of the
smug and pampered bourgeoisie of 1912. Stadler was spared the
knowledge of that rift in Western civilization itself which
Siegfried Sassoon exposed in *Does It Matter?*:[9]

Does it matter? – losing your legs? . . .
For people will always be kind,
And you need not show that you mind
When others come in after hunting
To gobble their muffins and eggs . . .

or D. H. Lawrence in his retrospective epigram, *The Late War*:[10]

The War was not strife
it was murder
each side trying to murder the other side
evilly.

Knowledge of that kind was to damp and divide the inter-national Futurism to which Stadler subscribed. The dominant inter-war 'isms' tended to be more political than aesthetic, and to impose narrowing limits on the area in which a poet could innocently pursue that quarrel with himself out of which, as Yeats said, poetry is made. Stadler's poem *Der Aufbruch*, for instance, came to be censured for its 'militarism,' and his celebration of the 'dark gods' of the blood became suspect on related grounds. The individualism that was a pre-condition of innovation in the arts – and even the aspiration towards a new community or 'communion' so pervasive in Stadler's work – was soon to be open to pressure and attacks from every side.

4 Blaise Cendrars, whose most vital poetry was written between 1912 and 1918, though he survived both wars, wrote an almost Dadaist 'war poem' in 1916, *La Guerre au Luxembourg*. The whole poem is like a farcical elaboration of Stramm's 'murder on murder/blinks/in childish eyes,' for this war is waged by children in the Luxembourg Gardens. Despite the controversy as to whether it was Cendrars or Apollinaire who first evolved the stylistic features common to Apollinaire's *Zone* and Cendrars's *Les Pâques à New-York*, Cendrars called Apollinaire 'the only poet in France for the last twelve years' (*Hamac*, 1913) – and, after Apollinaire's death, commemorated him in a poem that is also a celebration of the era in which both poets flourished. The international spirit of that era, true, is projected into the future, and Apollinaire's French patriotism fused with his internationalism as though there were no contradiction between them:

> Il s'amusait à vous jeter des fleurs et des couronnes
> Tandis que vous passiez derrière son corbillard
> Puis il a acheté une petite cocarde tricolore
> Je l'ai vu le soir même manifester sur les boulevards
> Il était à cheval sur le moteur d'un camion américain et
>   brandissait un énorme drapeau international déployé
>   comme un avion
> VIVE LA FRANCE...[11]

> (He amused himself by throwing you flowers and garlands
> While you were following his hearse

Then he bought a little tricoloured rosette
That same night I saw him demonstrate on the boulevards
He was straddling the bonnet of an American truck and
    waving an enormous international flag spread out
    like an aeroplane
LONG LIVE FRANCE...)

Yet that contradiction did not become irreconcilable until patriotism turned into the new nationalism of the twenties and thirties; and Cendrars's magical resurrection of his dead friend presents him exactly as he was, with all his complexities and his redeeming naïveté. What Cendrars could not foresee in November 1918, when he wrote *Hommage à Guillaume Apollinaire*, is that Apollinaire would have little progeny of the kind envisaged in the poem:

Des petits Français, moitié anglais, moitié nègre, moitié russe, un
    peu belge, italien, annamite, tchèque
L'un a l'accent canadien, l'autre les yeux hindous
Dents face os jointure galbe démarche sourire
Ils ont tous quelque chose d'étranger et sont pourtant bien de
    chez nous
Au milieu d'eux, Apollinaire, comme cette statue du Nil, le père
    des eaux, étendu avec des gosses qui lui coulent de partout
Entre les pieds, sous les aisselles, dans la barbe
Ils ressemblent à leur père et se départent de lui
Et ils parlent tous la langue d'Apollinaire

(Little Frenchmen, half English, half Negro, half Russian, a bit
    Belgian, Italian, Annamite, Czech
One with a Canadian accent, the other with Indian eyes
Teeth face bones joints outlines gait smile
They all have something foreign about them and yet all belong
    to us
In their midst, Apollinaire, like that statue of the Nile, Father of
    Waters, stretched out with children flowing from every part of
    him
Between his feet, under his armpits, inside his beard
They look like their father and look unlike him
And they all speak the language of Apollinaire)

In the Paris of the twenties and early thirties a good many poets did continue to speak the language of Apollinaire. So did poets in Russia, Germany and Italy, though under the shadow of new political developments that were to silence many of them, if they did not recant and 'reform,' as Marinetti recanted his international Futurism when he became a Fascist. Mayakovsky's suicide in 1930 ended that poet's attempt to reconcile international Futurism with service to the Communist Party and its increasingly nationalistic régime in Russia. Two other Russian innovators of the same generation, Velemir Klebnikov and Sergei Yesenin, had died in 1922 and 1925, even less capable than Mayakovsky of meeting official demands on the arts. Osip Mandelstam was repeatedly arrested, sent to Siberia, and prevented from publishing his work after 1928. Even his death was never recorded or made public, though it now seems likely that he died at Vladivostok in 1938, changed beyond recognition and almost driven out of his mind by the treatment he had suffered. Lorca was murdered by Spanish Fascists, his younger contemporary Miguel Hernández starved and tortured to death in the prison of Alicante in 1942. The gifted Hungarian poet Miklós Radnóti died in a German extermination camp in 1944. The German poet Gertrud Kolmar was last known to be alive in 1943, when she was working in a forced-labour camp. The Turkish poet Nazim Hikmet was sentenced to twenty-nine years of solitary confinement in 1929 and forced to take refuge in Russia after his release in 1951. The great majority of the German modernists who survived until 1933 ended their lives in exile, more than one of them by suicide. The Spanish poets of Lorca's generation, as well as Antonio Machado and Juan Jiménez, were similarly dispersed after the Civil War. Apollinaire's friend Max Jacob was arrested in his religious retreat at Saint-Benoît-sur-Loire and died in a German concentration camp. There is no need to continue that list or to bring it up to date. The few cases mentioned should be more than enough to show that the post-1918 era was very different indeed from Cendrars's anticipation of it in his tribute to Apollinaire.

5   The near-apotheosis of Guillaume Apollinaire in Cendrars's poem is as true to the spirit of the era that ended when the poem was written as it is true to the spirit of Apollinaire, who brought back the confessional and autobiographical preoccupations condemned by the advocates of

pure or absolute poetry. Apollinaire delighted in celebrations of his own life and exploits, half-mythologizing himself with a kind of zest more reminiscent of Byron, if not of Villon, than of his immediate predecessors or successors in France. When Apollinaire wrote:

> Hommes de l'avenir souvenez-vous de moi
> Je vivais à lépoque où finissaient les rois[12]

> (Men of the centuries to come, remember me
> I lived in the epoch that abolished kings)

he claimed the same kind of intimacy with the Zeitgeist as Brecht, with very different premises but with the same Villonesque precedents claimed in poems like *Vom armen B.B.* (Of Poor B.B.) and *An die Nachgeborenen* (To Posterity). Both poets were eclectic, availing themselves of any model or convention that could be renovated or adapted for their own purposes. Needless to say, the Villonesque convention did not allow them to render the whole of their personalities, for these were as complex and many-sided as the personality of Pessoa; but it did enable them to exercise a historically representative function that had long seemed incompatible with modern poetic practices. Deliberate simplifications of his poetic self – inevitable if Guillaume Apollinaire, the cosmopolitan poet of mixed, foreign and mysterious parentage, was to be adopted by France as a representative figure – are more evident in his later poems than in his pre-war work. Although the naïve mode, with echoes not only of Villon, but of folk poetry, Ronsard and a variety of other models, was as genuine and essential a feature of Apollinaire's earlier innovations as his happy use of the contemporary vernacular, *Zone* and *La Chanson du mal-aimé* are self-discoveries rather than self-projections. Despite its direct appeal to posterity, even *Vendémiaire* continues that exploration by presenting the poet in terms of the experiences that have formed him. The claim

> Je suis ivre d'avoir bu tout l'univers

> (I'm drunk with drinking the whole universe)

is aptly substantiated by vivid details of what the poet has drunk. When, in another poem from *Alcools*, *Cortège*, Apollinaire addresses himself

> Je me disais Guillaume il est temps que tu viennes

> (I told myself Guillaume it is high time you arrived)

the context, once more, is one of self-discovery, self-confrontation, and it seems no less natural that Apollinaire should address himself, or his double, by name than that he should talk to himself at all, as in the very opening line of the collection *Alcools*:

> A la fin tu es las de ce monde ancien

> (In the end you are tired of this ancient world).

Throughout these poems Apollinaire was indeed presenting not only his own complex person but a great deal of the modern world at a turning-point which he understood as well as any poet writing at the time, with a prescience especially remarkable in the poem *Cortège*:

> Rien n'est mort que ce qui n'existe encore
> Près du passé luisant demain est incolore

> (Nothing is dead save that which is still to come
> Beside the luminous past tomorrow is colourless).

As a poet who looked back as much as he looked forward, who vacillated between a Futuristic delight in anything that was new and a weary longing for that 'ceremony of innocence' which many of the twentieth-century innovations served to 'drown,' Apollinaire had no need to emphasize his representative status. His very desire to be a representative figure and to combine 'perfection of the life' with 'perfection of the work' was strangely anachronistic, more reminiscent of Victor Hugo than of Hugo's successors. It was also a naïve ambition; and the same naïveté that makes Apollinaire so attractive a character accounts for many of his shortcomings as a poet – his tendency to plagiarize, for instance, or his inability to resist conventional rhetoric and lyricism of a kind not truly compatible with his equally genuine passion for modernity. These shortcomings seem to be more apparent to his French critics than to his foreign ones; and there is a connection between Apollinaire's somewhat insecure standing in France, as compared with his international reputation, and the basic personal insecurity that made him try too hard to compensate for his illegitimate foreign birth. Apollinaire never came to terms with it. Hence his excessive desire to be appreciated and accepted – whether by the Parisian 'avant-garde' or by the Académie Française – his paranoia, his exaggerated patriotism and his fits of utter dejection. Even his death at the age of thirty-eight might well have been avoided but for his compulsion to compensate for his rootlessness by insisting on leaving the comparative safety of the artillery so as to qualify for a commission, though the mere sense of belonging to the French Army seemed to have almost staunched the inner wound.

These biographical considerations are not irrelevant to the case of a poet who never tried to keep his empirical self out of his poems, and who felt the need to ask posterity for the same appreciation and acceptance that he needed as a man:

> Je lègue à l'avenir l'histoire de Guillaume Apollinaire
> Qui fut à la guerre et sut être partout[13]

> (I bequeath to the future the story of Guillaume Apollinaire
> Who was in the war and had learnt to be everywhere).

Even in his fine valedictory poem *La Jolie rousse*, which concludes his collection *Calligrammes*, Apollinaire's self-consciousness obtrudes in the 'Mais riez, riez de moi' ('But laugh at me'), an invitation to his readers that detracts from a poem that would otherwise demand no indulgence on any reader's part, since it presents the sum of Apollinaire's experience with a directness and unpretentiousness broken only by those very pleas for indulgence and pity. One could excuse the banality of Apollinaire's reference to the war as an 'effroyable lutte' – a description contradicted by other poems in *Calligrammes*, such as

> Ah Dieu! que la guerre est jolie![14]

> (My God, how pretty is war!)

> Que c'est beau ces fusées qui illuminent la nuit[15]

> (How lovely they are, these rockets that light up the night)

because the conversational tone of the poem permits a certain slackness in the choice of words; and the self-portrait as such is convincing, even when Apollinaire, once more, related himself to the age:

Je sais d'ancien et de nouveau autant qu'un homme seul pourrait des
                                                              deux savoir
Et sans m'inquiéter aujourd'hui de cette guerre
Entre nous et pour nous mes amis
Je juge cette longue querelle de la tradition et de l'invention
        De l'Ordre et de l'Aventure

(I know as much of the old and the new as one man could know of
                                                              both
And without worrying today about this war
Between ourselves and on your behalf my friends
I judge this long quarrel between tradition and invention
        Between Order and Adventure).

That summary is to the point; but in the lines that follow
Apollinaire weakens it by appealing to those whose 'mouths are
fashioned in the image of God,' and craving their indulgence
towards the generation that sacrificed order to adventure. As
often as not Apollinaire's false steps as a poet were obeisances to
conventions and orders which he was not adventurous enough
to leave behind, and it is these lapses that account for many
impurities of diction, structure and gesture in his poetry. For
all his enthusiastic championing of a succession of modernist
movements, even Apollinaire's manifestos and critical essays
show that his break with Romantic-Symbolist practices was a
restoration as much as it was a revolution. This can be seen in
his earliest articles of 1903, as in his late essay *L'Esprit nouveau
et les poètes*, with its warnings against 'cosmopolitan lyric expression' that would 'yield only shapeless works without character
or individual structure.' Both Dadaism and the most recent
Concrete poetry might be the subject of another reservation in
the same essay: 'I think it wrong that a poem should be composed merely of imitations of a noise to which no lyric, tragic or
pathetic significance can be attached.' Yet Apollinaire's
originality sprang from a new awareness that was essentially
cosmopolitan, an awareness that permitted shock effects like

> Et moi j'ai le coeur aussi gros
> Qu'un cul de dame damascène[16]
>
> (And my heart is as heavy as
> A Damascan lady's backside)

or the topographical shifts and juxtapositions of *Zone*.

If posterity, on the whole, has accorded Apollinaire the indulgence which he so frequently asked for, it is not only because of the charm of his personality – present in everything he wrote, in strict contravention of Symbolist austerity in this regard – but because his very uncertainties and defects were to prove as exemplary as his successful innovations. Apollinaire's extraordinary prescience caused him to write in 1917: 'The use of literary liberty in society will become increasingly rare and precious. The great democracies of the future will not be very liberal towards writers.'[17] His own poetry anticipates this trend in its directness of utterance, its reversions to traditional modes and conventions, its shrinking back from innovations felt to be too individualistic or too cosmopolitan. All these are characteristics of the work produced after the First World War by poets under corporate pressure, whether this pressure came from totalitarian régimes or from their own ideological commitments.

Like very few poets of his time, Apollinaire created a legendary role for himself, by an uneasy marriage between the empirical and poetical selves that had scarcely been attempted since Wordsworth's 'egotistical sublime' or Victor Hugo's more egotistical, but not always sublime, ambition to act as a 'legislator of mankind,' or at least as the mouthpiece and conscience of a people. Apollinaire's styles are almost as various and heterogeneous as those of Fernando Pessoa, but what prevents them from falling apart – sometimes within the confines of a single longer poem – is the very biographical unity which Pessoa was adventurous enough to discard. From the point of view of the legend, Apollinaire's death in November 1918 could not have been more accurately timed. Blaise Cendrars was not alone in feeling it to be the end of an era. Max Jacob wrote: 'Truthfully, neither the success of my friends nor those of our victorious country can bring to life again what his death has withered in me for ever. I did not know that he was "my life" to this extent. For me something has broken somewhere. If I were a little more sensitive I should feel that I myself had died.'[18]

Apollinaire's exemplary significance in the immediate pre-war era of international innovation in the arts can be taken for granted. What is not so obvious is the extent to which his work prefigures later developments. I have already mentioned two

poems in which Bertolt Brecht presents himself – or an image
and legend of himself – to posterity. The earlier of those poems
– *Vom armen B.B.* (1919) – contains this stanza:

> Gegen Morgen in der grauen Frühe pissen die Tannen,
> Und ihr Ungeziefer, die Vögel, fängt an zu schrein.
> Um die Stunde trink ich mein Glas in der Stadt aus und schmeisse
> Den Tabakstummel weg und schlafe beunruhigt ein.

> (In the grey light before morning the pine-trees piss
> And their vermin, the birds, raise their twitter and cheep.
> At that hour I drain my glass in town, then throw
> The cigar butt away and worriedly go to sleep.)

More than any other word here the shock effect of 'piss' serves
to create that image of the hard-bitten, unsentimental,
thoroughly urban and would-be proletarian character whom
Brecht's poem is designed to project. The same word and effect
occur in these lines from Apollinaire's poem *Les Fiançailles*,
dedicated to Picasso and going back to 1902:

> Les becs de gaz pissaient leur flamme au clair de lune
> Des croque-morts avec des bocks tintaient des glas.

> (Into moonlight the gas-lamps pissed their flames
> Undertakers with beer glasses rang the knell.)

Apollinaire's lines are romantic where Brecht's are strenuously
anti-romantic since the much more appropriate 'pissing' of the
gas-lamps conveys the squalor of the modern city and the whole
poem laments the 'extermination' of lambs and shepherds, the
'drowning' of one 'ceremony of innocence.' Unlike the 'I' of
Brecht's poem, the 'I' of Apollinaire's 'drinks the stars by the
glassful,' a metaphor in stark contrast both with the beer glasses
of the undertakers in his poem and with Brecht's draining of his
glass. But the two poets were alike not only in their eclecticism
and plagiarisms, but in their use of shock effects. 'Surprise is
the most powerful modern device,' Apollinaire wrote in an essay.

Another early poem by Apollinaire, *Merlin et la vieille femme*
in *Alcools*, is dominated by the polarity of two images, that of the
'bleeding light' that makes 'clouds flow like a menstrual flux'
and that of the 'hawthorn in flower.' This poem, still very much
in the Symbolist manner, with a special debt to the hermetic
poems of Gérard de Nerval, invests the recurrent image of

'l'aubépine en fleurs' with a regenerative significance contrasted with the cruelty of merely physical 'birth, copulation
and death.' The same image re-appears in a poem of the
Second World War, in Louis Aragon's *Santa Espina*:[19]

> Et l'on verra tomber du front du Fils de l'Homme
> La couronne de sang symbole du malheur
> Et l'Homme chantera tout haut cette fois comme
> Si la vie était belle et l'aubépine en fleurs
>
> (And from the brow of the Son of Man we'll see
> The crown of blood symbol of suffering fall
> And this time loud will Man sing out as though
> Life were worth living and the thorn in flower).

These war-time poems by Aragon broke with his earlier
practice both as a Surrealist poet and as one who applied avant-
garde techniques to Communist propaganda as crude as this
from *Front-rouge* (1930):

> Voici la catastrophe apprivoisée
> Voici docile enfin la bondissante panthère
> l'Histoire menée en laisse par la Troisième Internationale
> Le train rouge s'ébranle et rien ne l'arrêtera
> UR
> SS
> UR
> SS
> UR
> SS
> Il n' y a personne qui reste en arrière
> agitant les mouchoirs Tout le monde est en marche
> UR
> SS ...
>
> (Here is the catastrophe tamed
> Here is the leaping panther tamed at last
> History led on the leash by the Third International
> The red train moves off and nothing will stop it ...
> No one will stay behind
> waving handkerchiefs
> The whole world's on the move ...)

and so forth. André Gide welcomed the break as a 'renaissance'
of 'direct poetry,' as opposed to 'cerebral poetry,' and Cyril

Connolly described Aragon as 'the first poet of the United Nations to make music out of the war.' If that 'renaissance' came to nothing, the specious rhetoric of the passage quoted from *Santa Espina* – different from the rhetoric of *Front-rouge* only in its deliberate resort to traditional lyrical clichés and stock responses more patriotic and religious than international – tells us why.

Apollinaire cannot be blamed for this particular concurrence, but his later poems did provide a precedent for the pastiche 'renaissance' hailed by André Gide, as well as for such genuine lyricism as Aragon's *Le Crève-coeur* and *Les Yeux d'Elsa* also contain. Apollinaire's basic naïveté – maintained despite much that is 'cerebral,' deliberate and 'faux-naïf' in his work – redeems many of his lapses, even in the sequences of love and war poems written towards the end of his life. It was the inter-war period, with its demands for a total ideological commitment, that tended to 'drown' the 'ceremony of innocence' everywhere and make naïveté a crime. The political utopianism so striking in the modernist movements of the pre-1914 era had given poetic imagination a scope and impetus that rarely outlasted the experience first of mass slaughter, then of perpetually clashing ideologies, factions and national ambitions throughout the next half-century. But for those utopian premises, the realistic war poems of Wilfred Owen, Isaac Rosenberg and Siegfried Sassoon would have lacked the sharp edge of pity and anger that distinguishes them from most of the poetry written by combatants in the Second World War.

6   A comprehensive survey of twentieth-century war poetry would have to embrace the political poetry of the twenties and thirties, both militant and pacifist, and especially the poetry occasioned by the Spanish Civil War. For the same reason it would have to embrace the German and Russian 'war poetry' and anti-war poetry written after the Second World War, as well as poems occasioned by the wars in Korea and Vietnam; and it would have to consider poems about war written before the event, such as Georg Heym's apocalyptic poem *Der Krieg*, written in 1911. Much of the most durable war poetry of the Second World War was written by non-

combatants or by men of the Résistance, like Paul Eluard and René Char. In the era of total politics, in fact, war poetry has become continuous, ubiquitous and hardly distinguishable from any other kind of poetry.

Apart from resistance poetry – which includes work produced by reluctant conscripts, by the victims of totalitarian discrimination and by civilians or guerillas in occupied countries – the only war poetry that matters by combatants in the Second World War was the British and American, since no other combatants in the war still had the same freedom to write and publish what they pleased as their predecessors in the First World War.

> To fight without hope is to fight with grace,
> The self reconstructed, the false heart repaired.

Those lines from Herbert Read's *To a Conscript of 1940*[20] are written from the point of view of a survivor of the First World War, and one who had never ceased to reflect on his experiences of it. Yet their mood is extraordinarily similar to that of T.S. Eliot's *Four Quartets* – the work of a poet who was a combatant in neither war – and to that of the young British and American poets of the generation to which the poem is addressed. Behind the stoicism of those lines one senses the experience not only of active service in 'the war to end all wars' but of the never-ending war that began in 1917. Their stoicism was shared by Keith Douglas, the most mature and receptive of the British poets, who died on active service in the Second World War. Douglas was not a pacifist, neither was he an Anarcho-Syndicalist like Herbert Read, or a Christian, like T.S. Eliot; but Douglas fought 'without hope' and 'with grace.' In a letter to his friend J.C. Hall he wrote: 'To be sentimental or emotional now is dangerous to oneself and to others. To trust anyone or to admit any hope of a better world is criminally foolish, as foolish as it is to stop working for it.'[21] Behind that statement, too, lies the awareness of what has gone before, and it is this awareness – not only of what had been happening in literature internationally, an awareness quite as marked in the work of Sidney Keyes, but of what had been happening to the very fabric of Western civilization – that sets Douglas apart from the other British 'war poets' of his generation. Replying to the charge that he had failed as a poet, in the same letter of 1943, Douglas himself made that point: 'Only someone who is out of touch, by which I mean first hand touch, with what has happened outside England – and from a cultural point of view I wish it had affected English life more – could make that criticism.'

That Keith Douglas was also aware of his predecessors of the First World War is attested by his tribute to Isaac Rosenberg – 'Rosenberg I only repeat what you were saying' – in *Desert Flowers*. Yet unlike the debt of Alun Lewis to Edward Thomas or the debt of Sidney Keyes to Yeats, Rilke, Eliot and other poets, the literary influence on Keith Douglas did not prevent him from responding to the immediate experience of his wartime life. He had the advantage both of a painter's eye for significant detail and of a maturity far in advance of his years. (Douglas was only twenty-four when he was killed in June 1944, but his *Collected Poems* includes work written at the age of fourteen, and his skill, assurance and range of observation had steadily increased ever since that precocious beginning.) The very roughness of structure and texture which J.C. Hall felt to be unpoetic – or, as Douglas corrected him, unlyrical – in his later poems has to do with the openness to experience that was his strength, as it was the strength of Isaac Rosenberg and other poets of the First World War. Once again it was Douglas himself who explained why smoothness and euphony would have been inappropriate:

I don't know if you have come across the word Bullshit, it is an army word and signifies humbug and unnecessary detail. It symbolizes what I think must be got rid of – the mass of irrelevancies, of 'attitudes,' 'approaches,' propaganda, ivory towers, etc. . . . that stands between us and our problems and what we have to do about them. To write about the themes which have been concerning me lately in lyric and abstract form would be immense bullshitting. . . . I suppose I reflect the cynicism and the careful absence of expectation (it is not quite the same thing as apathy) with which I view the world. . . . I never tried to write about war . . . until I had experienced it.[21]

The 'cynicism' and 'careful absence of expectation' have already been connected with Douglas's awareness of what had preceded the war. The same awareness told him that, however necessary and worth fighting, this war would not finally resolve the conflicts or eradicate the evils from which it sprang. For all his courage and efficiency as a soldier, therefore, Douglas remained partly detached. The persistent premonition that he would not survive the war made him at once adventurous and ironic. Because he fought 'without hope' and 'with grace' – that is, with an old-fashioned gallantry that left him free at times to convert his tank into an ambulance for wounded men, as he records in his prose account of desert warfare, *Alamein to Zem Zem*[22] – his critical intelligence made him wary of 'humbug' even in himself. *Alamein to Zem Zem* begins like this:

> To say that I thought of the Battle of Alamein as an ordeal sounds pompous: but I did think of it as an important test, which I was interested in passing. I observed these battles partly as an exhibition – that is to say that I went through them a little like a visitor from the country going to a great show, or like a child in a factory – a child sees the brightness and efficiency of steel machines and endless belts slapping round and round, without caring or knowing what it is all there for. When I could order my thoughts I looked for more significant things than appearances; I still looked – I cannot avoid it – for something decorative, poetic or dramatic. . . . I never lost the certainty that the experience of battle was something I must have.

That balance between involvement and detachment is as characteristic of Douglas as the way in which he combined ironic observation with a search for 'more significant things than appearances,' a search apparent not only in metaphysical poems like *Time Eating* but in his love poems and war poems proper. At first sight his poem *Aristocrats* reads only like a satirical exposure of upper-class British attitudes carried over from school playing fields and the codes of civilian life into the business of war:

> The noble horse with courage in his eye
> clean in the bone, looks up at shellburst:
> away fly the images of the shires
> but he puts the pipe back in his mouth.
>
> Peter was unfortunately killed by an 88:
> it took his legs away, he died in the ambulance.
> I saw him crawling on the sand; he said
> It's most unfair, they've shot my foot off.
>
> How can I live among this gentle
> obsolescent breed of heroes, and not weep?

> Unicorns, almost,
> for they are falling into two legends
> in which their stupidity and chivalry
> are celebrated. Each, fool and hero, will be an immortal.[23]

It is Douglas's historical awareness, as well as his refusal to be hoodwinked, that gives this poem a pathos made more poignant by its ironies. Douglas himself was very much a product of pre-war upper-class England, with all the virtues and gallantry of that 'obsolescent breed of heroes,' but without the stupidity that could take its code for granted. Yet Douglas knew that the very virtues which he and his fellow officers were fighting to defend could not long survive even a victorious war. *Aristocrats* is more than a satirical poem, and more than a compassionate poem, because in it Douglas confronts the hopelessness and the grace of his own part in the war that cost him his life. It is a quarrel not only with others, but with himself; and a memorial not only to the heroism of others, but to his own. Perhaps Douglas also knew in his heart that his own truthfulness in the face of corporate experience owed a good deal to his upbringing, to a liberalism and individualism that were no less in danger of becoming obsolete than the reliance on fair play which the same institutions served to inculcate. The liberalism and individualism, in any case, are inseparable from Douglas's response to an illiberal and largely totalitarian war; and all his wartime poems as well as *Alamein to Zem Zem* show that he had no illusions about the anomaly of his own involvement in that war.

There is less ambivalence in Randall Jarrell's *The Death of the Ball Turret Gunner*. In this poem the individual serviceman is seen as a mere accessory in a mechanized war, and the gunner of the poem could just as well be a German or a Russian as an American because it is assumed that the claims of the State on the individual are as total as those of the modern war machine. The serviceman's attitude to the war becomes an irrelevance, since his moral assent is not required by either machine:

> From my mother's sleep I fell into the State
> And I hunched in its belly till my wet fur froze.
> Six miles from earth, loosed from its dream of life
> I woke to black flak and the nightmare fighters.
> When I died they washed me out of the turret with a hose.[24]

The inhumanity of the State and war machines is suggested by the word 'fur' in the second line, with its animal associations which the rest of the poem does not explain or elaborate; but the last line implies that even the animal order has more grace than the mechanical, for the gunner is now reduced to so much waste matter that must be removed in the interest of efficiency.

When Keith Douglas, in the last stanza of *Aristocrats*, wrote about his British officers that 'the plains were their cricket pitch/ and in the mountains the tremendous drop fences/brought down some of the runners,' he was making a tacit comparison between 'these obsolescent' sportsmen 'with their famous unconcern' and every other kind of participant in the Second World War, including its civilian victims and such conscripts as the one commemorated in Randall Jarrell's poem. Douglas himself could 'fight with grace' because he retained his moral freedom and integrity, thanks to a code incomprehensible to those others, the majority no longer dying 'like cattle' – as in Wilfred Owen's poem of the First World War – but turning into refuse like metal parts that have sprung a leak. Jarrell's poem, on the other hand, could never have been written but for a tacit comparison of his totally mechanized order with one that permits a measure of freedom and grace.

8

A PERIOD LOOSE AT
ALL ENDS

1   THE lines by Herbert Read, Keith Douglas and
Randall Jarrell quoted in connection with the Second World
War are alike in being stylistically unadventurous, if not
positively retrogressive, in comparison with the innovations of
the period that ended in 1917. All three examples have a
metrical freedom close to speech rhythms, but the dilution of
Imagist practice is especially striking in Herbert Read's resort to
discursive or abstract statement, to end rhymes and stanza form,
and even to a simile in the concluding line: 'As he stood against
the fretted hedge, which was like white lace.' All three poems
achieve what Herbert Read calls 'organic form,' but the simile
in the last line of his poem does suggest a loss of faith in the
power of the bare image to embody meaning; and the condemnation of 'vague generalities' in the *Imagist Manifesto* of 1913
might well be applied to the words 'death and darkness and
despair' in the fourth stanza:

> We went where you are going, into the rain and the mud;
>> We fought as you will fight
> With death and darkness and despair;
>> We gave what you will give – our brains and our blood.

One reason is that *To a Conscript of 1940* clearly aspires to the
condition of public poetry, like many poems written in the
same period by W.H.Auden, Stephen Spender and Cecil Day
Lewis, by Louis Aragon and Pierre Emmanuel, and by a great

number of poets with no ambition to be innovators or modernists. Paul Eluard, on the other hand, could write distinctly
public poems like his *Poésie et vérité 1942*, without modifying
his style, a style evolved out of Dadaist and Surrealist experiment. What is more relevant than the distinction between
private and public poetry is the widespread tendency towards
retrenchment already apparent in the poetry of the twenties
and thirties. More often than not this retrenchment included a
return to national traditions, as opposed to the international
Futurism and modernism of 1912. Even T.S. Eliot's *Four Quartets*
– poems which it would be crude and inadequate to describe as
public poems – participate in the general trend towards an
explicitness incompatible with the more extreme innovations of
modernism, whether Symbolist, Imagist, Expressionist or
Surrealist; and with some of Eliot's own earlier practices, for
that matter. The emphasis on tradition in Eliot's critical
writings is in line with the general trend in so far as it is an
emphasis on national tradition, on religious and cultural homogeneity, and on an impersonality opposed to the individualism
of the pre-1914 era. What the First World War brought home
to everybody, to conservatives and revolutionaries alike, is the
extent to which collective forces could overwhelm the individual
and overrule his choices, just when the liberty of the individual
seemed more secure than ever. It is true that this security had
been questioned by poets before 1914, especially by those who
recognized that it was the privilege of a social minority in
countries similarly privileged; but even those pre-war poets
who revolted against the security, or foresaw the coming era
of mass movements and mass pressures, as Apollinaire did,
could not help taking their own conditions for granted.

   In England, America, Germany, France, Russia, Italy and
Spain the avant-garde movements disintegrated under the
pressure of political ideologies, in many cases before their
actual suppression by totalitarian governments. 'In the late
1920s,' Frederick Brown wrote in his essay *On Louis Aragon:
Silence and History*,[1] 'the Surrealist movement began to collapse.
Its ranks were thinned by suicides, personal quarrels, and defec-
tions to the Communist party which, almost from the beginning,
had coerced the Surrealists to question and justify their existence
as a revolutionary group.' Frederick Brown demonstrates the

inevitability of this collapse by tracing Louis Aragon's attempts to reconcile the aesthetic of Surrealism with a political commitment that culminated in the writing of Aragon's poem *Front-rouge*. The Surrealists, Brown shows, 'wished to short-circuit the world' by 'equating mind and world.' He quoted André Breton's *Second Manifesto*:

> It is clear ... that Surrealism is not seriously interested in whatever is being produced next door under the pretext of art or of anti-art, of philosophy or of anti-philosophy, in a word, in anything whose end is not the annihilation of being in a flash, interior and blind. ... What could those people who harbour some concern about the place they will occupy *in the world* expect to gain from the Surrealist experiment?

In other words, Surrealism insists on the autonomy of the conscious and subconscious minds of individuals, at the expense of the very social and economic realities on which Communist dogmatism insists with an unprecedented exclusiveness. André Breton's comments on *Front-rouge* sum up the quarrel between the assumptions of two eras, assumptions which Aragon vainly tried to bring together in a poem at once ideologically directed and structurally free:

> I owe it to myself to declare that *Red Front* does not open a new path in poetry; and it would be idle to offer it as a model for poets living in the present age simply because, in such a realm, an objective starting-point cannot avoid being an objective end-point, as in this poem *which returns to the exterior subject*. ... It was already true a century ago (of Hegel's Aesthetics) that, in the more advanced forms of poetry, the subject must inevitably appear as something irrelevant; since then it has even become impossible to state the subject in advance. ...

That two eras as well as two basic artistic principles are at odds in Aragon's practice here is also brought out by Frederick Brown's final comment on 'the apocalyptic assumptions of a previous generation, the sublime optimism that made an Aragon, as creator, adhere first to Surrealism, then to Communism.' These, Frederick Brown concludes, 'strike us as belonging to some violent childhood.'

2   The distinction between public and private poetry is valid if we apply it not so much to subjects or themes as to the relationship between poet and reader posited by the very structure and texture of poems on any subject whatever. The very absence of subjects or theme in Surrealist poetry – or the impossibility of categorizing and rationalizing its subjects or themes – points back to its Romantic-Symbolist ancestry and to its essentially exploratory nature. That is why André Breton objected to the 'objective starting-point,' which must also be an objective 'end-point,' in Aragon's *Front-rouge*. Most of the English 'political' poetry of the thirties could make little use of Surrealist or other modernist innovations because its primary aim was not exploratory, but hortatory or descriptive; it posited a relationship between poet and reader based on common experience, common attitudes, common knowledge. (Its weaknesses often sprang from the circumstance that this community did not really exist, because the poets in question were divided and protected from most of those on whose behalf they would have liked to speak, by the barriers of class and education.) It was from the point of view of an exploratory poet that Ezra Pound could write in 1931: 'All the developments in English verse since 1910 are due almost wholly to Americans. In fact, there is no longer any reason to call it English verse, and there is no present reason to think of England at all.'[2] Some thirty-five years later, in his Introduction to the revised *Faber Book of Modern Verse*, its American editor, Donald Hall, remarked: 'Sometimes I wonder if England ever came to modern art at all. While Stravinsky and Picasso and Henry Moore – to mention one Englishman at least – were inventing forms and techniques, W. H. Auden was "experimenting" with sonnets and off-rhyme and Anglo-Saxon metres.' Auden and Dylan Thomas are the only British-born poets represented in H. M. Enzensberger's international *Museum of Modern Poetry* (1960), as compared to ten American-born, sixteen French, five Polish and four Czechoslovak poets, to pick out a few of the nationalities represented there. Yet Britain would undoubtedly be well represented in any international anthology of the best poems written during the same period, if modernity were not the criterion; and Enzensberger himself has argued that the modern poetry exhibited in his 'museum' is a

183

thing of the past, that it 'can be continued only as a conventional game.'

This brings us back to the difference between a primarily exploratory or experimental poetry and one primarily concerned with its function as a means of communication. It was an excellent American poet, Robert Frost, who formulated the basic premise of those non-modernists whose work tends to be public in the sense suggested above: 'In literature it is our business to give people the thing that will make them say, "Oh yes, I know what you mean." It is never to tell them something they don't know, but something they know and hadn't thought of saying. It must be something they recognize.'[3] Needless to say, too rigid an insistence on that principle would severely restrict the scope of twentieth-century poets, as it has restricted the scope of lesser poets than Robert Frost, even where no totalitarian programme for the arts enforced its extreme application. Robert Frost himself offered a corrective and acknowledged the degree to which all good poetry must be exploratory, when he wrote: 'For me the initial delight is the surprise of remembering something I didn't know I knew.'

The difference, then, is a difference of degree, and it has to do with what kind of inner and outer realities a poet considers himself free to explore. The Surrealists set no limit to their freedom, at least as far as inner realities, including the subconscious, are concerned; and Dylan Thomas too exercised that kind of freedom in his earlier poems, not only telling people something they didn't know, but telling them something he didn't know before the poem brought it to light. What Robert Frost forgot to include in his statement is that even the things which people don't know about themselves, or about anything else, can be recognized when they appear in a poem, though Frost implies as much when he speaks of the delight of 'remembering something I didn't know I knew.' That is why poets who cared as little as Dylan Thomas did about being understood, about speaking for others rather than for themselves, could awaken a wider and deeper response than other poets scrupulously conscious of what their readers might be expected to know and not to know.

However concerned with their moral and social functions, therefore, the best poets of the inter-war period achieved a balance between personal and public utterance, between exploration and reference, between the poem's freedom merely to 'be' and the inescapable tendency of words to convey or imply meaning. This is as true of Mayakovsky and Pasternak in Soviet Russia as of Montale and Ungaretti in Fascist Italy, though the greater the public pressure on poets to conform, the greater was their need to safeguard a little area of freedom by resorting to a 'hermetic' art. The cultural bureaucrats responded by assuming, quite rightly in most cases, that anything they could not understand must be subversive and heterodox. Even Bertolt Brecht, the most consistent theorist and practitioner of a politically committed poetry that was also modern and intelligent, availed himself of Chinese models in order to escape the consequences of living under a Communist régime, writing short poems whose imagery could not easily be translated into unambiguous statements; and Brecht had become a master of subterfuge long before he exposed himself to that danger.

3   In the middle twenties Brecht began to evolve a theory of poetry directly opposed both to Romantic-Symbolist conceptions of 'pure' or 'absolute' poetry and to the individualistic premises of early twentieth-century modernism. Like the theories of most poets, Brecht's were preceded by practice, by his own poems written since the end of the war, a representative selection from which was published in 1927 in his book *Hauspostille* (Manual of Piety). In the same year Brecht, who had been invited to act as judge for a poetry competition, reported on the work of some four hundred poets who had submitted entries, and refused to award a prize. In the report Brecht wrote that 'apart from my own productions I have never been especially interested in lyrical poetry'; and he went on to declare that 'poetry undoubtedly ought to be something that can easily be assessed for its utility value. . . . All great poems have a documentary value. They contain their authors' way of speaking, that of important men.'[4] Brecht admitted that he thought little of the poetry of Rilke, Stefan George and Franz Werfel, three of the most widely read and imitated German poets of the time, a dislike substantiated in a much later note (1940): 'The poet now represents only himself. In George the

The Truth of Poetry

pontifical line, under the mask of contempt for politics, becomes openly counter-revolutionary, i.e. not only reactionary, but an active and effective instrument of the counter-revolution.'⁵ In another comment on his report of 1927 Brecht insists that the poetry written under the influence of the three poets mentioned is neither useful nor beautiful.

I don't wish to make Stefan George responsible for the World War. But I see no reason why he should isolate himself. I believe that this naïve sage wanted to show all those who share his opinions that he was incomparable and unique. After a brief examination of his aesthetic value I had to conclude that he was fit for police duties. And for a policeman an attitude of pure enjoyment in the midst of an intricate nexus of crimes is not the right one. It is not a police-man's business merely to register certain conflicting emotions on his face. . . . I go on to assert that almost all the poetry of the declining bourgeoisie, but certainly its representative part, shows too many class-war tendencies to have a purely aesthetic value.

Even in this radical application of Marxian principles to literary criticism (or polemics) Brecht pays lip service at least to considerations of beauty rather than utility; and it is important to bear in mind that Stefan George, Brecht's principle target here and elsewhere, did assume the active function of prophet and leader of a cultural élite, despite his early beginnings as a disciple of Mallarmé and his professions of a pure aestheticism. Nor does Brecht deny the value of poetry as the expression of personality, though his notions of what constitutes an 'important man' clearly differ from those of the 'declining bourgeoisie.' What his own notions were can be deduced from the 'prole-tarian' image of himself in the poem *Of Poor B.B.* in *Hauspostille*. What is much more crucial, Brecht's definitive edition of the *Hauspostille*, prepared in the last decade of his life and published after his death,⁶ includes his three *Psalms*, prose poems whose free imagery derives from the visionary poems of Rimbaud and is close to Surrealist practice:

6. Das ist der Sommer. Scharlachene Winde erregen die Ebenen, die Gerüche werden Ende Juni masslos. Unge-heure Gesichte zähnefletschender nackter Männer wandern in grossen Höhen südwärts. . . .

7. In den Hütten ist das Licht der Nächte wie Lachs. Man feiert die Auferstehung des Fleisches.

(6.   This is summer. Scarlet winds stir up the
plains, the smells at the end of June grow boundless.
Monstrous visions of teeth-gnashing naked men travel
southwards at great heights. . . .

7.   In cottages the nocturnal light is like salmon.
The resurrection of the flesh is celebrated.)

Other 'psalms' and poems written in the same manner, in 1920
and 1921, were collected posthumously in the second and eighth
volumes of Brecht's *Gedichte*. In a note of 1938[7] Brecht mentions
that he sang the psalms to a guitar accompaniment and defends
himself against the charge of 'formalism.' 'Because I am an
innovator in my field, some people keep on shouting that I'm
a formalist. They do not find the old forms in my work, and,
worse, they find new ones, and then they infer that it is the forms
that interest me, but I have discovered that I'm rather inclined
to deprecate the formal element. I have studied the old forms
of poetry, story-telling, drama and theatre at various times and
only given them up when they stood in the way of what I
wanted to say.' As Brecht knew as well as anybody, contemporary poets not fortunate enough to be living and working
outside Russia, as Brecht was, were simply not free to say what
they wanted to say; and in the fifties Brecht became explicit
about the need for new forms, though in a note not published
in his lifetime: 'Only new contents permit new forms. Indeed
they demand them. For if new contents were forced into old
forms, at once you would have a recurrence of that disastrous
division between content and form, because the form that is old
would separate from the content that would be new. The life
which is everywhere assuming new forms in our society, in
which the foundations are being shifted, can be neither rendered
nor influenced by a literature in the old form.' The same division
between form and content, Brecht argues, is a characteristic of
the 'bankruptcy of literature in the late capitalist epoch.' In the
same way Brecht warned against the narrow interpretation of
'realism' that was cramping, and still cramps, Communist
literature. As an example of social, if not socialist realism, *avant
la lettre* he cites Shelley's *The Mask of Anarchy*, which he also
translated – a striking instance of Brecht's ability to make use
of the most diverse models, from ancient Greek drama to

187

Arthur Waley's translations from the Chinese, from Villon to Kipling, from Luther's Bible to jazz lyrics and cabaret songs. It was almost certainly with his own practices in mind that Brecht argued against the suppression of 'destructive and anarchistic poetry' by the State, which 'damages pro-State literature if it suppresses anti-State literature.'[8] A retrospective note of 1940 on his own *Hauspostille* judges it to be not only anarchic but 'dehumanized,' since in these poems 'beauty adheres to wrecks, rags become delicate. The sublime rolls in the dust, meaninglessness is saluted as a liberator. The poet has lost solidarity even with himself: risus mortis. But it's not without strength.'[9]

Brecht's most revolutionary act as a poet was what he called his 'language-washing.' It was by stripping his diction of ornamental and sentimental accretions that he avoided the pitfalls of 'committed' verse, and so assumed an exemplary importance for so many younger poets after the Second World War. Although his extraordinarily varied poetic output – which fills some two thousand pages in the posthumous collected edition, with more poems likely to be added – includes a good deal of didactic political verse, he maintained his own freedom to say what he wanted to say. His theoretical statements, too, are truly dialectic. 'Art *is* an autonomous realm,' he wrote in 1940, 'though in no circumstances an autarchic one'; and this in connection with another Romantic poem of the 'bourgeois era,' Wordsworth's 'She was a Phantom of Delight.'[10] A note of 1944 on Arthur Waley's translations from the Chinese demonstrates that 'there is no difference between didacticism and entertainment. . . . In its didactic as in its other works, poetry succeeds in enhancing our enjoyment of life. It sharpens the senses and turns even pain into pleasure.'[11]

By far the greater part of Brecht's poetry is designed to give people 'something they recognize'; but Brecht's directness could serve to make a point as devastating in its exposure of Communist smugness as so many of his other political poems are in their exposure of capitalist exploitation or Fascist militarism. His poem on the workers' uprising in East Berlin, *Die Lösung*,[12] is a good example of Brecht's ability to say the unexpected thing about public affairs:*

* Permission to quote the text of this poem here was refused by the copyright holder.

The Solution
After the uprising on June 17th
The Secretary of the Authors' Union
Had leaflets distributed in the Stalinallee
Which said that the people
Had forfeited the government's confidence
And could only win it back
By redoubled labour. Wouldn't it
Be simpler in that case if the government
Dissolved the people and
Elected another?

This poem was not included in the selection from his *Buckower Elegien* which Brecht published in his *Versuche 13* of 1954, and Brecht's dealings with political authorities and powers of every kind are reminiscent of James Joyce's motto, 'Silence, exile and cunning.' Yet *Die Lösung* is direct enough, making its point without recourse to metaphor, heightened language or formal prosody. From the *Hauspostille* onwards, effrontery had always been part of Brecht's poetic gesture. In late poems like *Die Lösung* the effrontery is conveyed not by posturizing, strong words and forceful rhythms, but by the seeming laxity and randomness of the presentation. It is as though the poet could not be bothered to turn his prose into 'poetry'; but in their own way those lines answer almost all the demands of the *Imagist Manifesto*: 'To use the language of common speech, but to employ always the exact word, not merely the decorative word. To create new rhythms as the expression of new moods. To allow absolute freedom in the choice of subject. To present an image. We are not a school of painters, but we believe that poets should render particulars exactly and not deal with vague generalities. To produce poetry that is hard and clear, never blurred and indefinite. Finally, most of us believe that concentration is the very essence of poetry.' One could cavil about the fourth clause, 'to present an image,' if the later practice of the Imagists themselves had not shown that lyrical verse is one thing, political verse another.

That Brecht was aware of the chief author of the *Imagist Manifesto*, Ezra Pound, is attested by a short poem written in the early forties, *E.P. Auswahl seines Grabsteins*, which takes issue not with Ezra Pound's later political affiliations but with the aestheticism which Brecht must have regarded as their premise:

> *E.P. Auswahl seines Grabsteins*
> Die Herstellung von Versteinerungen
> Ist ein mühsames Geschäft und
> Kostspielig. Ganze Städte
> Müssen in Schutt gelegt werden
> Und unter Umständen umsonst
> Wenn die Fliege oder der Farn
> Schlecht plaziert wurde. Überdies
> Ist der Stein unserer Städte nicht haltbar
> Und auch Versteinerungen
> Halten sich nicht sicher.[13]

> (*E.P. L'Election de Son Sépulchre*
> The production of petrifactions
> Is an arduous business and
> Expensive. Whole towns
> Must be reduced to rubble
> And at times in vain –
> If the fly or the fern
> Was badly placed. Furthermore
> The stone of our towns is not lasting
> And even petrifications
> Can't be relied on to last.)

Here the satire is as cryptic and indirect as it is open and direct in *The Solution*, because the subject itself is comparatively esoteric, as well as being delicate. What is evidently implied is a dialectical relationship between art intended to be autarchic and the social conditions required to sustain it. 'Petrifaction' or fossilization stands for the process by which living organisms – including human lives – are transmuted by such an art into monuments. Brecht's implicit alternative is an art that transmutes as little as possible, insisting on the primacy of immediate human needs. With a number of blatant exceptions, due to his own political affiliations, Brecht's poetry avoided monumentalism and the 'production of petrifactions,' because his social consciousness did not need to be projected ideologically, but informed his responses to every kind of experience, every phenomenon touched upon in his work. Although it is conceivable that the casualness which was his alternative to

monumentalism will reduce much of his poetry to the order of
occasional verse, his occasions remain relevant and crucial
enough, his tone of voice distinctive enough behind all the
stylistic masks and conventions of which he made use, to have
justified his claim, 'I need no gravestone,' until now.

> *Ich benötige keinen Grabstein*
> Ich benötige keinen Grabstein, aber
> Wenn ihr einen für mich benötigt
> Wünschte ich, es stünde darauf:
> Er hat Vorschläge gemacht. Wir
> Haben sie angenommen.
> Durch eine solche Inschrift wären
> Wir alle geehrt.[14]

> (I need no gravestone, but
> If you need one for me
> I wish the inscription would read:
> He made suggestions. We
> Have acted on them.
> Such an epitaph would
> Honour us all.)

Only one other twentieth-century poet I can think of,
William Carlos Williams, succeeded as well as Brecht in inte-
grating his poetic and social selves to the extent of really
overcoming the Romantic-Symbolist dichotomies. Both became
masters of the seemingly off-hand, seemingly effortless manner
that leaves no gaps between the thing said and the way of
saying it, between what the poem enacts and the person who
enacts it. Of the two, Williams was by far the more sensuous and
visual poet, and he presented 'images' rather than moralities;
but both poets made a new purity out of the very stuff which
most of their predecessor poets had condemned in advance as
impure, because it was ordinary and workaday. The similarity
of tone is striking as soon as Williams addresses himself to the
community, instead of applying himself to the individual people
and things that constitute it. So in *Tract*:

> No wreaths please –
> especially no hot-house flowers.
> Some common memento is better,
> something he prized and is known by:

> his old clothes – a few books perhaps –
> God knows what! You realize
> how we are about these things,
> my townspeople –
> something will be found – anything
> even flowers if he had come to that.
> So much for the hearse.[15]

Because Brecht had to pass through a phase of individualistic revolt – that of his play *Baal* and the poems in *Hauspostille* – before becoming identified with ordinariness, Williams succeeded much better than he in the rendering of 'all trades, their gear and tackle and trim,' and indeed of the 'pied beauty' celebrated by Gerard Manley Hopkins. Here Brecht was inhibited by his political preoccupations, his concern with those realities which could almost turn 'a conversation about trees' into a crime; and for a long time, gentleness and the kind of sympathy that flows freely into other persons and things seemed suspect to him, because of their associations with 'bourgeois' sentiment, the luxury of people whose feelings and energies are otherwise unemployed. Brecht did write poems in praise of people, things, places and – repeatedly – trees; and his poem *Die Liebenden* (from his opera *Mahagonny*) is the most memorable of many in which harsh realities yield a tenderness of their own. Brecht's poem *An die Nachgeborenen* (To Posterity) refers to the circumstances that make such poems stand out from the body of his work:

> Dabei wissen wir doch:
> Auch der Hass gegen die Niedrigkeit
> Verzerrt die Züge.
> Auch der Zorn über das Unrecht
> Macht die Stimme heiser. Ach, wir
> Die wir den Boden bereiten wollten für Freundlichkeit,
> Konnten selber nicht freundlich sein. . . .

> (And yet we know well:
> Even hatred of vileness
> Distorts a man's features.
> Even anger at injustice
> Makes hoarse his voice. Ah, we
> Who desired to prepare the soil for kindness
> Could not ourselves be kind.)

4   The historical importance of Brecht's reversal of the dominant poetic trends since Baudelaire – and indeed since Romanticism – needs little emphasis. Most of his poetry is public to a degree reminiscent of classical eras, and much of it is popular without condescension, even where Brecht had deliberate recourse to media, like the ballad, sonnet and song, that seemed incapable of being truly revived and modernized. Unlike the poetry of William Carlos Williams, little of Brecht's is impersonal in the sense suggested by Pasternak when he wrote: 'In art the man is silent and the image speaks.' Brecht's personality, his wily intelligence and his moral toughness, are present even in poems that come close to being pastiche; but not obtrusively so in the later poems, because the personality itself has been stripped down to essentials.

Pasternak too had to revise his early reliance on the image and on the music of poetry. 'We drag everyday things into prose for the sake of poetry. We entice prose into poetry for the sake of music,' he wrote in *Safe Conduct* (1931), but also: 'Poetry as I understand it flows through history and in collaboration with real life.'[16] The autonomous image and the music of poetry had to be reconciled with a historical consciousness that had become inescapable in the age of total politics. In an interview given shortly before his death, Pasternak said: 'In writing as in speaking the music of the word is never just a matter of sound. It does not result from the harmony of vowels and consonants. It results from the relation between the speech and the meaning. And meaning – content – must always lead.'[17]

Except where poetry insulated itself against this historical consciousness, or was preserved from it by a continuity of traditions and institutions – in countries relatively undisrupted by war or revolution – the old dispute about the primacy of form or content assumed a new urgency and a new complexity. The question itself is rather like the one as to which came first, the chicken or the egg; but the answer in each individual case, the exact balance, to be struck by each poet between conscience and imagination, public and private concerns, communication and discovery, became truly difficult and problematic. National differences, too, asserted themselves with a vengeance after the international Futurism of 1912. In French, Italian and Spanish poetry, for instance, the primacy of 'form' was maintained much more stubbornly than in English, American, Russian and German poetry, for reasons not only social and political, but cultural and linguistic. Though the Surrealist movement broke up, Surrealist practice retained its hold on French poets up to the fifties and sixties – as in the work of Paul Eluard, Pierre Jean Jouve, Pierre Reverdy, Henri Michaux and René Char – while the public, popular and social poetry of Jacques Prévert was rarely taken as seriously by French critics as it was by critics outside France.

Dadaism, too, proved tenacious long after it had gone underground (to emerge after the Second World War). The sound poems of Kurt Schwitters set a precedent for much that seemed most new a decade after his death. Jean (or Hans) Arp, better known as a sculptor, wrote and published poems over a period of sixty years, beginning in 1903 with poems that anticipate Surrealism despite their *art nouveau* features. In his Dadaist poems proper, written from 1916 to shortly after the First World War, 'words, catchwords, sentences from daily newspapers and especially their advertisements became the basis for poetic constructions,' as Arp explained. Chance became an artistic principle, because Arp identified chance with reality and nature, as opposed to all that is willed and deliberate in conventional art. That principle, too, was to be revived by Concrete poetry, like Arp's use of verbal collage and his permutations of words and idioms. 'dada,' Arp wrote in 1931 or 1932, 'is for nonsense that doesn't mean stupidity. dada is nonsensical like nature and life. dada is for nature and against art. dada like nature wants to give everything its essential place.'[18] Most of those poems by Arp which he called 'unanchored,' because their words and things are not tied down to a preconceived meaning, are untranslatable, because they play too freely with their material, which is language. But in the twenties some of Arp's poems began to reveal an anchor that could be metaphysical or social:

> während die einen mit ihrer rechten hand auf
> ihre linke hand
> und mit ihrer linken hand auf ihre rechte hand
> zeigen
> beide hände voll zu tun haben
> und dennoch auf keinen grünen zweig kommen

wachsen die andern auf bäumen in den himmel
obwohl jemand da ist der dafür zu sorgen hat
dass die bäume nicht in den himmel wachsen. . . .[19]

(while some point with their right hands to their left hands
and with their left hands to their right hands
have their hands full
and so can't get to the top of the tree
others grow on trees into the sky
although there is someone whose business it is to see
that trees don't grow up to the sky. . . .)

Even here Arp plays changes on German idioms in a way that
cannot be fully rendered; but the anchor is visible in any
language, as in this passage from the same sequence:[20]

als ihm der boden unter den füssen fortgenommen wurde
heftete er sich mit seinen blicken an die decke
und sparte seine schuhe
so hing er regungslos wie ein scharadensack
und frönte dem abc des herren- und damenlosen leibes
es drängte ihn nicht einen befiederten schabrackenhiatus
                                        zu wichsen
er strebte weder danach ein held des tages noch ein
                                held der nacht zu werden. . . .

(when the ground was taken from under his feet
he attached himself to the ceiling with his eyes and
                                        saved his shoes
like that he hung motionless like a charade sack
and served the abc of the masterless and mistressless body
he was not impelled to wax a plumed caparison hiatus
he did not aspire to become either a hero of the day
                                or a hero of the night. . . .)

The anchoring of such poems is given away in the same
sequence, when Arp calls a shoe 'the emblem of senseless busy-
ness.' By 1930, when he wrote his sequence *Das Tagesgerippe*
(The Skeleton of Day), the exuberant nonsense of the Dada
period had yielded to a more sober, elegiac and largely retrospective mood, and even the verbal play had been discarded, as
in Section 7:[21]

wo sind die blätter
die glocken welken

es läutet nicht mehr in der erde
wo wir einst schritten
ist das licht zerrissen
die spuren der flügel führen ins leere
wo sind die lippen
wo sind die augen
grauenvoll zerschlug sich ihr herz zwischen den
häuptern
der letzte atemzug fällt aus dem körper wie ein
stein
wo wir einst sprachen flieht das blut aus dem feuer
und der gestaltlose kranz dreht sich im schwarzen
grund
unsichtbar für immer ist die schöne erde
die flügel schweben nie mehr um uns

(where are the leaves
the bells wilt
no ringing is heard in the earth
where once we walked
the light is torn
the wakes of wings lead into the void
where are the lips
where are the eyes
their heart between heads was horribly dashed to pieces
the last breath drops from the body like a stone
where once we talked our blood flees from the fire
and the shapeless wreath turns in the blackness below
for ever invisible is our beautiful earth
never again will the wings hover around us).

In the later poems, written in the next three decades, Arp's nonsense rarely lacks an ironic sting or an elegiac undertone. The principle of fortuitousness had lost most of its impact on people whose complacency was being thoroughly shaken up without the help of the arts, if it was not incapable of being shaken up by anything whatever. The sequence *Blatt um Feder um Blatt* of 1951–2 contains an epigram that could not be more explicit:

Nun hat die Angst die meisten Menschen verlassen,
und die Unendlichkeit hat kein gutes Wort
kein ängstigendes Wort mehr für sie.
Gähnende Leeren wachsen neben gähnenden Leeren.

(Now fear has abandoned the greater part of men
and infinity hasn't one kind word,
one fearful word to say to them.
Yawning voids grow next to yawning voids.)

Yet in the same sequence Arp still writes that 'Chance frees us
from the net of meaninglessness,' and 'We take refuge in deeper
games,' a statement literally true of the poems he continued to
write until shortly before his death in 1966.[22]

Arp's insistence on chance has more in common with the
Surrealist practice of 'automatic writing' than with the more
rigorously 'scientific' experiments in verbal analysis, verbal pat-
terning and verbal permutation of the Concrete poets. Another
way of putting it is that Arp's reliance on chance gave the
greatest possible scope to his imagination, as well as to his
ingenuity, since his games with words and idioms did not
exclude the free association of images. Just as William Carlos
Williams's reliance on minutely observed realities did not
prevent him from concluding that 'only the imagination is real,'
Arp's starting-point at the opposite end did not prevent him
from anchoring many of his poems in recognizable realities; and
even where Arp did not impose a preconceived meaning on his
poems, the nature of language saw to it that meanings were
released by his verbal structures.

Arp's identification of chance with nature implies a faith in
meanings which our normal use of language cannot apprehend;
and long before he became a master of comic nonsense Arp was
a visionary poet of a more conventional kind. In a poem written
in the late thirties, *Lied des Roten*,[23] Arp recalls the artists in the
Café Odéon of 'twenty years ago.' They vanish again and
'smoking eggs lie in their place.' The poem continues:

> wenn ich nicht acht gebe
> entsteht nun ein gedicht.
> trinken und singen fällt mir ein
> wir trinken und singen
> und die zeit vergeht.
> es singt und weht
> und wandert im licht.
> eines tages rascheln wir wie welke blätter fort
> zerfallen zu staub
> und werden wieder funken und sterne

und singen und trinken
und wandern selig in feurigen mänteln.

(if I'm not careful now
I shall write a poem.
drinking and singing occur to me.
we drink and sing
and time goes by.
it sings and wafts
and walks in the light.
one day we all rustle off like dead leaves
crumble to dust
and turn again into sparks and stars
and sing and drink
and blissfully walk in our fiery mantles.)

The subject of 'it sings and wafts' is not 'time.' The 'it' is impersonal, and its identity is not revealed. The cosmic and Biblical allusions in the poem point back to Arp's earliest, pre-modernist and pre-Dadaist, visions. Arp's 'nature' was never that of the naturalists, but a super-reality which words could not name but only let through when they had been shaken and broken up, as they were by Arp's nonsense. Despite the anchors, a concession to historical consciousness, Arp's use of language remained as different as possible from that of Brecht, who picked up his words and idioms where he found them and treated most of them as a solid, reliable currency.

5   A poem by Pedro Salinas renders the misgivings about names that have troubled so many modern poets and impelled them to resist demands for straightforward communication:

Por qué tienes nombre tú
día, miércoles?
Por qué tienes nombre tú
tiempo, otoño?
Alegría, pena, siempre
por qué tienes nombre: amor?

Se tu no tuvieras nombre,
Yo no sabría qué era,
ni cómo, ni cuándo. Nada.

Sabe el mar cómo se llama,
que es el mar? Saben los vientos
sus apellidos, del Sur
y del Norte, por encima
del puro soplo que son?

Si tu no tuvieras nombre,
todo sería primero,
inicial, todo inventado
por mí
intacto hasta el beso mío.
Gozo, amor: delicia lenta
de gozar, de amar, sin nombre.

Nombre, qué puñal clavado
en medio de un pecho cándido
que sería nuestro siempre
si fuese por su nombre![24]

(Why do you have a name,
day, Wednesday?
Why do you have a name,
season, autumn?
Happiness, pain, why always
do you have a name: love?

If you had no name
I should not know who it was
nor how nor when. Nothing.

Does the sea know what it's called,
that it is the sea? Do the winds know
their descriptions, south
and north, as well as
the pure breath that they are?

If you had no name
all would be primal,
pristine, all be invented by me
untouched before my kiss.
Joy, love: slow delight
of enjoying, loving, without a name.

Name, you dagger pushed
into the innocent breast
that would always be ours
but for its name!)

Here names stand for connotations, rather than denotations,
and it is conventional connotation of which words must be
stripped before the essential phenomenon can be experienced.
A poem by Jorge Guillén, *Los Nombres*, might seem to contradict
the poem by Salinas, by denying that 'a rose by any other name
would smell as sweet':

Albor. El horizonte
Entreabre sus pestañas
Y empieza a ver. Qué? Nombres.
Están sobre la pátina

De las cosas. La rosa
Se llama todavía
Hoy rosa, y la memoria
De su tránsito, prisa,

Prisa de vivir más.
A largo amor nos alce
Esa pujanza agraz
Del Instante, tan ágil

Que en llegando a su meta
Corre a imponer Después!
Alerta, alerta, alerta,
yo seré, yo seré!

Y las rosas? Pestañas
Cerradas: horizonte
Final. Acaso nada?
Pero quedan los nombres.[25]

(Dawn. The horizon
half-raises its eyelashes,
and begins to see. What? Names.
They are on the patina

of things. The rose
still is called
rose today, and the memory
of its passing, haste,

haste to live more.
Love drives us further
under the harsh blows
of the moment, so lithe

that to arrive at its end
it imposes its Afterwards!
Be careful, be careful, be careful.
I shall be, I shall be!

And the roses? Their lashes
shut tight: horizon
ended. Nothing left perhaps?
Yet the names last.)

The names of Guillén's poem last because he sees them as part of the 'patina of things,' of their essences. Whereas Salinas wants to capture essence in the phenomenon itself, Guillén suggests that our subjection to time makes that impossible, because our most intense 'epiphanies' (in James Joyce's sense of the word) are in the future or in the past tense – they are anticipations or recollections of experience. Yet the names celebrated by Guillén are not those deplored by Salinas. Both poets reach out beyond connotations and beyond history for an essence akin to what Arp called 'nature,' for an order in which things are what they are, not what we have made them. That reaching out for a pristine order relates the dawn of Guillén's poem to the 'innocent breast' in Salinas.

Jorge Guillén's belief in names as a repository of essence accounts for the degree of abstractness or generality that is bound to strike an English reader in all his poetry, as indeed in much modern Spanish, Italian and French poetry. This very important characteristic, which could easily be taken to indicate a lack of historical consciousness or an indifference to what is going on in the world, has to do with language itself and with ways of thinking and feeling scarcely affected by the quarrel between modernism and traditionalism. The difference has greatly occupied the French poet Yves Bonnefoy, whose Shakespeare translations brought him up against them, and I shall have more to say about Bonnefoy's observations. The briefest comparison of Brecht's manner with that of Pablo Neruda, or Paul Eluard, or Salvatore Quasimodo – poets with a political commitment hardly less pronounced than Brecht's – would also point to differences of that kind.

6   Like most of the Spanish poets of his generation, Federico García Lorca was as much concerned with the tradition of Spanish poetry as with international modernism. His interest in reviving the Andalusian *canto jondo* goes back to 1922. Four years later he took part in the Góngora revival connected with the tercentenary of Góngora's death, lecturing both on Góngora and on Soto de Rojas, a Góngorist poet. In those lectures, Lorca closely identified his own aims with the practice of the baroque mannerists. He developed a theory of 'anti-naturalism, anti-spontaneity.'[26] Like Valéry, Lorca insisted on the value of conscious and deliberate craftsmanship; the poet's main business is to 'restrict himself' (limitarse), examine his consciousness and study the mechanics of his creation. 'Only metaphor,' Lorca says, 'can raise style to a kind of permanence.' Although Lorca's use of imagery often resembled that of the Surrealists, his emphasis on the conscious control and elaboration of metaphor does not accord with modernist practices, least of all with those of the Surrealists. Unlike Arp, Lorca had little use for nature in this phase: 'The poet clearly recognizes that nature as God made it is not nature as it must appear in the poem.' Lorca therefore also redefined inspiration, quoting Paul Valéry's argument against it and writing: 'Inspiration is a state of contemplation, not of creative dynamism. From inspiration one returns as from a distant country. The poem is an account of the journey. Inspiration provides the image but not its dress. In order to clothe it the quality and sound of each word must be weighed up with equanimity and without an endangering passion.'

Two years later, in his lecture *Imagination, Inspiration, Evasion*, Lorca reviewed this position, considerably modifying the importance attached to imagination or fancy in the Góngora lecture. Nature and reality are now given their due. 'A grotto considered as a geological phenomenon, our recognition and understanding of the water's action, are more poetic than the fancy that giants were the builders of that grotto.' Specific phenomena become more important than the artifice that imposes order on them and mythologizes them. Yet a limit is set to the demands of reality on poets by the principle of 'evasion' or 'escape,' two of whose modes are irony and mysticism.

In 1930 Lorca lectured on the peculiarly Spanish notion of the *duende*, a kind of national genius characterized by its obsession with death or by what Unamuno called 'the tragic sense of life.' With his *Romancero gitano* (1928) Lorca had already proved not only that he himself had the *duende* but that Spanish poetry could still be popular if it was 'open to death.' The emphasis on ingenuity in the Góngora lecture was thoroughly revoked at this point: 'Intellect is often the enemy of poetry because it imitates too much.' Lorca's new conception of poetry as a medium that includes the public, almost as an active participant in its composition, breaks as drastically with Romantic-Symbolist theory as the work of Brecht, though Lorca had some difficulty in extending the application of his ideas to poetry other than Spanish. 'Spain is at all times obsessed with *duende* . . . because . . . it is a country that opens to death. In all other countries death is an end. It comes and one draws the curtains. Not in Spain. In Spain a dead man is more alive as a dead man than anywhere else in the world: his profile wounds like a razor blade.' Not very convincingly, Lorca suggests that the Italian counterpart of the *duende* is the Angel, its German counterpart the Muse; but Lorca does extend the application when he writes: 'The *duende* wounds and the tendency of that wound, which never closes, distinguishes the creative man.' This psychological insight corresponds to Edmund Wilson's in his study *The Wound and the Bow*, a book not concerned with Spanish literature at all.

In *The Poetic Image* (1932) Lorca dismisses the dichotomy between inspiration and invention, emotion and intellect, deliberate and spontaneous art. His definition of the poetic image – 'a poetic image is always a transference of meaning' – still stresses its metaphorical character at the expense of that realism at which English and American poets have excelled. Much of the imagery in the earlier poems of William Carlos

Williams, for instance, does not transfer meaning, because the things in those poems – 'the red wheelbarrow,' the 'plums in the icebox,' 'the rumpled sheet of brown paper' – are not metaphors. Lorca's stress on the metaphorical function of images is also apparent when he writes: 'Two conditions are necessary to give life to an image: form and a range of development: a cerebral nucleus and the perspective around it.'

Yet in his sequence *Poeta en Nueva York* (1929–30) Lorca had already grappled with a theme that brought him up against the limitations of traditional metaphor, just as it brought him up against the limitations of those ballad and song forms which he had so successfully revived. New York and America were nothing less than the modern experience, a confrontation with everything which Spanish life and Spanish tradition were not. Whether he liked it or not, Lorca had to come to terms with the cosmopolitan awareness that had informed the pre-1914 poems of Apollinaire and Cendrars; and his capacity to transform what he experienced was put to a new test. The Spanish 'openness to death' was one thing; the mass production of meat in America, another:

> ... los interminables trenes de leche,
> los interminables trenes de sangre,
> y los trenes de rosas maniatadas
> por los comerciantes de perfumes.
> Los patos y las palomas
> y los cerdos y los corderos
> ponen sus gotas de sangre
> debajo de las multiplicaciones;
> y los terribles alaridos de las vacas estrujadas
> llenan de dolor el valle
> donde el Hudson se emborracha con aceite.
> Yo denuncio a toda la gente
> que ignora la otra mitad,
> la mitad irredimible
> que levanta sus montes de cemento
> donde laten los corazones
> de los animalitos que se olvidan
> y donde caeremos todos
> en la última fiesta de los taladros.[27]

(... the interminable milk trains
the interminable blood trains
and the trains of roses handcuffed
by the dealers in perfume.
The ducks and the pigeons
and the hogs and the lambs
shed their drops of blood
underneath the multiplications;
and the terrible outcry of cattle squeezed together
fills the valley with grief
where the Hudson gets drunk on oil.
I denounce all those people
who ignore the other half,
the irredeemable half
that raises the mountains of concrete
under which beat the hearts
of those little forgotten creatures
and where we shall all go down
in the ultimate feast of the drills. ....)

What outraged Lorca about those 'milk trains' and 'blood trains' was the alienation of the modern urban masses from the very thing they live on. That's why the same poem *Vuelta a la ciudad* (Return to the City) includes statistics, real or invented, of the number of ducks, pigs, cows, lambs, etc., butchered each day in New York. The Spanish *duende* could not accommodate those 'multiplications' and industrializations of death:

No es el infierno, es la calle.
No es la muerte, es la tienda de frutas. ...
Qué voy a hacer, ordenar los paisajes?
Ordenar los amores que luego son fotografías,
que luego son pedazos de madera y bocanadas de sangre?
No, no; yo denuncio,
yo denuncio la conjura
de estas desiertas oficinas
que no radian las agonías,
que borran las programas de la selva,
y me ofrezco a ser comido por las vacas estrujadas
cuando sus gritos llenan el valle
donde el Hudson se emborracha con aceite.

(This is not hell, this is the street.
This is not death, this is a fruit stall. ....

What shall I do? Order the landscape?
Order the loves that soon will be photographs,
that soon will be splinters of wood and mouthfuls of blood?
No, no; I denounce,
I denounce the conspiracy
of these deserted offices
that do not radiate agonies,
that blot the forest's programmes,
and offer myself to be eaten by the cattle squeezed together
when their cries fill the valley
where the Hudson gets drunk on oil.)

The order which the poetic imagination imposes by metaphor
breaks down in face of such experience; and it is Lorca's capitu-
lation here to realities which he cannot order or transform that
makes this poem truly modern. Lorca's response to the American
processing of death might seem excessive if it did not anticipate
the 'blood trains' that were soon to be filled with human
'material' for slaughter, multiplied into abstraction, and admini-
stered in offices that 'radiated no agonies.' Lorca's Spanish
duende demanded the dignity of tragic sacrifice, present even in
the bull-ring, because the man and the bull meet there as
adversaries. This sterilized, depersonalized death made Lorca
feel that his own humanity had been annulled; hence his urge
to offer himself as a sacrifice.

The uncertainties and inconsistencies of style in *Poeta en
Nueva York* as a whole arise from the clash between Lorca's
assumptions as a Spanish poet and the strange, estranging
realities that confronted him in America. Surrealist imagery,
rhetorical accumulations of metaphor and hyperbole alternate
with a new plainness of diction. Lorca still attempts to master
and order his material imaginatively, as in the poem *Cementario
judio* (Jewish Cemetery), an apocalyptic interpretation not of
the cemetery but of the passage to America of the immigrants
buried there. In the *Ode to Walt Whitman* the alternation of the
two styles is especially marked because Lorca switches from a
realistic registering of observed phenomena to a similar interpretation of the United States as a whole, stressing the alienation of
urban Americans from the land on which they have settled:

  ... Pero ninguno se dormía,
  ninguno quería ser el río,

ninguno amaba las hojas grandes,
ninguno las lengua azul de la playa.

(... But no one slept,
no one wanted to be the river,
no one loved the large leaves,
no one the long blue tongue of the beach.)

In the same poem the description of New York – 'New York
of filth/New York of cables and death' – gives way to the
Surrealism of

Qué ángel llevas oculto en la mejilla?
Qué voz perfecta dirá las verdades del trigo?
Quién el sueño terrible de tus anémonas manchadas?

(What angel do you keep hidden in your cheek?
What perfect voice will speak the truths of wheat?
Who the terrible dream of your tainted anemones?)

Yet nothing could be more direct than

y la vida no es noble, ni buena, ni sagrada

(and life is not noble, nor good, nor holy).

7   The same alternation of styles is found in the work
of Pablo Neruda, especially in poems that attempt the mythical
view of a region or country which unifies *Poeta en Nueva York*. A
still closer parallel is presented by Hart Crane's *The Bridge*, a
poem sequence almost exactly contemporary with Lorca's and
related to it not only in theme and locality but in that aspiration
towards a mythical comprehensiveness and finality. Hart Crane
had the advantage of an American background and a knowledge
of American history; but even the alienation which Lorca
suffered in New York has its parallels in Crane's poem, despite
Crane's evident intention to glorify the very features of American
civilization which horrified and alienated Lorca. Both poets
applied an essentially Romantic sensibility to a task which
William Carlos Williams, in his *Paterson*, was to approach more
pragmatically and realistically, unencumbered with Lorca's
Spanish traditionalism or Crane's hankering after a Keatsian
or Miltonic grandeur difficult to blend with the American
vernacular. Walt Whitman is invoked in both poems, but as a
pioneer of the American myth rather than as a pioneer of the

American idiom, as a prophet rather than as a commentator. In both poems there is an extreme tension between empiricism and imagination.

Like Lorca, once more, Crane began as a 'pure' poet, with no inclination towards social or political commitment in poetry. Commenting on his early poem *Black Tambourine* in a letter to Gorham Munson, Crane wrote: 'The value of the poem is only, to me, in what a painter would call its "tactile" quality, – an entirely aesthetic feature. A propagandist for either side of the Negro question could find anything he wanted in it.'[28] *Black Tambourine* begins:

> The interests of a black man in a cellar
> Mark tardy judgment on the world's closed door.
> Gnats toss in the shadow of a bottle,
> And a roach spans a crevice in the floor.[29]

Aesop occurs in the next stanza, to 'insinuate' – the word Crane used in the same letter – that the Negro's place '(in the popular mind)' is 'somewhere between man and beast.' The word 'mid-kingdom' in the next stanza, as Crane points out, is 'perhaps the key word to what ideas there are' in the poem:

> The black man, forlorn in the cellar,
> Wanders in some mid-kingdom, dark, that lies,
> Between his tambourine, stuck on the wall,
> And, in Africa, a carcass quick with flies.

The comma after 'lies' is an extraordinary instance of Crane's reluctance to allow his poem to fall into the syntax of prose discourse and give anything away to 'the propagandist for either side.' The reason is not so much that 'what ideas there are' in this poem do not matter – the whole poem hinges on an analogy no less intellectual than aesthetic and 'tactile' – as that Crane does not want his myth to be disturbed by topical concerns. His position, basically, is that of the Romantic-Symbolist poets; his special affinities are with Mallarmé, Rimbaud, Valéry, and Wallace Stevens in his own time and country. Hart Crane's judgement on his time was 'a period that is loose at all ends, without apparent direction of any sort. In some ways the most amazing age there ever was. Appalling and dull at the same time.'[30] His early artistic purism was adopted in opposition to a period in which the autonomy of the arts was called in question with an almost unprecedented vehemence and thoroughness.

Even when Crane had begun to work on *The Bridge*, a poem whose very conception demanded the inclusion of history and hence of a more than aesthetic commitment, he defended the 'negative capability' of poets against the moral and philosophical strictures of his friend Gorham Munson:[31]

The tragic quandary (or agon) of the modern world derives from the paradoxes that an inadequate system of rationality forces on the living consciousness. I am not opposing any new synthesis of reasonable laws which might provide a consistent philosophical and moral program for our epoch. Neither, on the other hand, am I attempting through poetry to delineate any such system. If this 'knowledge,' as you call it, were so sufficiently organized as to dominate the limitations of my personal experience (consciousness) then I would probably find myself automatically writing under its 'classic' power of dictation, and under that circumstance might be incidentally as philosophically contained as you might wish me to be. . . . But my poetry, even then – in so far as it was truly poetic – would avoid the employment of abstract tags, formulations of experience in factual terms, etc. – it would necessarily express its concepts in the more direct terms of physical-psychic experience.

The Bridge, therefore, could only be written in modern sequence form, like Eliot's *The Waste Land* or Lorca's *Poeta en Nueva York*. A single long poem would have called for the kind of unity which Crane found neither in the age nor in himself. (His friend and editor Waldo Frank wrote of Crane: 'His person sense is vacillant and evanescent'[32] – a characteristic of modern poets, ever since Keats, that is closely bound up with the philosophical and moral scepticism of Crane's letter. 'No wonder Plato considered the banishment of poets,' he observed in it; '– the reorganization of chaos on a basis perhaps divergent from his own threatened the logic of *his* system, itself founded on assumptions that demanded the very defence of poetic construction which he was fortunately able to provide.')

Crane's basic difficulty over *The Bridge* was much the same as Lorca's over his New York sequence. It has to do with the evaluation of contemporary America and the quality of its civilization:

The form of my poem rises out of a past that so overwhelms the present with its worth and vision that I'm at a loss to explain my delusion that there exist any real links between that past and a future destiny worthy of it. The 'destiny' is long since completed, perhaps the little last section of my poem is a hangover echo of it – but it hangs suspended somewhere in ether like an Absalom by his hair. The Bridge as a symbol today has no significance beyond an economical approach to shorter hours, quicker lunches, behaviorism and toothpicks. . . . If only America were half as worthy today to be spoken of as Whitman spoke of it fifty years ago there might be something for me to say. . . .[33]

The preponderance of the past in Crane's poem corresponds to the preponderance of traditional grandeur and eloquence in its diction. Laforgue and Eliot, Crane wrote, 'whimpered fastidiously,' as opposed to Rimbaud, 'the last great poet that our civilization will see.' Lorca's Spanish *duende* and his pervasive sense of a life in which men are organically and meaningfully related to their environment, including their natural environment, made it easier for him to sympathize with American Negroes than with the 'blancos del oro,' white men obsessed with money. The American past, back to the Indian past celebrated in the *Powhatan's Daughter* section of *The Bridge*, had similar significance for Crane; and despite his reservations about Eliot, he could no more build a stylistic bridge from the spoken vernacular of his time to the past glories of English verse than Eliot could in *The Waste Land*, but had to resort to contrast by juxtaposition, just as Eliot did. So in *Cutty Sark*:

> 'It's S.S. *Ala* – Antwerp – now remember kid
> to put me out at three she sails on time.
> I'm not much good at time any more keep
> weakeyed watches sometimes snooze – ' his bony hands
> got to beating time . . . 'A whaler once –
> I ought to keep time and get over it – I'm a
> Democrat – I know what time it is – No
> I don't want to know what time it is – that
> damned white Arctic killed my time . . .'
>
> *O Stamboul Rose – drums weave –*
>
> 'I ran a donkey engine down there on the Canal
> in Panama – got tired of that –

then Yucatan selling kitchenware – beads –
have you seen Popocatepetl – birdless mouth
with ashes sifting down – ?

and then the coast again . . .'

Rose of Stamboul O coral Queen –
teased remnants of the skeletons of cities –
and galleries, galleries of watergutted lava
snarling stone – green – drums – drown –[34]

The juxtaposition here is delicate and the context less wilful
and stark than in Eliot, because Crane's imagination was indeed
less fastidious than Eliot's, more generous towards his own age.
Yet when Crane deals specifically with the past, as in the *Ave
Maria* section about Columbus, the Miltonic echoes become as
insistent in his verse as the Shakespearean echoes do in Eliot's:

O Thou who sleepest on Thyself, apart
Like ocean athwart lanes of death and birth,
And all the eddying breath between dost search
Cruelly with love thy parable of man –
Inquisitor! incognizable Word
Of Eden and the enchained Sepulchre,
Into the steep savannahs, burning blue,
Utter to loneliness the sail is true.[35]

In *The Harbor Dawn* section of *Powhatan's Daughter*, on the
other hand, the remote past and the present are completely
fused in verse so subtly allusive that one is scarcely aware of the
transitions. The formal iambics merge easily into the free verse of

your hands within my hands are deeds;
my tongue upon your throat – singing
arms close; eyes wide, undoubtful
dark
drink the dawn –
a forest shudders in your hair![36]

just as the dream of the Indian past blends with sounds still to
be heard on the East Coast of America:

. . . The long, tired sounds, fog-insulated noises:
Gongs in white surplices, beshrouded wails,
Far strum of fog horns . . . signals dispersed in veils.[37]

Although Crane did not avail himself of Ezra Pound's metrical innovations, and iambics dominate the rhythmic structure of *The Bridge*, his rhymed or blank iambics are varied not only by line length but by a tendency to split up within the line into separate rhythmic units. It is in the *Cape Hatteras* and *The Tunnel* sections that the rhythmic tension and modulations enact the most intense degree of ambivalence in Crane's vision of modern America, of the technology and industrialization whose dynamism he affirmed but whose direction he dreaded as much as Lorca did. The invocation of Whitman in *Cape Hatteras* is followed by the sinister presence of Edgar Allan Poe in *The Tunnel*, and the bridge is replaced by the underworld of the subway. Here, too, Crane comes closest to T.S. Eliot's negative vision of the modern world, using snatches of overheard talk in the manner of *The Waste Land*:

> 'But I want service in this office SERVICE
> I said – after
> the show she cried a little afterwards but –'[38]

The iambic verse almost disintegrates in the passage beginning 'The intent escalator lifts a serenade/Stilly/Of shoes, umbrellas, each eye attending its shoe, then ...'

In a few of his later short poems, like *Moment Fugue*, Crane completed his liberation from conventional prosody. That poem captures a moment of contemporary life ('The syphilitic selling violets calmly/and daisies ...') and gives it a vast extension by a masterly disposition of pauses and suspense. The organization of lines, rhythms and syntax there recalls the practice of William Carlos Williams, though the skill and subtlety with which Crane combined visual and musical effects were surpassed by no American poet of his time.

8   'Where are my kinsmen and the patriarch race?' Crane asked in the *Quaker Hill* section of *The Bridge*, and that question resounds even through those passages in which he tied the 'loose ends' of the period to the past or imaginatively projected them into the future. Crane's Romantic-Symbolist assumptions could not be denied, any more than Lorca's or Eliot's; and no poet of that period could feel wholly positive towards the age without as drastic a revision of premises, attitudes and expectations as that accomplished by Brecht or William Carlos Williams – and even their misgivings remained, as in Brecht's laconic late poem:

> *Der Radwechsel*
> Ich sitze am Strassenrand
> Der Fahrer wechselt das Rad.
> Ich bin nicht gern, wo ich herkomme.
> Ich bin nicht gern, wo ich hinfahre.
> Warum sehe ich den Radwechsel
> Mit Ungeduld?[39]

> (*Changing the Wheel*
> I sit on the roadside verge
> The driver changes a wheel.
> I do not like the place I have come from.
> I do not like the place I am going to.
> Why with impatience do I
> Watch him changing the wheel?)

Even ideologically committed poets could succumb to the doubts about a period 'without any apparent direction of any sort.' At such times the programmes and certainties of Communism were replaced for poets by that 'principle of hope' expounded by the Marxist philosopher Ernst Bloch, the utopian principle that had sustained the impatient humanism of an earlier, less knowing generation, as it continued to sustain that of Lorca and Crane.

Poets who had no use for the positivism of political programmes were more likely to attach their hopes to bare nature, human or non-human, like D. H. Lawrence or Stadler before them. Crane's vitalism was of that kind, and so was that of Eugenio Montale, whose early work was influenced by the writings of Bergson and Boutroux. 'Miracle was for me as evident as necessity,' Eugenio Montale has written, and the miracle which his poems praise is often that of sheer energy maintained in the teeth of forbidding obstacles.

Montale's early poem *Non Chiederci la parola* (from his first collection *Ossi di seppia* of 1925) renders the refusal to attach his hopes to a positive and positivist programme:

Non chiederci la parola che squadri da ogni lato
l'animo nostro informe, e a lettere di fuoco
lo dichiari e risplenda come un croco
perduto in mezzo a un polveroso prato.

Ah l'uomo che se ne va sicuro,
agli altri ed a se stesso amico,
e l'ombra sua non cura che la canicola
stampa sopra uno scalcinato muro!

Non domandarci la formula che mondi possa aprirti,
sí qualche storta sillaba e secca come un ramo.
Codesto solo oggi possiamo dirti,
ciò che *non* siamo, ciò che *non* vogliamo.[40]

(Do not ask us for the word that squares off, every side,
our shapeless life-urge, and in characters of fire
proclaims it and shines out like a crocus
lost half-way down a dusty field.

Oh the man who goes by with confidence
a friend to others and to himself
and never gives a thought to that shadow of his
the dog-days brand there on a flaking wall!

Do not ask us for the formula to open worlds,
some twisted syllable, yes, one dead-dry as a branch.
Nowadays we can tell you only this,
what we are *not*, what we do *not* want.)[41]

As in so many modern poems, negatives and negations assume a crucial importance here. Not only the poet's capability, but his identity and purpose, are defined by negatives. Psychologically, this scepticism towards rational definition assures an openness to what Arp called 'nature' or the psychologist Groddeck the 'It' – Montale's 'amorphous mind' rendered by his translator as 'life-urge,' an interpretation more in keeping with what is known about Montale's philosophical interests than with this particular context and the image of the 'dry branch' which becomes 'dead-dry' in the English version; and in the sequence *Mediterraneo* (1924), poems in which the 'weak life' of the speaker confronts the stronger life of the sea, it becomes clear that the force celebrated by Montale demands the extinction of individual life, its return to the flux of nature:

> Non sono
> che favilla d'un tirso. Bene lo so: bruciare,
> questo, non altro, è il mio significato.

> (I am no more
> than a spark from a beacon. Well do I know it: to burn,
> this, nothing else, is my meaning.)[42]

Yet a poet like Montale, whose strength is openness to experience of every kind, cannot be tied down to a philosophical system. Against his constant preoccupation with flux Montale sets his 'occasions,' minute realities perceived and rendered with a delicacy and precision from which his melancholy does not detract:

> La vita è questa scialo
> di triti fatti, vano
> piú che crudele.

> (Life is this squandering
> of banal events, vain
> rather than cruel.)[43]

It is his awareness of such events that makes his sensibility akin to T.S.Eliot's despite blatant differences of background and outlook. The kinship is most striking in Eliot's shorter and less 'philosophical' poems, such as the five *Landscapes* which he relegated to his 'minor poems,' though they are as fine as anything he wrote.

In Montale's *Casa sul mare* (House on the Sea) the flux yields to a timelessness or eternity that seems to transcend nature as it transcends the 'foam or wrinkle' of the sea; but one cannot be sure, because Montale differs from Eliot in being less intent on recognizable 'objective correlatives' – or subjective correlatives – of observed phenomena. Montale's imagination moves more freely, providing fewer data that are common property. His poetry almost always has a physical quality that engages and concerts all the senses. Montale's preoccupation with the sea remained as constant as Ungaretti's, at least throughout the twenties and thirties, but the sea of *Casa sul mare* is not the sea of his poem *Eastbourne*, with its hints of historical disaster blended, as always in Montale, with personal themes and immediate observations. What Montale has called 'religious penetration of

the world' has enabled him to break down all the barriers
between private and public poetry, between a poetry of personal
experience and a poetry of ideas. Only the title of his *La
primavera hitleriana* (Hitler Spring) makes this a primarily
'political poem'; its texture and imagery are as subtly and
intricately modulated as the texture and imagery of his 'love
poems' or 'nature poems,' categories equally irrelevant to
Montale's work. For the same reason Montale is at once a pure
and a committed poet.

Of Montale's admirable poem *L'anguilla* (The Eel), too, it is
difficult to say whether it celebrates the life-force which is also
the 'life-urge' in use, or a transcendental, spiritual principle.
The eel is characterized as

> torcia, frusta,
> freccia d'Amore in terra
> che solo i nostri botri o i disseccati
> ruscelli pirenaici riconducono
> a paradisi di fecondazione;
> l'anima verde che cerca
> vita là dove solo
> morde l'arsura e la desolazione,
> la scintilla che dice
> tutto comincia quando tutto pare
> incarbonirsi, bronco seppellito . . .

> (torch, whiplash,
> arrow of love on earth
> which only our gullies or the dried-up
> Pyrenean streams lead back
> to a paradise that fecundates;
> the green soul questing
> life where nothing but
> blazing heat and desolation gnaw,
> the spark that is saying
> everything begins when everything seems
> to char black, a buried stump . . .)[44]

If the capital letter of 'Amore,' the word 'anima' and the word
'paradiso' arouse associations with the last line of Dante's *Divina
commedia*, the physical details and the word 'fecondazione' belong
to nature and biology; but Montale's 'religious penetration of
the world,' a penetration at once pantheistic and Christian,

links the two orders – most explicitly in the concluding lines of the first section:

> l'iride breve, gemella
> de quella che incastonano i tuoi cigli
> e fai brillare intatta in mezzo ai figli
> dell'uomo, immersi nel tuo fango, puoi tu
> non crederla sorella?

> (short-lived iris, the rainbow, twin-sister
> of the one your forehead sets
> and you let shine entire among the sons
> of men plunged in your mire, can you
> not take her for a sister?)

where the internal rhyme 'gemella/quella' and the end-rhyme 'cigli/figli' enact the kinship or twinship of eye and rainbow and eel and the Biblical 'sons of man' – as well as the 'you' of the poem, unidentified as in so many poems by Montale.

Movement and quest are still affirmed in Montale's *Conclusioni provvisorie* (Provisional Conclusions) of 1953–4. The 'spark' of the early poem *Dissipa tu se lo vuoi* and the iridescence in *L'anguilla* correspond to the 'traccia madreperlacea di lumaca' ('mother-of-pearl track of a snail') in *Piccolo testamento* (Little Testament); and Montale's still earlier refusal to speak in 'characters of fire' is confirmed by the same poem's insistence that the sustaining radiance

> non è lume di chiesa o d'officina
> che alimenti
> chierico rosso, o nero

> (is no light from church or factory
> nourished
> by red prelate or by black)

but 'a hope that burnt more slowly /than the heavy log in the grate.' That image of combustion points back to the poems of *Mediterraneo* and leads to the 'provisional conclusions' here that

> uno storia non dura che nella cenere
> e persistenza è solo estinzione.

> (a story lives on in its ashes alone
> and persistence is simply extinction.)

Another summary of Montale's development and a brief inner biography occur in his *Botta e riposta* (Thrust and Reply) of 1961, with greater emphasis on the 'Augean stables' of the age and 'the swirling upon/turd rafts.' The 'hermeticism' of Montale's manner has never been an escape from the most unpleasant realities of his time. It is a hermeticism not of experience or sensibility – the whole political history of Europe from the twenties to the sixties of this century can be gathered from what his poems say and do not say – but of language and gesture, and it has served to preserve that essential autonomy of poetry which even Brecht recognized and respected. Just as Brecht could be cryptic when it suited him, Montale could be direct, both in the rendering of physical phenomena and in the statement of ideas and conclusions; but it was the needs of each poem that determined its degree of explicitness, not a compulsion to compromise with the language and functions of prose.

The last section of Montale's poem *Xenia* (1964–6), a sequence dedicated to the memory of his wife, could not be more direct or explicit; yet it is a justification of all that has made much of Montale's poetry difficult and elusive:

> Dicono che la mia
> sia una poesia d'inappartenenza.
> Ma s'era tua era di qualcuno:
> di te che non sei più forma, ma essenza.
> Dicono che la poesia al suo culmine
> maginifica il Tutto in fuga,
> negano che la testuggine
> sia più veloce del fulmine.
> Tu sola sapevi che il moto
> non è deverso dalla stasi,
> che il vuoto è il pieno e il sereno
> è la più diffusa delle nubi.
> Così meglio intendo il tuo lungo viaggio
> imprigionata tra le bende e i gessi.
> Eppure non mi dà riposo
> sapere che in uno o in due siamo una sola cosa.[45]

> (They say that mine
> is a poetry of not-belonging.
> But if it was yours it was anyone's:
> yours who are not a shape now, but essence.

They say that poetry at its peak
glorifies the All in its flight,
and they deny that the tortoise
is faster than lightning.
You alone knew that motion
is not different from stasis,
that the void is fullness, and calm
is diffuse as no other cloud.
This brings me closer to understanding your long voyage
encased in bandages and plaster.
Yet it gives me no peace to know
that as one or as two we're a single thing.)

The charge of 'not-belonging' must have been directed against the difficulty of Montale's work, due to the way in which private and public experience are interwoven in the texture of his poems, exactly as they are interwoven in the texture of a human life. Yet Montale's poetry does 'glorify the All in its flight,' the cosmic flux as well as the stasis, though in a quiet voice wary of the rhetorical generalities that come so easily to most Italian poets; and his poetic 'I,' like Eliot's, is one that has been so thoroughly stripped of circumstantial accretions that it functions impersonally, as a medium rather than as a subject (in either sense of the word). Montale, therefore, belongs to his poems, and his poems belong to any reader prepared to entrust himself to their exploratory courses. What Montale does not provide is confirmation of commonplaces, a guided tour of the recognized 'sights.'

For that reason, most of Montale's poetry does not 'belong' in yet another respect: it does not belong to the trend which has created a new international style since 1945, a style that owes much to Brecht's break with Romantic-Symbolist assumptions. If the easy conversational tone of *Xenia* is a development in line with that trend, Montale does not go so far as to renounce exploration in favour of a language so thoroughly purged of idiosyncrasy as to amount to a new kind of 'anti-poetry' which imposes very severe limits on the imagination.

9

A NEW AUSTERITY

1   THE new anti-poetry – a product of the Second World War, as the very different anti-poetry of Dadaism was a product of the First – arose from an acute distrust of all the devices by which lyrical poetry had maintained its autonomy. For the new anti-poets it was not enough that poetry should be as well written as prose. It should also be capable of communicating as directly as prose, without resort to a special language mainly distinguished by its highly metaphorical character. As in the case of Brecht, who anticipated these later developments, political and social concerns were at the root of the new austerity; but something of the new austerity is to be found not only in poets preoccupied with Marxism and the Marxist 'politicization of art,' but in the T.S.Eliot of the *Four Quartets* and the later plays, as in the post-1945 poems of Gottfried Benn or of Eugenio Montale.

In Montale's *Dora Markus* or *Eastbourne*, poems written in the thirties, allusions to the political realities of the time are not explicit enough to advertise themselves as a 'theme,' much as only the title of *La primavera hitleriana* promises a 'political poem.' The new directness and literalness assert themselves in a poem by Montale's younger contemporary Salvatore Quasimodo, despite remnants of a Romantic rhetoric and hyperbole. *Milano, agosto 1943* sticks to its theme:

> Invano cerchi tra la polvere,
> povera mano, la città è morta.

E morta: s'è udito l'ultimo rombo
sul cuore del Naviglio. E l'usignolo
è caduto dall'antenna, alta sul convento,
dove cantava prima del tramonto.
Non scavate pozzi nei cortili:
i vivi non hanno più sete.
Non toccate i morti, cosi rossi, cosi gonfi:
lasciateli nella terra delle loro case:
la città è morta, è morta.

> (*Milan, August* 1943
> In vain you grope in the dust,
> poor hand, the city has died.
> Has died: the last uproar has faded
> in the Naviglio's heart. And the nightingale
> dropped from the aerial mast, high up above the convent,
> where it sang before the disaster.
> Dig no more wells in the courtyards:
> the living have lost their thirst.
> Do not touch the dead, so swollen and so red:
> leave them to rot in their houses:
> the city has died, has died.)

Compared with the poems of Brecht on related subjects, this poem falls short of the new austerity, because its gesture and imagery are dominated less by the event recorded than by the poet's response to it, and this response does not come from a sensibility as thoroughly politicized as Brecht's. (Brecht could speak in the first person and yet speak publicly and politically. That first person was a *persona*, like any Symbolist's, but a *persona* that had been conditioned, simplified and modified by the uses to which it was put.) Yet for all its echoes of Leopardi's elegiac cadences, Quasimodo's poem is a step towards the 'impure poetry' advocated by Pablo Neruda.

This impure poetry, Neruda wrote in 1935, was to be 'ravaged by the labour of our hands as by an acid, saturated with sweat and smoke, a poetry that smells of urine and of white lilies, a poetry on which every human activity, permitted or forbidden, has imprinted its mark.'

A poetry impure as a suit of clothes, as a body, soiled with food, a poetry familiar with shameful, disgraceful deeds, with dreams, observations, wrinkles, sleepless nights, presentiments; eruptions of hatred and love; animals, idylls, shocks; negotiations, ideologies, assertions, doubts, tax demands . . .[1]

At this time, before he had joined the Communist Party, Neruda's conception of impure poetry had a place not only for dreams but also for 'melancholy, for threadbare sentimentality, fruits of marvellous, forgotten human potentialities, impure, perfect, thrown away by literary men in their delusion: the light of the moon, the swan at nightfall . . . To be afraid of bad taste is to be frostbitten.' The very style of the manifesto accords with the ebullience of Neruda's earlier poetry, with its long breath and its delight in the proliferation of images. Yet Neruda's insistence on the 'reek of the human' in poetry – a reek that includes the smell of white lilies, even before they have festered – links his practice to Brecht's. With his characteristic dryness and austerity Brecht drew up a similar programme in a poem written in the thirties, but published only after his death:[2]*

Von allen Werken

Von allen Werken die liebsten
Sind mir die gebrauchten.
Die Kupfergefässe mit den Beulen und den abgeplatteten Rändern
Die Messer und Gabeln, deren Holzgriffe
Abgegriffen sind von vielen Händen: solche Formen
Schienen mir die edelsten. So auch die Steinfliesen um alte Häuser
Welche niedergetreten sind von vielen Füssen, abgeschliffen
Und zwischen denen Grasbüschel wachsen, das
Sind glückliche Werke.

*It was Hans Magnus Enzensberger who drew attention to the parallel in his *Einzelheiten*, Frankfurt, 1962, p. 321. What Neruda has called 'impure poetry' corresponds to what I have called 'anti-poetry' in the post-1945 era. The term 'anti-poems' was used by the Chilean poet Nicanor Parra in exactly the sense that I have in mind for his collection *Poemas y antipoemas*, written from 1938 to 1953 and published in 1956. Unlike the anti-poems of the Dadaists and Surrealists, Nicanor Parra's anti-poems are distinguished by their cultivation and penetration of ordinariness, by a diction deliberately quotidian and the introduction of *personae* defined by their functions within a recognizable social order.
Poems for people who don't read poems is the title chosen by Hans Magnus Enzensberger for the English selection from his work (New York and London, 1968), and that title sums up the paradox of anti-poetry at its most extreme. For the anti-metaphorical tendencies of the new anti-poetry, see Enzensberger's *sommergedicht* (summer poem) in that volume, pp. 144–5 ('throw away those metaphors/ they're a thing of the past').

Eingegangen in den Gebrauch der vielen
Oftmals verändert, verbessern sie ihre Gestalt und werden köstlich
Weil oftmals gekostet. . . .

(Of All Works

Of all works I prefer
Those used and worn.
Copper vessels with dents and with flattened rims
Knives and forks whose wooden handles
Many hands have grooved: such shapes
Seemed the noblest to me. So too the flagstones around
Old houses, trodden by many feet and ground down,
With clumps of grass in the cracks, these too
Are happy works.

Absorbed into the use of the many
Frequently changed, they improve their appearance, growing
    enjoyable
Because often enjoyed. . . .)

The broken statues and 'half-dilapidated buildings' that follow
in Brecht's poem are absolved from their associations with
'bourgeois' romanticism and sentimentality both by Brecht's
tone and by his emphasis on change and growth, that utopian
principle in Communism which he upheld even in the teeth of
a petrified bureaucracy. Neruda's moonlight and swans were
never to Brecht's liking; and it was not until Neruda had joined
the Communist Party in 1943 that the Chilean poet, too, began
to strip his poetry of its 'bourgeois' effects – with disastrous consequences for a while, since he did not discard the traditional
rhetoric of Spanish poetry even in his polemics against the
'Gidean intellectualists, Rilkean obfuscators of life, specious
existentialist jugglers, surrealist poppy flowers, bright only in
your graves, europeanizing modish carcasses, pale maggots in
the cheese of capitalism.'[3] The drastic change of style which
Neruda's change of heart demanded was announced in his
lecture on *Obscurity and Clarity in Poetry* delivered in 1953. His
recognition that he was writing for 'ordinary people, people so
modest that very often they have not learnt to read,' led to his
advocacy of a 'poetry like bread that can be shared by all,
learned men and peasants alike, by our entire, immeasurable,
wonderful extraordinary family of peoples.' He declared: 'It

was a great effort for me to sacrifice obscurity to clarity, for obscurity of language has become the privilege of a literary caste in our country. . . . I have resolved to become more and more simple in my new poems, more simple each day.' Even the most sincere resolutions of poets, private as well as public, are rarely worth very much, simply because 'the wind bloweth where it listeth'; but Neruda's baroque imagination has made genuine concessions to the new austerity in his later poetry. One reason is that the public declaration came after the event.

2   The struggle between Neruda's 'obscure' and 'clear' styles can be seen in the *Heights of Macchu Picchu*[4] sequence of his *Canto general*, written in 1945. Section IX, for instance, is a series of asyntactic images and metaphors, many of which may be easily mistaken for 'Surrealist poppy flowers' by a reader unfamiliar with the baroque strand in Spanish poetry. The forty-three lines of this section do not contain a single statement or active verb that would serve to 'explain' those images and metaphors or relate them to an argument not implicit in them. This makes them autonomous, in the manner of 'pure' poetry, though the context of the whole sequence adds to their significance. Whereas a few of them are almost literally descriptive of the mountain city and its surroundings, like the 'bastion perdido' (lost bastion) of the second line, most of them are imaginative transmutations of the things seen, like

Caballo de la luna, luz de piedra.

(Horse of the moon, stone light.)

In Section XII of the same sequence, on the other hand, not only is the diction far less metaphorical, the syntax regular, but such metaphors as do occur are subordinated to an unambiguous argument. This seeming inconsistency of style adds to the range of the sequence, for in Section IX Neruda is concerned with the natural world, in Section XII with the human, historical world, that of the workmen who built the city. Autonomous images without a syntax that would relate them to historical time and to an order not of their making are perfectly appropriate to the natural phenomena of Section IX, just as directness is called for in the poet's attempt to identify himself with the builders of the city to the extent of inviting them to 'speak through my words and through my blood.'

The vatic assumption behind that invitation is the key to Neruda's difficulties in evolving the clear and unrhetorical style which his political and humanitarian commitments demanded. Brecht, as I have suggested, had to strip not only his diction, but his poetic person, of all that he felt to be excessively individualistic. A similar process can be observed in Neruda's later poetry – as in the later, discursive poetry of another politically committed poet, Hugh MacDiarmid, whose *In Memoriam James Joyce*[5] comes close to being anti-poetry of the special post-1945 kind – a poetry deliberately impure, akin to prose in its subordination of rhythm and imagery to argument.

Neruda's empirical self becomes prominent in the collection of poems published in England as *We Are Many*,[6] with translations by Alastair Reid. The rhetoric and the vatic gestures have been discarded, though there is much self-questioning, and Neruda is very much aware that so rich and multiple a poetic personality as his has always been cannot easily be reduced to an empirical self representative of the man in the street. His resolution of 1953 is taken up in the short opening poem, *Nada más* (Nothing More):

> ... Quise ser como el pan:
> la lucha no me encontró ausente.
>
> Pero aquí estoy con lo que amé,
> con la soledad que perdí :
> junto a esta piedra no reposo.
>
> Trabaja el mar en mi silencio.
>
> (... I wished to be like bread:
> The struggle never found me wanting.
>
> But here I am with what I loved,
> with the solitude I lost.
> In the shadow of that stone, I do not rest.
>
> The sea is working, working in my silence.)[7]

The Truth of Poetry

What this poem implies is that the social and political
functions of poetry cannot engage the whole of Neruda's
imagination, that a 'conversation about trees,' or only a contemplation of trees in silence and in solitude, is a human need
as real, if not quite as general, as the need for bread, even if the
silence is one 'about so many misdeeds,' as Brecht wrote. In the
poem *Pido silencio* (I Ask for Silence) Neruda makes the need
explicit:

> No puedo ser sin que las hojas
> vuelan y vuelvan a la tierra.

> (I cannot exist without leaves
> flying and falling to earth.)

The difficulty of reducing both his poetic and empirical selves
to a generally human lowest common denominator, in accordance with a creed that makes this lowest common denominator
an economic one, is most apparent in the little poem *Muchos
somos* (We Are Many).

> De tantos hombres que soy, que somos
> no puedo encontrar a ninguno:
> se me pierden bajo la ropa,
> se fueron a otra ciudad.

> Cuando todo está preparado
> para mostrarme inteligente
> el tonto que llevo escondido
> se toma la palabra en mi boca.

> . . . .
> Cuando arde una casa estimada
> en vez del bombero que llamo
> se precipita el incendiario
> y ése soy yo. No tengo arreglo.
> Qué debo hacer para escogerme?
> Cómo puedo rehabilitarme?

> (Of the many men who I am, who we are,
> I cannot settle on a single one.
> They are lost to me under the cover of clothing.
> They have departed for another city.

When everything seems to be set
to show me off as a man of intelligence,
the fool I keep concealed on my person
takes over my talk and occupies my mouth.

. . . .

When a stately home bursts into flames,
instead of the firemen I summon,
an arsonist bursts on the scene,
and he is I. There is nothing I can do.
What must I do to single out myself?
How can I put myself together?)

The candour, relaxation and directness of Neruda's manner
in that poem – as in *El miedo* (Fear) in the same collection, a
poem that deflates the hero-image of the vatic poet, or *El
perezoso* (Lazybones), which contrasts the poet's sensuous delight
in what this earth has to offer him with the urge of others to
'violate the gentle moon' and 'set up their pharmacies there' –
are very much in line with international developments after
1945 in that they serve to close the gap between the empirical
selves and the projected selves of poets. Yet the very simplification of Neruda's manner has brought him up against old
complexities and dilemmas, like the recognition of multiple
personality in *Muchos somos*, and these complexities and dilemmas are treated rather too complacently to produce the shock
of recognition. Neruda's self-explorations provide a corrective
to simplifications of a different kind to be found in the ideological
verse of his brief Stalinist phase; but they do not grapple with
the assumption on which that verse was based. In *El perezoso*,
therefore, he can write:

Mi casa tiene mar y tierra
mi mujer tiene grandes ojos
color de avellana silvestre . . .

(My house has both the sea and the earth
my woman has great eyes
the colour of wild hazelnut . . .)

lines that lay themselves open to obvious non-literary objections
of the kind raised by Neruda against 'Gidean' and 'Rilkean' and
other 'pale maggots in the cheese of capitalism.' Because the 'I'
that appears in these poems has not been reduced, as Brecht's

was, to its socially relevant and representative constituents, the 'bread' of his plain style may well have proved more indigestible to 'ordinary people' than the rhetoric or the self-sufficient imagery of his earlier work, if only because most 'ordinary people' turn to poetry not for bread, but for cream cakes, if they turn to it at all.

The most memorable passages of these poems are not those in which Neruda is at home to his readers, careful to avoid poses yet conscious that this informality is being exposed to cameras, but those in which he returns to the real business of his life – a business whose processes are necessarily private and solitary, though its products are not. Such a passage occurs in *El perezoso*:

> El primer vino es rosada,
> es dulce como un niño tierno,
> el segundo vino es robusto
> como la voz de un marinero
> y el tercer vino es un topacio
> una amapola y un incendio.

> (The first wine is pink in colour,
> is sweet with the sweetness of a child,
> the second wine is able-bodied,
> strong like the voice of a sailor,
> the third wine is a topaz, is
> a poppy and a fire in one.)

3   Another South American poet of Neruda's generation, César Vallejo, broke with the tradition of 'pure' and 'obscure' poetry under the pressure of his social and political conscience, to the extent of forbidding himself that sensuous response to the things of nature and civilization which has always distinguished Neruda's best work. Already in Vallejo's first collection, *Los heraldes negros* (1918), social compassion was at odds with the style of 'advanced' poetry, still predominantly Symbolist at that period as far as Peru was concerned. The complete breakthrough occurred in his next collection, *Trilce*, published only four years later in Peru, fourteen years later in Spain also. His third and fourth collections, *Poemas humanos* and *España, aparte de mi este caliz*, were published posthumously in Paris, where Vallejo died in obscurity and poverty in 1938. Poem XXVI of *Trilce* contains a kind of poetic manifesto:

> Rehusad, y vosotros, aposar las plantas
> en la seguridad dupla de la Armonia.
> Rehusad la simetría a buen seguro.
>
> (Refuse to place your footsteps
> in the dual safety of Harmony.
> Refuse to let symmetry make you sure.)

In Vallejo's poems social compassion and self-portraiture are not separable, since his concern with others became a consuming obsession, as the very cadences and vocabulary of his verse, their harshness and roughness, attest. So in *El pan nuestro* (Our Daily Bread), a poem from his first collection:

> Todos mis huesos son ajenos;
> yo tal vez los robé!
> Yo vine a darme lo que acaso estuvo
> asignado para otro;
> y pienso que, si no hubiera nacido,
> otro pobre tomara este café!
> Yo soy un mal ladrón.... A dónde iré!
>
> Y en esta hora fría, en que la tierra
> trasciende a polvo humano y es tan triste,
> quisiera yo tocar todas las puertas,
> y suplicar a no sé quién, perdón,
> y hacerle pedacitos de pan fresco
> aquí, en el horno de mi corazón....[8]
>
> (Every bone in me belongs to others;
> and maybe I stole them!
> I went to take for my use a thing
> that may have been meant for another;
> and I think that if I had not been born
> another poor man would have drunk this coffee!
> I'm a sly thief.... And what can I do?
>
> And at this cold hour, when the earth
> smells of human dust and is so sad,
> I wish I could knock on all the doors
> and beg I don't know whom to forgive me
> and make little bits of fresh bread for him
> here, in my heart's oven...!)

The implications of Vallejo's 'bread' are similar to those in the statement and poem by Neruda; and Brecht, too, was to make much the same point in a poem written some twenty years after Vallejo's:

Man sagt mir: Iss und trink du! Sei froh, dass du hast!

Aber wie kann ich essen und trinken, wenn
ich dem Hungerden entreisse, was ich esse, und
mein Glas Wasser einem Verdurstenden fehlt?
Und doch esse und trinke ich. . . .[9]

(They tell me: Eat and drink. Be glad that you can!

But how can I eat and drink, when
From the hungry man I snatch what I eat and
my glass of water deprives the man dying of thirst.
And yet I eat and drink. . . .)

One difference is that Vallejo renders the emotion of compassion, Brecht its dialectic, completed by the laconic and matter-of-fact fifth line. Brecht was less interested in the quality of his own feelings, in the 'oven' of his heart, than in a dilemma that must be resolved by political action, the abolition of poverty. In his dedication of another early poem, *Los dados eternos* (The Everlasting Dice), to Manuel Gonzales Prada, Vallejo called it 'this fierce and extraordinary feeling – one of those for which the great master has enthusiastically praised me.' Vallejo's later poems put less emphasis on the emotional gesture, but his political commitment never turned him into a mainly didactic or impersonal poet. Even *Un hombre pasa* (A Man Passes), which explicitly contrasts the bread with the cream cakes offered by 'advanced' thought and art in Vallejo's time, is a poem of experience rather than of ideas:

Un hombre pasa con un pan al hombro.
Voy a escribir, después, sobre mi doble?

Otro se sienta, ráscase, extrae un piojo de su axila, mátalo.
Con qué valor hablar del psicoanálisis?
. . . .
Un cojo pasa dando el brazo a un niño.
Voy, después, a leer a André Bretón?
. . . .

Otro busca en el fango huesos, cáscaras.
Cómo escribir, después, del infinito?

Un albañil cae de un techo, muere y ya a no almuerza.
Innovar, luego, el tropo, la metáfora?
. . . .
Alguien pasa contando con sus dedos.
Cómo hablar del no-yo sin dar un grito?[10]

(A man goes by with a loaf on his shoulder.
How, then, can I write about my double?

Another sits down, scratches himself, extracts a flea from his
    armpit, kills it.
What's the use of talk about psychoanalysis?
. . . .
A man with a wooden leg goes by holding a child by the hand.
Will it help to read André Breton?
. . . .
Another searches the mud for potato peels and for bones.
How, all the same, can I write of the infinite?

A labourer falls from the scaffolding and will not eat breakfast
    again.
What about tropological changes, a new use of metaphor?
. . . .
Someone goes by and counts on his fingers.
How discuss the non-ego now, and not scream?)

The allusions here to tropology and metaphor are especially
significant, since the new anti-poetry, beginning with much of
Brecht's, was to reduce poetic diction to those elements which
no longer strike one as metaphorical or figurative, because they
belong to the stock of prose usage. The invention of metaphors
and similes was felt to be a luxury, a self-indulgence, if poetry
could do without such personal linguistic accretions. That
particular austerity is one of the most characteristic features of
the social and political poetry written in many languages after
1945, and indeed of poetry not overtly social or political in
theme, but shaped by a social and political consciousness.
Vallejo did not attain that degree of austerity. Even his compassion remained personal and individualistic, whatever its
ideological implications. In the early poems pity moves Vallejo

to a revolt not against society, but against God and against life itself. So in *Los dados eternos*:

Dios mío, estoy llorando el ser que vivo;
me pesa haber tomádote tu pan;
pero este pobre barro pensativo
no es costra fermentada en tu costado:
tú no tienes Marías que se van!

Dios mío, si tú hubieras sido hombre,
hoy supieras ser Dios;
pero tú, que estuviste siempre bien,
no sientes nada de tu creación.
Y el hombre sí te sufre: el Dios es él!

. . . .
Dios mío, y esta noche sorda oscura,
ya no podrás jugar, porque la Tierra
es un dado roído y ya redondo
a fuerza de rodar a la aventura,
que no puede parar si no en un hueco
en el hueco de inmensa sepultura.[11]

(My God, I'm weeping for the life I live;
it grieves me to have taken your bread;
but this poor thinking clay that I am
is no crust that leavened in your side:
you have no Marys that go away!

My God, if you had been a man
today you would know how to be God;
but you, who have always lived well,
feel nothing at all of your creation.
And the man who suffers you: God is he!

. . . .
My God, this dark and damped night
you cannot go on playing, because this Earth
is a die flawed and already round
with haphazard rolling,
and it will never stop unless in a hollow,
in the hollow of an immense tomb.)

The personal revolt and pity are quite as marked in later poems like *La colera que quiebra al hombre en niños* (The Anger That Breaks Down a Man into Children) and even in those occasioned by the Spanish Civil War. *Cuidate, España, de tu propia España* (Take Care, Spain, of Your Essential Spain) contains a warning against those 'a hundred per cent loyal,' the party executives and bureaucrats who were not motivated by Vallejo's compassion; and many of his last poems returned to a personal or existential anguish, that of *El alma que sufrió de ser su cuerpo* (The Soul That Suffered from Being a Body), the title of a poem written in the last year of Vallejo's life.

4 Although he was a politically committed poet, Vallejo stopped short of the new austerity. The starkness and directness of his diction did not prevent most of his work from being 'the metaphor of a feeling' – Hölderlin's definition of lyrical poetry. In the new anti-poetry, on the other hand, both feeling and metaphor were subordinated to an 'objective' function, to the presentations of socially relevant realities. Vallejo's *Un hombre pasa* anticipates and uncovers one of the sources of this anti-poetry, the bad conscience of poets whose inherited specialization made them the purveyors of exquisite artifacts to a privileged minority. Hence the insistence on bread both in Vallejo and in Neruda. Yet Vallejo's poems on the Spanish war, collected as *España, aparte de mi este caliz* (1939), show how aware he was that an extreme reaction to this dilemma might prove as dangerous to society as to the art of poetry. If commitment to a political ideology left no place for the sensibility and imagination of poets, there was something wrong not only with the poets but with the ideology.

'What do I care for the art of poetry as such?' the Hungarian poet Attila József wrote in his poem *Ars Poetica* (1937), contrasting his 'great gulps of reality' with the 'bogus imagery' of other poets; but his 'gulps of reality,' too, is a metaphor, and his whole poem 'the metaphor of a feeling,' a verbal gesture whose effect depends on his capacity to make his 'realities' emotionally convincing, since they cannot now be tested empirically. That brings us back to József's own imagery and to the art of poetry. Whether the imagery of the poets he had in mind really was 'bogus' makes no difference to the gesture which his poem enacts: we imagine those poets to have been less familiar than József with certain facts of life, those brought

233

home to József by his proletarian status in a society still partly feudal; and as far as the poem is concerned, it is enough for us to imagine something of the kind.

Although the new anti-poetry (which József did not write) has an obvious connection with Marxism, a distrust of trope and metaphor is to be found in modern poets decidedly non-Marxist or anti-Marxist, even in a poet as remote from social realism, let alone socialist realism, as Wallace Stevens. A tendency towards anti-poetry is inseparable from almost every variety of twentieth-century modernism, including Ezra Pound's impatience with the merely decorative word; and behind every such tendency there was the uncomfortable awareness rendered in Marianne Moore's *Poetry*:[12]

> I, too, dislike it: there are things that are important beyond all
>> this fiddle.
>> Reading it, however, with a perfect contempt for it, one
>>> discovers in
>> it after all, a place for the genuine.
>>> Hands that can grasp, eyes
>>> that can dilate, hair that can rise
>>>> if it must, these things are important not because a
>
> high-sounding interpretation can be put upon them but because
>> they are
>> useful. When they become so derivative as to become
>>> unintelligible,
>> the same thing may be said for all of us, that we
>>> do not admire what
>>> we cannot understand: the bat
>>>> holding on upside down or in quest of something to
>
> eat, elephants pushing, a wild horse taking a roll, a tireless wolf
>> under
>> a tree, the immovable critic twitching his skin like a horse that
>>> feels a flea, the base-
>> ball fan, the statistician –
>>> nor is it valid
>>> to discriminate against 'business documents and
>
> school-books'; all these phenomena are important. One must
>> make a distinction
>> however: when dragged into prominence by half poets, the

result is not poetry,
nor till the poets among us can be
'literalists of
the imagination' – above
insolence and triviality and can present

for inspection, 'imaginary gardens with real toads in them,' shall
we have
it. In the meantime, if you demand on the one hand,
the raw material of poetry in
all its rawness and
that which is on the other hand
genuine, then you are interested in poetry.

I have quoted this poem in full because it says almost all there is to be said about the tendency towards anti-poetry in the work of modernists without Marxist affiliations. What is more, *Poetry* is itself an anti-poem, whatever it may assert in favour of poetry. It is an anti-poem because it subordinates music and feeling to argument, and could have been written in prose without losing more than a little of its elegance, succinctness and invention. This is not to deny that a great deal of art and skill have gone into the writing; but the art and the skill, including the strict metre and the carefully placed rhymes – rather less abundant here than in many of Marianne Moore's poems – serve an essentially non-lyrical end. The syllabics of the metre, to begin with, produce a mathematical regularity that is lost on the ear, since syllabics take no account of the weight and length of sounds, and the rhythms of *Poetry* are prose rhythms to the ear. At the same time the syllabic, semantic and syntactic structure produces line-breaks like 'are/useful,' 'to/eat' (between two stanzas!), 'of/the imagination,' and even 'base-/ball.' The poem's form, therefore, becomes the opposite of what Herbert Read has called 'organic form,' and its very intricacy serves to remind us of the difference between the poem's 'raw material' and the poet's ordering of it. The similarity with Brecht is very striking, because this reminder amounts to what Brecht called an 'alienation effect.' The deliberate prosiness, too, of phrases like 'all these phenomena are important' is exactly like Brecht's, as are the line endings on prepositions and conjunctions, though Brecht did not write in syllabics.

The unexpected similarity is mainly due to Marianne Moore's uncomfortable awareness of the vast non-poetry-reading public with no time for 'all this fiddle.' To Brecht that public was the proletariat and the peasantry, since he grew up in a country whose 'cultured' middle classes prided themselves on admiring even what they could not understand. Marianne Moore's obeisances to baseball fans and statisticians – perfectly sincere obeisances, by the way, as all her poetry confirms – point to social preoccupations no less acute, but shaped by the peculiar character of American democracy, in which 'culture' – or 'Kulchur,' as Pound significantly spelled it – was widely felt to be a rather sinister foreign invention. 'Business documents' and even 'school-books,' on the other hand, were decidedly useful, since but for school-books business documents might have proved as 'unintelligible' as poems or as the animals, both native and exotic, listed in the poem. The listing of those animals as instances of 'what we cannot understand' – instances, not metaphors, in this context – may point to another American peculiarity, the degree to which many urban Americans are alienated from nature: in other societies a statistician might well seem a much less familiar, less intelligible phenomenon than a bat.

There are many different reasons why modern poets have disliked poetry. Marianne Moore's is the opposite of the frustration experienced by 'pure' poets in their struggle to prevent words from meaning something. The 'too' of 'I, too, dislike it' establishes an immediate complicity not with poets like Mallarmé confronted with the blank paper 'defended by its whiteness' but with the pragmatic American majority. Hence Marianne Moore's insistence on the literalness that links her anti-poetry to that of Brecht and other Marxist poets. Unlike these, she was saved from the danger of the sort of non-poetry, as distinct from anti-poetry, produced by renegades of the avant-garde reacting too strongly and too deliberately against their 'bourgeois' subjectivity and individualism. Unlike the Europeans among them, she was also unable to fall back on traditional or popular verse forms in order to create an easy *rapport* with a majority public, baking synthetic bread for general distribution. Yet this is the dilemma of her anti-poetry, an anti-poetry decidedly for eggheads, since the same scrupulous truthfulness that has made her work literal has also made it cerebral and austere. For all her quotations from newspapers and magazines, her sincere obeisances to baseball fans and statisticians, Marianne Moore's sacrifice of lyricism has not endeared her work to the pragmatic majority. Paradoxical though it may seem, it is the utterly subjective lyricism of Dylan Thomas that is more likely to lure statisticians away from their statistics, baseball fans from their baseball, businessmen from their business documents. Marianne Moore's astringency, her precise and scrupulous literalness, are most fully appreciated by those who have come to 'dislike it' only after liking it too much, to the point of surfeit. It is they who can count the cost of her self-denial.

Yet Marianne Moore's work also makes one wonder whether verse, even anti-verse, is the best medium for the kind of observations and moralities at which she excels. The prose pieces in her book *Tell Me, Tell Me*[13] are as witty, elegant and inventive as her verse, and quite as idiosyncratic. Poetry, on the other hand, can be made out of the very lack of the substance which Marianne Moore so liberally provides.

The Brazilian poet Carlos Drummond de Andrade, for instance, is obsessed with doubts about the very nature of reality, doubts that one might suppose incompatible with the literal attention that Marianne Moore has given to human affairs.

> O imperio do real, que não existe
>
> (The empire of the real which does not exist)

he has written in his poem *Procura* (Search), a poem as rich in minute particulars, nonetheless, as Marianne Moore's work. Another of his poems, *Especulações em tôrno da palavra homen* (Speculations about the Word Man), concludes a long series of questions with the characteristic one, 'does man exist?' ('mas existe o homen?'). Those unpragmatic doubts have not prevented Drummond de Andrade from writing a poetry full of mundane ironies and insights about human life, or a poem as incisively topical as the long poem *The Bomb* (*A bomba*)[14] which begins:

> A bomba
>   é uma flor de pânico apavorando os floricultores
> A bomba

> é o produto quintessente de um laboratório falido
> A bomba
> é miséria confederando milhões de misérias. . . .

> (The bomb
> is a flower of panic that frightens the horticulturists
> The bomb
> is the quintessential product of a bankrupt laboratory
> The bomb
> is misery in league with a million other miseries. . . .)

Here, as elsewhere, Drummond de Andrade's ontological uncertainties give greater depth and sharpness to his observations of real phenomena. His very negations become poetically positive. A short poem in his first collection, *Alguma poesia* (1930), applies a truthfulness as rigorous as Marianne Moore's to the poetic process itself, but in order to show how a poet makes something out of a nothing which in turn was something:

> *Poesia*
> Gastei uma hora pensando um verso
> que a pena não quer escrever.
> No entanto êle está cá dentro
> inquieto, vivo.
> Ele está cá dentro
> e não quer sair.
> Mas a poesia dêste momento
> inunda a minha vida inteira.[15]

> (I have wasted an hour thinking up a line
> which my pen refuses to write.
> And yet it is here inside me
> unquiet, alive.
> It is here inside me
> and won't come out.
> Yet the poetry of this moment
> floods my whole life.)

Even 'beyond all this fiddle' – and Drummond de Andrade is not a poet of vague emotive gestures – the 'raw material' of poetry includes moments like the one recorded here, moments that burn up the very material, words, of which poems are made. Much of the anti-poetry written after 1945 is dry, laconic and austere not only because its authors are 'literalists of the imagination' but because the imagination itself has come up against barriers of an unprecedented kind. The experience of silence in face of the unspeakable is one of them. 'What we cannot speak about, of that we should be silent,' Wittgenstein wrote;[16] and 'Objects can only be *named*. Signs are their representatives. I can only speak *about* them: I cannot *put them into words*. Propositions can only say *how* things are, not *what* they are.'[17] One of the functions of poetry had always been to do what Wittgenstein calls impossible here, to 'put objects into words,' rather than 'speaking about them.' Where the impossibility has been recognized and confronted, poetry has tended to confine itself to a bare naming of things, without any claim to the sacred and creative significance which another twentieth-century philosopher, Martin Heidegger, attributes to the process of naming.

This has led to a new self-identification with things, as in the work of Francis Ponge:

Objects, landscapes, events and people give me much pleasure. They convince me completely. For the simple reason that they don't have to. Their presence, their concrete evidence, their solidity, their three dimensions, their palpable, not-to-be-doubted look . . .; (this does not invent itself, but lets itself be seen), their look: 'it is beautiful because I should not have invented it; I should have been incapable of inventing it'; they are my only *raison d'être*, more precisely my *pretext*: and *the variety of things is what actually composes me*. This is what I want to say: I am composed of their variety, which would allow me to exist even in silence. As if I were the place around which they exist. But in relation to only one of them, to each of them in particular, *if I consider one only*, I disappear, it annihilates me.[18]

In practice the hyper-realism of Francis Ponge can produce effects akin to Surrealism or to the pure fantasies of Henri Michaux, since Ponge's realism is not a social realism and his self-identification with things leads to discoveries that are also self-discoveries. The reciprocity on which his poems and prose poems hinge becomes magical. Yet the concrete and the literal are his starting-point.

5   The continued absence of a recognizable social context in much French poetry sets it apart from the dominant

trends elsewhere. Drummond de Andrade's doubts as to whether man exists, reality exists, have not detracted from the social relevance of his poetry, but given a special poignancy to his human sympathies. In Italian poetry, too, a 'hermetic art' has given way to social and political preoccupation, as in the work of Franco Fortini, who sums it up in the poem *Riassunto* (Retrospect):[19]

> Ho lavorato tutti gli anni, ho veduto
> poco mutar le stagioni dietro i vetri, lavorando
> per l'auto, i giornali, i medici, il cibo e la casa.
> Non quello che dovevo ma nemmeno
> quello che mi piacera, facendo; non con l'animo
> lento dei savi, nè con l'occhio lucente
> nè con la mente allegra.
>
> Ma l'acqua buia oltre l'avvenire,
> il lago fermo che in solitudine sta,
> io l'ho saputo dire; e voi che siete
> esitanti su queste parole sappiate che è,
> dietro il pianto superbo e la debole ira,
> in voi eguale e in me.

> (*Retrospect*
> I have worked all these years, have seen
> the seasons change little behind the window panes, working
> for the car, the papers, the doctors, for food and the house.
> Doing not what I ought to have done, but neither
> what I should like to have done; not with the slow mind
> of the wise, nor with bright eyes,
> nor with a glad heart.
>
> But the dark water beyond the future,
> the still lake that lies unvisited there,
> of that I knew how to speak; and you
> that hesitate over these words should know:
> behind the proud complaint and the feeble anger
> it is one in you and in me.[20])

Here, too, the empirical and poetic selves have met again, not without tensions and differences, but with no pretences on either side. The diction is as bare and simple as that of Drummond de Andrade's poem, yet in neither poem has collo-quialism been carried to the length of anti-poetry. Fortini's grave, classical cadences can accommodate his motorcar and newspapers as easily and naturally as the 'still lake.' In the same way, his poetic self, imaginative and utopian as even the most politically realistic poets rarely cease to be at heart, is included in Fortini's gesture of solidarity with others, avoiding those condescending winks at ordinariness, if not vulgarity, character-istic of so many who have assumed the new *persona* of poet-as-man-in-the-street.

The acknowledged influence of English poetry on Drummond de Andrade has something to do with his preference for the observed and specific detail; but other Latin American poets, and even the Spanish poet Blas de Otero, have come to share that preference. It is the French poets who are almost alone in having little use for the experience of their empirical and social selves in poetry, often out of an attitude towards the function of naming much more like Heidegger's than like Wittgenstein's. One explanation for this has been put forward by Yves Bonnefoy in several essays and lectures that have sprung from his concern with English poetry, especially as a translator of Shakespeare.

His essay *La Poésie française et le principe d'identité*[21] makes radical distinctions between the two languages and literary traditions, distinctions hinging on different modes not only of speech, but of thought and perception. Significantly the essay records an 'epiphany' – in Joyce's sense of the word – occasioned by seeing a lizard* on the wall of a ruined house. The prosaic uses to which that perception might be put confront the poet with 'the agonizing tautology of the common word,' with the 'sudden mutism of the universe' and 'the idea of death.' In order to name his lizard poetically he has to resort to a 'freedom' within himself, a freedom that recalls Rilke's notion of transformation as well as Heidegger's 'institution' of being on the poet's part; and indeed Yves Bonnefoy speaks of 'being,' of the logos, of 'the universe,' of an 'impulse towards salvation.' The real has to be 'interiorized,' made inward, by the poet's search for 'the threads that unite things *within me*.' In French poetry, Yves Bonnefoy goes on to show, not all words are poetic, and some resist poetry

---

*The word used is 'salamandre' and, with empirical pedantry, I have pointed out to M. Bonnefoy that this popular designation for a gecko is not precise enough in his context, since a salamander, strictly speaking, is an amphibian that does not climb walls.

to a degree not true of English poetry. The reason is that English poetry begins with 'aspects' or appearances whereas French poetry begins with 'essences.' It was the essence of that lizard which had to be captured by the poet, discovered within himself.

A poem in Yves Bonnefoy's *Du Mouvement et l'immobilité de douve*[22] is very relevant to his essay:

> La salamandre surprise s'immobilise
> Et feint la mort.
> Tel est le premier pas de la conscience dans les pierres,
> Le mythe le plus pur,
> Un grand feu traversé, qui est esprit.
>
> La salamandre était à mi-hauteur
> Du mur, dans la clarté de nos fenêtres.
> Son regard n'était qu'une pierre
> Mais je voyais son coeur battre éternel.
>
> O ma complice et ma pensée, allégorie
> De tout qui est pur,
> Que j'aime qui resserre ainsi dans son silence
> La seule force de joie.
>
> Que j'aime qui s'accorde aux astres par l'inerte
> Masse de tout son corps,
> Que j'aime qui attend l'heure de sa victoire,
> Et qui retient son souffle et tient au sol.
>
> (The lizard surprised grows motionless
> and feigns death.
> Such is the first step of consciousness in stones,
> The purest myth,
> A great fire crossed, which is spirit.
>
> The lizard was half-way up
> The wall, in the brightness of our windows.
> His gaze was only a stone
> But I saw his heart beat eternal.
>
> O my accomplice and my thought, emblem
> Of all that is pure,
> How I love him who compresses thus in his silence
> The sole power of joy.

How I love him who accords with the stars in the inert
Mass of all his body,
How I love him who awaits the hour of his victory
And holds his breath and clings to the soil.)

The identification of poet and lizard effected in this poem
would not strike many English readers as an example of
reciprocity, because the lizard's 'aspects' and appearances are
too thinly sketched to constitute more than a 'pretext' – as
Francis Ponge calls it – for a process of self-exploration that is
also a personal search for salvation. (If Yves Bonnefoy's 'salamandre' *is* a lizard or gecko, not a salamander, the allusion to
fire in the fifth line becomes even more subjective; and an
English reader, in any case, would expect sensuous data
amounting to an exact specification – data which the French
poet would feel to be prosaic.) Gerard Manley Hopkins or Ted
Hughes would have begun by rendering the lizard's 'quiddity'
in terms not of abstractions but of concrete particulars. If they
ended by extracting an essence, this essence, too, would have
been inherent in the particulars, or at least prefigured in them
to a much greater degree. Yves Bonnefoy's poem is remote from
almost every idiom of contemporary English or American
poetry, because its language functions in a radically different
way, its movement proceeds in a radically different direction;
and above all, because it assumes an order of pure ideas, or of
pure subjectivity, that can be evoked poetically with a minimum
of sensuous substantiation. True, the cosmology implicit in the
poem becomes much more palpable in the context of the whole
book of poems, which has the character of a sequence; and it
would be absurd to read Bonnefoy's poem as the 'animal poem'
which it patently is not. Yet the poem bears out what Bonnefoy
says about the differences between French and English poetry.

Bonnefoy sums them up when he points out that English
poetry arises from the tension between multiple appearances
and the desire to discover essences. He quotes Coleridge's
remark: 'Beautiful is that in which the many still seen as many
becomes one.' With John Donne in mind, Bonnefoy writes:
'People often repeat that English poetry "begins with a flea and
ends with God." To that I reply that French poetry reverses the
process, beginning with God, when it can, to end with love of
no matter what.' Much English poetry seems trivial to French

readers; and Bonnefoy remarks on the preference of English and American readers for Corbière and Laforgue, poets whom French criteria relegate to minor status. All this has to do with language itself, with what Bonnefoy calls the 'semi-transparency' of French words, as compared with the earthy opaqueness and body of the Anglo-Saxon. Because Latin was the language of theology, liturgy and mysticism, 'leaves and nightingales' lost their sacred associations in French. 'In every practical instance this was bound to make this experience, however direct, of the absolute in French words infinitely fragile and private.' Bonnefoy, therefore, is very conscious of the deficiencies and dangers of his own language for poets, because, 'if in the words we employ there is that virtuality of presence, that great hope, it follows that we shall speak under that sign, as though inebriated, without having criticized, as we should, our practice towards things. But to name the tree too facilely is to take the risk of remaining captive to a poor image of the tree, or at least to an abstract one that cannot grow in the space of the absolute without beginning with one of the aspects retained in isolation – absentmindedly – of the thing.' 'French poetry,' Bonnefoy remarks, 'has no Mercutio to recall its Romeo to "the duty of triviality," from that beauty of words into which they may have put no more than the phantom of things.'

In his later poems Bonnefoy has struggled against that 'fault,' as he calls it, to the point of a declaration of war against the 'beauty' that seduced the French Symbolists, whose art he had described in the essay as 'narcissistic and sterile.'

> Celle qui ruine l'être, la beauté
> Sera suppliciée, mise à la roue. . . .[23]
>
> (She who ruins being, beauty
> Will be tortured, put to the wheel. . . .)

In another poem, *L'Imperfection est la cime*, he has written:

> Ruiner la face nue qui monte dans le marbre,
> Marteler toute forme toute beauté.
>
> Aimer la perfection parce qu'elle est le seuil,
> Mais la nier sitôt connue, l'oublier morte,

L'imperfection est la cime.[24]

(Destroy the naked face that rises in marble,
Smash every form every beauty.

Love perfection for being the threshold,
But deny it as soon as it is known, forget it when dead,

The summit is imperfection.)

Bonnefoy's later collections, *Hier régnant désert* (1958) and *Pierre écrite* (1964), have profited by the struggle, without any loss of that 'passionate intensity' that has always distinguished his practice, because of his conviction that poetry has to do with truth and with salvation. Like Francis Ponge, Guillevic and Philippe Jaccottet, he has become deeply involved with the visible world, though not primarily with its social phenomena. His struggle against a beauty too dependent on abstraction is his own contribution to the new austerity, and this contribution can be understood only against the background of French poetry between Symbolism and the Surrealism that was Bonnefoy's starting-point.

The participation of post-1945 French poets in the new austerity, then, is of a kind that still leaves them remarkably free from what has been recognized as an 'international style' in poetry. A reviewer in the *Times Literary Supplement*[25] gave this unsympathetic and cursory description of it: 'Now, in his latest book, Mr Merwin seems to have abandoned himself to whatever approximates in poetry to the "international style" in painting: that is, the non-narrative, neo-imagistic exercise which fits equally well, or equally badly, into English, French, Spanish, German or Japanese, a cold collation of tentative, repetitive, sometimes almost stammering incoherence.' Well, this style does not 'fit equally well' into the languages listed; and it is rarely 'neo-imagistic,' because one of its distinguishing characteristics is a distrust of figurative devices that extends to a use of imagery to be found in Imagism at its purest, as in T.E. Hulme's famous simile in *Autumn*:

I walked abroad,
And saw the ruddy moon lean over a hedge
Like a red-faced farmer.

The reviewer goes on to quote a few lines from poems by W.S. Merwin, and comments: 'They might be translations of Sernet or Heissenbüttel or Tamura Ryuichi; or they might be Eluard translated by Creeley, or Lorca "imitated" by Wieners.' The lumping together of all these names shows only ignorance or insensitivity to essential differences. 'Imagism' apparently will do as a synonym for 'modern,' good enough for Lorca and Eluard, Creeley and Heissenbüttel – a poet whose verbal, grammatical and semantic permutations have about as much in common with Robert Creeley's lyrically expressive poems as either has with Lorca's work: and Lorca, as it happened, wrote narrative ballads when it suited him. Something like a new international style in poetry does exist, apart from the programmatically international movement known as 'Concrete poetry,' with which Helmut Heissenbüttel's work is connected. I have suggested that French poetry still tends to be an exception, because so much of it excludes all explicit evidence of social and political concerns. Yet Philippe Jaccottet is another French poet who has worked towards 'a poetry without images,'[26] by which he means a poetry without metaphor, since he distinguishes 'necessary' from 'ornamental' images. The necessary images, the images that 'count,' are those pertaining to the 'epiphany' recorded in the poem, not to an argument that might arise from the epiphany. I use the word 'epiphany' once more because Jaccottet is not a descriptive poet, though his epiphanies arise from intense encounters with visible phenomena, with the air and light that surround them, with 'inscapes' rendered as minutely and lovingly as Hopkins rendered them. Yet, like Bonnefoy, Jaccottet insists on the relation of all such phenomena to the inner life. He, too, is looking for what he calls a 'centre,' a revelation of essences, to be found *through* the things of nature rather than *in* them. He attempts 'to situate what I have seen in a certain air. That, at first, seems simpler than anything, when it is just the most difficult and the rarest thing of all, that moment when poetry, without seeming to do so, because it is stripped of all brilliance, attains what to me is its highest point.'[27] At that moment 'poetry becomes the bare naming of things,' and this is where Jaccottet, too, moves towards the new austerity, a poetic phenomenalism far more radical than that of the Imagists. This short poem from Jaccottet's *Airs*[28] exemplifies the reduction he has practised in order to render no more than a moment of perception, but a moment that expands in the mind:

> Le souci de la tourterelle
> c'est le premier pas du jour
>
> rompant ce que la nuit lie
>
> (The turtledove's care
> is the first footfall of day
>
> severing that which night binds).

This is a simplicity at once new and old, since it complements Sappho's perception about dusk and Hesperus gathering 'what bright sunrise scattered.'

6   The new austerity is most rigorous in those poets whose experience of total war and total politics has shaken them out of the assumptions – so essential to the work of Bonnefoy and Jaccottet, but also to that of American poets such as Robert Duncan – that personal feeling and personal imagination still accord with general truths of a meaningful kind; that the purest and most intense perceptions of poets remain exemplary because they find names for that which would otherwise remain un-named. At its most extreme, the new austerity is not only anti-metaphorical but anti-mythical; and one of Yves Bonnefoy's most ambitious later poems, *Le Dialogue d'Angoisse et de Désir*, re-interprets the myth of Persephone's descent to the under-world. To the Polish poet Tadeusz Rózewicz, for instance, myths and archetypes are as suspect as the traditional language of poetry: 'I regard my own poems with acute mistrust,' he has written; 'I have fashioned them out of a remnant of words, salvaged words, out of uninteresting words, words from the great rubbish dump, the great cemetery.' The 'great rubbish dump' and 'the great cemetery' are the realities to which the Second World War had reduced Rózewicz and many other European poets.

The same poet has formulated his distrust of poetic metaphor:

The more intricate, ornate and surprising the poem's exterior, the more dubious is its interior, the lyrical event, which often fails to penetrate the ornaments fabricated by the poet. It follows that the art of creating images becomes meaningless at a certain stage, although it presupposes much culture, diligence, originality and other qualities so greatly valued by our critics. So I think that the function of metaphor as the best and fastest mediator between an author and his audience is very problematical. A poet really uses images to illustrate his poems. The image, therefore, is a detour, where events in the realm of feeling wait to reveal themselves directly; where they suddenly appear in their unambiguous entirety, and wait to confront the reader. The image, the metaphor, then, does not speed up, but delays the reader's encounter with the true meaning of a poetic work.[29]

Rózewicz, of course, uses images; and he blurs the issue by not distinguishing between images and metaphors, or between decorative and functional metaphors, since all language itself is metaphorical up to a point.

Rózewicz makes his practice most clear in his poem, *My Poetry*:

> translates nothing
> explains nothing
> expresses nothing
> embraces no totality
> fulfils no hope
>
> creates no new rules
> takes part in no amusement
> it has a definite place
> which it must fill
>
> if it is not esoteric
> if it is not original
> if it does not astonish
> then that's how it must be presumably
>
> it obeys its own necessity
> its own possibilities
> and limitations
> is overruled by itself

> it replaces no other
> cannot be replaced by any other
> is open to all
> without secrets
>
> it has many tasks
> to which it is never equal.[30]

This is anti-poetry at its barest, stripped not only of metaphor but of that beauty which Robert Duncan still believes to be identical with truth. 'What I produced,' Rózewicz has said, 'is poetry for the horror-stricken. For those abandoned to butchery. For survivors. We learnt language from scratch, those people and I.' It is anti-poetry written out of a state of mind which Rózewicz explained in 1960: 'I cannot understand that poetry should survive when the men who created that poetry are dead. One of the premises and incentives for my poetry is a disgust with poetry. What I revolted against was that it had survived the end of the world, as though nothing had happened.' His banal vocabulary – 'I had to rehabilitate banality,' he said in 1966 – has to do with an extreme revulsion against individuality, hence against the principle of invention. What he aspired to was 'anonymity; lack of creative personality; absence of every kind of originality.' In another poem on poetry, *Nowy Wiersz* (New Verse), his son wakes up and asks him what he is doing. 'Nothing,' he replies, and:

> I am correcting
> the new
> superfluous poem.

When he 'listens to the dreary voice' inside himself, what he hears is:

> someone will come
> to wipe
> the talking mould
> from your skins.

'The production of "beauty" to induce "aesthetic experiences", ' he said in 1966, 'strikes me as a harmless but ludicrous and childish occupation.'

Another Polish poet, Tymoteusz Karpowicz, has rendered a

similar experience, though not without resorting to metaphor and allegory of a kind in order to deflate metaphor and allegory:

> *Dream*
> What horrible dream
> made the poet
> jump out of his sleep
> like a stag from a burning forest?
>
> – The butterfly from his metaphor
> had covered him with its wings
>
> and the door knob that he had described
> has moved.[31]

The limitations of so strict a literalism are indicated by Rózewicz himself in his *A Sketch for a Modern Love Poem*,[32] which begins:

> And yet whiteness
> can best be described by greyness
> a bird by a stone
> sunflowers
> in December
> . . . . .
> the most palpable
> description of bread
> is that of hunger
> there is in it
> a humid porous core
> a warm inside
> sunflowers at night
> the breasts the belly the thighs of Cybele
> . . . . .
> lack hunger
> absence
> of flesh
> is a description of love
> is the modern love poem.

Imagination, in other words, is needed in order to render even such stark realities as starvation and sexual deprivation; and beauty, too, may creep in by the back door, because rightness of any kind – especially that which results from the proper adaptation of means to a function – is felt to be beautiful. In Rózewicz's poem *Fear*[33] the fourth line is decidedly metaphorical, though the metaphor is not decorative but functional:

> Your fear is great
> metaphysical
> mine is small
> a clerk with a briefcase ...

And oxymoron is another poetic and rhetorical device which Rózewicz cannot do without:

> I shall speak to all
> who do not read me
> nor hear nor know
> nor need me
>
> They do not need me
> but I need them.[34]

Yet the severe literalness of this new anti-poetry does make it truly international in so far as its matter and assumptions are shared. Both personal idiosyncrasy and the national idiosyncrasies of language are subordinated to a bareness of utterance always close to the silence from which its minimal stock of words has been 'salvaged.' Such anti-poems, therefore, can be translated with relatively little loss. Yet their effect depends on each reader's ability to accept their precondition, a precondition that can be summed up in T.W.Adorno's statement that after Auschwitz poems can no longer be written. The work of Rózewicz and many other European poets of his generation is the answer of those who agree with that statement, who have made themselves at home in the silence which it prescribes. Their anti-poetry does not contradict it.

Zbigniew Herbert, another Polish poet, writes *persona* poems that seem far removed from Rózewicz's literalism of the imagination and close to the historical monologues written in an earlier period by Cavafy, Pound and Eliot; but Herbert's intricately allusive art in *Tren fortynbrasa* (Elegy of Fortinbras) or *Apollo and Marsyas* has grown from the same 'great rubbish dump' and 'great cemetery,' passing through the same silence.

The romantic conception of the poet who lays bare his wounds, who intones his own unhappiness, still has many adherents today, despite the changes in style and in literary taste. They believe that it is the artist's sacred right to be self-centred and to exhibit his sore ego. If there were such a thing as a school for literature, it would have to set exercises in the description of things before all, not that of dreams. Beyond the poet's ego there extends a different, obscure but real world. One should not cease to believe that we can grasp this world in language and do justice to it.

In the same comment on his poem *Dlaczego klasicy* (Why Classics) Herbert said: 'Poetry as a verbal art bored me' – exactly the position of the anti-poets; and about his recourse to history, as well as literary and mythical personages, he had this to say: 'I turn to history not for lessons in hope but to confront my experience with the experience of others and to win for myself something which I should call universal compassion, but also a sense of responsibility, a sense of responsibility for the state of the human conscience.'[35]

Although Herbert has chosen an indirect approach to the realities which his poems grasp, whereas Różewicz has tried to make do with an almost unprecedented directness, their work has a common base, and that base is common to poets writing in many languages, under many different political and social conditions. This is not to claim that there is, or should be, a uniform international style reduced to a drably functional austerity. The Yugoslav poet Miodrag Pavlovic, whose work shows a distinct kinship with that of Herbert in its recourse to history and myth – as in his *Gathering of the Dogs in Knossos*, *Pindar Walking* and *Watchmen before Athens*[36] – has explicitly dissociated himself from what he calls 'the tendency to a formal universality of the poetic idiom . . . the symptom of a superficial standardization of products in our industrial age.'[37] No such 'formal universality' is needed, since the common base does not forbid divergence or diversity. The common base is no more than a point of departure and return, where silence has to be confronted, all the verbal equipment of poetry stripped down and put to the test of silence.

7   William Carlos Williams, Marianne Moore, Bertolt Brecht are a few of the poets who anticipated the new austerity because their social awareness made them 'literalists of the

imagination' well before Auschwitz. The dynamic principle of 'open form' in Williams was to prove especially useful to his successors, since the new austerity needed a substitute for the richly wrought texture which its practitioners were to deny their poems. Williams's definition of the poet in *The Wind Increases* declares and enacts this principle:

> . . . . .
> Good Christ what is
> a poet if any
>   exists?
>
> a man
> whose words will
>   bite
>   their way
> home – being actual
>
> having the form
>   of motion . . .[38]

Here, too, the words are plain to the point of self-effacement, of transparency; what we see through them is a gesture, a process of thought and feeling, a 'motion' as Williams says. In *Paterson* there is also the insistence on 'relations' rather than dreams:

> Be reconciled, poet, with your world, it is
> the only truth!
> . . . . .
> – the language is worn out.[39]

and:

> The province of the poem is the world.[40]

The context of these statements in the long poem is dramatic, so that they are saved from didactic one-sidedness; and the same is true of this rendering of the anti-poetic complex:[41]

> Doctor, do you believe in
> 'the people,' the Democracy? Do
> you still believe – in this
> swill-hole of corrupt cities?
> Do you, Doctor? Now?

> Give up
> the poem. Give up the shilly-
> shally of art.

The 'swill-hole of corrupt cities' had once impelled poets to cultivate a 'pure,' 'absolute' or 'hermetic' art. Here the social consciousness, the sense of community, is such that the value of poetry becomes dependent on a faith in the people, just as it was a corporative disaster that invalidated the very language of poetry for European poets after 1945.

It is Hans Magnus Enzensberger, a West German poet – and translator of William Carlos Williams – who has revolted most violently against his own language, often to the point of a deliberate anti-poetry, as in his poem *landessprache* (*man spricht deutsch*),[42] with its bitterly mocking quotation from Rilke and its angry misquotation from Hölderlin. The very rhetoric of this poem has a deflatory function. Although, unlike Rózewicz, Enzensberger draws on the full resources of his language, that language is identified with

> diesem land
> dahin mich gebracht haben meine älteren

> (this country
> to which my elders brought me),

a country characterized elsewhere in the poem:

> auf diesem arischen schrotthaufen,
> auf diesem krächzenden parkplatz,
> wo aus den ruinen ruinen sprossen,
> nagelneu ruinen auf vorrat, auf raten,
> auf abruf, auf widerruf:
> . . . .
> in dieser mördergrube,
> wo der kalender sich selber abreisst vor ohnmacht und hast,
> wo die vergangenheit in den müllschluckern schwelt
> und die zukunft mit falschen zähnen knirscht. . . .

> (on this aryan dump of scrap,
> on this croaking parking lot,
> where from ruins ruins sprout
> brand new ruins, ruins in stock, ruins by standing order,
> by instalments, by sale or return:
> . . . .

in this murderer's den
where in haste and impotence the calendar tears its own leaves,
where the past rots and reeks in the rubbish disposal unit
and the future grits its false teeth. . . .)

The satirical, self-generating and self-deflating hyperbole of this poem serves only to confront the silence, 'the great rubbish dump, the great cemetery,' and to grope its way out. The full resources of the German language are employed against the German language, and against a poetic tradition which is indicted of complicity in creating the rubbish dump and the cemetery because it was a tradition of 'power-protected inwardness,' as Thomas Mann called it. The moral austerity implicit in Enzensberger's hyperbole becomes evident in his shorter and later poem *schattenreich* (shadow realm), which begins:

i

hier sehe ich noch einen platz
einen freien platz,
hier im schatten.

ii

dieser schatten
ist nicht zu verkaufen.

.   .   .   .

(i

here even now i see a place
a free place,
here in the shadow.

ii

this shadow
is not for sale.)

.   .   .   .

This is the plain, bare, minimal diction of the new anti-poetry, without the technical terms, foreign phrases, literary and vernacular borrowings to which Enzensberger resorts elsewhere for satirical or sociological purposes. His 'shadow realm' itself is one largely defined by negatives, like love and bread in Rózewicz's poem or Andrei Voznesensky's *Antiworlds*:

> . . . .
> Long live Antiworlds! They rebut
> With dreams the rat race and the rut.
> For some to be clever, some must be boring.
> No deserts? No oases, then.
>
> There are no women –
>   just anti-men.
> In the forests, anti-machines are roaring. . . .[43]

Like Enzensberger in *shadow realm* and other later poems, Voznesensky is acutely conscious of the smallness and precariousness of the 'free place' still available to individuals in the age of total politics, total economics, total mechanization: so in *A Beatnik's Monologue: The Revolt of the Machines*:[44]

> O predatory creatures of our age,
> the soul's been vetoed.
> We retreat to the mountains, we hide in our beards.
>
> We dive naked into water,
> but the rivers are drying
> up; in the seas the fish are dying.
> Women give birth to Rolls-Royces throughout the nation –
> radiation.
>
> My soul, helpless, hunted animal –
> . . . .

The Beatnik of this poem should not be identified with the poet; but Voznesensky's long poem *Cza*, similarly masked though it is by its subtitle, leaves little doubt as to the urgency of the poet's own concern with the 'continuing radiance they used to call/the human soul' under the pressure of bureaucracy and industrialization:

> Of Stalin do not sing;
> We are more than nuts and bolts;
> And no more shall we choke
> On his blue-bearded smoke.[45]

Throughout the poem robots and 'programmed animals' are

contrasted with the one thing constant on earth, 'the human soul'; and Voznesensky speaks in his own voice when he asserts:

> The world is not junk for auction.
> I am Andrei, not just anyone.
> All progress is retrogression
> If the process breaks a man down.[46]

To remember the 'great rubbish dump,' junk yard and cemetery of the recent past, while doing all they can to prevent the creation of others, is one of the functions that has come to unite poets in almost every part of the world; and the 'international style' of anti-poetry has been one of their media. Yet the assertion of individuality is part of the same function. Even where Romantic individualism, the 'egotistical sublime,' has been as thoroughly discarded as the diction and euphony of Romantic prosody, there has been an inevitable tension between the aspiration of anti-poetry towards 'anonymity' and the need of each poet to be true to his own experience, imagination and sensibility. This assertion of the personal principle has been most vehement where collective pressures have been greatest, as in East Germany. Wolf Biermann's *Rücksichtslose Schimpferei* (Invective with no Holds Barred)[47] opens with a significant repetition of the first person singular:

> *Ich Ich Ich*
>
> bin voll Hass
> bin voll Härte
> der Kopf zerschnitten
> das Hirn zerritten
>
> (*I I I*
>
> am full of hate
> am full of hardness
> my head all gashed
> my brain half smashed)

and this folk singer's declaration of war against Communist bureaucracy includes the claim: 'The collective has detached itself from me!' Here Biermann is speaking for the individual as such as well as for himself, and a separate section serves to qualify the superb insolence of his tirade:

4

Ich will beharren auf der Wahrheit
ich Lügner

(I will insist on the truth
liar that I am).

The concluding section, on the other hand, proceeds with no
holds barred:

Ich habe euch lieb
Hier habt ihr den Schrieb
schwarz auf weiss
ich liebe euch heiss
aber jetzt lasst mich bitte allein sein
auf der schiefen Linie
getrennt vom Kollektiv
Ich liege eben schief
Ich lieg bei meiner Frau
und die kennt mein Herz

(I love you all
Here is the scrawl
in black and white
I love you all right
but now please leave me alone
on the deviating line
detached from the collective
that's how I happen to live
I don't lie straight with my wife
and she knows how I feel).

Paradoxically, the very assertion of the personal principle
here owes its direction and candour to the reduction of personality which permits Biermann to claim 'I am the individual.'
The self presented in this poem is anyone's, however non-
conformist, just as the diction of this poem is anyone's. Biermann
claims no privilege as an 'exceptional person' or as a poet. His
invective owes its strength to the ordinariness of its language
and the absence of any claim to distinction or superiority. His
voice is a collective voice demanding freedom from the collective.

This peculiarity becomes very striking if one turns from
Biermann's poems to those of another East German 'devi-
ationist,' the much older poet Peter Huchel, whose last collection

appeared only in West Germany.[48] The book contains no
protest poems and no overt references of any kind to the régime
under which Huchel chose to live, at the cost of silence and
public disgrace. *Der Garten des Theophrast* (The Garden of
Theophrastus) is one of these later poems, and it is dedicated to
the poet's son:

> Wenn mittags das weisse Feuer
> Der Verse über den Urnen tanzt,
> Gedenke, mein Sohn. Gedenke derer,
> Die einst Gespräche wie Bäume gepflanzt.
> Tot ist der Garten, mein Atem wird schwerer,
> Bewahre die Stunde, hier ging Theophrast,
> Mit Eichenlohe zu düngen den Boden,
> Die wunde Rinde zu binden mit Bast.
> Ein Ölbaum spaltet das mürbe Gemäuer
> Und ist noch Stimme im heissen Staub.
> Sie gaben Befehl, die Wurzel zu roden.
> Es sinkt dein Licht, schutzloses Laub.

> (When at noon the white fire of verses
> Flickering dances above the urns,
> Remember, my son. Remember the vanished
> Who planted their conversations like trees.
> The garden is dead, more heavy my breathing,
> Preserve the hour, here Theophrastus walked,
> With oak-bark to feed the soil and enrich it,
> To bandage with fibre the wounded bole.
> An olive tree splits the brickwork grown brittle
> And still is a voice in the mote-laden heat.
> Their order was to fell and uproot it,
> Your light is fading, defenceless leaves.)

The very resort to a *persona* here, like the formal diction and
the classical cadences, removes the poem from that public and
common ground to which Biermann's belongs by virtue of its
manner, regardless of what either poem argues or asserts. In
Huchel's poem the domain of poetry is a garden, and a garden
threatened by an unidentified 'they.' We do not need to attribute a topical identity to this 'they.' The sadness, resignation
and pride of the poem's gesture recall an attitude familiar to us
from a line of poets that goes back to Horace and beyond him.
Nor do we need to know who Theophrastus was in order to
sense that the poem posits a special relation between the art of

poetry and the phenomena of nature. What the poem is and does suffices to make it a poem thoroughly out of key with the age; and the isolation which it enacts is a more thorough one than the isolation which Biermann demands.

That the personal principle should be reaffirmed by poets living under Communism, while many poets living in relatively individualistic societies are still depersonalizing the language and assumptions of poetry, would be paradoxical only if poets were conformists, if poets were wholly independent of the paradoxes of history itself, or if the development of poetry proceeded in straight lines, rather than dialectically, out of conflicts and tensions. Political commitments are invalidated by political realities; just as political programmes are invalidated not only by the temptations of office but by the sheer cussedness of unpredictable circumstance. The sadness of Huchel's poem is matched by that of Franco Fortini's *Traducendo Brecht* (Translating Brecht), published in the same year as Huchel's;[49] but Fortini, writing in a non-Communist country, needs no disguise either for his own person or for the cause of his sadness:

> Un grande temporale
> per tutto il pomeriggio s'è attorcigliato
> sui tetti prima di rompere in lampi, acqua.
> Fissavo versi di cemento e di vetro
> dov'erano grida e piaghe murate e membra
> anche di me, cui sopravvivo. Con cautela, guardando
> ora i tegoli battagliati ora la pagina secca
> ascoltavo morire
> la parola d'un poeta o mutarsi
> in altra, non per noi più, voce. Gli oppressi
> sono oppressi e tranquilli, gli oppressori tranquilli
> parlano nei telefoni, l'odio è cortese, io stesso
> credo di non sapere più di chi è la colpa.
>
> Scrivi, mi dico, odia
> chi non dolcezza guida al niente
> gli uomini e le donne che non te si accompagnano
> e credono di non sapere. Fra quelli dei nemici
> scrivi anche il tuo nome. Il temporale
> è sparito con enfasi. La natura
> per imitare le battaglie è troppo debole. La poesia
> non muta nulla. Nulla è sicuro, ma scrivi.

(All afternoon
a thunderstorm hung on the rooftops,
then broke, in lightning, in torrents.
I stared at lines of cement, lines of glass
with screams inside them, wounds mixed in and limbs,
mine also, who have survived. Carefully, looking
now at the bricks, embattled, now at the dry page,
I heard the word
of a poet expire, or change
to another voice, no longer for us. The oppressed
are oppressed and quiet, the quiet oppressors
talk on the telephone, hatred is courteous, and I too
begin to think I no longer know who's to blame.

Write, I say to myself, hate those
who gently lead into nothingness
the men and women who are your companions
and think they no longer know. Among the enemies' names
write your own too. The thunderstorm,
with its crashing, has passed. To copy
those battles nature's not strong enough. Poetry
changes nothing. Nothing is certain. But write.)

Fortini's poem is about politics and poetry, about political commitment and its frustration by the complexity of events. Its wisdom and honesty, confirmed by the dialectical twist at the end, enable Fortini to combine the language of anti-poetry with the traditional dignity of Italian verse; to be more realistic than Huchel, less strident than Biermann.

Yet a similar balance has been struck by poets writing in Communist countries, including East Germany; and this balance has included one between social preoccupations and the personal principle. Such younger East German poets as Günter Kunert, Heinz Kahlau, Karl Mickel and Volker Braun have maintained the freedom to criticize and the freedom to write in an individual manner, without feeling compelled to re-assert a drastically individualistic creed. Günter Kunert's work has exemplified the 'humanizing' function of poetry to which he referred in a statement,[50] ascribing it to 'a dialectical process in which the tension-fraught lyrical ego and the reader's ego become identified and yet, at the same time, not identified; one alienates the other and yet simultaneously fuses with it. The poem rubs off on the reader's psyche but the reader's image in turn rubs off on the poem.'

8   Many of Kunert's British and American contemporaries would accept this cautiously dialectical definition of the relation between poetry and its readers; and Biermann's protests, of course, also have their counterpart in America, Britain and West Germany. British poets, on the whole, have not gone as far in the direction of anti-poetry as their contemporaries in other countries; but, notoriously, they have not gone as far in any direction whatever for a very long time. '*Foreign poetry! No!*' was the characteristic response of Philip Larkin in an interview for *The London Magazine*;[51] and Kingsley Amis has made the same point no less emphatically. Yet Larkin, Amis and many other British poets have tried to effect the very identification with the 'man in the street' to which international anti-poetry has aspired, even if it had to be a British man in the street, and British class structure has complicated the operation in a uniquely British way.

'The greatest danger lies in the poet believing in poetry,'[52] Roy Fuller remarked in the same issue of *The London Magazine*; and that was another pointer to the anti-poetic complex that has been prevalent in British poetry since W. H. Auden and the thirties, despite David Gascoyne's profession of faith in the 'Christ of Revolution and of Poetry'[53] and Dylan Thomas's in his 'craft or sullen art.' The 'literalism of the imagination' that goes with the new austerity has long been firmly established in British poetry; and Philip Larkin affirmed his adherence to the *literal* truth of poetry in his interview with Ian Hamilton: 'I suppose I always try to write the truth and I wouldn't want to write a poem which suggested that I was different from what I am. . . . For instance, take love poems. I should feel it false to write a poem going overboard about someone if you weren't at the same time marrying them and setting up house with them. . . . I think that one of the great criticisms of poets of the past is that they said one thing and did another – a false relation between art and life. I always try to avoid this.' That, precisely, is the new anti-poets' quarrel with 'poets of the past,' with those poets who believed in poetry. It goes without saying that Philip

Larkin's inclusion of the poet's empirical self in this literalism is a severe limitation, though he overcomes it in many of his poems by identification and sympathy with other people's empirical selves. Yet Larkin has also observed: 'A very crude difference between novels and poetry is that novels are about other people and poetry is about yourself.' The danger arises where poets try too hard to let the reader's image rub off on their poems, especially where that image is conditioned by class differences and characterized by a set of attitudes morally and intellectually inferior to the poet's.

A very decided interest in foreign poetry – shared to some extent and in different ways by Donald Davie, D.J. Enright, Charles Tomlinson, Geoffrey Hill, Thom Gunn, Jon Silkin and Ted Hughes among British poets prominent since 1945 – underlies Christopher Middleton's summary of post-war trends in his interview. 'Modernism in Central Europe and Spain,' he said,[54] 'was at most points connected with a strong sense of social revolution, a catastrophic view of history, in which poets affiliated themselves to the progressive democratic and left-wing movements. In English-language modernism, on the other hand, we have never really had a democratic tradition. Eliot and Pound's poetry of that time was concerned with re-defining and purifying traditional values rather than with trying to generate ideas which would point forward.' If the new austerity is included among modern trends, despite its reaction against certain forms of modernism, English-language poetry since the thirties seems not less but more democratic than most of that written in other languages, if only because of a preoccupation with the ethics and 'ambiance' of personal relationships attested in Philip Larkin's reference to love poems. This preoccupation has been more persistent than preoccupations with formal innovation on the one hand, political change on the other; but the diction and *personae* of British poetry especially anticipated the international trend towards a closing of the gap between personal vision and public concerns. In America, too, William Carlos Williams was not alone in maintaining a democratic tradition. Middleton is certainly right when he says that Eliot and Pound 'were worried about culture, not about people'; but Williams was worried about people and culture.

The parochialism of English poetry is another matter. Philip

Larkin is proud of it. Middleton has said: 'There are very few English poets who seem to have any sense of history as something happening in me and you and all around us all the time: they've steered off into a parochial corner of the universe and have lost their historical sense.' Charles Tomlinson, too, spoke of 'the suffocation that has affected so much English art since the death of Byron.'[55] From a particular American point of view, Robert Bly wrote in 1962:[56] 'Current poets in the United States seem to be perishing on either side of a grey division between century-old British formalism on the one hand and a vandalism of anti-poetry on the other.' But a certain kind of parochialism can be a source of strength, if it is combined with Middleton's 'sense of history.' The poetic revival to which Tomlinson, Middleton and Bly have contributed has done away with 'century-old British formalism' but not with an often intense involvement in particular localities and ways of life. 'I believe that poetry is one means of discourse which takes one not into dream, not into clouds, but into realities beyond normally observable realities,' Christopher Middleton affirmed. Minute observable realities can lead to them; and even dreams can lead to them, if their peculiar kind of truth is rendered as scrupulously as any other.

Reviewing *A Group Anthology* in 1963, an anonymous contributor to *The Times Literary Supplement*[57] summed up his over-all impression of the contents in terms of what Northrop Frye has called 'the low mimetic,' characterizing them as follows: 'Poets no longer imitate the actions of gods or heroes, or allegorical representatives of ideal virtues, or states of *bourgeois* well-being, or intense and exciting states of subjective feeling: they imitate the untidy, shabby, incoherent pattern of every-day life as it is, and this imitation arouses in them no strong positive or negative feelings, but rather a peculiar and rather low-toned feeling, like the feeling of somebody swallowing with a grimace a tepid and flocculent half-pint of bitter beer, towards the dimness and yet the necessity of things as they are.'

What, for lack of a better word, I have called the new 'anti-poetry' is an extreme form of the 'low mimetic,' austerely dedicated to rendering 'things as they are' in the language of people as they speak. This kind of verse is anti-poetic if our norm is Romantic-Symbolist poetry, and its aspiration 'to the condition of music.' Yet our understanding of modern poetry is incomplete and inadequate if we forget that every movement towards pure, absolute autotelic or hermetic art arose from a quarrel with 'things as they are,' from a polar tension, such as Baudelaire's, between the world of 'spleen' and the 'ideal.' That tension may be low in much English verse of the fifties and sixties; but, from Baudelaire onwards, modern poetry has vacillated between collaboration with the *Zeitgeist* and defiance of it. Collaboration meant 'low mimesis' and irony, the realism not only of Laforgue and Corbière and Eliot, but of Baudelaire himself in lines like 'Eldorado banal de tous les vieux garçons'[58] ('Trite Eldorado of every old bachelor's dreams'). The force of that line, of course, derives from the tenacity of Baudelaire's adherence to the opposite pole, that of high art and of 'ideal virtues.' Baudelaire's 'dandyism' defied the *Zeitgeist* and prepared the way for the 'dehumanized' art of Mallarmé; but his realism collaborated with the *Zeitgeist* and humanized poetry by admitting characters, places and things excluded by his wholly Romantic predecessors. Out of a similar quarrel with himself Wallace Stevens, much of whose earlier poetry seemed the embodiment of a Baudelairean dandyism, came to declare, 'It must be human,' where the 'must' can be understood either as an imperative or as the confirmation of an inescapable fact; and William Carlos Williams, a master of the 'low mimetic,' came to declare, 'Only the imagination is real.'

W. H. Auden, too, has perpetuated the quarrel, suppressing the lines that contained one of his best-known professions of 'commitment':[59]

> All I have is a voice
> To undo the folded lie,
> The romantic lie in the brain
> Of the sensual man-in-the-street
> And the lie of Authority
> Whose buildings grope the sky;
> There is no such thing as the State
> And no one exists alone;
> Hunger allows no choice
> To the citizen or the police;
> We must love one another or die.

That too explicit, too easy profession was cancelled by another, equally explicit, in Auden's *New Year Letter*:

> Art is not life and cannot be
> A midwife to society.

Commenting on Auden's attempt to resolve the contradiction in theory by positing two kinds of art, 'escape art' and 'parable art,' Colin Falck has written:

Art, in other words, is not the creation of forms which symbolize and make sense of feelings in real life. It is a second, escape world cut off from the real life altogether. And rendering unto Caesar is not a matter of using the discoveries of art for the saner management of life: it is the adulteration of art itself with the philosophy of life that the artist already holds. Responsible poetry therefore becomes a kind of war-time fruit cake, with the raisins of escape thinly distributed in a daily bread of parable. Many people would feel that these rather prosaic theories have left their mark on Auden's poetry. But is the truer story perhaps that it happened the other way round? Inside the Auden we know, that is to say, there was once a Romantic-Symbolist signalling to be let out; something happened to the signals, and the poet began casting around for an external authority which would free him from the authority of poetry itself. . . .60

As Colin Falck implies in the same essay, the 'authority of poetry itself' permits no convenient division of loyalties to 'parable art' on the one hand, 'escape art' on the other, though it permits, or positively demands, a permanent tension between the two poles. In that respect 'modern poetry' is no different from poetry of any other period, though the two poles have moved farther apart since Heinrich Heine's lines about the unending battle between 'truth' and 'beauty,' 'barbarians' and 'Hellenes,' 61 a battle fought out not only between opposing schools of poets and critics, but within every poet who matters, from poem to poem, and from line to line.

10

TOWN AND COUNTRY: PHENOTYPES AND ARCHETYPES

1   I F A humane and humanistic poetry is one that 'marches fraternally between science and philosophy,' as Baudelaire put it, the poetry written since his time might be expected to have come to terms both with machines and with the predominantly urban character of a mechanized civilization. Some modern poetry has; but it is one thing to assert with F. T. Marinetti and other Futurists that a 'roaring motor-car is more beautiful than the Nike of Samothrace,' or to make sure that one's landscapes contain the obligatory pylon, quite another to attune the mind, sensibility and imagination to an urban and technological order which they stubbornly resist – out of the very antagonism to specialization that motivated Baudelaire's pronouncements against the growing specialization of art. Baudelaire is often said to have initiated a poetry of the modern city. If he did so, he also initiated a response to it ambivalent at best, but more often like the grimace with which the Group Anthology poets are described as swallowing their 'tepid and flocculent half-pint of bitter beer.' Baudelaire celebrated Paris as he celebrated her prostitutes, beggars, drunkards, underdogs and criminals. Indeed, he celebrated Paris as a whore; and in an unfinished poem intended for the second edition of *Les Fleurs du mal*,[1] he wrote:

> Car j'ai de chaque chose extrait la quintessence,
> Tu m'as donné ta boue et j'en ai fait de l'or.

(From each thing I gathered its quintessence,
You gave me your mire, and I turned it into gold.)

Like Rimbaud after him, Baudelaire saw himself as an 'alchemist of the world,' not merely collecting the base matter of the modern city, but transmuting it: and right up to the snatches of pub talk in Eliot's *The Waste Land*, very few of Baudelaire's successors have found any other use for the raw material of modern city life. Wordsworth was able to celebrate London as he did because the time of day and the perspective of Westminster Bridge exempted him from moral involvement in everything which 'that mighty heart' activated when it was not 'lying still.' In poems such as the verse *Epilogue* to *Petits poèmes en prose* Baudelaire tried hard to contemplate Paris from an aesthetically soothing distance and vantage point, but already by the third line of his *Epilogue* not only have a 'hospital' and 'brothels' detached themselves from his aerial view of the city as a whole, but these literal data have been joined without transition by a metaphorical 'purgatory' and 'hell.' The poem ends as a declaration of love for the 'infamous capital,' its 'courtesans' and 'bandits,' with a salutation, on the way, to Satan, 'patron' of Baudelaire's 'distress' – because only that perverse resort enabled Baudelaire to extract aesthetic gold from the moral mire that was his raw material.

Nor was it an accident that the first poet to grapple with the modern city both as an artist and as a moralist should be driven to resorts like Baudelaire's pseudo-theology of Satanism, or his related efforts to persuade himself that artifice was superior to nature. This cult of artifice, consciousness and deliberateness – adapted by Baudelaire from the writings of Edgar Allan Poe and passed on to a variety of later poets, from Mallarmé and Wilde to Stefan George and the Yeats of the Byzantium poems – might easily have constituted one link between modern poetry and modern technology. The author of *Axel*, a classic of 'decadent' aestheticism, also wrote one of the early classics of science fiction, *L'Eve future*; but Villiers de l'Isle-Adam's interest in modern inventions, like Poe's, was aesthetic and psychological. Baudelaire and his successors could approve the ingenuity that went into scientific inventions, and their utopian potentialities; what they could not accept was the utilitarian functions and ends of modern technology. Despite his lip service to the cult of artifice, therefore, Baudelaire's imagery tended to draw on nature for symbols of the 'ideal,' on the phenomena of modern civilization for symbols of the fallen, depraved and neurotic condition which he called 'spleen.' However hard he tried, he could not be more modern in this regard than William Blake, whose response to 'dark Satanic mills' or the 'marks of weakness, marks of woe' on every city-dweller's face differed from Baudelaire's only in being unambiguous in its opposition to the utilitarian principle.

Many later poets have shown a similar incapacity to march 'fraternally' beside a science that applied itself to providing new means of economic exploitation. One reason for it may be that 'the imagination is conservative,' as Hofmannsthal said; but the 'conservative' must not be understood in a narrowly political sense. The imagination can also be politically radical, like William Blake's, or revolutionary, as in so many poets since Baudelaire. Yet even at its most utopian or apocalyptic, the imagination is conservative in its recourse to norms and archetypes. The Good City is one of those norms and archetypes; but since few or no modern cities have been found good enough by their poets, nature is the norm to which poetry has returned again and again, with a persistency not diminished but intensified by urban and industrial encroachments on the countryside. As David Wright has emphasized,[2] English Romantic nature poetry, too, was a reaction to the industrial revolution and to modes of thought consonant with it. Even those twentieth-century poets who have achieved a thorough break with Romantic-Symbolist premises have found it impossible to accept technical advances that could lead to the destruction of all nature, as well as all civilization, on this planet – 'the best that we have,' as Günter Kunert has called it in his sardonic epigram *Laika*.[3] This is true even of the most politically progressive and scientifically minded of the post-1945 poets, with the possible exception of some of the Concrete poets, whose very methods are scientific or mechanistic in as much as they experiment with verbal material at once morally neutral and semantically fortuitous, as though aspiring to the conditions of computers.

Machines are prominent in the poetry of Hans Magnus Enzensberger, who has taken immense trouble to keep up with scientific and technical developments, just as he has made it his business to know what is going on in politics and society all over the world. Yet he has done so not in order to 'march fraternally' beside the technicians but to know what they are up to, and to oppose them. That he, too, is on the side of nature can hardly be doubted by readers of his poem *das ende der eulen* (the end of the owls) :[4]

> ich spreche von euerm nicht,
> ich spreche vom ende der eulen.
> ich spreche von butt und wal
> in ihrem dunkeln haus,
> dem siebenfältigen meer,
> von den gletschern,
> sie werden kalben zu früh,
> rab und taube, gefiederten zeugen,
> von allem was lebt in lüften
> und wäldern, und den flechten im kies,
> vom weglosen selbst, und vom grauen moor
> und den leeren gebirgen:
>
> auf radarschirmen leuchtend
> zum letzten mal, ausgewertet
> auf meldetischen, von antennen
> tödlich befingert floridas sümpfe
> und das sibirische eis, tier
> und schilf und schiefer erwürgt
> von warnketten, umzingelt
> vom letzten manöver, arglos
> unter schwebenden feuerglocken,
> im ticken des ernstfalls.
>
> wir sind schon vergessen.
> sorgt euch nicht um die waisen,
> aus dem sinn schlagt euch
> die mündelsichern gefühle,
> den ruhm, die rostfreien psalmen.
> ich spreche nicht mehr von euch,
> planern der spurlosen tat,
> und von mir nicht, und keinem.
> ich spreche von dem was nicht spricht,
> von den sprachlosen zeugen,
> von ottern und robben,
> von den alten eulen der erde.

(i do not speak of what's yours,
i speak of the end of the owls.
i speak of turbot and whale
in their glimmering house,
in the sevenfold sea,
of the glaciers –
too soon they will calve –
raven and dove, the feathered witnesses
of all that lives in the winds
and woods, and the lichen on rock,
of impassable tracts and the grey moors
and the empty mountain ranges:

shining on radar screens
for the last time, recorded,
checked out on consoles, fingered
by aerials fatally florida's marshes
and the siberian ice, animal
reed and slate all strangled
by interlinked warnings, encircled
by the last manoeuvres, guileless
under hovering cones of fire,
while the time-fuses tick.

we are already forgotten.
don't give a thought to the orphans,
expunge from your minds
your gilt-edged security feelings
and fame and the stainless psalms.
i don't speak of you any more,
planners of vanishing actions,
nor of me, nor of anyone.
i speak of that without speech,
of the unspeaking witnesses,
of otters and seals,
of the ancient owls of the earth.)

The depreciation of humanity here is rhetorical and ironic. Yet the playing off of men against nature, of technical contraptions against the 'grey moors,' points to one of Enzensberger's constant and serious preoccupations. The extreme confrontation of the two orders occurs in a later poem, *lachesis lapponica*; and there the 'greyness' of a Scandinavian landscape calls in question the very human and moral commitments that have impelled Enzensberger in the direction of anti-poetry. Nor is Enzensberger alone among poets of his time in experiencing the natural order as an alternative to civilization. Whereas the Romantics tended to look for a harmony between men and nature, post-Nietzschean poets have been tempted to dismiss all civilization as a botched job, to turn their backs on history and to look at human affairs *sub specie naturae*. Enzensberger has not given in to this temptation, but he has clearly felt it. The example of predecessors like Gottfried Benn, who drew on his scientific training for writings not only drastically hostile to science but atavistic in their longing for pre-conscious nature, served as a warning. Yet well-meaning calls for fraternal marches and the happy cohabitation of 'the two cultures' have become not less but more inept since Baudelaire's time. Many poets have done their best to become more scientific; but many technicians and technocrats now perform functions as incompatible with the human ends of science as with those of poetry.

2   Needless to say, an anti-scientific, anti-positivist bias has also persisted among poets.

> ... But they have named all the stars,
> trodden down the scrub of the desert, run the white moon to a
>   schedule,
> Joshua's serf whose beauty drove men mad.
> They have melted the snows from Erebus, weighed the clouds,
> hunted down the white bear; hunted the whale the seal the
>   kangaroo
> they have set private enquiry agents on to Archipiada :
> What is your name? Your maiden name?
> Go in there to be searched. I suspect it is not your true name.
> Distinguishing marks if any? (O anthropometrics!) ...

This passage from Basil Bunting's *Villon*,[5] written in 1925, renders a whole complex of traditional poetic antagonisms – to scientific positivism, to the interference of men in the life of nature, to the interference of technically aided administrations in the lives of individuals. The same poet, characteristically, has resisted the anti-poeticism that demands direct statement couched in the vocabulary and syntax of current prose usage.

'Poetry is seeking to make not meaning but beauty,' Basil Bunting has said;[6] 'or if you insist on misusing words, its "meaning" is of another kind, and lies in the relation to one another of lines and patterns of sound, perhaps harmonious, perhaps contrasting and clashing, which the hearer feels rather than understands; lines of sounds drawn in the air which stir deeper emotions which have not even a name in prose. This needs no explaining to an audience which gets its poetry by ear.' Apart from the question of whether poetry should be read or heard – and the present revival of spoken poetry, on the whole, has favoured not Bunting's kind of poetry but the kind that conveys instant and obvious 'meaning' with little regard for 'beauty' – Bunting's statement defines the position of a poet who will not collaborate with the *Zeitgeist*, a position reminiscent of the modernism of 1912. His very use of the unfashionable word 'beauty' reminds us that the truths of modern poetry need not be the truths of newspapers, nor its concerns the concerns of politicians. Bunting's highly developed sense of place, and of particular ways of life rooted in particular localities, is another characteristic that sets his work apart from anything that could be described as a new 'international style' in poetry.

Of all the values which the imagination of twentieth-century poets has conserved – whether with the literalism of Enzensberger or the intricate allusiveness of earlier modernists – none has been as consistently and unanimously upheld as the seemingly lost cause of nature. Ideas of the Good City have differed, since they depend on religious, ethical and political assumptions. Edwin Muir's poem *The Good Town*[7] exemplifies one such idea, but in retrospect and by contrast with those things that had turned the good town into a bad one; and Edwin Muir's entire work arose from a duality not unlike Baudelaire's, a duality that contrasts the phenomena of experience with the archetypes of the imagination. Something of the ambivalence of Baudelaire's response to his city has attached to much of the specifically urban poetry written since his time – even, as I have suggested, to Hart Crane's *The Bridge*, for all its affirmative and laudatory designs.

Eliot's *The Waste Land* is far from being the only poem of its period in which the modern city becomes infernal. Eliot's German coeval Georg Heym, who died in 1912, devoted a poem to the demons of the cities (*Die Dämonen der Städte*), and this is only one of many apocalyptic visions of megalopolitan infernos in his work and that of his contemporaries, Georg Trakl, Ernst Stadler, Jakob van Hoddis, Alfred Lichtenstein and Yvan Goll. In a poem by Hoddis, *Morgens* (In the Morning), girls going to work in factories, 'to the machine and dreary drudgery,' are juxtaposed with the 'tender light' of morning and 'the tender green of the trees,' the 'screaming' of urban sparrows with 'the singing of skylarks' 'out there in the wilder fields.' Georg Trakl's relatively slight experience of Vienna and Berlin gave rise to visions of evil more stark than those of either Eliot or Baudelaire, as in his short poem *An die Verstummten* (To the Silenced):

> O, der Wahnsinn der grossen Stadt, da am Abend
> An schwarzer Mauer verkrüppelte Bäume starren,
> Aus silberner Maske der Geist des Bösen schaut;
> Licht mit magnetischer Geissel die steinerne Nacht verdrängt.
> O, das versunkene Läuten der Abendglocken.
>
> Hure, die in eisigen Schauern ein totes Kindlein gebärt.
> Rasend peitscht Gottes Zorn die Stirn des Besessenen,
> Purpurne Seuche, Hunger, der grüne Augen zerbricht.
> O, das grässliche Lachen des Golds.
>
> Aber stille blutet in dunkler Höhle stummere Menschheit,
> Fügt aus harten Metallen das erlösende Haupt.
>
> (Oh, the great city's madness when at nightfall
> The crippled trees gape by the blackened wall,
> The spirit of evil peers from a silver mask;
> Lights with magnetic scourges drive off the stony night.
> Oh, the sunken pealing of evening bells.
>
> Whore who in icy spasms gives birth to a dead child.
> With raving whips God's fury punishes brows possessed,
> Purple pestilence, hunger that breaks green eyes.
> Oh, the horrible laughter of gold.
>
> But silent in dark caverns a stiller humanity bleeds,
> Out of hard metals moulds the redeeming head.)

The antagonism of all these poets to cities that owed their expansion to commerce and industry could be ascribed to Romantic-Symbolist attitudes. Trakl also wrote an early poem,

Die schöne Stadt (The Beautiful City), about Salzburg, and in
that poem there is no moral or aesthetic condemnation of towns
as such. In the town of that poem pealing bells and organ music
blend quite happily with 'march rhythms' and 'guard calls,'
just as the smells of incense and lilac blend with the smell of tar.
Trakl's pre-1914 Salzburg, like Edwin Muir's Prague before
the Communist coup of 1948, could still be reconciled with ideas
of the Good City. Yet the Communists among the German poets
of Georg Trakl's generation were no less antagonistic to big
cities than those who were liberals or Christian; and a generation earlier the politically 'progressive' poet Richard Dehmel
had written his *Predigt ans Grossstadtvolk*[8] (Sermon to the
Inhabitants of Large Cities), calling on the new urban proletariat to revolt by leaving the cities and taking possession of the
countryside! Again, the utopian Communism of the pre-1918
era, especially its German variants, must be distinguished from
later party dogma; but Bertolt Brecht, who remained a Communist throughout the Stalin era and did his utmost to purge
his poetry of every kind of residual bourgeois romanticism,
also presented visions of the doom of large cities, from the early
Vom armen B.B. (Of Poor B.B.) with its reference to 'those tall
boxes on the island of Manhattan' –

Von diesen Städten wird bleiben: der durch sie hindurchging, der
Wind!

(Of those cities will remain: what passed through them, the wind!) –

to more cautious or cryptic allusions to this theme right up to
his last poems, as in his apology for country retreats, *Sommerurlaub
in Buckow* (1953),[9] which concludes with the dialectical justification: 'Principles are kept alive by being broken.' In his poem
of the mid-twenties, *Von der zermalmenden Wucht der Städte*[10] (Of
the Crushing Impact of Cities), Brecht's manner is still modernistic, visionary and idiosyncratic; the free association of images
recalls Rimbaud:

> Aber die Händelosen
> Ohne Luft zwischen sich
> Hatten Gewalt wie roher Äther.
> In ihnen war beständig
> Die Macht der Leere, welche die grösste ist.

275

Sie hiessen Mangel-an-Atem, Abwesenheit, Ohne-Gestalt
Und sie zermalmten wie Granitberge
Die aus der Luft fallen fortwährend.
Oh, ich sah Gesichter
Wie in schnell hinspülendem Wasser
Der abtrünnige Kies
Sehr einförmig. Viele gesammelt
Gaben ein Loch
Das sehr gross war.

Immer jetzt rede ich nur
Von der stärksten Rasse
Über die Mühen der ersten Zeit.

Plötzlich
Flohen einige in die Luft
Bauend nach oben; andere vom höchsten Hausdach
Warfen ihre Hüte hoch und schrien:
So hoch das nächste!
Aber die Nachfolgenden
Nach gewohnten Daches Verkauf fliehend vor Nachtfrost
Drangen nach und sehen mit Augen des Schellfischs
Die langen Gehäuse
Die nachfolgenden.
Denn zu jener Zeit in selbiger Wändefalt
Assen in Hast
Vier Geschlechter zugleich
Hatten in ihrem Kindheitsjahr
Auf flacher Hand den Nagel im Wandstein
Niemals gesehn.
Ihnen wuchs ineinander
Das Erz und der Stein.
So kurz war die Zeit
Dass zwischen Morgen und Abend
Kein Mittag war
Und schon standen auf altem, gewöhnetem Boden
Gebirge Beton.

(But the handless
Without air between them
Had the strength of crude ether.
In them was constant
The vacuum's power, the greatest power of all.
They were called Lack-of-Breath, Absence, No-Shape

And they crushed like mountains of granite
That fell from the air without end.
Oh, I saw faces
Like renegade pebbles
Left behind in swift-rinsing water
Very uniform. Many of them assembled
Made a hole
That was very large.

Always now I am speaking
Of the strongest race only
Of the first phase's labours.

Suddenly
Some of them fled into the air
Building upwards; others from the highest rooftop
Flung high their hats and shouted:
As high as the next!
But their successors
Fleeing from night frost after the sale of familiar roofs
Pressed on behind them and see with a haddock's eyes
Those long receptacles
That succeeded houses.
For within the same walls at that time
Four generations at once
Gulped down their food
And in their childhood year
Had never seen
On flat palms the nail in the wallstone.
So brief was that time
That between morning and evening
There was no noon
And already on the old, familiar site
Loomed mountains of concrete.⟩

That myth of the building of modern cities is connected not
only with the brief reference to Manhattan in the earlier poem
but also to Brecht's poem *Diese babylonische Verwirrung* (This
Babylonian Confusion) probably written towards the end of the
twenties. Essentially different though it is from the apocalyptic
visions of cities in poems written by the early Expressionists
before the First World War – most of which carried implications
of judgement, even where Lichtenstein's mundane irony made

'handsome homosexuals' tumble out of bed, rather than invoking doom upon Sodom and Gomorrah – Brecht's myth is no more favourable to the modern city. Nor is the related short poem *Von den Resten älterer Zeiten* (Of the Remnants of Former Times) in which the moon that 'still hangs above the new buildings at night' becomes 'the most useless/Of the things made of copper' and the 'great new aerials,' already present in *Of Poor B.B.*, 'know nothing of a former time.'

The Swedish poet Lars Gustafsson (born 1936) has filled his poems with detailed descriptions of ingenious machines; but these machines turn out to be museum pieces, with the romantic glamour of vintage cars or the ruins of Victorian factories. It is the British poets, from Auden, Spender, MacNeice and Day Lewis in the thirties to Philip Larkin in the fifties and sixties, who have done most to naturalize the really functional gadgets of their time in poetry – without too obtrusive a grimace in a few striking instances, such as Larkin's poem *Here*[11] with its 'cut-price crowd, urban and simple.' Needless to say, even Larkin's acceptance of this crowd and its technical accessories has been wrested from expectations and preferences more traditionally 'poetic,' as the Baudelairean spleen that pervades most of his later poetry attests; but Basil Bunting's archetypes, too, would lose half their significance without their contraries, the 'private enquiry agents' and the 'anthropometrics.' It was a poet, William Blake, who said, 'Without Contraries is no progression.' Without contraries there would be no poetry either. Every modern poet worth reading contains an anti-poet, just as every modern anti-poet worth reading contains a Romantic-Symbolist poet. The wider and the more strongly charged the field of tension between them, the greater a poet's potentialities of achievement and progression.

3   The urban crowd which Philip Larkin's poems can sometimes accept is not that of London or 'Megalometropolis,' as David Gascoyne called London in his *Night Thoughts*,[12] the most Baudelairean exploration of an urban inferno written since the last war. Gascoyne's archetypes in that poem are not so much those of nature as those of the Good City, but that does not make his vision either more conciliatory or less ambivalent than Baudelaire's. The Battersea Power Station's 'giant stacks' become

> The pillars of a temple raised to man-made power and light

so that a sort of Promethean or Luciferian grandeur is granted to Gascoyne's city despite the 'fumes that rise from the abyss.' Yet, since archetypes dominate Gascoyne's vision, his megalo-metropolis remains infernal.

Poets whose vision is dominated by the archetypes of nature, on the other hand, have been able to accept and even to celebrate cities, perhaps because moral judgement is less incumbent on their imagination. Two contemporaries of the early Expression-ists, Oskar Loerke and Wilhelm Lehmann, are remarkable for a poetry that subordinates all temporal and spatial differences to a Nietzschean cosmology of recurrent identity, a cosmology based on the cycles of nature and on the archetypes of myth. Both poets could accept and assimilate many phenomena of modern civilization not because of a special commitment to them but because almost any phenomenon fitted into an order so capacious. I say 'almost,' because the phenomena of National Socialist rule reduced Loerke to despair and Lehmann to silence. Neither nature nor mythology provided models for that kind of civilization, though Loerke drew on the animal world and the 'realm of shades' in his attempts to render the self-destructive futility of the war.[13] Wilhelm Lehmann survived both world wars to write poems in which Marlene Dietrich and Claire Bloom are effortlessly juxtaposed with Aphrodite and Artemis, the minutiae of observed reality – and Lehmann's knowledge of botany and zoology alone gives a scientific precision to his observations – with their recurrent archetypes. After a visit to England at the age of eighty-two, his first for almost half a century, Lehmann wrote a poem called *London* (1964).[14] The poem does not characterize, let alone judge, the city as a whole. From the opening lines:

> Jahrhundertespät
> Novemberkühl
>
> (Centuries late,
> November-cool)

it moves to a 'chaplinesque old man' playing jazz records to the

city crowd from an old pram, his bowler hat pressed down over
a thin face, then to the Zoo and to an East Asian owl, the tilt
of whose head is like that of the old man's head. But at that
point the archetypes effect a transformation and reversal:

> Sie übersieht mich,
> La Belle Dame sans merci,
> Ich bin der Greis,
> Die Göttin sie.

> (She overlooks me,
> La belle Dame sans merci,
> I'm the agèd man,
> The goddess she.)

In Lehmann's work – and to a lesser extent in Loerke's – the
function of natural and mythical archetypes is mainly conciliatory, because they suspend historical and generic differences
even where particulars are scrupulously adduced. Edwin Muir
is another poet who celebrated recurrent fables, situations and
types, but with a dual vision as alive to contrasts and conflicts
as to similarities; and those contrasts and conflicts, of course, are
inseparable from the human condition of 'living in time.'

Living in Time was the title of one of Kathleen Raine's early
books of poems.[15] The same poet is now almost alone, at least
among her English and American contemporaries, in both
writing and advocating a poetry of pure types, the archetypes
of nature, myth, religion and metaphysics. In her essay *On the
Symbol* she takes issue with the critical writings of William
Empson, which she considers 'consistent with the positivist
philosophy' of Cambridge: 'For all the complexities and ambiguities and relationships which he discerns are upon the same
plane of the real. There is one type of complexity which he fails
to consider, that resonance which may be present within an
image of apparent simplicity, setting into vibrations planes of
reality and of consciousness other than that of the sensible world:
the power of the symbol and symbolical discourse.'[16] Here
Kathleen Raine is in partial agreement with Philippe Jaccottet
who has also remarked on the 'apparent simplicity of the
greatest poetry'; but in practice, and this applies to some of the
poems in Kathleen Raine's collection *The Hollow Hill*,[17] symbols
derived from esoteric philosophy may be as inaccessible to

readers not familiar with it as the ingenious ambiguities and complexities in William Empson's poems; and there is also the danger that tension may be lost if the particulars of experience are either too rigidly excluded or too directly identified with the archetypes.

In his later collection of essays, *L'Entretien des Muses*,[18] Philippe Jaccottet has been careful to strike the right balance between the extremes of pure and impure poetry, including the kind of purity that goes straight to the archetypes. In the work of René Char, for instance, Jaccottet finds a tendency towards a poetic 'narcissism' that is one of style, not of attitude, and considers Char's best passages to be those 'distinguished by being relatively closer to the common language.' Jaccottet still believes in poetry as 'a simple object of knowledge': 'The poet's eye is the battering-ram which demolishes his walls and, if only for a moment, gives us back the real and, together with the real, *a possibility of life.*' But this reality need not be esoteric, especially at a time when the most ordinary phenomena of the 'sensible world' are losing their reality. 'The eye of modern poets is one of the sharpest and most attentive that exists (whether it falls on objects close or distant, on interior or exterior space, poles which, in any case, he tends to interchange or reverse).' Above all, Jaccottet never forgets this essential polarity of the poetic mode of perception. He defines 'the sort of *realism* relevant to modern poetry' as one that is not 'merely a minute inventory of the visible, but an attention to it so profound that it must inevitably end by coming up against the limits of the visible.' In other words, poetic realism is not incompatible with 'symbolic discourse,' since in poetry the most concrete image tends to assume symbolic connotations, which need not be conscious, systematic or intended. Kathleen Raine, too, has a scientist's knowledge of the particulars of nature; and it is this concentration on particulars that distinguishes twentieth-century nature poetry, regardless of whether those particulars are rendered for their own sake or within a cosmological, metaphysical or symbolic framework.

If 'nature poetry' has become a dispensable category, it is not because the sensibility and vision of poets has become predominantly urban. In the work of Ted Hughes, for instance, historical experience is inseparable from a new concern with the ferocity of predatory animals. Ted Hughes did not need to draw elaborate analogies between his hawk, whose 'manners are tearing off heads,' and the human proclivities that have given him his peculiar power to identify with hawks, pike, thrushes, otters or water-lilies; the single word 'manners' is enough to make the connection. Even Ted Hughes's snowdrop is 'brutal' in the pursuit 'of her ends.' Since the animal and plant poems of *A Hawk in the Rain* and *Lupercal* Ted Hughes, in any case, has been extending the same vision to human affairs, especially to war, as in the sequence *Scapegoats and Rabies*[19] or the sequence *Out*.[20] A cruel cosmology and ontology has also been emerging in poems like *Pibroch* and *Goat-Psalm*. If these are 'nature poems' they are also civilization poems of the post-Auschwitz, post-Hiroshima era, instances of the 'extremist art' which A. Alvarez has found in the work of Robert Lowell, John Berryman, Sylvia Plath and Anne Sexton.[21] The stricture of anthropomorphism, too, has become inapplicable to the animal poems of Ted Hughes, as to the *Flower Poems*[22] of Jon Silkin, because one could just as easily complain that Hughes's poems about human beings are 'zoomorphic'; and comparisons, implicit or explicit, between human and non-human behaviour have come to favour the non-human orders. In Ted Hughes's *View of a Pig*[23] there are no references to the political world; yet the pig's behaviour – conditioned in any case by what men have made of the original animal, by its breeding and domestication – is related to human behaviour towards the pig:

> ... Pigs must have hot blood, they feel like ovens.
> Their bite is worse than a horse's –
> They chop a half-moon clean out:
> They eat cinders, dead cats.
> . . . .
> I stared at it a long time. They were going to scald it.
> Scald it and scour it like a doorstep.

Theodore Roethke's earthy flower poems have a good deal in common with those written a generation later by Ted Hughes and Jon Silkin. Although Roethke seemed content to render the greedy self-assertiveness of plants without looking for human analogies, his poem *Orchids* shows the same concern and familiarity with non-human behaviour or 'manners' – a concern and familiarity almost totally lacking in Romantic nature poetry.

Roethke's orchids are 'devouring infants,' 'Lips neither dead nor alive/Loose ghostly mouths/Breathing':

> They lean over the path,
> Adder-mouthed,
> Swaying close to the face,
> Coming out, soft and deceptive,
> Limp and damp, delicate as a young bird's tongue;
> Their fluttery fledgling lips
> Move slowly,
> Drawing in the warm air. . . .[24]

All the descriptive epithets and similes of this poem enact the process of devouring; and since any successful description in lyrical poetry presupposes a measure of self-identification with the thing described, all Roethke's plant and greenhouse poems tell us something about human nature. In a sense, they are part of Roethke's autobiography, an exploration of those subconscious layers of the personality which remain intimately related to the animal, vegetable and even mineral orders. Stephen Spender has said: 'The unconscious mind from which poetry derives – or to put it more old-fashionedly, the imagination – believes in whatever it animates.'[25] This can also be put the other way round: the unconscious mind or imagination animates that to which it feels related; and although machinery and gadgets may occupy our conscious mind, because we use them or tinker with them or are used by them, modern poetry proves conclusively that our kinship with organic nature can only be repressed, never eradicated. The more it is repressed, the greater its threat to the civilization that represses it.

'The modernist tradition, though it was neglected between about 1935 and 1955, is again very much alive,' Louis Simpson wrote in 1964.[26] One of the outstanding American contributors to that revival, Gary Snyder, has explained how little that revival owes to the quality of industrial civilization in his country. 'My own opinion,' he wrote in his essay *Passage to More than India,*[27] 'is that we are now experiencing a surfacing (in a specifically "American" incarnation) of the great Subculture which goes back as far perhaps as the late Paleolithic.' This surfacing has to do with the rediscovery that 'mankind's mother is Nature and Nature should be tenderly respected; that man's life and destiny is growth and enlightenment in self-disciplined freedom; that the divine has been made flesh and that flesh is divine; that we not only should but *do* love one another.' One manifestation of the surfacing is the recognition of the American Indian past: 'The American Indian is the vengeful ghost lurking in the back of the troubled American mind. . . . That ghost will claim the next generation as its own. When this has happened, citizens of the USA will at last begin to be Americans, truly at home on the continent, in love with their land.' Gary Snyder's prediction is based on the view that 'industrial society indeed appears to be finished.' Even if that view is tinged with wishful thinking – and Snyder supports it with the most various evidence – the wish is one that should be taken seriously by politicians, sociologists and town planners. In the new American poetry, not least in Gary Snyder's, it has become vital and fertile; where it remains inarticulate or unconscious, destructive violence is its one release.

One common and unifying feature of much new American poetry is its dynamism – 'art as process,'[28] as Charles Olson has called it. This aesthetic is naturalistic not in the sense of imitating nature, but of wanting art to *be* nature. Much of this poetry is highly individual, to the point of idiosyncrasy, but it is not individualistic, because the poet's self is conceived as part of nature. Indeed, Olson has also written of 'getting rid of the lyrical interference of the individual ego.' The first person is freely used as an indispensable vehicle in the process of apprehending objective realities. As Robert Creeley puts it, 'the question becomes, *what is real* – and what is of that nature? The most severe argument we can offer against the "value" of some thing or act, is that it is *not* real, that is has no given place in what our world has either chosen or been forced to admit. So it is the *condition* of reality which becomes our greatest concern.' Olson defines this reality as one 'without interruption' – like the reality of nature – and it is the poet's business to treat 'the objects which occur at every given moment of composition (of recognition, we can call it) . . . exactly as they do occur therein and not by any ideas or preconceptions from outside the poem. . . .' Robert Duncan has made the same point both in his analysis, quoted by Creeley, of conventional form 'significant in so far as it shows control' – a kind of form that he found inadequate – and in this explanation of his own practice:

'Central to and defining the poetics I am trying to suggest here is the conviction that the order man may contrive or impose upon the things about him or upon his own language is trivial beside the divine order or natural order he may discover in them.'[29] It is hardly necessary to stress the connection between that principle of discovering, not imposing, order, and Gary Snyder's view that 'industrial society indeed appears to be finished.' The assumptions behind this new aesthetic are not anti-scientific – Duncan's authorities include the scientists Whitehead and Schrödinger – but they are anti-technological. 'It is a changing aesthetic,' Duncan says, 'but it is also a changing sense of life. Perhaps we recognize as never before in man's history that not only our own personal consciousness but the inner structure of the universe itself has only this immediate event in which to be realized. Atomic physics has brought us to the threshold of such a – I know not whether to call it certainty or doubt. . . . The other sense that underlies the new form is one that men have come to again and again in their most intense and deepest vision, that the Kingdom is here, that we have only now in which to live.'[30]

Robert Creeley also stresses the importance of place and of things in a kind of writing whose nature is 'to move in the field of its recognitions, the "open field" of Olsen's *Projective Verse*.' This place, he says, 'is not now more than activity'; and Gary Snyder's work is the most remarkable instance of how both place and things can become integral parts of activities re-enacted in words, in poems that convey the very rhythms of physical labour. This aspect of the new poetry is also brought out by Edward Dorn in his essay on Olson's *Maximus Poems*, especially where he opposes description for description's sake, which Creeley calls 'that practice that wants to "accompany the *real*" but which assumes itself as "objectively" outside the context in some way.' Creeley also quotes Louis Zukovsky: 'This does not presume that the style will be the man, but rather that the order of his syllables will define his awareness of order. For his . . . major aim is not to show himself but that order that of itself can speak to all men.'

Since the new aesthetic insists on a poetry 'where the whole physiology of a man is at work in the poem'[31] stylistic differences do become operative again, despite the agreement of all those poets over basic principles. Robert Creeley's poems, for instance, are not only taut and spare, compared to those of Olson or the more recent poems of Edward Dorn,[32] but the processes they enact are mainly inner processes. Things and places, therefore, are less prominent in them and Creeley shows affinities with European poets of the new austerity in his almost total avoidance of metaphor. When Creeley writes of Olson, as compared with Pound, that 'he wanted to see the organization of the poem become *something more than an ego system*,' he raises crucial questions not about the intentions but about the practice of some of these poets, especially in their longer poems. Duncan has praised Olson for his 'leisurely and exact talking,'[33] but one limitation of the new aesthetic is that it does away with the principle of selection; this can lead to garrulity, the besetting sin of American verse in the Whitman lineage. Olson is certainly right in insisting that 'art does not seek to describe but to enact.'[34] Yet the exclusive stress on energy and process does not allow for the inescapable differences between art and nature or for the quality of what a poem enacts.

Robert Bly believes that this new aesthetic has hardened into an orthodoxy as rigid as the academicism which it set out to displace and blames 'the American love of technique.'[35] Bly has both advocated and practised a poetry of the 'deep image,' and his models have been European rather than American. Of the new American poets he writes that they are now 'about half-free' – only half-free because 'their poetry tends to restrict itself to certain mapped out sections of the psyche. The reason is that this fourth generation instead of going to the sources of "free verse" in Europe, have modelled themselves basically on Eliot, Pound and Williams. . . . We have not yet regained in American poetry that swift movement all over the psyche, from conscious to unconscious, from a fine table to mad inward desires, that the ancient poets had, or that Lorca and others gained back for poetry in Spanish. Why not? Every time we get started, we get sidetracked into technique.'

Despite the theoretical agreement among poets of the Black Mountain and Beat groups, the practice of some of them is close to that of Robert Bly, James Wright, Louis Simpson, W.S. Merwin and Donald Hall, who belong to neither group. Denise Levertov and Cid Corman, like Robert Creeley, write mainly short poems, often with a psychic freedom conducive to the 'deep image.' The same poets, on the other hand, have written political poems in which that psychic freedom is restricted by the need to drive home a point, though their best political poems retain as much of it as the medium permits.[36] Nor is a sense of process lacking in them or in other poets who are not 'projectivists.' Robert Bly's *Driving through Minnesota during the Hanoi Bombings* is an attempt to enact two experiences simultaneously, the one involving the poet physically and immediately, the other sympathetically and imaginatively; in this poem, too, the first person is used as a vehicle, not as a subject.

The return to nature in American poetry – and by that I mean not only the rural setting of much new poetry but also what I have called its naturalistic aesthetic – is closely bound up with the need to get rid of 'ego systems.' That need, anticipated by Brecht, has also informed the new austerity of European poets; but in those countries where corporative pressures have been greatest, under Stalinist and Fascist régimes, poets have felt an opposing need to reassert the personal principle. In *A Precocious Autobiography*[37] Yevgeny Yevtushenko wrote of the 'substitution of the "we" for "I" by the Proletarian Culture movement – the "we" that drummed and thundered from the printed page drowning out the music, subtle and inimitable, of the human individuality. Long after the disintegration of the movement many poems written in the first, the singular, the unique person still bore the hallmark of that gigantic stage prop "we." The poet's "I" was purely nominal.' The grammatical person makes little difference. What matters, in poetry, is the use to which it is put; and Yevtushenko's point is that poetry demands 'nothing less than truth.' The corporative 'we' was inadequate because 'Soviet poets wrote nothing of their own ideas, their own conflicts and complexities and therefore nothing of the difficulties and conflicts of others. . . . When Mayakovsky says "we," he is still Mayakovsky. Pasternak's "I" is the "I" of Pasternak.' In other words, any reduction of the *moi haïssable* must proceed from a genuine recognition of its limits, not from the imposition from without of a simplified and falsified 'we.' Not only social order but 'the divine or natural order' of which Robert Duncan has written brings poets up against the limits of their own consciousness.

287

4   Broadly speaking, the new American poetry has
distinct affinities with the new European poetry, because both
tend towards an immediacy that was lacking in Romantic-
Symbolist practice. In European poetry of the austere kind this
immediacy is one mainly of diction – a diction as close as
possible to the language of contemporary speech; but any change
in diction means a change in assumptions and attitudes, a change
in the gestures of poetry. More specifically, the adoption of a
deliberate 'unpoetic' idiom, of the 'low mimetic,' means a
sacrifice of personal discreteness; and it is no accident that such
a sacrifice should be characteristic of poets, like Rózewicz or
Enzensberger, whose style was formed in response to a political
and social crisis. The American emphasis on action, and so on
the 'field' explored by a poem, on breath units and sentence
structure, often goes together with a similar use of the demotic
vernacular. Both practices are naturalistic in their approach to
the real, though the reality in question may be primarily
external or primarily internal. Where 'ego systems' have been
done away with, this distinction ceases to be a crucial one. What
does remain crucial is the tension between particulars and
generalities, between the phenotypal and the archetypal image.
That tension will vary from poet to poet, from case to case; and
no theory or group technique can regulate it.

   A remarkable variation in that regard is to be found in the
post-war work of the German poet Günter Eich, from the well-
known inventory poem, listing his possessions as a prisoner of
war, in *'Abgelegene Gehöfte* (1948), to the 'nature' poems of
Botschaften des Regens (1955) – poems in which natural phenomena do indeed convey coded messages of human and moral
relevance – to the cryptic and laconic short poems in *Zu den
Akten* (1964) and *Anlässe und Steingürten* (1966). This development
runs counter to the dominant trend in that the early poem
served as a model to younger practicians of the austere style,
whereas the later poems are both personally idiosyncratic and
free in their association of images. The poetry of Günter Grass
has moved in the opposite direction, from an almost neo-
Dadaist playfulness of metaphor and imagery to a manner
seemingly direct, realistic and austere.[38] Such variations are
especially apt to occur where private and public concerns do

not easily accord, as in West Germany, with its special burden of political responsibility assumed by almost every poet who has been writing since 1945. The special tension between 'conscience and creation,' as Christopher Middleton once called the two poles, bequeathed by German history, can be traced in the work of Ingeborg Bachmann, an Austrian poet whose sensibility and imagination were not predisposed to political or social themes. Erich Fried, a poet born in Austria but resident in England since before the war, has become the most thoroughly and prolifically political poet writing in German; but much of Fried's earlier work, especially the longer sequences collected in his *Reich der Steine*,[39] was linguistically and semantically exploratory, closer to the verbal play of James Joyce or Dylan Thomas than to the austerities of didactic and exhortatory verse.

Conscience and creation are admirably integrated in the work of the East German poet Johannes Bobrowski, whose poetry confounds all the categories, antinomies and trends. Bobrowski's war poems are also 'nature' poems. His poems about places are also poems about people, his poems about people also poems about history and nature. Very little of his poetry is overtly didactic, yet all of it, as he said, was written as an act of expiation. He was a Christian and a Socialist, a traditionalist and an innovator. His diction was as plain and bare as that of the extreme anti-poets – out of an impersonality and aversion to self-display which he shared with them – but his plain words are disposed in such a way as to give his work a depth peculiar to the purest poetry. His East European landscapes are invoked rather than described, in accordance with a German lyrical tradition that extends from Klopstock and Hölderlin to Trakl, yet the effect is one of palpable precision. Above all, Bobrowski's awareness of his own time, including the war in which he had been a reluctant participant, was enriched by a historical imagination at home in almost any era and any place. His poem *Absage* (Forgoing) moves effortlessly from the ancient Pruzzians, a Slav people exterminated by the mediaeval Order of the Teutonic Knights, to this depersonalized, self-effacing character-ization of Bobrowski's function as a man and poet:

> Dort
> war ich. In alter Zeit.
> Neues hat nie begonnen. Ich bin ein Mann,

> mit seinem Weibe ein Leib,
> der seine Kinder aufzieht
> für eine Zeit ohne Angst.
>
> (There
> I was. In an age long past.
> Nothing new has ever begun. I am a man,
> one flesh with his wife,
> who raises his children
> for an age without fear.)

The spatial disposition of Bobrowski's simple words – including his natural archetypes, his rivers and hills and lakes – was determined by the temporal range of his imaginative sympathies. Together they create the dimension of depth in which all his phenomena have their being. His art was one of exact relations, of poetic 'architecture,' as Hölderlin once called it; and in its combination of plainness with mystery, of concreteness with universality, it accords with Philippe Jaccottet's definition of the highest lyrical intensity.

That 'extremist art' – and all art informed by an intense awareness is extremist in our time – need not take the form of personal confession, as in Robert Lowell's *Life Studies*, Sylvia Plath's *Ariel* or John Berryman's *Dream Songs*, can also be seen in the work of Paul Celan. His early poem *Todesfuge* (Death Fugue), perhaps the only decisive proof that poems could be written not only after Auschwitz but about the cold horrors perpetrated there, does not contain the word 'I,' though Celan wrote it out of direct personal experience, and not long after the event. The intricate musical structure, like the archetypal, partly Surrealist, imagery, serves to distance the poem from historical events. For the same reason the poem is instrumented rather than vocalized. Such a theme can be taken up only with a reticence that leaves the unspeakable unspoken.* Celan's extremism in his late work hinges on the question of what can still be said or no longer be said in poetry. If he has written anti-poems his anti-poems are as far removed as possible from the 'low mimetic.' Ordinary language will not serve him. His diction vacillates between archaism and neologism. His images

---

* In the work of Nelly Sachs, too, its treatment is more mythical or mystical than realistic.

are as plainly generic as Bobrowski's – 'stone' is a recurrent one – yet their connotations are cryptically idiosyncratic. Again and again his later poems – 'language grilles' according to the title of one of his collections[40] – come up against the unspeakable. Silences and hiatuses are part of what they render and enact. Yet, in their own inimitable and difficult way, Celan's poems are attempts to communicate, 'ways of a voice to a receptive you,' as he put it once,[41] a 'desperate dialogue' and 'a sort of homecoming.' Johannes Bobrowski, too, whose short lines and hesitant syntax are akin to those of Celan's later poems, wrote of his

> Sprache
> abgehetzt
> mit dem müden Mund
> auf dem endlosen Weg
> zum Hause des Nachbarn.
>
> (language
> hunted down
> with a weary mouth
> on its unending way
> to the neighbour's house.)[42]

Celan's doubts about ever arriving there are more persistent and more acute.

> :es sind
> noch Lieder zu singen jenseits
> der Menschen
>
> (:there are
> still songs to be sung on the other side
> of humankind)

is a 'tree-high thought' in one of his later poems.[43] The same section of the book contains a poem in which Celan reflects on the way that his words are taking:

> Weggebeizt vom
> Strahlenwind deiner Sprache
> das bunte Gerede des An-
> erlebten – das hundert-
> züngige Mein-
> gedicht, das Genicht.

Aus-
gewirbelt,
frei
der Weg durch den menschen-
gestaltigen Schnee,
den Büsserschnee, zu
den gastlichen
Gletscherstuben und -tischen.

Tief
in der Zeitenschrunde,
beim
Wabeneis
wartet, ein Atemkristall,
dein unumstössliches
Zeugnis.

(Etched away from
the ray-shot wind of your language
the garish talk of rubbed-
off experience – the hundred-
tongued my-
poem, the noem.

Whirled
clear,
free
your way through the human-
shaped snow,
the penitents' snow, to
the hospitable
glacier rooms and tables.

Deep in time's crevasse
by the alveolate ice
waits, a crystal of breath,
your irreversible
witness.)

A reviewer in *The Times Literary Supplement*[44] quotes one passage of this poem – 'the hundred-/tongued my-/poem, the noem' – and calls it a moment of despair, 'when the poem (Gedicht) seems mocked by an echo suggesting nothingness (Genicht).' But Celan is contrasting his own practice with that of other poets, adherents of the 'low mimetic': the 'hundred-tongued my-poem,' which is a non-poem or 'noem,' is theirs, not Celan's. His way is to cleanse his poems of the 'garish talk of rubbed-off experience' and make for the 'hospitable glacier rooms and tables.' The near-impossibility of translating such poems becomes apparent when the same reviewer goes on to interpret a related neologism in the concluding poem, which he renders as follows:

> Einmal,
> da hörte ich ihn,
> da wusch er die Welt,
> ungesehn, nachtlang,
> wirklich.
>
> Eins und Unendlich,
> vernichtet,
> ichten.
>
> Licht war. Rettung.
>
> (Once
> I heard him
> as he washed the world,
> unseen, nightlong,
> real.
>
> One and Infinite,
> annihilated,
> ihilate.
>
> Light was. Salvation.)

The word 'ichten' does indeed seem a positive counterpart to the 'nothing' in 'vernichtet' – and in Middle High German there was still a positive 'icht' or 'aught' corresponding to the negative 'nicht' or 'naught' – but this translation misses the connection with the 'my-poem' of the other passage, the possessive ego-principle that turns poems into 'noems.' Paul Celan has pointed out to me that 'ichten' primarily is a verbal formation derived from the pronoun 'ich.' If the infinitive of the verb were 'ichen,' 'ichten' would be the third person plural of the past tense of a verb 'to I':

> One and Infinite,
> annihilated,
> ied.

Yet that rendering too would set off misleading reverberations, beginning with 'eye' – another of Celan's recurrent words – and its English verbal form. On the poem as a whole the same reviewer commented: 'Celan speaks of this epiphany as having occurred at some definite moment in the past – but his poem embodies it, recreates it, and this takes it out of time. Who was heard, who washed the world, who brought salvation, we do not know.' Whatever the primary sense of 'ichten,' we still shall not know even if Celan's own interpretation strengthens the sense of an assertion and manifestation of an identity other than the poet's. 'In spite of frequent use, here as elsewhere, of terms and images hallowed by Christian and Jewish tradition,' the reviewer went on to say, 'no doctrine will accommodate the mysterious presences of Celan's poetry, presences born out of despair, out of a sense of deprivation, out of a post-Nietzschean conviction that the God worshipped by former ages is now dead.'

Celan provides no evidence of such a conviction. One way in which his art is traditional has to do with its function of bearing witness, a religious function which it shares with the poetry of Johannes Bobrowski; but its extremism – an extremism greater than that of the American confessional poets or the 'low mimetic' of the new anti-poetry, with its resort to a diction that guarantees a measure of human community – does point to a post-Nietzschean situation. What remains difficult is the degree to which Celan's art is anachronistic, as well as extreme, because he acknowledges no break in the development of modern poetry, no consolidation or revision of modernism. Celan's genitive metaphors, for instance, link his work to the later poetry of Rilke and to French Surrealism; and a clue to his artistic extremism, an extremism of diction and syntax, occurs in his address *Der Meridian*,[45] where he suggested the possibility of 'thinking Mallarmé to his logical conclusion.' Both Mallarmé's and Rilke's assumptions were decidedly post-Nietzschean: and with Mallarmé Celan shares a strong aversion to the merely phenomenal and accidental, as opposed to the essential and archetypal.

Celan began by rendering extreme experience – that of a poet born into a Jewish German-speaking community in Roumania, fed on the 'black milk' of terror under the German and Russian occupations and surviving that terror to become a resident of France. Although he writes in German, his artistic purism has closer parallels in contemporary French than in either West or East German poetry. This artistic purism is content with nothing less than 'raids on the inarticulate.' It would be impertinent to speculate how much of Celan's later practice is due to extreme experience, how much to the artistic rigour of an unrepentant modernist. What is certain about Celan's later poems is that they explore the limits of language and the limits of consciousness, groping their way towards a communion that may be religious or mystical, since their starting-point is total solitude and their destination 'on the other side of humankind.'

5   'Post-Nietzschean convictions,' which may or may not be Celan's, ought to preclude religion of a transcendental or other-worldly kind; hence their proclivity to natural archetypes and the celebration of existence on this earth – Rilke's 'Hiersein ist herrlich.' Yet Rilke had to invent his own angels; and many other post-Nietzscheans have proclaimed: 'God is dead. Long live God!' There is a nature mysticism and a nature occultism.

A consistently post-Nietzschean naturalism has been expounded by the Scottish poet Kenneth White, whose French translator, Pierre Leyris, has described him as 'passionately in love with this world and unconditionally rejecting any other. . . . Completely opposed to the pseudo-fatality of History. Conceding to cities only the most accidental parts of his being, between two visits to his mother, Earth.'[46] White himself has distinguished between religious and cosmic poetry, as between 'nature poems' and 'earth poems.' What he says about communication may be relevant to Paul Celan's poetic practice: 'It is not communication between man and man that matters, but communication between man and the cosmos. Put men in touch with the cosmos and they will be in touch with one another.' Kenneth White insists on 'immediate life,' which he believes to be almost lost to modern urban man. 'What, after all, does the world amount to for the modern man – or perhaps a modern man does not even give a thought to the world, has no experience of the world, is in fact *absent* from the world, hostile to it? Or should I say absent from the earth rather than absent from the world? Nothing worth the trouble of living there – a megalopolitan nightmare: that is the *modern* world.' Modern artists, too, move between 'the abstract and the vulgarly personal.' Kenneth White longs for the end of modern art. According to him 'the poet is not concerned with art but with reality. The poet is human, but he is also something more than human – he has cosmic affinities. . . . Poetry is affirmation of reality, no more, no less.' White has written poems and prose about the modern city, more specifically about Glasgow, but in his poems, too, urban civilization is negative, 'abstraction and ugliness,' the sun in *Winter Evening* 'a beetroot thrown in mud.' His positive, that is, his immediate experience of the cosmos is rendered in *White Wood*:

> So I have put away the books
> and I watch the last apples fall
> from the frosty trees
>
> . . . and suddenly
> suddenly in the midst of the winter wood
> I knew I had always been there
>
> before the books
> and after the books
> there will be a winter wood
>
> and my heart will be bare
> and my brain open to the wind.[47]

White's diction here enacts the bareness. Where the sense of cosmic relation fails him, 'immediate life' ceases, as in the poem *Now in This Tomb*:

> . . . the mind,
> is empty of sense, no alliance
>
> can be made between self and things
> and the self is weary of its masks
> its verbal conjugations and no longer asks
> for the poison pit of conscience
>
> for the world of perpetual beginnings . . .[47]

In other post-Nietzschean poets, including Ted Hughes, the impulse towards a nature mysticism or nature occultism is stronger. Kenneth White shows little awareness of the greed and cruelty of nature, or of the very great difficulties that arise in any attempt to derive models for human existence from non-human nature alone. Perhaps ideas of the Good City are a necessary complement to a poet's 'cosmic affinities'; and such ideas are in fact implicit in the work of most major poets whose primary concern is with nature.

Even St-John Perse, a post-Nietzschean poet of 'eternal recurrence,' of natural processes and primitive human experience, has defended poetry as a 'way of knowledge,' claiming that science and poetry 'put the same questions to the same abyss.'[48] 'For if poetry is not itself, as some have claimed, "absolute reality," it is poetry which shows the strongest passion and the keenest apprehensions of it, to that extreme limit of complicity where reality seems to shape itself within the poem. . . . Poetry is not only a way of knowledge; it is even more a way of life – of life in its totality.' To Perse the poet is 'the guilty conscience of his time,' because 'the real drama of this century lies in the growing estrangement between the temporal and untemporal man.' It is one limitation of Perse's poetry that it has so little to offer 'the temporal man'; its cosmic affinities have little room either for a sense of individual life, or for historically and socially conditioned experience of a specifically modern kind. This also limits the relevance of Perse's defence of modern poetry, as when he writes: 'Its alleged obscurity is due not to its own nature, which is to enlighten, but the darkness which it explores, and must explore: the dark of the soul herself and the dark of the mystery which envelops human existence.' The alleged obscurities of modern poetry are of many different orders; they can be due not to an exploration of darkness, but to the complexities of the daylight world which poets share with the next man. They can be due to complexities of diction and style or to a transparent simplicity that eschews the abstractions of logical discourse, and 'puts away the books.' They can be due to the rendering of exceptional or extreme experiences, as in the hallucinated poems of Henri Michaux, or to the intellectualization of generally recognizable experience, as in the poems of William Empson and some of W. H. Auden's.

A preoccupation with the things of nature does not necessarily preclude any of these modes of difficulty or 'alleged obscurity.' Nature, too, can be treated archetypally or phenomenally, with many immediate degrees of realism and symbolism. Yet almost all modern poets agree that a concern with nature is not an escape from more urgent concerns; and the progress of urbanization and industrialization has given rise to a new feeling which Jules Supervielle called 'le regret de la terre' – 'regretting the earth.'

> Un jour la terre ne sera
> Qu'un aveugle espace qui tourne,
> Confondant la nuit et le jour.
> Sous le ciel immense des Andes
> Elle n'aura plus de montagnes,
> Même pas un petit ravin.
>
> De toutes les maisons du monde
> Ne durera plus qu'un balcon
> Et de l'humaine mappemonde
> Une tristesse sans plafond.
> De feu l'Océan Atlantique
> Un petit goût salé dans l'air,
> Un poisson volant et magique
> Qui ne saura rien de la mer.[49]
>
> (One day the Earth will be
> Only blind revolving space
> Confounding night and day.
> Under the vast Andean sky
> There will be no mountain left,
> Not even one little ravine.
>
> Of all the world's houses no more
> Than one balcony only remains,
> Of the human map of the world
> A sadness without a ceiling.
> Of the late Atlantic Ocean
> A faint salty tang in the air,
> A magical flying fish
> That will have forgotten the sea.)

In Supervielle's poem concern with the things of nature makes for plainness and naturalness of diction, though his responses to nature have a modern sophistication, complexity and irony, even when he apostrophizes natural phenomena as in the late poem *Pins*[50] (Pines):

O pins devant la mer,
Pourquoi donc insister
Par votre fixité
A demander réponse?
J'ignore les questions
De votre haut mutisme.
L'homme n'entend que lui,
Il en meurt comme vous.
Et nous n'eûmes jamais
Quelque tendre silence
Pour mélanger nos sables,
Vos branches et mes songes.
Mais je me laisse aller
A vous parler en vers,
Je suis plus fou que vous,
O camarades sourds,
O pins devant la mer,
O poseurs de questions
Confuses et touffues,
Je me mêle à votre ombre,
Humble zone d'entente,
Où se joignent nos âmes
Où je vais m'enfonçant,
Comme l'onde dans l'onde.

(O pines in front of the sea,
Why do you insist
By your immobility
On demanding an answer, then?
I do not know the questions
Which your lofty mutism asks.
Men understand only men,
And die of that, as you do.
And we have never had
A tender silence in which
We might have mixed our sands,
Your branches and my dreams.
But I let myself go so far
As to speak to you in verse,
I am more mad than you,

O my deaf companions,
O pines in front of the sea,
O you that put questions
That are confused and thick,
I commingle with your shade,
A humble zone of agreement
Where our souls are joined,
Where I go and lose myself
As wave does in wave.)

The self-conscious irony and lightness of those lines do not disguise Supervielle's real need to communicate with his trees, and one of his last poems begins

Laissez-moi devenir olivier de Provence.

(Let me turn into an olive tree of Provence.)

Reservations about a Romantic anthropomorphism are part of the tone and argument of *Pins*; and indeed the poem is also one about the differences between men and trees.

H.D.'s poem *Sigil*[51] permits no reservations, no irony. The identity of human and non-human nature is conveyed without argument, by stylistic means derived from Imagist practice:

Now let the cycle sweep us here and there,
we will not struggle;
somewhere,
under a forest-ledge,
a wild white-pear
will blossom;

somewhere,
under an edge of rock,
a sea will open;
slice of the tide-shelf
will show in coral, yourself,
in conch-shell,
myself;

somewhere,
over a field-hedge,
a wild bird
will lift up wild, wild throat,
and that song, heard,
will stifle out this note.

In a poem that reads and looks like free verse, rhyme is used to enact the identity, directly in the end-rhyme 'tide-shelf' – 'yourself,' unobtrusively in the partly internal rhyme 'ledge' – 'edge' – 'hedge' that links all the three stanzas. *Sigil* can be read as a 'nature poem' or as a 'love poem'; its post-Nietzschean cosmic sense – explicit in the 'cycle' of the first line – cuts through those outmoded categories.

Clearly such poems are very far removed from what most people now take to be the assumptions and aims of scientists. To those who believe that the business of science is not to know and understand nature but to change and manipulate it, the poets' inveterate fondness for 'conversations about trees' must seem a harmless anachronism at best, a reactionary crime at the worst; and Supervielle's poem is a conversation *with* trees. The reverse side of that need for the things of nature is an equally persistent rejection of the modern city. In Luis Cernuda's *Cemeterio de la ciudad* (City Graveyard) even the dead are alienated:

> Ni una hoja ni un pájaro. La piedra nada más. La tierra.
> Es el infierno así? Hay dolor sin olvido,
> con ruido y miseria, frío largo y sin esperanza
> Aquí no existe el sueño silencioso
> de la muerte, que todavía la vida
> se agita entre estas tumbas, como una prostituta.
> prosigue su negocio bajo la noche inmóvil.
>
> Cuando la sombra cae desde el cielo nublado
> y el humo de las fábricas se aquieta,
> en polvo gris, vienen de la taberna voces,
> y luego un tren que pasa
> agita largos ecos come un bronce iracundo.
>
> No es el juicio aún, muertos anónimos.
> Sosegados, dormir; dormir si es que podéis.
> Acaso Dios también se olvida de vosotros.
>
> (No leaf here, no bird. Stone, only stone. And earth.
> Is hell like this? There is pain here, without oblivion,
> squalor and noise, a coldness wide, without hope.
> Here you'll not find the unbroken sleep
> of death, with life all around
> moving between these graves like a whore
> plying her trade under a motionless night.

> When darkness falls from the cloudy sky
> and the factory smoke settles
> as grey dust, voices drift from the pub
> and a passing train's echoes
> vibrate far off like an angry bell.
>
> It is not judgement, you anonymous dead.
> Sleep on indifferent, sleep if you can.
> Perhaps even God will come to forget you.)

Yet almost all modern poets insist that poetry, among other things, is a 'way of knowledge,' that it enacts truths of a kind, though these truths may be subjective, paradoxical, esoteric or fantastic. The Hungarian poet Gyula Illyes said about the 'alleged obscurity' of modern poetry: 'The language that sways the world's destiny is more abstruse than that of the poets.'[52] And St-John Perse is not alone in believing that science and poetry 'put the same question to the same abyss.' Cernuda's poem about truth and lies, *Dejadme solo* (Leave Me Alone), puts it like this:

> . . . pero nunca pronuncian verdades o mentiras su secreto torcido
> verdades o mentiras
> son pájaros que emigran cuando los ojos mueren
>
> (. . . but never do truths or lies give away their crooked secret
> truths or lies
> are birds that migrate when our eyes die)

and that, too, is a truth drawn from experience.

'Science and poetry are alike,' May Swenson has also affirmed; 'or allied it seems to me, in their largest and main target – to investigate any and all phenomena of existence beyond the flat surface of appearances. . . . The poet's material has always been nature – human and otherwise – all objects and aspects of our outer environment as well as the "climate of the soul" and the "theatre of the emotions." The poet is the great anti-specialist.'[53] Although May Swenson's most characteristic poems are about animals and landscapes, she concludes that 'poetry can help man to be human.' The scientist P.B. Medawar not only agrees with Miss Swenson about the 'main target' of the two pursuits but considers the scientific way of knowledge essentially akin to poetry:

What I think I can say is that the imaginative process as it occurs in science is very much like any other intuitive or inspirational process as it occurs perhaps in the creation of a work of art. The hypothesis one thinks up to explain what would otherwise be totally mysterious phenomena is only a draft solution of whatever problem it was intended to clarify. .... The general impression I wanted to try to leave with you is that science is an exploratory process. It's an exploration guided by, given direction by, an imaginative precon- ception of what the truth might be; but the imaginative process is always under critical pressure, always under threat of refutation. Above all, it is important to realize that science is not a compilation of facts, nor a classified inventory of factual information. It is a vulgar error to think so.[54]

Applied science, of course, can lose sight of its targets; and poets, too, can become specialists, as Baudelaire feared they would in his time, out of an aestheticism that made life subser- vient to art. Yet the very medium of poetry sets a limit to that specialization. Whatever its programmes, preoccupations and techniques, poetry has continued to relate the inner world to the outer; and that is one way in which it 'can help man to be human.' Only bad and false poetry is as abstruse as 'the language that sways the world's destiny.' As Edwin Muir wrote, 'it is easy for the false imagination to hate a whole class; it is hard for the true imagination to hate a single human being.'[55]

6   One respect in which poetry, like all art, differs from science is an element in it which I have only touched upon, the element of sheer play. That element is most apparent in non- sense poetry, from Lewis Carroll, Edward Lear and Alfred Jarry to Christian Morgenstern, Joachim Ringelnatz, Kurt Schwitters, Gertrude Stein, Edith Sitwell and a good deal of later experimental verse. In connection with the practice of Jean Arp I remarked on the principle of fortuitousness adopted by the Dadaists. In recent visual and sound poetry that very prin- ciple of fortuitousness has been turned into a quasi-mechanical method. To the funny nonsense, serious nonsense and fantastic nonsense of their predecessors the new Concrete poets have added a good deal of pretentious nonsense; and they have worried those of their critics who believe that the human relevance of poetry is threatened by an art that approximates to abstraction by using words as a semantically neutral material. Such an art could indeed sever the connection – preserved to a greater or lesser extent in every other variety of modern poetry – between the inner and outer worlds. The new poet would be at once a player of verbal games and a technician 'feeding' random material into irresponsible machines.

One worried critic is Erich von Kahler, a humanist distinguished by his obstinate refusal to become a mere specialist in any of the fields to which he has made valuable contributions. It is his fear that the poet will cease to be 'the great anti-specialist' that has moved Kahler to attack the new experimental poetry:

> More recently, however, a boundless predominance of this exploratory function of art has led to a critical point, where the survival of art as it was known through the millennium is in jeopardy. . . . The completely objectified rendition of a more and more externalized world and the total elimination of human motivation and sentiment, this is an artistic proceeding of utmost reduction; it can be undertaken only by means of keenest analytical pursuance of a factuality that is unreal in its not only imperceptible, but actually imaginary minutiae. . . . It leads to a formalism, a skeletal form, in which all vital substance has faded away. A ghostly consciousness is confronted with itself.[56]

Kahler, here, is writing about the *nouveau roman*, but his strictures apply just as much to the experimental poetry of Helmut Heissenbüttel and Franz Mon which he analyses in the same chapter, *The Disintegration of Form*. Kahler wonders

whether poetry will be able to maintain itself much longer amidst 'ultra-intelligent machines,' how long it will be left time and space and a natural soil to grow from in the young. We see the poetic urge arise from inner revolt in oppressed countries, we still sense it breaking through the intellectual thicket in the distress and rebellion of Western poets. But it is high time, I believe, to warn our youth of a grave and vital danger: the overall dominance of scientism, i.e. scientistic mentality (to be distinguished from science itself, its inestimable value, though not limitless validity); to warn them of that common inclination to see all our life, indeed all reality, as a complex of detectable, and ultimately predictable and reproducible mechanisms.

This danger, it seems to me, is more theoretical than real, like the danger of 'dehumanization' in the poetry of an earlier modernism. Where the new experimental writing is half as mechanical as it sets out to be it is also tedious to a degree that makes it a bitter medicine rather than a pernicious drug. Those readers ascetic enough to swallow it for the sake of keeping up to date show an admirable fortitude: and one can be pretty sure that artists will cease to aspire to the condition of computers as soon as computers offer them serious competition, by doing what they do, only better or as well. Even from a humanist's point of view, many of the Concrete poets deserve every sympathy for trying to rid poetry of its atavistic assumptions. If poetry too disappears in that process, as it frequently does, not only do we discover more about the nature and limits of poetry, but the gap is sure to be filled by poets of a different kind.

Nor are the new poets really new. Corbière's poem *Epitaphe*[57] is prefaced by a little piece of prose that might have been written half a century later by Gertrude Stein, or nearly a century later by Helmut Heissenbüttel. It can be translated as follows:

Except for those lovers beginning or finished who want to begin at the end there are so many things that end at the beginning that the beginning begins to end by being the end, the end of it will be that the lovers and others will end by beginning to recommence with the beginning which will have ended by being no more than the end reversed, and that will end by being indistinguishable from eternity which has no end and no beginning and will also end by being finally indistinguishable from the rotation of the earth so that one will end by no longer distinguishing where the end begins from where the beginning ends which is the whole end of the whole beginning indistinguishable from the whole beginning of the whole end which is the final beginning of the infinite defined by the indefinite. That equals an epitaph which equals a preface and conversely.

The structure of that piece is exactly the structure of certain texts in Helmut Heissenbüttel's *Textbücher*, those in *Textbuch* 5[58] in which this method of permuted repetition becomes an effective means of social and political comment. So in this passage from *Klassenanalyse* (Class Analysis):

. . . a thingumy of that kind is conditioned by his regarding every thingumybobness as something better his thingumybobness is conditioned by his seeing not himself in the thingumy that he is but something better and this conditioning makes him determined to rise above himself he fulfils his conditions in that his conditioning leads not to self-knowledge but to something better and if he really regarded a thingumy as a thingumy and saw himself in that thingumy he would regard it as something worse for assuming that a thingumy regarded a thingumy only as a thingumy and not as something better but saw himself in it as something worse as something he did not want to regard himself as he would be forced to regard a thingumy as something neither better nor worse but simply as that sort of thingumy and that would really amount to self-knowledge. . . .

Because these permutations are guided and controlled by a critical intellect they are neither mechanical nor humanly irrelevant. On the contrary, they convey moral judgement that could not be conveyed as tellingly in any other way. Both the tedium and the funniness of that syntactical *perpetuum mobile* are exactly matched to the vicious circle which they enact and analyse. Neither Corbière's nor Heissenbüttel's piece is poetry, of course; and Heissenbüttel has explained why his texts no longer observe a borderline between poetry and prose: 'The development of the arts in the twentieth century shows this characteristic, among others, that it advances sporadically into realms where every artistic act comes up against the frontier of any other.'[59] Another characteristic of twentieth-century poetry which Heissenbüttel stresses is the degree to which it makes language autonomous. Of the longer poems or sequences of Pound, Guillén and Olson, he says that they are not 'a picture of the world but a world of language and nothing but language.' This is less true of the poets he mentions than of his own work and of Concrete poetry; and it is not the whole truth about all of his own work. *Klassenanalyse*, for instance, does not merely serve to 'duplicate the world linguistically, to multiply it.' What Heissenbüttel and other linguistically experimental poets do exclude is the subjectivity of lyrical poetry, its projections of feelings and moods; but as long as they choose the linguistic material which will then be left to its own devices – to grammatical permutations, to divisions into syllables or letters and new combinations of these components, or whatever their game may be – the autonomy of language is not a total one. As I have already implied, it is the selection and control of the initial word material that redeems their procedures from an automatism that would be totally boring.

Similar distinctions arise over experimental poetry written at least two decades before the institution of a Concrete poetry movement in the post-1945 period. Because play preponderates in the verbal permutations of Gertrude Stein, with their real or assumed naïveté of tone, their emulation of child's play, at times they are close to the autonomous language of Concrete poetry, to Dadaist fortuitousness or to Surrealist automatic writing. Many of her word sequences at least appear to be semantically unanchored. Yet much the same technique of verbal repetition and permutation was adopted by Laura Riding in parts of a collection as outstanding now as in 1930 for its intellectual tautness, its sophistication and its psychological searchingness, her *Poems: A Joking Word*.[60] Parallels with Heissenbüttel's use of that technique for satire and social comment are most striking in Laura Riding's poem *Fine Fellow Son of a Poor Fellow*. Verbal experiment goes to the extreme of an asyntactical continuum in the next poem from the same collection of poems written between 1919 and 1929, *What to Say When the Spider,** and this practice, too, prefigures that of Heissenbüttel elsewhere and of many Concrete poets.

That the verbal permutations in Laura Riding's poems are not nonsense, or that they are nonsense of the most serious and responsible kind, could be demonstrated only by relating the whole poem to Laura Riding's work in general and to the more traditionally lyrical or reflective poems that precede and follow it in the same collection; and Laura Riding's thinking about language, society, personal relations and personal identity in the shadow of death – to mention only a few of her dominant themes – was at once so intricate and so daring as to forbid this undertaking here. What these two poems will show at once is that the techniques of Concrete poetry are not as new as some of its promoters believe or assert; and that even its diversity is not without precedent in the work of earlier experimental poets.

Heissenbüttel too begins with doubts about language, doubts about what can, and cannot any longer, be said. That is his link

---

*Laura Riding refused the author permission to quote from these two poems, disagreeing with the context of discussion and insisting that her renunciation of poetry should have been mentioned here.[61]

not only with precursors like Laura Riding but with more purely lyrical poets like Paul Celan among his contemporaries and with the new anti-poetry (as distinct from the non-poetry that sometimes seems to be his objective). 'Today, when everything is mixed up, it is no longer possible simply to say that I am writing the truth when I am opposing untruth.' That statement points to Heissenbüttel's concern with the writings of Wittgenstein. He goes on to speak of 'the doubt as to whether what can be said is still sayable at all,' a doubt 'that is now critically directed against the conventional prejudices of language.' Yet a criticism of language – and that is what Heissenbüttel's texts constitute, though to a considerable degree his language is left free to criticize itself, to expose the assumptions and prejudices inherent in general usage – militates against total autonomy. In other words, Heissenbüttel's 'scientism' is one of method, and it is not incompatible with a commitment beyond that method. That is why he can write: 'Literature is knowledge: that, for our epoch, means among other things: a means of radical enlightenment.'

Helmut Heissenbüttel represents the austere and philosophical wing of the new linguistic poetry. His work is dedicated to the end of 'penetrating and establishing a foothold in a world that still seems to evade language' and of 'reaching the frontier of that which is *not yet* speakable.' What is new about his practice is its intellectual rigour, not its playfulness; but this has not prevented him from writing texts that combine extraordinary insights into human behaviour with effects decidedly comic and grotesque.

The sound poems of Ernst Jandl, on the other hand, seem to glorify the principle of play. His best-known poems, and those most immediately effective when read aloud by their author, have been onomatopoeic enactments of a single word, like *schmerz durch reibung* (pain through friction)[62] composed of the consonant and vowel sounds in the word 'frau,' or *schtzngrmm*, based on the consonant sounds in the word 'Schützengraben' (trench). Poems of this kind need to be heard rather than read, since the letters on the page are a mere notation more difficult to take in through the eye than a musical score; and it is doubtful whether anyone but the poet can vocalize such pieces exactly as they are intended to be vocalized. The last line of *schtzngrmm*, for instance, is 't-tt,' which on the page one would take to be an onomatopoeic rendering of rifle or machine gun fire, whereas in the poet's reading it also conveys a dying fall and the German word 'tot' (dead). Although sound poems preponderate in Jandl's principal collection, *Laut und Luise*, these may be witty or serious, mimetic or fantastic, satirical or expressive; and there are prose poems, like the sequence about England, *prosa aus der flüstergalerie* (prose from the whispering gallery), more akin to some of the semantic explorations of Helmut Heissenbüttel, as well as sequences whose main appeal is to the eye or to the intellect. Ernst Jandl's sound permutations draw on a great variety of idioms, particularly on Viennese dialect – a source also drawn on by Hans Carl Artmann, another Austrian experimental poet, for entirely different effects – and on Jandl's response to the sounds of the English language. Elsewhere some of the sources are literary, as when phrases from Goethe and Hölderlin are taken up in the sequence *zehn abendgedichte* (ten evening poems) and in the longer set of variations, *klare gerührt*.

In connection with Jandl's work Helmut Heissenbüttel has written that experiment and tradition need not be incompatible or irreconcilable. Quite apart from the circumstance that Jandl himself has also written, and continues to write, lyrical poems of a non-experimental kind, many of Jandl's experimental poems can be seen as developments of recognized and time-honoured media. Nor, unlike other Concrete poets, can Jandl be accused of narrowing the scope of lyrical poetry as such. Despite the seeming preponderance of sheer exuberant play in his work, observations, reflections, feelings and ingenuity contribute to its effect, even where his material has been reduced to the components of a single word; and his range extends to prose poetry on the one hand, to miniature drama on the other. Heissenbüttel is right to point out that Jandl's verbal poems are not absolutely different from any other poems written in the past; by which he does not mean only the 'tradition of the new' and the precedent set half a century ago by the onomatopoeic verse of August Stramm or the sound poems of Kurt Schwitters.

Ernst Jandl is innocent of 'scientism'; he also avoids the tendency towards tautology, truism and banality that makes much verbal poetry boring, in the same way as much post-Wittgenstein philosophy is boring to all but professional logicians. Even Franz Mon, a distinguished and many-sided experimental poet, could include the following variations on the obvious in his *Lesebuch*:63

> der tisch ist oval
> das ei ist oval
> nicht jeder tisch ist oval
> jedes ei ist oval
> kaum ein tisch ist oval
> kaum ein ei ist nicht oval
> dieser tisch ist viereckig
> dieses ei ist nicht viereckig
> viele tische sind viereckig
> viele eier sind nicht viereckig
> die meisten tische sind viereckig
> die meisten eier sind nicht viereckig
>
> (the table is oval
> the egg is oval
> not every table is oval
> every egg is oval
> scarcely one table is oval
> scarcely one egg is not oval
> this table is square
> this egg is not square
> many tables are square
> many eggs are not square
> most tables are square
> most eggs are not square).

Such logical exercises may well be an instance of 'radical enlightenment.' Franz Mon's *Lesebuch* is intended to be educational, and Helmut Heissenbüttel attributes its educational value to the absence of a design on the reader. Mon's is a primer, he writes, 'that does not canonize anything but leaves everything open. It is a primer that turns its back on edification, an irritating primer. Not certainty but uncertainty is what its examples convey.'64

7   That, of course, defines the 'radical enlightenment' of which Heissenbüttel writes elsewhere. Uncertainty, or scepticism, is what contemporary philosophers and contemporary

scientists recommend as the proper attitude to their material; as such it is the mid-twentieth-century counterpart of the high moral seriousness of nineteenth-century poets. It is also an attitude which anti-totalitarian intellectuals everywhere have adopted towards political ideologies. Heissenbüttel's 'openness,' in short, characterizes the truthfulness which he considers fitting in poets of his time; and that very mentality preserves the didactic functions of poetry. Of all the poets writing a hundred years after Baudelaire only those of the Concrete school, or some of them, can be said to produce work that 'marches fraternally between science and philosophy.'

My study began with a contradiction. It will end with a paradox and an irony, since it is those very poets who have alarmed the humanists. The reason, I think, is that science and philosophy themselves have become the province of specialists, and those poets too are specialists in their material, words. Their moral neutrality or 'openness' – implied in Heissenbüttel's defence of Mon's exercises but never wholly realized as long as poets choose their verbal material – is a specialist's virtue, or a specialist's vice, according to those who regard the moral neutrality of specialists as the greatest of threats to the survival of man on earth.

The paradox and the irony have a further twist. Baudelaire's opposing principle – art as an end in itself, art as play – has also triumphed in the practice of the very same school, especially those members of it who use words to make patterns and shapes mainly addressed to the eye. Valéry wrote: 'The most striking characteristic of a *work of art* can be called uselessness. . . . From another point of view considerations of our possible acts leads us to juxtapose (if not to conjugate) with this concept of *uselessness* . . . that of arbitrariness'; with the important corollary that 'the invention of Art has consisted in trying to confer on the first,' that is, on 'useless sensations,' 'a sort of usefulness; on the second,' that is, on our 'arbitrary acts,' 'a sort of *necessity*.'[65] Either 'radical enlightenment' or arbitrary play may seem to preponderate in the work of any one Concrete poet, but the two principles are inextricably interlocked in the various processes that are peculiar to the school as such. Baudelaire's antinomy, then, would appear to have been resolved or suspended in the latest experimental work: and that, precisely, is what is wrong with so much of it. Valéry's corollary has not been observed. Where the principle of arbitrariness does not come up against a semblance of necessity, the tension of poetry is lost; and in lyrical poetry the semblance of necessity has always been created by a sense of emotional urgency, by the poet's personal involvement in the material of his art. Baudelaire's antinomy is still a source of tension in other kinds of poetry; and there are good reasons for claiming that much of the purest Concrete poetry is not poetry at all, because poetry must be something more than an irritating – or boring – exercise in logic on the one hand, a quasi-abstract visual pattern on the other.

Something of the same ambivalence attaches to another development in poetry since 1945, the ability of certain poets to win and captivate large audiences of a kind denied to poets for centuries. This is a cultural and social phenomenon rather than a purely poetic one; and it is its cultural implications that could make it no less alarming to humanists than the 'scientism' of Concrete poetry. If the rift between poets and public seems to be closing at last, a concomitant is the widening rift between poetry intended for the inner ear and poetry mainly intended for public performance – and instant consumption. There are excellent poets, like Robert Creeley, whose public readings bring out the thews of their poems with an immediacy that adds to the printed text, because the breath units that control their structure and movement cannot be as clearly enacted on paper as by the living voice of the man. Yet other poets noted for their readings are those who sacrifice the difficult truth of poetry to facile effects or an assumption of shared beliefs that may be false or shoddy. If the state of technically advanced societies left poets with a choice only between language laboratories and the entertainment industry, the prospect would indeed be bleak. Even now a good many poets owe their reputations more to the aura that surrounds performers than to the quality of their work. Some of these poets need not concern us, since they belong to 'the history of publicity rather than of poetry,' as F.R.Leavis said of the Sitwells, who were eminent performers in their time, and incomparably better poets than some of their successors; but it is one thing to discount cynical careerists, another not to care about their audiences or about the genuine talents of poets too naïve to distinguish between truly popular art and its commercialized surrogates.

At its best, 'beat,' 'pop' and 'underground' poetry has a spontaneity, ingenuousness and imaginative ease rarely to be found in the laboratories or the academies. Yet not only are all those groups uncommonly mixed in themselves, but a two-way traffic connects them with groups and individual poets who would not wish to be labelled 'beat,' 'pop' or 'underground.' The traffic is one in time also. Some of the 'beat,' 'pop' and 'underground' poets are distinctly old-fashioned or eclectic in style; and the innovations of others do not differ essentially from those effected by modern poets of every other school, or of no school at all. What is 'pop,' 'beat' or 'underground' today will be academic tomorrow – if it survives the night; if it is not marred, that is, by the slackness that comes of relying on a predictable audience response, or of sheer incompetence. In other words, the new phenomenon reduces itself to a problem of standards; and the problem has to do with the new audiences for poetry rather than with the poetry in question. Perhaps even that problem is not a new one, since bad or mediocre poets have long tended to have a larger public than good ones. It is the peculiar fluidity of the present situation, with so much good will and eagerness on both sides, and so little discrimination, that makes the new response to poetry as alarming as it is gratifying.

No prediction will be offered here. If a true poet could predict what poetry he will be writing next year, or in the next decade, there would be no need for him to write it. In that sense every poem is experimental, or not worth writing. Poetry is a seeking and a finding of the unpredictable, within limits and conditions beyond the poet's control, because they depend on the complex interaction of external and internal processes. If poetry now is in a state of crisis, so it has been ever since Baudelaire; yet the century since Baudelaire's death has been one so rich in various developments that only a few of them could be traced or exemplified here. In another sense poetry is always about the same thing; that is why it has returned to archetypes after every sort of involvement in the phenomenal world, every mode of apprehending it or of enacting it in words. As long as poetry is written at all – written, not assembled by machines or produced out of a performer's hat to titillate an audience – it will continue to enact such truth as it can and must enact.

If my study has shown anything, it is how many kinds of truth poets have felt called upon to render or enact over the past century and more – not excluding the most literal and the most self-evident. The necessary interrelationship of beauty and truth in poetry remains tantalizingly paradoxical, if not mysterious; for the 'literalists of the imagination' have been brought up against the knowledge that the peculiar truth of poetry may have to be rendered by fictions, or by what, literally, amounts to lies; and absolutists of the imagination have been brought up against the knowledge that 'it must be human.' The paradox alone remains constant and perennial.

As recently as 1967 Keats's controversial equation of beauty with truth was re-affirmed in a poem by Paul Roche, *The Function of Art*,[65] with a bare conversational literalness that ends by confounding the literal mind. ('I thought art was beautiful,' she said./'Of course – by how it tells the truth:/Necessarily – by lying.') The terms of the equation are always being transposed and re-arranged; but the solution remains a paradox.

POSTSCRIPT

FOURTEEN years after its completion, I can make no apology for offering this text once more with no alterations beyond the correction of misprints. Since the book was not a history, let alone a compendium, of poetry written in the century or so before 1968, but a study of specific poems in relation to specific questions about the nature of poetry, to 'up-date' it would be a pointless exercise, not only because the 'up-dating' in turn would be out of date by the time of publication. If my investigations into many kinds of twentieth-century poems proved anything at all—and they were not intended to arrive at a foregone conclusion—it was that the tensions out of which poetry is produced remain constant for long periods, though the terminology may change from decade to decade, from year to year.

If I were to write such a study now, fourteen years later, a few of my exemplars and names might well be different ones, simply because I have been reading other work and forgotten much of what I read in the 'fifties and 'sixties; but I could not write such a study now. Any sequel to it would spring from different preoccupations, from an exacerbated awareness of the crisis that embraces far more than the production and functions of poetry. The last thing I should wish to do in such a book is to survey the latest developments in this or that national literature.

Even in 1968 I made no attempt to be up to date in my 'coverage' of poets and poems. As far as my home literature is concerned, I had decided decades earlier never to write about the work of my immediate contemporaries and coevals, so as to keep out of the gang warfare that passes for criticism of new work in the journals. Foreign literature was a different matter, because foreignness itself created the distance needed for critical judgement; and a more urgent incentive was the discovery that if I did not write about some of these foreign authors, nobody would. That applied to certain American poets also; and I refrained from writing about those American poets, such as Lowell, Berryman and Ginsberg, who had received adequate attention in this country and were not especially relevant to my themes. Where my British coevals were touched upon, it was because my themes required it. In a few other instances, too, I have broken my rule from time to time, writing about British and American contemporaries when I had special reasons for doing so; but these brief pieces do not belong to the context of this book, and will be collected in a companion volume of other writings on poetry.

One of these exceptions was the later work of W. S. Graham, who emerged from long silence with poems that made me question some of my earlier assumptions. In the last chapter of *The Truth of Poetry* I had seen a danger in the two extremes of commercialization of poetry in the entertainment industry on the one hand, its rarification in the language laboratories on the other. Without adopting the procedures of 'concrete' or experimental poetry, W. S. Graham's later work makes the most extraordinary use of 'laboratory' experience—the poet's struggle with the material of his art, language—in a way that is never tediously methodical but engrossing, moving and alive. This made me think again about the essential impurity of the medium of poetry—as compared to the medium of music—and poetry's traditional need for subject matter. If good poetry can be made out of the struggle to write good poetry, it seemed to me, poetry may be capable of a greater degree of autonomy than I had been prepared to admit; or, in other words, its subject matter is less important than I had believed, provided that humanity is not excluded by a mechanistic application of methods and procedures. Language, in any case, is so crucial and essential a component of humanity as to qualify as fit subject matter outside the laboratories. So what makes the difference between a good and a bad poem, or a live and a dead poem, about the behaviour of language turns out to be a matter not of the what, but the how—not the theme, but the treatment and development of the theme; and that brings poetry closer to music once more, despite the bother about meaning.

As for the other danger of popularization—instant poetry for instant consumption in performance—that, too, worries me less than it did in 1968. Because the language of true and searching poetry is a particular medium that demands a particular kind of attention—just as music and painting or sculpture demand a particular kind of attention—and the development of particular faculties in the recipients, it seems likely that the majority of that minority which turns to it at all will always turn to it with expectations to do with the what rather than the how. Hence the continuing appeal to readers who buy no other poetry books but anthologies of 'nature poems', 'love poems', 'cat poems' or whatever—when every true poet and reader of poems knows in his or her heart that those are meaningless divisions, that the 'cat poem' may be a love poem or a sociological poem or a metaphysical poem. If such readers also confuse the titillations of celebrity appearance with the quality of work offered in performances, at best that could be a stage in the development of their faculties, leading them to look for more enduring satisfactions. If not, they will soon lose interest in any sort of verse; and the heyday of poetic celebrity shows, in any case, seems to have passed, at least in Britain and North America.

If I had not had to draw the line somewhere, I should also have had to deal with poetry in English written by poets neither British nor American. My reason for not doing so was that to write about African, Australian, New Zealand, Caribbean, or Canadian poets one needs some understanding of their background conditions, both linguistic and otherwise, and I had never so much as visited any non-European country other than the U.S.A., with excursions to Canada. At least one Australian poet, Les Murray, might have tempted me to cross the line if I had known his work at the time of writing this book, or been able to read his illuminating account of his situation as an Australian cultivator of his own vernacular—a chink of light in my ignorance, but opened too late for the book. Much the same is true of a number of Canadian poets whose work was unknown to me in 1968. Yet it would have been reckless of me to stray beyond the fairly wide limits I had set myself. Many readers will think them too wide as it is.

When *The Truth of Poetry* first appeared, it was attacked in one weekly paper for being a contribution to 'comparative literature'. My response to that attack was rather like M. Jourdain's on being told that he had been speaking prose all his life. In order to write this book, and do the necessary reading, I had indeed given up an academic career, but as a teacher of German literature. The required specialization in that discipline proved incompatible with the writing of a book conceived and begun more than ten years before its publication. In all that time I had only the vaguest notion of the existence of that other academic discipline, 'comparative literature'. If I had chosen to write about poems in more than one language, it was because it seemed—and still seems—self-evident to me that in trying to understand what poetry does, can and cannot do, one must draw one's exemplars from as wide a range of it as possible. My writings on German literature, too, had always proceeded from an awareness of other literatures; and the very assumption that national literatures should be studied in isolation is a dubious one of relatively recent provenance. As far as Europe is concerned, literatures with closed frontiers have been the exception, not the rule; and, in that regard at least, Britain is part of Europe. A mere glance at the history of English literature from mediaeval times to the beginning of the Romantic Movement—or to the death-throes of the Romantic Movement in the early decades of this century—shows that the deliberate insularity advocated in certain quarters at present is a desperate simplification.

That does not mean that my book was a plea for internationalism in poetry. It has as much to say about the real and necessary differences between one cultural tradition and another as about confluences or parallels; and its total avoidance of those theoretical obsessions that continue to dominate not only criticism, but the very practice of imaginative writers, in France and Italy, must make it look parochially and amateurishly British wherever the act of writing has been made subservient to fashionable theories of what literature ought to be. Both in manner and matter, then, *The Truth of Poetry* is the work not only of a non-specialist, but an anti-specialist, convinced now as at the time of writing that what threatens the survival of poetry is what threatens the survival of civilization itself, of any kind of truth, any kind of meaningful activity—our fragmenting and fragmented specializations, bureaucratic, technical, economic and political. As long as that threat is contained, poetry of one kind or another is likely to be written, for it is as tough and adaptable as its maker, *homo faber*; and its truths will remain at once relative to the conditions of its survival and absolute in its need to transcend them.

It is the theory, the jargon and the prescriptions that have changed in those fourteen years. Where these are taken more seriously than they are in Britain, so has the critical attention given to this or that poet or group of poets. In West Germany, for instance, the neo-Brechtian minimal poetry of political and social comment was displaced in the early 'seventies by a more expansive 'new subjectivity' that found a place once more for individual consciousness and immediate personal experience; but this swing of the pendulum merely brought such poetry closer to the sort of work that had been done in the preceding decades by American and British poets. Two of the most gifted practitioners of this 'new subjectivity', Rolf Dieter Brinkmann and Nicolas Born, died prematurely when the trend was at its height. During the same period there was a mass exodus of East German poets to West Germany or Switzerland, precipitating a shift in the balance between these politically divided literatures and confronting the emigrants with drastic reorientations, only less extreme than that with which Joseph Brodsky has been confronted since his emigration to the U.S.A. in not involving their language. During that period, too, a West German poet, Ernst Meister, who had taken little notice of the changing trends and received very little notice in consequence, came into his own belatedly, and died on the very day he received notice of the award to him of the prestigious Büchner Prize.

The black irony of that coincidence would have been less acute if West Germany were not one of the European countries where serious literature is taken seriously in public—with a due of lip-service, at least, even from politicians, industrialists and the media—where unpopular writers are not despised or ignored, but respected, for maintaining their own standards, and where the profession of literature is still distinguished from the trade. Such a state of affairs may or may not be good for the souls of poets, some of whom fail to learn the lessons of humility and persistence in the teeth of indifference so freely granted to their counterparts in countries where poets know their (commercial) place; but it is good for the state of poetry. Ernst Meister, it happened, could afford to hold out and remain productive on his own terms—with only trends and fashions against him. Elsewhere the odds against major poetry have become overwhelming for different reasons—because major work is not wanted, aspiration is treated as presumption, and the too closely knit body of academics and journalists who manipulate reputations will delight in disparaging it. In Britain a searching poet like the late John Riley never penetrated that barrier before his death, because the critics relegated him to an 'underground' or fringe that does not qualify for notice in most of the general press, regardless of merit. No doubt, like Basil Bunting or Roy Fisher before him, John Riley would have emerged from that limbo in his lifetime but for his early death by murder, but the barrier has become less penetrable than it was in 1968. The immediate present, too, looks like 'a period loose at all ends'—apart from the growing threat of one end beyond the scope of this book. Not only the sheer number of working poets—which Yeats cannily recognized as an obstacle the best part of a century ago, and made quite sure of getting out of his way—but their diversity, and the failure of critics to sift the diversity other than by partisanship, are among the obvious causes. The less obvious are bound up with the general state of society and education, of manners and morals as much as taste and sensibility. Anything to do with the reception and function of poetry cannot be dealt with internationally—though comparisons could be interesting—but calls for detailed analysis of the social and cultural structures in question. That, too, is a subject for another book—perhaps for another author more competent than I am to deal with it.

All such shifts and events—and countless, innumerable ones are taking place at the moment of writing all over the world—belong to the history this book could only touch upon here and there, as particular heightenings of the tensions that are its subject. That these tensions can become catastrophic was part of the awareness out of which the book was written; and any reader of it can extend whatever useful insights it may contain to later developments, as to the many poets and poems that could have been, but were not, included, for reasons not to do with chronology.

Although neither nationally nor internationally there has ever been such a thing as linear progress in the arts, and it was as clear in 1968 as it is in 1982 that the various modernist movements had lost much of their impetus, one significant difference between the two decades is that there is far less excitement now about *avant-gardes* in most of the literatures from which my exemplars were drawn. One simple explanation for that may be that where survival is at stake, progress becomes something of a luxury. Yet on the level of individual achievement, development remains as indispensable in the arts as in other activity, because the alternative is stagnation and decay. We have more and more reason to be sceptical about eighteenth- and nineteenth-century beliefs in perpetual advances on all fronts—and 'avant-garde' is a military term; but no good reason at all to deprecate the authentic and necessary innovations of the modernist era. In every climate of opinion and belief it is the business of poets to add something to the resources of their medium, language, though that can be done by looking back as well as by looking forward—as long as the looks are searching ones. 'Art concerns itself with the difficult and the good', Goethe noted after a lifetime of looking in all directions. No change of mood or situation will make any difference to the truth of that synoptic remark.

M. H.
Suffolk, January 1982

REFERENCES

CHAPTER I
1 Letter, 5 May 1871.
2 In *Variété* II, Paris, 1930, p. 142.
3 This point is made by Walter Benjamin, to whose important essay on Baudelaire (*Schriften*, Frankfurt, 1955) I am greatly indebted (English translation in Walter Benjamin: *Illuminations*, New York, 1968, pp. 157 ff.)
4 '... volontiers je n'écrirais que pour les morts.' Dedication to *Les Paradis artificiels* (1860).
5 Henry James: 'Sincerity seems to us to belong to a range of qualities with which Baudelaire and his friends were but scantily concerned.' *French Poets and Novelists*, London, 1884, pp. 58–9, New York, 1964, pp. 58–9.
6 Jean-Paul Sartre: *Baudelaire*, translated by Martin Turnell, London and New York, 1950.
7 *Gautier: Sa vie et son oeuvre*, in *L'Art Romantique*, Paris, 1923, p. 97.
8 Note on *Les Liaisons dangereuses. Oeuvres posthumes*, Paris, 1908, p. 176.
9 *L'Ecole païenne* (1851), in *L'Art Romantique*, Paris, 1923, p. 327.
10 *Guys: le peintre de la vie moderne* (1863), in *L'Art Romantique*, p. 210.
11 Charles Baudelaire: *Correspondence I. 1841–63*, Paris, 1933, p. 440.
12 To Ancelle, 18 February 1866.
13 Henry James: op. cit., p. 62.
14 Mallarmé: *Oeuvres complètes*, Paris, 1945; p. 378.
15 Mallarmé: *Oeuvres en prose*, Geneva, 1946, p. 13.
16 Ibid., p. 137.
17 Comte de Lautréamont: *Oeuvres complètes*, Paris, 1938, pp. 303, 308.
18 *Briefwechsel zwischen George und Hofmannsthal*, Munich and Düsseldorf, 1953, p. 87.
19 *Mon coeur mis à nu*, in *Oeuvres posthumes*, Paris, 1908, p. 107.
20 Letter of 4 October 1887. First published in *Cahiers de la Quinzaine*, 1902.
21 Essays on Guys, loc. cit., p. 248. Cf. Baudelaire's essay on Wagner (ibid., p. 288): 'I feel sorry for poets guided by instinct alone. I consider them incomplete.'
22 Edwin Muir: *Latitudes*, London and New York, 1924, p. 147.

References

23 Erich Heller: *The Disinherited Mind*, Cambridge, 1952; New York, 1957, pp. 170–1.

24 Ibid., p. 151.

25 Ibid., p. 155.

26 *Culture and Anarchy*, London, 1869, p. viii; New York, 1924.

27 From *Rasselas*. Quoted by T.S.Eliot: *On Poetry and Poets*, New York and London, 1957, p. 179.

28 *Können Dichter die Welt ändern?* (1930), in Gottfried Benn: *Werke* IV, Wiesbaden, 1961, p. 215.

29 *Le Peintre de la vie moderne*, in *L'Art Romantique*, p. 244.

30 *Mon coeur mis à nu.*

31 *Fusées*, last entry.

32 A.E.Housman: *The Name and Nature of Poetry*, Cambridge and New York, 1933.

CHAPTER 2

1 *Ovid and the Art of Translation* (1680), in John Dryden: *Dramatic Poesy and Other Essays*, London, 1912, p. 154; *Dramatic Essays*, New York, 1912, p. 154.

2 A.E.Housman: *The Name and Nature of Poetry*, Cambridge and New York, 1933, p. 34.

3 London, 1955. See especially pp. 9, 56, 67, 148, 158.

4 Ibid., p. 192.

5 London, 1961, pp. 280, 46, 67; New Haven, 1960.

6 *Problems of Art*, London and New York, 1957, pp. 26, 160.

7 Ibid., p. 180.

8 In *Poésie vivante*, Geneva, November-December 1965.

9 W.H.Auden: *The Dyer's Hand and Other Essays*, London, 1963, p. 336; New York, 1963, p. 337.

10 New, enlarged edition, Hamburg, 1967.

11 Op. cit., p. 36.

12 Ibid., p. 110.

13 Ibid., p. 150.

14 Werner Vortriede: *Novalis und die französischen Symbolisten*, Stuttgart, 1963, pp. 149, 156 and *passim*.

15 In William Carlos Williams: *Collected Later Poems*, New York, 1963, p. 7.

16 In *Pictures from Brueghel and Other Poems*, New York, 1962, p. 109.

17 Ibid., pp. 93–4.

18 In *ELH, a Journal of English Literary History*, Vol. 25, No. 4, December 1956, pp. 279–98.

[19] Letter to Ronald Lane Latimer, 26 November 1955. *Letters of Wallace Stevens*, New York, 1966; London, 1967.

[20] To Samuel French Morse, 13 July 1949. Ibid.

[21] To Barbara Church, 20 August 1951. Ibid.

[22] To Ronald Lane Latimer, 22 October 1935. Ibid.

[23] Ezra Pound: *How to Read*, London and New York, 1931, pp. 17, 18.

[24] Ibid., pp. 18, 19.

[25] Octavio Paz: *L'Arc et la lyre*, Paris, 1965, pp. 46, 40–41.

[26] Ibid., p. 246.

[27] *The Letter of Lord Chandos*, in Hugo von Hofmannsthal, *Selected Prose*, New York and London, 1952, pp. 129–41; and Donald Davie's comments on it in *Articulate Energy*, pp. 1–5.

CHAPTER 3

[1] Letter to Izambard, 13 May.

[2] *Ce qu'on dit au poète à propos de fleurs*, in *Oeuvres de Arthur Rimbaud*, Paris, 1947, pp. 72–8.

[3] Ibid., pp. 107–8.

[4] *Un voyage à Cithère*.

[5] Baudelaire's prose poem *Confiteor de l'artiste*.

[6] Letter to Richard Woodhouse, 27 October 1818 in *The Complete Works of John Keats* (ed. H.Buxton Forman), Vol. IV, Glasgow, 1901, p. 173.

[7] To George Keats, September 1819. Ibid., Vol. V, p. 121.

[8] *Literary Essays of Ezra Pound*, New York and London, 1954, pp. 13, 282.

[9] *Paria*.

[10] By K.L.Ammer, in 1900 and 1907. The same translator's versions of Villon and Rimbaud had a wide and pervasive influence on poets such as Georg Trakl and Bertolt Brecht, to mention only the more prominent and well-documented instances. See Reinhold Grimm: *Strukturen*, Göttingen, 1963, pp. 124–5.

[11] From *Twenty Prose Poems of Baudelaire*, translated by Michael Hamburger, London, 1968, p. 28.

[12] Letter to Charles Henry, May 1882.

[13] *Complainte d'une convalescence en mai*.

[14] *Ballade*.

[15] *Complainte des crépuscules célibataires*.

[16] Ibid.

[17] *Regards sur le monde actuel*, Paris, 1931, pp. 84–9.

[18] *Auf den Tod des Schauspielers Hermann Müller* (1899).

References

CHAPTER 4
1 Paul Valéry: *Monsieur Teste*, Paris, 1927, p. 99; Hugo von Hofmannsthal: *Ad me Ipsum*, in *Aufzeichungen*, Frankfurt, 1959, p. 215.
2 Preface to *Mélange*, Paris, 1941, p. 8.
3 Translated by David Paul in Paul Valéry: *Plays*, New York and London, 1960, pp. 51–2. (The ellipses are Valéry's except for the last two.)
4 Ibid., p. 59.
5 Ibid., pp. 169–71.
6 Ibid., p. 204. ('Ce que l'on peut conter ne compte que fort peu.')
7 *Poésie et pensée abstraite*, in *Variété*, Paris, 1924, p. 72. English version by Denise Folliot in Valéry: *The Art of Poetry*, New York and London, 1958, p. 22.
8 Hofmannsthal: *Silvia im 'Stern'* (ed. Martin Stern), Bern and Stuttgart, 1959, p. 114.
9 *Monsieur Teste*, p. 63.
10 *Concerning Adonis*, in *The Art of Poetry*, p. 18.
11 *Memoirs of a Poem*, in *The Art of Poetry*, p. 120.
12 *Poetry and Abstract Thought*, ibid., p. 105.
13 Ibid., p. 79.
14 *Memoirs of a Poem*, ibid., p. 111. And in *Poetry and Abstract Thought*, where he speaks of *Le Cimetière marin* as having begun in him as a 'certain rhythm, that of the French line of ten syllables, divided into four and six.'
15 Ibid., *A Foreword*, p. 48.
16 *Memoirs of a Poem*, ibid., p. 125.
17 *Pure Poetry*, ibid., p. 185.
18 Ibid., *A Foreword*, p. 46.
19 From *Mélange*, Paris, 1941, pp. 117–31.
20 Oxford, 1939, p. 8; in *The Art of Poetry*, p. 58.
21 Op. cit., pp. 288, 324–5. See also Elizabeth Sewell: *Paul Valéry*, Cambridge, 1952.
22 Jorge Guillén: *Cántico* (bi-lingual selection), Boston and London, 1965.
23 Jorge Guillén: *Language and Poetry*, Cambridge (Mass.), 1961, pp. 207, 208–9.
24 *Au Sujet d'Adonis*, in *The Art of Poetry*, pp. 8–9.
25 Stefan George: *Tage und Taten*, 2nd edition, Berlin, 1925, p. 85.
26 London, 1927.
27 *Per Amica Silentia Lunae*, London, 1918, pp. 22, 26, 28, 40; New York, 1918, limited edition.

324

28 *Autobiographies*, London, 1955, p. 11. *The Autobiography of William Butler Yeats*, New York, 1953, p. 7.

29 *Essays and Introductions*, London and New York, 1961, p. 522.

30 *Letters on Poetry from W.B. Yeats to Dorothy Wellesley*, London, 1940, pp. 8, 119, 143, 157, 196; New York, 1940.

31 Mallarmé: *Crise de vers*, Paris, 1951, p. 366.

32 For an admirable exposition of these assumptions see Frank Kermode: *Romantic Image*, London, 1957; New York, 1958.

33 Introduction to *The Oxford Book of Modern Verse* (1936), p. xxxvi.

34 *Letters to Dorothy Wellesley*, p. 124.

35 P. xxxv.

CHAPTER 5

1 *Autobiographies*, p. 487; American edition, p. 297.

2 Riding and Graves, op. cit., pp. 227, 254–5.

3 *The White Goddess*, London, 1951, p. 14.

4 *On the Modern Mind*, in *Encounter*, Vol. XXIV, No. 5, p. 18.

5 *Yeats and Fascism*, in *The New Statesman*, 26 February 1965; reprinted in *Excited Reverie*, London, 1965.

6 In *Partisan Review*, Vol. XXXIII, No. 3, pp. 339–61.

7 From *High Talk. Last Poems and Plays*, London, 1940, p. 73; *The Collected Poems of William Butler Yeats*, New York, 1956, p. 331.

8 *Essays and Introductions*, pp. 339, 225, 203, 511, 526.

9 From *Meru. A Full Moon in March*, London, 1935, p. 70; *The Collected Poems*, New York, 1956, p. 287.

10 *Autobiographies*, p. 469; American edition, pp. 284 f.

11 *Tel Quel II*, Paris, 1943, p. 65.

12 Ibid., p. 43.

13 *Regards sur le monde actuel*, Paris, 1931, pp. 95, 101; *History and Politics*, p. 248.

14 Walter Benjamin: *Das Kunstwerk im Zeitalter seiner technischen Reproduzierbarkeit*, in *Schriften*, Frankfurt, 1955, Vol. I, p. 397; English version by Harry Fohn, in Benjamin: *Illuminations*, New York, 1968, pp. 243 f.

15 *Regards sur le monde actuel*, p. 174; *History and Politics*, p. 394.

16 *The Selected Writings of Juan Ramón Jiménez*, translated by H.R. Hays, New York, 1957, p. 214.

17 Ibid., pp. 188, 196, 200, 202.

18 Ibid., p. 251.

19 Ibid., p. 199.

20 Frank Kermode: *Puzzles and Epiphanies*, London, 1962, p. 4.

21 Paris, 1956.

References

22 Translated by Eudo C. Mason in *Rilke, Europe and the English-Speaking World*, Cambridge, 1961, p. 13. The same writer gives a full account of Rilke's political attitudes, their complexities and contradictions.

23 R.M.Rilke: *Gesammelte Werke*, Leipzig, 1927, Vol. III, p. 127.

24 From a letter dated Rodaun, 24 April 1927, unpublished as far as I know, given to me in a typed transcription by Hofmannsthal's widow, Gerty von Hofmannsthal, who copied it from the original.

25 Wallace Stevens: *Opus Posthumous*, New York, 1957, p. 158.

26 English version by David Luke in *Modern German Poetry: 1910–60*, London and New York, 1962, pp. 29–31.

27 Ibid., pp. 25–7.

28 Wallace Stevens: *The Necessary Angel*, New York, 1951, pp. 31, 30, 169, 4, 81.

29 *Opus Posthumous*, pp. xv, 158.

30 Ibid., pp. 160, 171, 227.

31 Ibid., p. 115.

32 *The Necessary Angel*, p. 116.

33 Ibid., p. 77.

34 Letter to R.L.Latimer, 31 October 1935; *Letters*, New York, 1966, p. 289.

35 *Opus Posthumous*, pp. 46–52.

36 *Sonette an Orpheus*, Leipzig, 1923, pp. 44, 53.

37 To Robert Pack, 28 December 1954. *Letters*, p. 863.

38 *Opus Posthumous*, pp. 86–8.

39 Kathleen Raine: *Defending Ancient Springs*, Oxford, 1967, p. 186.

40 *Poems 1923–54*, New York, 1954, p. 152; *Selected Poems 1923–58*, London, 1960, p. 11.

41 Ibid., New York, p. 397; London, p. 56.

42 Ibid., New York, p. 401; London, p. 58.

43 From *On Being Asked for a War Poem*, in *Later Poems*, London, 1931, p. 287.

44 To R.L.Latimer, 8 January 1935; *Letters*, p. 274.

CHAPTER 6

1 *Collected Poems*, London, 1955, p. 38; *Poems*, New York, 1959, p. 39.

2 *Problems of Art*, p. 122.

3 Quoted by H.R.Hays in his Preface to *Selected Writings of Juan Ramón Jiménez*, New York, 1957, p. xxv.

4 Foreword to *A Lume Spento, and Other Early Poems*, London and New York, 1966.

5 Ezra Pound: *Gaudier-Brzeska: A Memoir*, London, 1916, p. 98.

6 Donald Davie: *Ezra Pound: Poet as Sculptor*, London, 1965, p. 17; New York, 1964, p. 17.

7 Ibid., p. 244; and cf. p. 147.

8 London and New York, 1951, p. 14.

9 Ibid., p. 51.

10 Both in *Ezra Pound – A Collection of Essays* (ed. Peter Russell), London, 1950; New York, 1950, as *An Examination of Ezra Pound: A Collection of Essays*.

11 *The Paris Review*, No. 28, Summer-Fall, 1962, pp. 45–8; in *Writers at Work*, Second Series, New York, 1963, pp. 35–59.

12 Ibid., pp. 14–15.

13 E.P. *Ode pour l'Election de Son Sépulchre*.

14 *Mauberley* I, in Ezra Pound: *A Selection of Poems*, London, 1940, p. 55; Toronto, 1940.

15 *Literary Essays of Ezra Pound*, London and New York, 1954, p. 283.

16 *The Collected Essays, Journalism and Letters of George Orwell*, New York and London, 1968, Vol. 2, p. 239.

17 *The Unity of Eliot's Poetry*, in *The Review*, Oxford, No. 4, November 1962, pp. 16–27.

18 *The Literature of Politics*. Reprinted in T.S.Eliot: *To Criticize the Critic*, London and New York, 1965.

19 Reprinted in T.S.Eliot: *On Poetry and Poets*, London, 1957, pp. 89–102; New York, 1957, pp. 96–112.

20 Gottfried Benn: *Gesammelte Werke*, IV, Wiesbaden, 1961, p. 215.

21 Ibid., I, Wiesbaden, 1961, p. 510.

22 Paul Valéry: *Memoirs of a Poem*, in *The Art of Poetry*, London and New York, 1958, p. 108.

23 Benn: *Gesammelte Werke*, IV, p. 401.

24 Benn: *Ausdruckswelt*, Wiesbaden, 1949, p. 101.

25 Benn: *Gesammelte Werke*, IV, p. 68.

26 'For if there is still such a thing as transcendence, it can only be a bestial one.' *Akademie-Rede*, 1931, in *Gesammelte Werke*, I, p. 436.

27 W.H.Auden: *Selected Poems*, London, 1938, pp. 19–20; *Poems*, New York, 1934, p. 68.

28 Translation by Christopher Middleton, in Gottfried Benn: *Primal Vision*, New York, 1960, p. 289.

29 Translation by Michael Hamburger, ibid., pp. 238–9.

30 Rémy de Gourmont: *Promenades littéraires*, Paris, 1919, pp. 330–47.

31 Translated from Georg Rudolf Lind's German version in Fernando Pessoa: *Poesie*, Frankfurt, 1962, pp. 138 f.

32 From *O Guardor de Rebanhos V*, in Fernando Pessoa: *Obras completas*, Lisbon, Vols. 1–5, 1951. Subsequent quotations from Pessoa under his various names are also taken from this source.

References

33 *Fernando Pessoa: Présentation par Armand Guibert* (*Poètes d'aujourd'hui,* 73), Paris, 1960, p. 209.

CHAPTER 7
1 Ezra Pound: *Literary Essays,* London and New York, 1954, p. 288.
2 Wyndham Lewis: in *Blast II,* London, 1915, p. 5.
3 From *Otherworld,* London, 1920.
4 From *L'Allegria,* Milan, 1943.
5 Georg Trakl: *Die Dichtungen,* Zürich, 1946. Subsequent quotations from Trakl are also taken from this edition.
6 Margaret Davies: *Apollinaire,* London and New York, 1964, p. 219.
7 Cf. Introduction to *Modern German Poetry 1910-60* (edited by Christopher Middleton and Michael Hamburger), London and New York, 1962, pp. xxi-xliv.
8 English version in *Modern German Poetry 1910-60.* See my comments in *Reason and Energy,* London and New York, 1957.
9 Siegfried Sassoon: *Poems Newly Selected 1916-36,* London, 1940, p. 20; Toronto, 1940.
10 D.H.Lawrence: *Last Poems,* London, 1929, p. 59; New York, 1933, p. 52.
11 From *Hommage à Guillaume Apollinaire,* in *Blaise Cendrars: Oeuvres complètes,* Paris.
12 *Vendémiaire,* in *Alcools,* Paris, 1920, p. 161.
13 Apollinaire: *Oeuvres poétiques,* Paris, 1956, p. 272.
14 *L'Adieu du cavalier.* Ibid.
15 *Merveilles de la guerre.* Ibid.
16 *La Chanson du mal-aimé.* Ibid.
17 Preface to Apollinaire's selections from Baudelaire, Paris, 1917.
18 Quoted by Margaret Davies, op. cit., p. 304.
19 Aragon: *Le Crève-coeur,* London, 1942, p. 16.
20 Herbert Read: *Thirty-Five Poems,* London, 1940, p. 10; Toronto, 1940.
21 Keith Douglas: *Collected Poems,* London and New York, 1967, p. 150.
22 London, 1946; New York, 1968.
23 Keith Douglas: *Collected Poems.*
24 Randall Jarrell: *Little Friend, Little Friend,* New York, 1945.

CHAPTER 8
1 *The Southern Review,* Baton Rouge, Louisiana, Spring, 1967, pp. 311-21.

2 *How to Read*, London, 1932, p. 43.
3 *Modern Poets on Modern Poetry* (ed. J.Scully), London, 1966, pp. 50–1, 55.
4 Brecht: *Über Lyrik*, East Berlin, 1964, pp. 8–14.
5 Ibid., p. 114.
6 Bertolt Brecht: *Gedichte I*, Frankfurt, 1960.
7 *Über Lyrik*, pp. 16–17, 59.
8 Ibid., pp. 61–2.
9 Ibid., p. 91.
10 Ibid., p. 89.
11 Ibid., p. 60.
12 From *Buckower Elegien* (1953), in *Gedichte 7*, Frankfurt, 1964, p. 9.
13 *Gedichte 8*, Frankfurt, 1965, p. 193.
14 *Gedichte 7*, p. 116.
15 William Carlos Williams: *Collected Earlier Poems*, pp. 129–30.
16 Boris Pasternak: *The Collected Prose Works*, London, 1945, pp. 57, 111.
17 *Paris Review*, No. 24, Paris, 1960, p. 51.
18 *Strassburgkonfigurationen* in *Worte mit und ohne Anker*, Wiesbaden, 1957, p. 11.
19 Hans Arp: *Der gordische Schlüssel*, in *Gesammelte Gedichte I*, Wiesbaden, 1963.
20 Ibid., p. 153.
21 Ibid., p. 231.
22 See his poem *Das Rad* (The Wheel) of 1963 in *German Writing Today* (ed. Christopher Middleton), London, 1967, p. 19; New York, 1967.
23 *Gesammelte Gedichte I*, Wiesbaden, p. 248.
24 Pedro Salinas, *Poesias completas*, Madrid.
25 From Jorge Guillén: *Cantico*, Buenos Aires, 1950.
26 Erwin Walter Palm: *Kunst jenseits der Kunst, Akzente 3*, Munich, 1966, pp. 255–70.
27 F.Garcia Lorca: *Obras completas*, Madrid, 1955.
28 Letter of May 1961, in *The Poet's Vocation* (ed. William Burford and Christopher Middleton), Austin, Texas, 1967, p. 49.
29 Hart Crane: *The Collected Poems*, New York, 1933; London, 1938.
30 Letter of May 1961. *The Poet's Vocation*, p. 52.
31 Ibid., pp. 67–8; *Complete Poems and Selected Letters and Prose of Hart Crane*, New York, 1966, pp. 226 ff.
32 Introduction to *The Collected Poems of Hart Crane*, London, 1938, p. 15; New York, 1933.
33 Letter to Waldo Frank, 20 June 1926. *The Poet's Vocation*, pp.

References

68–9; *The Complete Poems and Selected Letters and Prose of Hart Crane*, p. 232.
34 *The Complete Poems*, etc., pp. 82 ff.
35 Ibid., p. 51.
36 Ibid., p. 56.
37 Ibid., p. 54.
38 Ibid., p. 110.
39 Brecht: *Gedichte 7*, p. 7.
40 Eugenio Montale: *Ossi di seppia*, Milan, 1925.
41 Translated by George Kay. From Montale: *Poesie/Poems*, Edinburgh, 1964, p. 11.
42 Ibid., p. 41.
43 Ibid., p. 49.
44 Ibid., pp. 213–15.
45 Text reprinted in *Quarterly Review of Literature*, Annandale-on-Hudson, Vol. XV, Nos. 1/2, pp. 7–9.

CHAPTER 9
1 *Sobra una poésia sin pureza* in the periodical *Caballo Verde*, Madrid, 1935. Reprinted in Pablo Neruda: *Las furias y las penas y otras poemas*, Santiago, 1947.
2 In *Gedichte 3*, Frankfurt, 1961, p. 177.
3 From *Canto general V*, Mexico City, 1950.
4 *The Heights of Macchu Picchu*, translated by Nathaniel Tarn, New York and London, 1966.
5 Glasgow, 1955.
6 London, 1967; New York, 1968.
7 This and subsequent translations of Neruda are by Alastair Reid. Neruda: *We Are Many*, London, 1967; New York, 1968.
8 From *Los heraldes negros*, Lima, 1918.
9 *An die Nachgeborenen* (To Posterity).
10 From *Poemas humanos*, Paris, 1939.
11 From *Los heraldes negros*.
12 From Marianne Moore: *Selected Poems*, New York, 1935.
13 New York, 1966.
14 In *Lição de Coisas*, Rio de Janeiro, 1962.
15 From *Alguma poesía*, Rio de Janeiro, 1930.
16 'Wovon man nicht sprechen kann, darüber muss man schweigen,' *Tractatus Logico-Philosophicus*, London and New York, 1961, p. 150.
17 Ibid., p. 23.
18 Francis Ponge: *My Creative Method* (1947–8). Translated by Lane

References

Dunlop in *Quarterly Review of Literature*, Annandale-on-Hudson, Vol. XV, Nos. 1 and 2, 1967, pp. 147–8.

19 From *Una volta per sempre*, Milan, 1963.

20 Translated by Michael Hamburger.

21 In *Un Rêve fait à Mantoue*, Paris, 1967, pp. 91–125.

22 Paris, 1953, p. 85.

23 *La Beauté*, in *Hier régnant désert*, Paris, 1958.

24 Ibid.

25 *International Anonymous*, 14 September 1967.

26 Philippe Jaccottet: *La Promenade sous les arbres*, Lausanne, 1957, p. 144.

27 Ibid., pp. 122, 125.

28 Paris, 1967.

29 Quoted by Walter Höllerer in *Akzente*, Munich, 1966.

30 *Moja Poeszia* (1965). Translated from the German version by Karl Dedecius: *Ein Gedicht und sein Autor*, Berlin, 1967, pp. 123–4. See also pp. 121, 132, 145.

31 Translation by Adam Czerniawski, in *Polish Writing Today*, London, 1967, p. 55.

32 Ibid., pp. 123–4. Translation by Czeslaw Milosz.

33 Ibid., p. 125.

34 From *An Address*, translated by Jan Darowski, ibid., p. 137.

35 *Ein Gedicht und sein Autor*, pp. 155, 156.

36 Translated in part by Christopher Middleton for his poem *Pavlovic Variations* (in Middleton: *Our Flowers and Nice Bones*, London and New York, 1970, pp. 59–64).

37 *Ein Gedicht und sein Autor*, p. 108.

38 *Collected Earlier Poems*, p. 68.

39 *Paterson*, Book II, New York, 1948, p. 103; London, 1964.

40 *Paterson*, Book III, New York, 1949, p. 122; London, 1964.

41 Ibid., p. 132 (New York ed.).

42 Hans Magnus Enzensberger: *poems for people who don't read poems*, London and New York, 1968.

43 Translation by Richard Wilbur from Andrei Voznesensky: *Anti-worlds*, New York, 1966, p. 40.

44 Translation by William Jay Smith, ibid., p. 69.

45 Ibid., p. 97.

46 Ibid., p. 106.

47 Wolf Biermann: Die Drahtharfe, Berlin, 1965, pp. 69–71. (English translation, *The Wire Harp*, New York, 1968.)

48 Peter Huchel: *Chausseen Chausseen*, Frankfurt, 1963.

49 In Fortini: *Una Volta per sempre*, Milan, 1963.

50 *Ein Gedicht und sein Autor*, p. 336.

References

51 Vol. 4, No. 8, 1964, p. 75.
52 Ibid., p. 30.
53 *Ecce Homo*, in David Gascoyne: *Poems 1937–42*, London, 1943.
54 *The London Magazine*, loc. cit., pp. 78–81.
55 Ibid., p. 84.
56 In César Vallejo: *Twenty Poems*, Madison, Minnesota, 1962, p. 10.
57 7 June 1963, p. 407.
58 In *Un Voyage à Cithère*.
59 1 September 1939, in *Another Time*, London and New York, 1940.
60 *Encounter*, August 1966, pp. 77–8.
61 In *Für die Mouche*. See Michael Hamburger: *Reason and Energy*, London and New York, 1957, pp. 161–2.

CHAPTER 10

1 *Oeuvres posthumes*, Paris, 1908, p. 20.
2 Introduction to *Penguin Book of Romantic Verse*, London, 1968.
3 In *Erinnerung an einen Planeten*, Munich, 1963.
4 In *landessprache*, Frankfurt, 1960.
5 In *Loquitur*, London, 1965.
6 In *Stand*, Newcastle-on-Tyne, Vol. 8, No. 2, 1966, p. 28.
7 In Edwin Muir: *The Labyrinth*, London, 1949.
8 In Richard Dehmel: *Ausgewählte Gedichte*, Berlin, 1905.
9 In Brecht: *Gedichte 8*, Frankfurt, 1965.
10 In *Gedichte 2*, Frankfurt, 1960.
11 In *The Whitsun Weddings*, London and New York, 1964.
12 London, 1956.
13 *Der Traum von den Raubtieren und von dem Schattenreich*, in Loerke: *Gedichte und Prosa I*, Frankfurt, 1958.
14 In Lehmann: *Sichtbare Zeit*, Gütersloh, 1967.
15 London, 1946.
16 In *Defending Ancient Springs*, London, 1967, p. 107.
17 London, 1965.
18 Paris, 1968, pp. 177, 179, 301, 304.
19 London, 1967.
20 In *Wodwo*, London and New York, 1967.
21 *The Times Literary Supplement*, 23 March 1967.
22 In *Nature with Man*, London, 1965.
23 In *Lupercal*, London and New York, 1960.
24 From *The Lost Son*, New York, 1948.
25 In *The London Magazine*, loc. cit., p. 37.
26 Ibid., p. 38.
27 In *Evergreen Review*, No. 52, New York, 1968, pp. 42, 89–90.

28 Charles Olson: *Selected Writings*, ed. Robert Creeley, New York, 1966, pp. 46, 24.
29 Introduction to *The New Writing in the USA*, London, 1967, pp. 19–20, 21, 22, 23, 24.
30 In *Contemporary American Poetry*, ed. by Howard Nemerov, Voice of America Forum Lectures, Washington, D.C., pp. 175, 182, 183.
31 Robert Creeley, in *The Review*, No. 10, Oxford, 1964, pp. 30, 31.
32 Edward Dorn: *The North Atlantic Turbine*, London, 1967; New York, 1968.
33 Robert Duncan: *The Review*, loc. cit., p. 36.
34 *Evergreen Review*, No. 5, New York, 1958, p. 97.
35 In *Stand*, Newcastle, Vol. 9, No. 1, 1967, pp. 11–12.
36 See James Wright's *Eisenhower's Visit to France*, 1959, in *The Branch Will Not Break*, Middletown, Connecticut, 1963; and Robert Bly's *Johnson's Cabinet Watched by Ants*, in *The Light around the Body*, London, 1968.
37 London, 1965, pp. 7–9; New York, 1964.
38 But compare my Introduction to Günter Grass: *Poems*, London, 1969.
39 Hamburg, 1963.
40 *Sprachgitter*, Frankfurt, 1959.
41 In *Der Meridian*, Frankfurt, 1961, pp. 22, 18.
42 *Sprache*, in *Wetterzeichen*, East Berlin, 1966.
43 *Atemwende*, Frankfurt, 1967, pp. 22, 27, 103.
44 7 December 1967, p. 1190.
45 P. 12.
46 Kenneth White: *En toute candeur*, Paris, 1964. This and the following quotations are taken from this source: pp. 10, 30, 68, 25, 23, 67, 69.
47 From *The Cold Wind of Dawn*, London, 1966.
48 *On Poetry*. Translated by W.H.Auden, New York, 1961, pp. 7, 9, 12, 11.
49 *Prophétie* (Prophecy), in *Gravitations*, Paris, 1925.
50 From *1939–45*, Paris, 1945.
51 *Selected Poems of H.D.*, New York, 1957.
52 In *The New Hungarian Quarterly*, Vol. VIII, No. 25, Budapest, Spring, 1967, p. 25.
53 In *Contemporary American Poetry*, pp. 191, 196, 199.
54 P.B.Medawar: *Scientific Method*, in *The Listener*, London, Vol. 78, No. 2011, 10 December 1967, pp. 455, 456.
55 Edwin Muir: *An Autobiography*, London and New York, 1954, p. 235.
56 Erich Kahler: *Out of the Labyrinth*, New York, 1967, pp. 173, 177,

198. And compare the same writer's lectures *The Disintegration of Form in the Arts*, New York, 1968, in which his argument is elaborated and substantiated.

57 *Les Amours jaunes*, Paris, 1947, p. 12.

58 Freiburg and Olten, 1965, pp. 44–5.

59 Helmut Heissenbüttel: *Über Literatur*, Freiburg and Olten, 1966, pp. 75, 198, 202, 231, 237.

60 London, 1930, pp. 112–18.

61 The reasons for Laura Riding's renunciation of poetry are indeed relevant to a book concerned with poetry and truth – as relevant as Rimbaud's renunciation of poetry, or Hofmannsthal's; but at the time of writing I had not seen the few statements about her renunciation which Laura Riding has published since her *Collected Poems* of 1938. Her introduction to a selection of her poems broadcast in the Third Programme of the BBC on April 1st 1962 explains why she has published no collection of poems since 1938: 'The final poems of that work concluded a long exploration of the possibility of using words in poetry with the true voice and the true mind of oneself. I had fervently believed that in poetry the way so to use words might be found – which had nowhere, yet, been found, completely. But after 1938 I began to see poetry differently, even to see it as a harmful ingredient of our linguistic life. . . . The equivalence between poetry and truth that I had tried to establish was inconsistent with the relation they have to each other as – the one – *art* and – the other – the reality. . . . But, what I achieved in this direction was ever sucked into the whorl of poetic artifice, with its overpowering necessities of patterned rhythm and harmonic sound-play, which work distortions upon the natural proprieties of tone and word. . . . I have learnt that language does not lend itself naturally to the poetic style, but is warped in being fitted into it; that the only style that can yield a natural and happy use of words is the style of truth, a rule of trueness of voice and mind sustained in every morsel of one's speech; that for the practice of the style of truth to become a thing of the present, poetry must become a thing of the past.'

Part of a longer, less personal statement on the subject, *Poetry and the Good*, appeared in the periodical *Chelsea* (No. 14, New York, Jan. 1964, pp. 38–47) under the title *Further on Poetry*. Here Laura Riding defined and analyzed what she calls the 'spiritual ineffectuality' of poetry: 'It is bound up with the appearance poetry has of being a mode of expressing what would otherwise be inexpressible, better described as the otherwise-unexpressed. This otherwise-unexpressed does not have real expression in poetry. It is adumbrated, suggested, implied; and a great deal of what in ordinary parlance would have explicit expression is given the same treatment. Meaning-content, in poetry, is more matter for surmise than for direct apprehension; and much more can, thus, seem to be said than in the ordinary way – so much more is left to be surmised. The effect of successful expression is created by a technique that might be called the poetic oblique. In poetry, the path of word-use necessarily veers from the path of natural linguistic difficulties (which, if persisted in, become the path of the true), to follow the line of art, which can seem straighter than the straight as it runs deviatingly on. A stylized failure-of-expression is the verbal heart of poetry's sacrosanctity. . . . Thus, with neither poets nor their words put to the proof (except with respect to the artificially created conditions of poetry itself), nothing is ever *in fact* spiritually defined, morally determined, linguistically resolved in poems. In no other field of human activity is there so much intensity of expectation and so little possibility of anything's happening to meet it. . . . The ultimate effect of poetry is to clarify nothing, to change nothing.'

62 In *mai hart lieb zapfen eibe hold*, London, 1965.
63 Neuwied and Berlin, 1967.
64 Ibid., p. 112.
65 Paul Valéry: *Notion générale de l'art*, in *Nouvelle Revue Française*, Paris, 1935, pp. 684–6.
66 In *To Tell the Truth*, London, 1967.

ACKNOWLEDGEMENTS

Author and publishers make grateful acknowledgement to those who gave their kind permission to quote from the following copyright material (except where otherwise stated all passages quoted in translation in this book were translated by the author):

Hans Arp, *Gesammelte Gedichte* (Limes Verlag, Wiesbaden). *Wortträume und schwarze Sterne* (Limes Verlag).

W.H.Auden, *Another Time* (Faber and Faber Ltd, London; Random House, Inc., and Alfred A. Knopf, Inc., New York, Copyright 1940 by W.H.Auden). *The Dyer's Hand and Other Essays* (Faber and Faber; Random House and Alfred A. Knopf. Copyright 1962 by W.H.Auden). *Selected Poems* (Faber and Faber). *Poems* (Random House and Alfred A. Knopf. Copyright 1934 by W.H. Auden renewed 1964 by W.H.Auden).

Twenty Prose Poems of Baudelaire, translated by Michael Hamburger (Jonathan Cape Ltd, London; Grossman Publishers, Inc., New York).

Gottfried Benn, *Gesammelte Werke in 4 Bänden* (Limes Verlag, Wiesbaden). *Primal Vision*, translated by Michael Hamburger (New Directions Publishing Corporation, New York).

Robert Bly, interview (*Stand* magazine, Newcastle on Tyne).

Yves Bonnefoy, *Du Mouvement et de l'immobilité de douve* and *Hier régnant désert* (© Mercure de France, Paris, 1958 and 1967).

Bertolt Brecht, *Gedichte* (Suhrkamp Verlag, Frankfurt).

Basil Bunting, *Collected Poems* (Fulcrum Press, London. Copyright © Basil Bunting 1968). Article (*Stand* magazine).

Paul Celan, *Atemwende* (Suhrkamp Verlag, Frankfurt).

Blaise Cendrars, *Oeuvres complètes* (© Editions Denoël, Paris, 1947).

The Complete Poems and Selected Letters and Prose of Hart Crane (Liveright Publishing Corporation. Copyright 1933, 1958, 1966 by Liveright Publishing Corporation, New York).

Robert Creeley (ed.), *The New Writing in the USA* (Penguin Books Ltd, London).

E.E.Cummings, *Selected Poems, 1923–1958* (MacGibbon and

Kee, London. *Poems 1923–1954* (Harcourt, Brace & World, Inc.).
Donald Davie, *Articulate Energy* (Routledge and Kegan Paul Ltd, London).

Margaret Davies, *Apollinaire* (Oliver and Boyd Ltd, Edinburgh).

Keith Douglas, *Collected Poems* (Faber and Faber; Chilmark Press, Inc., New York. © by Marie J. Douglas 1966).

T.S.Eliot, *Collected Poems 1909–1935* (Faber and Faber; Harcourt, Brace & World). *Four Quartets* (Faber and Faber; Harcourt, Brace & World). *The Elder Statesman* (Faber and Faber; Farrar, Straus and Giroux).

H.M.Enzensberger, *Landessprache* (Suhrkamp Verlag, Frankfurt). *Poems for People Who Don't Read Poems* (Martin Secker and Warburg Ltd, London; Atheneum Publishers, New York. Copyright © 1967 by Hans Magnus Enzensberger).

Colin Falck, article entitled 'The Exposed Heart' (*Encounter*).

Franco Fortini, *Una Volta per Sempre* (Arnoldo Mondadori Company Ltd, Milan).

Robert Graves, *The White Goddess* (Faber and Faber, London).

Jorge Guillén, *Cantico* (Editorial Sudamericana S.A., Buenos Aires).

Donald Hall, introduction to *The Faber Book of Modern Verse* (Faber and Faber).

H.D., *Selected Poems* (Grove Press, Inc., New York. Poem 'Sigil' copyright © 1957 Norman Holmes Pearson).

Erich Heller, *The Disinherited Mind* (Bowes and Bowes [Publishers] Ltd, London).

Hugo von Hofmannsthal, *Auf den Tod des Schauspielers Hermann Müller* (Insel Verlag, Frankfurt).

A.E.Housman, *The Name and Nature of Poetry* (Cambridge University Press, Cambridge).

Peter Huchel, *Chausseen, Chausseen* (Fischer Verlag, Frankfurt. © S. Fischer Verlag, Frankfurt am Main, 1965).

Ted Hughes, *Lupercal* (Faber and Faber; Harper and Row Publishers).

Philippe Jaccottet, *Airs* (© Editions Gallimard, Paris).

Randall Jarrell, *Complete Poems* (Farrar, Straus and Giroux, Inc. Copyright 1945 by Mrs Randall Jarrell).

Selected Writings of Juan Ramón Jiménez, translated by G.R.Hays (Farrar, Straus and Giroux. Copyright © 1957 by Juan Ramón Jiménez).

Poems by Tymoteusz Karpowicz and Tadeusz Różewicz in *Polish Writing Today* (Penguin Books Ltd) and *Postwar Polish Poetry* (Doubleday and Company, Inc.).

Frank Kermode, *Puzzles and Epiphanies* (Routledge and Kegan Paul; Chilmark Press. Copyright Frank Kermode 1962).

Susanne K. Langer, *Problems of Art* (Charles Scribner's Sons; Routledge and Kegan Paul).

D.H.Lawrence, *The Complete Poems of D.H.Lawrence*, Vol. II, edited by Vivian de Sola Pinto and F. Warren Roberts (Heinemann, London; The Viking Press, Inc., New York. Copyright 1933 by Frieda Lawrence. Reprinted by permission of Laurence Pollinger Limited and the estate of the late Mrs Frieda Lawrence).

Sir Peter Medawar, article entitled 'Scientific Method' (*The Listener*).

Christopher Middleton, interview with English poets (*London Magazine*).

Franz Mon, *Lesebuch* (Hermann Luchterhand Verlag GmbH, Neuwied).

Eugenio Montale, *Ossi di seppia* (Mondadori, Milan). *Poesie/Poems*, translated by George Kay (Edinburgh University Press). Poem 'Xenia' (*Quarterly Review of Literature*).

Marianne Moore, *Selected Poems* (Faber and Faber; The Macmillan Company. Copyright 1935 by Marianne Moore renewed 1963 by Marianne Moore and T.S.Eliot).

Edwin Muir, *Autobiography* (The Hogarth Press Ltd, London, and Mrs Willa Muir).

Pablo Neruda, *We Are Many*, translated by Alastair Reid (Cape Goliard, London; Grossman Publishers, Inc., New York. Permission covers the Spanish texts).

Conor Cruise O'Brien, article entitled 'Yeats and Fascism' (*New Statesman*).

Fernando Pessoa, *Obras completas* (Atica Editora, Lisbon. By permission of D. Henriqueta Rosa Dias, John N. Rosa and Louis M. Rosa, half-sister and half-brothers of the poet).

Michael Polyani, article entitled 'On the Modern Mind' (*Encounter*).

Ezra Pound, *A Lume Spento* (New Directions Publishing Corporation; Faber and Faber. © 1965 by Ezra Pound). *Personae* (New Directions; Faber and Faber. Copyright 1926 by Ezra Pound). *Lustra* (New Directions; Faber and Faber). *ABC of Reading* (Faber and Faber). *A Selection of Poems* (Faber and Faber). *The Cantos* (Faber and Faber). *Drafts and Fragments of Cantos CX to CXVII* (copyright © 1966, 1969 by Ezra Pound).

Salvatore Quasimodo, poem 'Milano, Agosto 1943' (Mondadori).

Kathleen Raine, *Defending Ancient Springs* (Oxford University Press, London).

339

Acknowledgements

R.M.Rilke, poems 'To Hölderlin' and 'Turning-Point' (original German by permission of Insel Verlag, Frankfurt. English translation from *Modern German Poetry 1910–1960*, edited by C. Middleton and M. Hamburger, MacGibbon and Kee; Grove Press. Copyright © 1962 by Michael Hamburger and Christopher Middleton). *Rilke, Europe and the English-speaking World*, translated by Eudo C. Mason (Cambridge University Press).

The Collected Poems of Theodore Roethke (Doubleday and Company, Inc., New York. Poem 'The Lost Son' copyright 1947 by Theodore Roethke).

Pedro Salinas, *Poesias completas* (© Soledad Salinas and Jaime Salinas).

Siegfried Sassoon, *Poems Newly Selected 1916–1936* (George Sassoon).

J. Scully (ed.), *Modern Poets on Modern Poetry* (quotations from Robert Frost by permission of Holt, Rinehart and Winston, Inc., New York. All rights reserved).

Elizabeth Sewell, *Paul Valéry* (Cambridge University Press).

Gary Snyder, essay entitled 'Passage to More than India' (Evergreen Review, Inc., New York).

Wallace Stevens, *Collected Poems* (Faber and Faber; Random House and Alfred A. Knopf; copyright 1954 by Wallace Stevens). *Letters of Wallace Stevens* (Faber and Faber; Random House and Alfred A. Knopf. Copyright 1966 by Holly Stevens). *The Necessary Angel* (Random House and Alfred A. Knopf; Faber and Faber. Copyright 1951 by Wallace Stevens). *Opus Posthumous* (Random House and Alfred A. Knopf. Copyright 1957 by Elsie and Holly Stevens).

Jules Supervielle, *Gravitations* (© Editions Gallimard, Paris). *1939–1945* (© Editions Gallimard, Paris).

Ungaretti, *L'Allegria* (Mondadori, Milan).

Paul Valéry, *The Art of Poetry*, translated by Denise Folliot (Routledge and Kegan Paul). *The Collected Works of Paul Valéry*, edited by Jackson Matthews (Princeton University Press; Routledge and Kegan Paul; © The Bollingen Foundation, 1958, 1960, 1965, 1968, 1969). *Plays*, translated by David Paul (Routledge and Kegan Paul). *Mélange* (© Editions Gallimard).

Andrei Voznesensky, *Antiworlds*, edited by Patricia Blake and Max Hayward, translated by William Jay Smith (Basic Books, Inc., Publishers, New York. © 1963 by Encounter Ltd, 1966 by Basic Books).

Kenneth White, *The Cold Wind of Dawn* (Jonathan Cape).

William Carlos Williams, *Collected Poems* (MacGibbon and Kee Ltd, London). *Collected Earlier Poems* (New Directions; MacGibbon and Kee. Copyright 1938 by William Carlos Williams). *Collected Later Poems* (New Directions. Copyright 1944 by William Carlos Williams). *Pictures from Breughel and Other Poems* (New Directions. Copyright 1954 and 1955 by William Carlos Williams). *Paterson* (New Directions. Copyright 1948, 1949 by William Carlos Williams).

Wittgenstein, *Tractatus Logico-Philosophicus* (Routledge and Kegan Paul; Humanities Press).

Writers at Work (Paris Review Interviews, Second Series. By permission of The Viking Press, Inc., New York. Copyright © 1963 by The Paris Review, Inc.).

W.B.Yeats, *Autobiographies* (Macmillan and Co., London). *The Autobiography of W.B.Yeats* (The Macmillan Company, New York. Copyright 1916, 1936 by The Macmillan Company renewed 1944 by Bertha G. Yeats). *The Collected Poems of W.B.Yeats* (Macmillan and Co., London; The Macmillan Company, New York. Poems 'Politics,' 'Under Ben Bulben,' 'The Circus Animals' Desertion,' 'High Talk' copyright 1940 by Georgie Yeats renewed 1968 by Bertha Georgie Yeats, Michael Butler Yeats, Anne Yeats. Poem 'Meru' copyright 1934 by The Macmillan Company renewed 1962 by Bertha Georgie Yeats. Poem 'Ego Dominus Tuus' copyright 1918 by The Macmillan Company renewed 1945 by Bertha Georgie Yeats). *Essays and Introductions* (Macmillan and Co., London; The Macmillan Company, New York. © Mrs W.B.Yeats 1961). *Letters on Poetry from W.B.Yeats to Dorothy Wellesley* (Oxford University Press, London). Introduction to the *Oxford Book of Modern Verse* (The Clarendon Press, Oxford).

Yevgeny Yevtushenko, *A Precocious Autobiography* (Collins Publishers, London; E.P.Dutton and Co. Inc., New York).

NAME INDEX

Name Index

Cortes-Rodrigues, Armando, 146
Crane, Hart, 140, 144, 207–9, 211–213, 273
Creeley, Robert, 122, 246, 284–6, 312
Cummings, E.E., 108–9

Dante, 15, 121–2, 216
d'Aurevilly, Barbey, 2
Davie, Donald, 22–4, 26, 118–19, 263
Davies, Margaret, 160
Day Lewis, Cecil, 180, 278
de Campos, Alvaro, 139–40, 143–6
Degas, Edgar, 29
de Gourmont, Rémy, 138
Dehmel, Richard, 275
Delacroix, Eugène, 8
de l'Isle Adam, Villiers, 7, 9, 17, 58, 94, 268
de Nerval, Gérard, 5, 172
de Otéro, Blas, 241
de Rojas, Soto, 202
Dewey, John, 88
Dietrich, Marlene, 279
Dobrée, Bonamy, 22, 26
Donne, John, 243
Dorn, Edward, 285–6
Dostoevsky, Fyodor, 85
Douglas, Keith, 175–80
Drummond de Andrade, Carlos, 237–8, 240–1
Dryden, John, 21, 126
Duncan, Robert,' 122, 247, 249, 284–7

Eich, Günter, 288
Eliot, T.S., 2, 13, 15, 28, 30, 32–3, 47–8, 51, 54–7, 60, 78, 85, 94, 100, 105–7, 114–15, 118, 121–31, 138, 144, 146, 175–6, 181, 209–12, 215, 219–20, 251, 263, 265, 268, 273–4, 286
Eluard, Paul, 48, 153, 175, 181, 194, 202, 246
Emmanuel, Pierre, 180
Empson, William, 35, 280–1, 297
Enright, D.J., 12, 263

Enzensberger, Hans Magnus, 72, 183, 222, 254–6, 269–73, 288

Falck, Colin, 266
Flint, F.S., 153–4, 156, 159
Fortini, Franco, 240–1, 260–1
Frank, Waldo, 209
Fried, Erich, 289
Friedrich, Hugo, 27–9, 38, 59
Frost, Robert, 115, 184
Frye, Northrop, 264
Fuller, Roy, 262

Gallarati-Scotti, Duchess Aurelia, 98–9
Gascoyne, David, 262, 278–9
Gautier, Théophile, 4, 18, 93
George, Stefan, 10, 28, 70–3, 85–6, 98, 100–1, 111, 150, 185–6, 268
Gide, André, 11, 173–4
Goethe, J.W. von, 13, 15, 309
Goll, Yvan, 151, 274
Góngora, Luis de, 202–3
Grass, Günter, 288
Graves, Robert, 72, 83–4, 152
Grenfell, Julian, 149
Groddeck, Georg, 214
Guillén, Jorge, 37, 69–70, 95, 112, 200–1, 306
Guillevic, Eugène, 245
Gunn, Thom, 263
Gustafsson, Lars, 278

Hall, Donald, 121, 183, 286
Hall, J.C., 175–6
Hamilton, Ian, 262
H.D. (Hilda Doolittle), 300
Heidegger, Martin, 239, 241
Heine, Heinrich, 43, 266
Heissenbüttel, Helmut, 246, 304–11
Heller, Erich, 12–14, 34, 70
Herbert, Zbigniew, 251–2
Hernández, Miguel, 166
Heym, Georg, 160, 174, 273
Hikmet, Nazim, 166
Hill, Geoffrey, 147, 263
Hoddis, Jakob von, 48, 160, 274

344